NINETEENTH-CENTURY
PHILOSOPHY OF RELIGION

Edited by Graham Oppy and N. N. Trakakis

⁂

VOLUME 4

THE HISTORY OF
WESTERN PHILOSOPHY OF RELIGION

ACUMEN

First published in 2009 by Acumen
First published in paperback by Acumen in 2013

Acumen Publishing Limited

4 Saddler Street
Durham
DH1 3NP

ISD, 70 Enterprise Drive
Bristol, CT 06010, USA

www.acumenpublishing.com

ISBN: 978-1-84465-684-4 (paperback Volume 4)
ISBN: 978-1-84465-679-0 (paperback 5 volume set)
ISBN: 978-1-84465-223-5 (hardcover Volume 4)
ISBN: 978-1-84465-181-8 (hardcover 5 volume set)

British Library Cataloguing-in-Publication Data
A catalogue record for this book is available from the British Library.

Typeset in Minion Pro.
Printed and bound in the UK by CPI Group (UK) Ltd, Croydon, CR0 4YY.

CONTENTS

EDITORIAL INTRODUCTION

Bertrand Russell's *History of Western Philosophy* (1946; hereafter *History*) provides a model for *some* of the significant features of the present work. Like Russell's more general history, our history of Western philosophy of religion consists principally of chapters devoted to the works of individual thinkers, selected because of their "considerable importance". Of course, we do not claim to have provided coverage of all of those who have made important contributions to Western philosophy of religion. However, we think that anyone who has made a significant contribution to Western philosophy of religion has either seriously engaged with the works of philosophers who are featured in this work, or has produced work that has been a focus of serious engagement for philosophers who are featured in this work.

Like Russell, we have aimed for contributions that show how the philosophy of religion developed by a given thinker is related to that thinker's life, and that trace out connections between the views developed by a given philosopher and the views of their predecessors, contemporaries and successors. While our primary aim is to provide an account of the ideas, concepts, claims and arguments developed by each of the philosophers under consideration, we think – with Russell – that this aim is unlikely to be achieved in a work in which "each philosopher appears as in a vacuum".

Again like Russell, we have only selected philosophers or religious writers who belong to, or have exerted a significant impact on, the intellectual tradition of the West (i.e. western Europe and the Anglo-American world). We realize that this selection criterion alone excludes from our work a number of important thinkers and religious groups or traditions, such as: Asian philosophers of religion, particularly those representing such religions as Hinduism, Buddhism, Confucianism and Taoism; African philosophers of religion; and individuals, texts and traditions emanating from indigenous religions, such as those found in the native populations of Australia and the Pacific Islands. Clearly, the non-Western world has produced thinkers who have made important, and often overlooked, contributions to the philosophy of religion. We have decided, however, not to include any entries on these thinkers, and our decision is based primarily on the (admittedly not incontestable) view that the Asian, African and indigenous philosophical and religious traditions have not had a great impact on the main historical narrative of the West. It would therefore have been difficult to integrate the various non-Western thinkers into the five-volume structure of the present work. The best way to redress this omission, in our view, is to produce a separate multi-volume work that would be dedicated to the history of non-Western philosophy of religion, a project that we invite others to take up.

Where we have departed most significantly from Russell is that our work has been written by a multitude of contributors, whereas Russell's work was the product of just one person. In the preface to his *History*, Russell claimed that:

> There is ... something lost when many authors co-operate. If there is any unity in the movement of history, if there is any intimate relation between what goes before and what comes later, it is necessary, for setting this forth, that earlier and later periods should be synthesized in a single mind. (1946: 5)

We think that Russell exaggerates the difficulties in, and underestimates the benefits of, having a multitude of expert contributors. On the one hand, someone who is an expert on the work of a given philosopher is bound to have expert knowledge of the relation between the work of that philosopher, what goes before and what comes after. On the other hand, and as Russell himself acknowledged, it is impossible for one person to have the expertise of a specialist across such a wide field. (Indeed, while Russell's *History* is admirable for its conception and scope, there is no doubt that it is far from a model for good historical scholarship.)

Of course, Russell's worry about a multiplicity of authors does recur at the editorial level: the editors of this work have no particular claim to expertise concerning any of the philosophers who are featured in the work. In order to alleviate this problem, we invited all of the contributors to read drafts of neighbouring contributions, acting on the assumption that someone who is an expert on a particular philosopher is likely to have reasonably good knowledge of contemporaries and near contemporaries of that philosopher. Moreover, each of the five volumes comes with an expert introduction, written by someone who is much better placed than we are to survey the time period covered in the given volume.

Obviously enough, it is also the case that the present work does not have the kind of narrative unity that is possessed by Russell's work. Our work juxtaposes contributions from experts who make very different theoretical assumptions, and who belong to diverse philosophical schools and traditions. Again, it seems to us that this represents an advantage: there are many different contemporary approaches to philosophy of religion, and each of these approaches suggests a different view about the preceding history. Even if there is "unity in the movement of history", it is clear that there is considerable disagreement about the precise nature of that unity.

Although our work is divided into five volumes – and despite the fact that we have given labels to each of these volumes – we attach no particular significance to the way in which philosophers are collected together by these volumes. The order of the chapters is determined by the dates of birth of the philosophers who are the principal subjects of those chapters. While it would not be a task for a single evening, we do think that it should be possible to read the five volumes as a single, continuous work.

* * *

Collectively, our primary debt is to the 109 people who agreed to join with us in writing the material that appears in this work. We are indebted also to Tristan Palmer, who oversaw the project on behalf of Acumen. Tristan initially searched for someone prepared to take on the task of editing a single-volume history of Western philosophy of religion, and was actively involved in the shaping of the final project. He also provided invaluable advice on the full range of editorial questions that arise in a project on this scale. Thanks, too, to the copy-editors and others at Acumen, especially Kate Williams, who played a role in the completion of this project, and to the anonymous reviewers who provided many helpful comments. We are grateful to Karen Gillen for proofreading and indexing all five volumes, and to the Helen McPherson Smith Trust, which provided financial support for this project. We also acknowledge our debt to Monash University, and to our colleagues in the School of Philosophy and Bioethics. Special thanks to Dirk Baltzly for his suggestions about potential contributors to the volume on ancient Western philosophy of religion and for his editorial help with the chapter on Pythagoras.

Apart from these collective debts, Graham Oppy acknowledges personal debts to friends and family, especially to Camille, Gilbert, Calvin and Alfie. N. N. Trakakis is also grateful for the support of family and friends while working on this project, which he dedicates to his nephew and niece, Nicholas and Adrianna Trakakis: my prayer is that you will come to share the love of wisdom cultivated by the great figures in these volumes.

Graham Oppy

N. N. Trakakis

CONTRIBUTORS

Douglas Anderson is the author of two books on the work of Charles S. Peirce: *Creativity and the Philosophy of C. S. Peirce* (1987) and *Strands of System* (1995). He is a past president of the Peirce Society and is presently editor-in-chief of the *Transactions of the Charles S. Peirce Society*.

Roland Boer is Research Professor of Theology at the University of Newcastle. Recent publications include *Marxist Criticism of the Bible* (2003), *Symposia* (2007), *Criticism of Heaven* (2007) and *Rescuing the Bible* (2007).

Yolanda D. Estes teaches philosophy at Mississippi State University. A specialist in German idealism and ethics, she is a founding member of the North American Fichte Society. With her colleague Curtis Bowman she is currently completing a book of translations of the writings of the atheism dispute accompanied by orginal commentaries on the controversy, *Fichte and the Atheism Dispute*. Her other writings about Fichte's philosophy of religion are published in the selected proceedings from the North American Fichte Society and the *Encyclopedia of Unbelief*.

Russell Goodman is Regents Professor of Philosophy at the University of New Mexico. He is the author of *American Philosophy and the Romantic Tradition* (1990) and editor of *Contending with Stanley Cavell* (2005). His papers on Emerson have appeared in the *Journal of the History of Ideas*, *ESQ: A Journal of the American Renaissance*, *The Oxford Handbook of American Philosophy* and in edited volumes on nature, friendship and Neoplatonism. In 2003 he directed a summer institute on Emerson for the National Endowment for the Humanities (NEH), and in 2005 he directed a summer seminar for the NEH devoted to reading Emerson's essays.

Adolf Grünbaum is the Andrew Mellon Professor of Philosophy of Science and Primary Research Professor of History and Philosophy of Science at the University of Pittsburgh, where he has also been the founder, director and now chairman of its Center for Philosophy of Science. He is the author of twelve books and of some 390 articles in anthologies and philosophical and scientific journals, dealing with the philosophy of physics, the theory of scientific rationality, the philosophy of psychiatry and psychoanalysis and the critique of theism. He has been President of the American Philosophical Association (1982–83), has delivered the Gifford Lectures at the University of St Andrews (1985) and is a Fellow of the American Academy of Arts and Sciences.

Van A. Harvey is Professor of Religious Studies (Emeritus) at Stanford University. His field of specialization is the relationship between religion and its critics in the nineteenth century. He is the author of *Feuerbach and the Interpretation of Religion* (1996), which won the American Academy of Religion 1996 award for excellence in constructive-reflective studies. His articles on Feuerbach have appeared in the *Stanford Encyclopedia of Religion* (online), the *New Encyclopedia of Unbelief* (2007), the *Encyclopedia of Protestantism* (2004) and in the volume *Theology at the End of Modernity* (1991), as well as in various journals.

Douglas Hedley is Senior Lecturer in the Philosophy of Religion at the University of Cambridge and Fellow of Clare College, Cambridge. He is a past secretary of the British Society for the Philosophy of Religion and past president of the European Society for the Philosophy of Religion. He is the author of *Coleridge, Philosophy and Religion* (2000) and *Living Forms of the Imagination* (2008), and editor of *Deconstructing Radical Orthodoxy* (with Wayne Hankey, 2005), *The Human Person in God's World* (with Brian Hebblethwaite, 2006) and *Platonism at the Origins of Modernity* (with Sarah Hutton, 2008).

H. S. Jones is Professor of Intellectual History at the University of Manchester. He has written widely on nineteenth-century French and British intellectual history, and is the editor and translator of Auguste Comte's *Early Political Writings* (1998).

Ian Ker is a Senior Research Fellow in Theology at St Benet's Hall, Oxford. He is the author of *John Henry Newman* (1988) and *The Achievement of John Henry Newman* (1990). He is also the editor of the Oxford critical edition of Newman's *An Essay in Aid of a Grammar of Assent* (1985).

Rudolf A. Makkreel is Candler Professor of Philosophy at Emory University. He is the author of *Dilthey, Philosopher of the Human Studies* (1975) and *Imagination and Interpretation in Kant* (1990), and co-editor of Dilthey's *Selected Works* (1985–2002). He was the editor of the *Journal of the History of Philosophy* from 1983 to 1998, and has been a recipient of fellowships from the NEH, DAAD, Alexander von Humboldt Foundation, Thyssen Stiftung and Volkswagen Stiftung. He is currently writing a book on critical hermeneutics and historical judgement.

Clancy Martin is Associate Professor of Philosophy at the University of Missouri in Kansas City. He works on nineteenth-century continental philosophy, especially Kierkegaard and Nietzsche. He has translated Nietzsche's *Thus Spoke Zarathustra* (2005) and is presently translating *Beyond Good and Evil* (forthcoming) as well as many shorter pieces by Kierkegaard and Nietzsche. He has published six books and many essays on ethics and the history of philosophy, and his two latest books, *Lies, Love and Marriage* (2009) and *The Philosophy of Deception* (2009), develop Nietzsche's ideas about religion, truthfulness, self-deception and deception.

William McDonald is Senior Lecturer in Philosophy at the University of New England, Australia. He is the translator of Kierkegaard's *Prefaces: Light Reading for Certain Classes as the Occasion May Require, By Nicolaus Notabene* (1989), the author of online articles on Kierkegaard in the *Stanford Encyclopedia of Philosophy*, the *Internet Encyclopedia of Philosophy* and the *Literary Encyclopedia*, and of numerous book chapters on Kierkegaard, and is currently co-authoring *A Kierkegaard Dictionary* (with Andrew Burgess, Steven Emmanuel and David Gouwens, forthcoming).

Philip A. Mellor is Professor of Religion and Social Theory at the University of Leeds. His research interests are in the Durkheimian tradition of the sociology of religion and social theories of human embodiment. His publications include *Religion, Realism and Social Theory* (2004), *The Sociological Ambition* (with Chris Shilling, 2001) and *Re-forming the Body* (with Chris Shilling, 1997). He is a member of the British Centre for Durkheimian Studies.

Kelly A. Parker is Associate Professor and Chair of the Department of Philosophy at Grand Valley State University, Michigan. He is a founder and current president of the Josiah Royce Society. His publications centre on the thought of Charles S. Peirce, Josiah Royce, William James and John Dewey, and on contemporary applications of pragmatism in education, environmental philosophy and ethics. Previous publications include "Josiah Royce on 'The Spirit of the Community' and the Nature of Philosophy" (*Journal of Speculative Philosophy*, 2000), "Josiah Royce" (*Stanford Encyclopedia of Philosophy*, 2004), and "Josiah Royce: Idealism, Transcendentalism, Pragmatism" (*Oxford Handbook of American Philosophy*, 2008).

Paul Redding is Professor of Philosophy at the University of Sydney. His researches have predominantly been directed to a revisionist reinterpretation of the metaphysical commitments of the German idealist tradition (*Hegel's Hermeneutics*, 1996; *Continental Idealism*, 2009), to reconstructing idealist approaches to the role of emotion in thought (*The Logic of Affect*, 1999), and to recent attempts within analytic philosophy to forge connections with the philosophy of Hegel (*Analytic Philosophy and the Return of Hegelian Thought*, 2007).

Michael Ruse is Lucyle T. Werkmeister Professor of Philosophy and Director of the Program in the History and Philosophy of Science at Florida State University. He is the author of many books on the history and philosophy of evolutionary theory, including *Darwinism Defended* (1982), *Taking Darwin Seriously* (1986), *Evolutionary Naturalism* (1995), *Can a Darwinian be a Christian?* (2001) and *The Evolution–Creation Struggle* (2005), and the editor of *Philosophy after Darwin* (2009).

Chris Ryan specializes in philosophy of religion, the history of nineteenth-century philosophy in Europe and the religions of India. He received his PhD from the University of Cambridge in 2007 and is now a trainee religious studies teacher at Roehampton University, London. His book *Schopenhauer's Philosophy of Religion* is due to be published in 2009.

Chin Liew Ten is Professor of Philosophy at the National University of Singapore. He is interested in issues relating to liberty and toleration, including religious toleration. He is the author and editor of several books, including *Mill on Liberty* (1980), *The Nineteenth Century* (1994), *Mill's Moral, Political, and Legal Philosophy* (1999), *Was Mill a Liberal?* (2004), *A Conception of Toleration* (2004), *Multiculturalism and the Value of Diversity* (2004) and *Theories of Rights* (2006). He is working on *A Historical Dictionary of John Stuart Mill's Philosophy*. He is a Fellow of the Australian Academy of the Humanities and a Fellow of the Academy of Social Sciences in Australia, and serves on the editorial boards of several journals in philosophy, politics and bioethics.

Colin Tyler is Senior Lecturer in Political Theory at the University of Hull. He edited the *Collected Works of Edward Caird* (1998) and produced a critical edition of the *Unpublished Manuscripts in British Idealism* (2005/2008). His most recent book is *Idealist Political Philosophy* (2006). He is co-editor of the journal *Collingwood and British Idealism Studies* and is joint director of Hull's Centre for the Study of Idealism.

Michael Vater is a retired Professor of Philosophy at Marquette University. His writings include editions and translations of Schelling's philosophy of identity – *Presentation of My System* (1801), *Further Presentations from the System of Philosophy* (1802) and *Bruno, or, On the Divine and the Natural Principle of Things* (1802) – and various essays on the philosophies of Fichte and Hegel. He now teaches Buddhist and Taoist meditation at the University of Wisconsin-Milwaukee and at Marquette University.

Theodore Vial is a member of the Iliff School of Theology in Denver, Colorado. He contributed the chapter "Schleiermacher and the State" to the *Cambridge Companion to Friedrich Schleiermacher* (2005). He is the author of *Liturgy Wars*

(2004) and "Friedrich Schleiermacher on the Central Place of Worship in Theology" (*Harvard Theological Review*, 1998). He is also a member of the steering committees of the Schleiermacher Group and the Nineteenth-Century Theology Group of the American Academy of Religion.

Robert Wicks is Associate Professor of Philosophy at the University of Auckland. He is the author of *Schopenhauer* (2008), the entry on Schopenhauer in the *Stanford Encyclopedia of Philosophy* and articles on Schopenhauer's philosophy in the *European Journal of Philosophy*, the *History of Philosophy Quarterly*, the *Journal of Nietzsche Studies* and the *Blackwell Companion to Schopenhauer*.

1

NINETEENTH-CENTURY PHILOSOPHY OF RELIGION: AN INTRODUCTION

Douglas Hedley and Chris Ryan

The predominant position of nineteenth-century philosophy of religion was conciliatory. Its main figures set out to confront, absorb and pass beyond the radical Enlightenment's critical assault on Europe's religious and metaphysical tradition by developing philosophical syntheses that, to a great extent, assimilated the main lines and presuppositions of these critiques, while simultaneously preserving the most important features of Europe's religious inheritance. This spirit of conciliation is as evident in the metaphysical systems of mainstream German idealism at the opening of the century, as it is in the neo-Kantian inspired division between fact and value that dominated philosophy of religion at its close. In the long term, however, this synthesis turned out to be as fragile as it was subtle; although it managed to weather the stormy changes and extremes that buffeted it for the greater part of the century, its elements were eventually torn apart by the extreme intellectual and cultural conditions that emerged with the killing fields of the First World War.

THE RADICAL ENLIGHTENMENT: SPINOZA AND HUME

The Enlightenment inaugurated a fundamental upheaval in the European tradition of philosophical reflection on religion, for it was during this period that philosophers developed perspectives on the theological inheritance of the West, and methods of analysing its main themes, that dispensed with the assumptions and sources of the great works of late medieval scholasticism, such as the *Disputationes Metaphysicae* (Metaphysical disputations) of Francisco Suárez (1548–1617) (*see* Vol. 3, Ch. 6). For the most part, these new perspectives and analytical methods were positive in both intention and effect, and a succession of mainstream early modern philosophers – René Descartes (1596–1650), John Locke (1632–1704), Gottfried Wilhelm Leibniz (1646–1716) and George Berkeley (1685–1753) (*see* Vol. 3, Chs 8, 12, 13, 14, respectively) – made significant contributions to the

European tradition of metaphysical reflection on the divine. However, parallel to this constructive tradition was another, one that was questioning, sceptical and often corrosive, the foremost representatives of which were Baruch Spinoza (1632–77) and David Hume (1711–76) (*see* Vol. 3, Chs 11, 19, respectively). Since the philosophers of religion of the nineteenth century paid greater attention to the objections of Spinoza and Hume than to the positive proposals of Descartes and Locke, we shall begin with a brief overview of Spinoza's and Hume's treatment of the main themes of classical theism.

Spinoza and Hume were in many ways philosophical antipodes – the former a rationalist metaphysician and the latter a mitigated sceptic – but their respective criticisms of classical theism have many points in common. In relation to natural theology, they set out to show that its conclusions overdetermine its data, for with a contrary intention they used its central premises to construct an image of divinity quite different from that preached from church pulpits across Europe. Spinoza's ontological argument demonstrated an impersonal God, coextensive with the whole face of nature, while Hume's critical survey of the traditional arguments for the existence of God led to the conclusion that the first cause of the universe may have some remote analogy to the human mind, but that its personal or moral predicates, on the basis of which it was presented as a being worthy of worship, the ground of morality and the guarantor of religious hopes, cannot be established through the methods of natural theology. The latter predicates are, instead, simply projections of vulgar imagination, hardly distinguishable from our "Inclination to find our own Figures in the Clouds, our Face in the Moon, our Passions & Sentiments even in inanimate Matter" (Hume 1993: 26). And having cast doubt on the personal picture of God, Spinoza and Hume attacked other doctrines associated with it, such as providence, teleology and the immortality of the soul.

Traditionally, a theist might have responded by conceding that natural theology demonstrates a metaphysical rather than a religious being, while also pointing out that this modest task of founding the lower storeys or 'preambles of faith' is merely the preliminary for raising upon them the upper storeys or edifice of classical theism, constructed from materials taken from revelation, which is in turn authenticated by the miracles it reports. However, Spinoza's and Hume's common commitment to epistemological and metaphysical naturalism led them to raise reasoned objections to this strategy also. Spinoza maintained that God is perfect, infinite substance, from which all things flow with necessity; to attribute to him the power or desire to interfere with the perfection of his ordained order, as miraculous events do, is to imply that his nature and will are contingent and therefore capable of change, which is tantamount to a denial of his perfection. In his *Tractatus Theologico-Politicus* (Theological-political treatise) Spinoza argued that the miracle stories of the Bible should be read not as historical records, but as imaginative pictures recommending moral practice, for the Bible was composed by sages with practical insight but no scientific understanding. Hume's essay "Of

Miracles" effectively established the same point, but by way of a sceptical argument that lacked the metaphysical underpinnings of Spinoza's criticisms. Hume reasoned that miraculous events are, by definition, unlikely, and that no testimony is sufficiently trustworthy to overturn our experientially grounded belief in the uniformity of nature (Hume 2000: 83–99).

These critiques of the 'externalist' or 'objectivist' sources of medieval scholastic theology – the possibility of making inferences from nature to God, religious scriptures and supernatural events – gave rise to the view that they could no longer be deemed self-validating, but were in need of a prior, immediate and more obviously self-grounding principle, by and through which they might be authenticated. For the mainstream exponents of nineteenth-century philosophy of religion, the turn to the subject initiated by Immanuel Kant (1724–1804) (*see* Vol. 3, Ch. 21) was a crucial step in re-establishing the intellectual respectability of the central themes of the European theological tradition.

FIRST ATTEMPT AT A SYNTHESIS: KANT

Although aware of Spinoza, Kant was little affected or shaken by his philosophical system. Kant's indebtedness to Hume, however, was very great, and he famously credited Hume with awakening him from his "dogmatic slumbers" or fidelity to the metaphysics of Leibniz (Kant 1997a: 4.260). Kant's contribution to the philosophy of religion of our period is, of course, immeasurable, and the degree of his influence is a consequence of the comprehensive rigour with which he prosecuted his critique of metaphysical theism. Whereas Spinoza and Hume set out to show that natural theology's arguments for the existence of God admit alternative conclusions, the target of Kant's critical philosophy was the very premises of these arguments.

From one perspective the radical nature of Kant's assault on natural theology might be presented as its strong point, while from another it might be seen as its main weakness. Kant's transcendental idealism is more fundamentally decisive in forbidding inferences from the world to God than Hume's scepticism, but for the same reason it more readily invites dismissal, in so far as it is founded on the counter-intuitive proposition that the world of experience is mere appearance, being the sum of the subject's synthesis of intuition and concept. Kant did, of course, subject the three main arguments of natural theology to exhaustive critical analysis: he questioned the validity of the main premise of the ontological argument, revealed the extent to which cosmological arguments depend on this doubtful premise, and – resuming the critique of metaphysical anthropomorphism initiated by Spinoza and Hume – objected that the argument from design (or, in his idiom, 'the physico-theological argument') establishes a finite architect of the world rather than an absolute creator God or *ens realissimum*. However, Kant's criticisms of the arguments of natural theology do, to a great extent, depend

3

on his exposure of the transcendental illusion on which they are based; namely, the category error of using concepts authoritative for reasoning on objects of sensibility for speculations passing beyond the bounds of sense.

In relation to the philosophy of religion, however, Kant is notoriously Janus-faced. Apart from sustaining and intensifying Spinoza's and Hume's criticisms of the externalist sources and anthropomorphic conceptions of natural theology, his thought contains a theologically constructive aspect. After mounting a comprehensive assault on the possibility of constitutive knowledge of metaphysical entities such as God, world and soul in the *Kritik der Reinen Vernunft* (Critique of pure reason) of 1781, seven years later, in the *Kritik der Praktischen Vernunft* (Critique of practical reason), he readmitted the *ideas* of such entities as postulates of practical reason or regulative beliefs, faith in which arises from "a need *of reason*" that we bestow unity on our thought and action (Kant 1997b: 5.142–3). Kant's regulative moral theology was, in part, stimulated by his encounter with Rousseau's theories of freedom and the will. However, the position he developed in his third critical work of 1790, the *Kritik der Urteilskraft* (Critique of the power of judgement), testified to the enduring influence of Leibnizian themes on his critical philosophy, for in the second portion of the work he used teleological ideas to present a symbolic picture of a purposive and providential universe in which the realms separated by his previous critical works – phenomenon and noumenon, nature and freedom – were ultimately harmonized.

Like his precursor Leibniz, Kant was fundamentally rationalist in temperament. In his view theology was the science (*logos*) of God (*theos*), and his notion of the divine was less that of the God of Abraham, Isaac and Jacob, whom one approaches on bended knees in fear and trembling, and more of an unchanging metaphysical *logos*, ground and guarantor of natural and moral law. Leibniz and Kant were both impressed by modern science, and convinced of its explanatory superiority over pre-modern Aristotelian physics. However, they also considered scientific accounts of nature insufficiently self-grounding and in need of a higher principle that satisfies reflection's tendency to completeness. Kant thought that only the concept of a supersensible basis of nature, in which mechanism and teleology are combined, could account for our intimation of the ultimate convergence of the natural and moral orders, and thereby justify our wonder at the starry heavens above and the moral law within (Kant 1997b: 5.161). Although Hume's sceptical criticisms of the anthropomorphism of dogmatic metaphysics disturbed Kant sufficiently for him to deny that we can obtain constitutive knowledge of such a principle or truly ascribe purposes to nature, his consistent interest in showing that reason – in both its theoretical and practical incarnations – requires regulative assent to notions such as God, freedom, immortality and teleology, testifies to Kant's post-critical attachment to the dominant themes of classical theism.

The influence of Leibniz on Kant can be detected in another conception central to the critical philosophy: that of subjectivity, or – in Kant's technical language –

the transcendental unity of apperception. This conception is functionally comparable to the monads of Leibniz, in so far as they are both universal conditions for the possibility of individual subjectivity and the existence of a personal ego. The universality of this ground was important for Kant, in so far as it enabled him to combine his idealism with the view that subjective experience is more than merely 'subjective', in the sense of relative to every individual. Experience is of a common world, since it is the effect of apperception's preconscious synthesis of intuition and concept in the judgement, which thereby establishes a criterion of objective truth. An important corollary of the way in which Kant conferred epistemological primacy and logical authority on subjectivity is that, from this time onward, all truth-claims, and especially those of a metaphysical or theological stripe, had to pass through its prism. Spinoza and Hume might have exposed the fragility of the objectivist or externalist theological scaffolding erected by the scholastics, but Kant opened up a new field for theological and metaphysical speculation, albeit one that lies within.

However, what we have referred to as Kant's synthesis was really a separation, for having surrendered the known realm to agnosticism, mechanism and determinism, he was obliged to sever any connection between ordinary experience and God, freedom, immortality and teleology, and relocate their *possibility* in the unknowable thing-in-itself. The reception of his philosophy in the early nineteenth century reflects these tensions. Many of his successors, especially those whose reputations were institutionally established and who therefore exerted the greatest immediate influence in the philosophy of religion, interpreted his assault on natural theology as a concession to the radical Enlightenment, and as a principled refusal to revert to pre-critical, scholastic defences of the tradition. These thinkers – Fichte, Schelling and Hegel – considered the most significant part of Kant's philosophy to consist of his moral theology and its themes of freedom and teleology. In the thought of Schelling and Hegel in particular, this aspect of Kant's work provided materials for rehabilitating the central conceptions of the Western metaphysical tradition, albeit on very new and very novel grounds.

A contrary evaluation of Kant's relation to theism was formulated by Arthur Schopenhauer, and although his view was initially marginal, it grew in influence after the 1850s. He considered Kant's significance to consist of his distinction between phenomenon and thing-in-itself and his assault on mainstream theological metaphysics, since these had cleared the way for a wholesale revision of the methods and aims of metaphysical enquiry. Schopenhauer claimed that Kant had applied his moral theology as a palliative to soothe the pain inflicted by his destruction of natural theology, and to avoid the rebuke of the censor. In the following section we shall see how Schopenhauer's estimation of the devastation inflicted on classical theism by Kant had been anticipated in the late eighteenth century.

THE SYNTHESIS UNRAVELS: JACOBI

After our previous survey of the history of philosophical reflection on theism from Spinoza through Hume to Kant, we now focus on the local and specifically German context in which the effects of these criticisms were measured, debated, fought over and either affirmed or dismissed. This narrowing of focus is important, in so far as these late-eighteenth-century debates established the main lines of the German idealists' conception of the difficulties to be resolved if the central themes of the religio-metaphysical tradition were to be reconciled with the altered conditions of the modern age.

Friedrich Heinrich Jacobi (1743–1819) is a figure who rarely features in Anglophone history of philosophy, but he played a central role in three intellectual scandals that greatly influenced philosophy of religion in the nineteenth century: the Spinozist, atheist and pantheist controversies.

In 1783 Jacobi entered into a dispute with a leading representative of the German *Aufklärung*, Moses Mendelssohn (1729–86), concerning the alleged Spinozism of Mendelssohn's recently deceased friend, Gotthold Ephraim Lessing (1729–81) (*see* Vol. 3, Ch. 22). Jacobi published his correspondence with Mendelssohn in 1785, along with a rigorous examination of Spinoza's metaphysical system. Jacobi credited Spinoza's metaphysics with being the most rigorous and consistent system of philosophy, in relation to which other self-proclaimed rational systems (such as Mendelssohn's) are simply instances of arrested development. However, Jacobi also claimed that Spinoza's philosophy is the epitome of rationalistic nihilism, a materialist system that methodically traces necessary relations between events in accordance with the principle of sufficient reason, and in the process denies a personal God, free subjectivity and the distinction between good and evil. It thereby supports atheism and moral fatalism, and stands as a cautionary tale for those who insist on the explanatory privileges of reason over the dictates of common sense and faith.

Jacobi's presentation of Spinoza as a materialist, atheist, nihilist and moral fatalist was not the only interpretation circulating in late-eighteenth-century Germany. Prominent figures of the *Sturm und Drang* movement, such as Johann Wolfgang von Goethe (1749–1832) and Johann Gottfried Herder (1744–1803), offered an interpretation of Spinoza the opposite of Jacobi's, one that assimilated the idealized language of Spinoza's pantheism and contrast between *natura naturata* (created nature) and *natura naturans* (creative nature) to their poetic nature mysticism. Herder in particular used ideas from Spinoza in the development of a pantheist cosmology, albeit one based on dynamic vital force as opposed to inert matter and that supplanted Spinoza's mechanical principles of explanation for teleological principles. He used this teleological monism to construct an organic theory of mind or spirit (*Geist*) that struck a middle path between Cartesian mind–body dualism and reductivist materialism. Herder's re-evaluation of Spinoza was an important influence on German idealism, and his theory of the mind's emergence from nature is an obvious precursor to Schelling's description of nature as "slumbering spirit".

During his controversy with Mendelssohn, Jacobi had often claimed Kant as an authority for his defence of the merits of faith over the dangers of rational speculation. However, in 1786 Kant intervened in the Spinozist controversy in order to distinguish his position from both Jacobi's and Mendelssohn's, after which Jacobi began to cast Kant's idealism in the role previously assumed by Spinozist naturalism in his polemics: as the embodiment of rationalism and nihilism. Jacobi attacked Kant's epistemology at the passage from intuition to concept, the point at which the subject transforms its contact with the external world into determinate knowledge of objects by subsuming sense-data under concepts of the understanding. In Jacobi's view, Kant's theory of the nature and genesis of knowledge is tantamount to solipsism, scepticism and nihilism because it represents knowledge as an effect of the subject's absorption of objective reality into its *a priori* categories. Kant's subject is therefore an isolated monad, locked into its own consciousness and creating its own merely formal world out of nothing. In a desperate bid to avoid these unwelcome consequences, Jacobi claimed that Kant had illicitly introduced the thing-in-itself as the extra-phenomenal *cause* of sensations, and had followed this up with an equally unwarranted appeal to the practical postulates of God, freedom and immortality in the second *Critique*.

In opposition to rationalism and the threat it posed to religion, common sense and morality, Jacobi proposed a fideist acceptance of the immediate intuitions of a personal God, subjectivity, freedom and the reality of moral distinctions.[1] Although the German idealists rejected Jacobi's solution to the difficulties raised by Spinoza's metaphysics and Kant's epistemology, his polemics established their understanding of their main task: to controvert Jacobi's dictum that the immediacy of freedom is incompatible with a systematic explication of being. In quick succession Fichte, Schelling and Hegel constructed systems in which the regulative themes of Kant's philosophy – God, freedom, immortality and teleology – were synthesized with Spinoza's systematic naturalism.

SECOND ATTEMPT AT A SYNTHESIS: GERMAN IDEALISM

Johann Gottlieb Fichte (1762–1814) first entered the stage of philosophical history in 1792, on the publication of his *Versuch einer Kritik aller Offenbarung* (Attempt at a critique of all revelation). This was a Kantian inspired work that developed a post-Enlightenment criterion for validating revelation that ruled that its authenticity is established through agreement with the *a priori* moral notions of the

---

1. In an odd reversal, Jacobi (following J. G. Hamann) claimed Hume's theory of natural belief as confirmation of his fideism, translating Hume's 'belief' with the German term for 'faith' (*Glaube*); see Jacobi (1787).

subject. Owing to a printer's error, Fichte's work was published anonymously, and was at first hailed as Kant's long-awaited work on the philosophy of religion. Kant disclaimed authorship and revealed that Fichte was the author, bringing the latter instant philosophical fame. A year later, in 1793, Kant published his *Religion innerhalb der Grenzen der blossen Vernunft* (Religion within the limits of reason alone), in which he defended a similar thesis concerning the role of subjectivity in warranting revelation.

Fichte followed up the success of his first book with a systematic work of 1794–5, the *Wissenschaftslehre* (Science of knowledge). It developed a philosophical scheme modelled on but also departing from Spinoza's monism, beginning not with substance but with the freedom of pure consciousness or the absolute I. In the first, theoretical section of the work, the absolute I posits (*setzen*) the not-I, or objective realm of nature, as a limiting sphere for finite subjectivity's cognition and action. At this point, Fichte's system appears to be a metaphysical extravagance, surpassing the worst excesses of pre-Kantian dogmatic metaphysics. However in the second, practical section of the work, it becomes clear that Fichte's absolute I is a regulative ideal towards which we move, rather than a constitutive, transcendent being or creator-God. Central to Fichte's practical philosophy is the concept of striving (*Streben*), the process by which the subject arrives at objective knowledge of nature by imposing its moral ideal of the absolute I on the not-I, thereby making subjectivity and freedom ascendant over objectivity and determinism.

In 1798 Fichte published an essay, "Über den Grund unseres Glaubens an eine göttliche Weltregierung" (On the basis of our belief in a divine governance of the world), in which he identified God with the moral order brought about by human striving. This attracted the charge of atheism and in the following year Fichte was forced to resign from his professorship at Jena. Although, after his appointment to the University of Berlin in 1810, Fichte's absolute I seems to have been "most obediently converted into the good Lord", as Schopenhauer (1974a: 141) commented, Fichte's influence on the philosophy of religion of our period is largely indirect. During the atheism controversy, Jacobi had used Fichte's philosophy as evidence of his charge that Kantian idealism leads to solipsism, and this left Fichte's immediate successors, Schelling and Hegel, with the impression that Fichte's practical idealism had simply ridden roughshod over the question of the relation between subject and object, concept and intuition, and the problem of our knowledge of the external world. However, both Schelling and Hegel took from Fichte's fusion of Spinoza and Kant the conception of philosophy as knowledge of the absolute, and the idea that Kantian apperception and subjectivity, rather than Spinozistic thinghood and substance, is the route to its cognition.

Friedrich Wilhelm Joseph Schelling (1775–1854) had collaborated with Fichte at Jena, but his thought soon developed in its own direction. He raised Fichte's regulative absolute to the level of constitutive reality, redefining it, with Spinoza, as the ground or inner being of nature or universe as a whole. However, Schelling's move was not a reversion to Spinoza's mechanical universe, but an elevation of Spinoza to Kant's and Fichte's practical or regulative philosophy, since Schelling ascribed the purposiveness of moral subjectivity to nature by reintroducing, as Herder had before him, teleological judgement. Although this step disregarded Kant's strictures against constitutive teleological judgement in the third *Critique*, Schelling considered his resurrection of teleology to be vindicated by recent scientific theories that postulated one single natural force to explain the actions of matter. In Schelling's *Naturphilosophie*, nature was presented as a dynamic and hierarchical system of various grades reflecting different levels of organization and development of one basic force. The highest development of this natural force is human consciousness, for nature is slumbering spirit and consciousness awakened spirit, so that human knowledge of nature is also nature's knowledge of itself. In this early system of Schelling, the absolute is the identity or indifference point in which subject and object, spirit and nature, the ideal and the real, are unified. Although the absolute thereby solves the problems of freedom and determinism in moral philosophy and subject and object in epistemology, Schelling maintained that it cannot be cognized directly itself, but only embodied in art.

Just as Schelling had collaborated with Fichte in the late eighteenth century, so G. W. F. Hegel (1770–1831) collaborated with Schelling in the first few years of the nineteenth century. In 1807, however, Hegel announced his independence with the publication of *Phänomenologie des Geistes* (Phenomenology of spirit; hereafter *Phänomenologie*), in which he notoriously (albeit only implicitly) caricatured Schelling's notion of the absolute as empty formalism, "abstract universality", and the night in which all cows are black (Hegel 1977: §16). Hegel had not rejected Schelling's organic conception of the absolute as the basis for subject–object identity, but his criticism was motivated by his growing concern that Schelling's definition of the absolute as the indifference or vanishing point between subject and object, inaccessible to conceptual thought, fails to give an account of how the absolute relates to and is embodied in its parts or modes: finite consciousness, the objective realm of nature and the events of history. It thereby implies that their existence is mutually extrinsic. In order to explain the relation between the absolute and its modes, Hegel formulated his dialectical logic, which traces the stages of mediation by which the oppositions known to the reflective understanding (*Verstand*) – infinite and finite, God and humanity, subject and object, freedom and determinism – confront and negate each other, before what is essential in each is raised to a higher level through the synthesizing activity of speculative reason (*Vernunft*).

Hegel offered his dialectical logic as more than simply rational method: he also saw it as a reflection of objective processes in nature, history and spirit. In the *Phänomenologie* Hegel employed the dialectic to chart the emergence of higher and more inclusive states of consciousness from the conflict and mediation of contradictions inherent within previous states. The work describes a very broad sweep, from the immediacy of sense-experience up to 'absolute knowing', the point at which all oppositions have been overcome and the absolute, or God, is self-luminous subject, or, like Aristotle's unmoved mover, thought thinking itself. For Hegel, therefore, the absolute or God is the completion of a process, something realized at the end of history, through and in the spiritual life of humankind. Hegel commended Christianity as the consummate religion on the grounds that it communicated the same content as his conceptual philosophy in the medium of pictures (*Vorstellungen*). In opposition to religions that define God as absolute existence or *ens realissimum*, Hegel claimed the Christian doctrine of God's incarnation and death on the cross as a confirmation of his contention that "negation itself is found in God" (Hegel 2006: 465). But this negation is simply the condition of the possibility of a higher synthesis, pictorially presented in Christian doctrine by the resurrection and its image of final reconciliation between God and humanity, infinite and finite, the absolute and its modes.

The philosophy of religion of the mainstream German idealists was, therefore, a middle way or path of mediation. In the wake of the criticisms of Spinoza, Hume and Kant, they accepted that the sources and methods of scholasticism were incompatible with the intellectual culture of modernity, and that fideism was simply a refusal to engage with the advanced spirit of the age. But while giving due consideration to the force of Enlightenment critiques, they also set out to preserve as many of the themes of Europe's tradition of metaphysical and theological reflection as possible, in the pursuit of which aim they made use of Spinoza's monist metaphysics and Kant's regulative ideas of God, freedom and teleology.

However, in their responses to Enlightenment critiques of classical theism, Schelling and Hegel drew on a number of sources apart from Spinoza and Kant. These included the speculations of the Rhineland mystics and Giordano Bruno (1548–1600), the mystical theology of Jakob Böhme (1575–1624), the Swabian pietism of Christoph Friedrich Oetinger (1702–82), and cabbalist interpretations of Spinoza's pantheism. The upshot was a conception of God that departed radically from the scholastic notion of *actus purus*. We have already referred to Hegel's contention that God must overcome negation in order to attain self-realization. In Schelling's work of 1809, *Philosophische Untersuchungen über das Wesen der menschlichen Freiheit* (Philosophical investigations into the nature of human freedom) – written when he was in close contact with Franz von Baader (1765–1841), a Christian cabbalist and scholar of Böhme – he replaced his earlier, abstract definition of the absolute as the point of indifference between subject and object with a theology in which God creates the world through self-division (*Entscheidung*). These alternative models, in which negation, potentiality and non-being are introduced as elements within God, enabled Schelling and Hegel to incorporate Trinitarian theology as a central element in their philosophical systems. In their view, the traditional image of a fully realized, transcendent creator-God outside the world was simply deistic. Although they revived Aristotelian teleology and used it to replace Spinoza's conception of the universe as a machine with the conception of it as an organism, their teleological laws are internal to rather than imposed on nature from the outside by a transcendent designer. As a consequence, the spectre of pantheism often plagued the reception of their philosophy. In a final bid to eradicate accursed rationalism, fatalism and nihilism from the face of the earth, Jacobi entered into a vitriolic and public disagreement over pantheism with Schelling in 1812. And as late as 1841, when Schelling had repudiated much of his youthful attachment to Spinoza in favour of his proto-existentialist 'positive philosophy', he was summoned to the chair of philosophy in Berlin to eradicate the "dragon's seed of Hegelian pantheism"[2] from the minds of German youth.

But an unexpected feature of the metaphysics of Schelling and Hegel, given their mutual opposition to a theology of transcendence and perfection and their flirtations with a Spinozist theological immanence, is their insistence on the personality of the absolute. Schelling's work of 1809 offered not merely a theology but also a theogony, in which God creates his personality, freedom and essence as love through organization of the forces at his basis or centre. This basis is the *Urgrund* or *Ungrund*, which, as pure will or desire, is the unthinkable element in God and nature: that which resists inclusion within a system of concepts. Hegel too emphasized the distinction between his conception of the absolute as subject from Spinoza's substance monism (Hegel 1977: §17). For both thinkers, personality was not a mere seeming or dispensable attribute, a superimposition of the anthropomorphizing imagination. It was, instead, central to metaphysics. For Hegel, personality arises through mediation, through being in relation with others, a mediation that brings about the ascent to spirit and freedom. Although both thinkers disputed what they considered to be crude representations of Spinoza's pantheism, they also distanced their own metaphysics from his impersonal and ontologically perfectionist image of the divine. In their attempt to reformulate and revise the classical tradition of theological metaphysics, Schelling and Hegel certainly changed many aspects of it, and simply excluded others. However, their common concern to preserve the themes of God's personality, freedom, teleology and the doctrine of the Trinity shows that they did not completely accept Spinoza's and Hume's criticisms of theological anthropomorphism, or Kant's argument that, since teleological judgement is based on analogy with our own conscious intentions, we cannot truly ascribe purposes to nature. Together they accepted Spinoza's and Hume's argumentative assaults on the integrity of theology's external sources, such as revelation, prophecy and miracles, and replaced them with spiritual, ideal or moral sources of religious knowledge. However, by synthesizing themes from mystical theology with Kant's turn to the subject, they formulated a new theology that supported the personality and freedom of God.

---

2. This is a phrase coined by the Prussian monarch Frederick William IV, and cited in the letter from the Ministry of Culture offering the position to Schelling (reprinted in Schelling 1977: 408–9).

During one of the last great periods of metaphysical speculation in Western philosophy, therefore, theological themes played a central and openly acknowledged role. Some commentators have disputed the sincerity of Schelling's and Hegel's theologies, arguing that they employed religious language prudentially, in order to avoid political censorship. Schopenhauer frequently characterized his fellow idealists as secret Spinozists who, as employees of the state, were obliged to pay lip service to the Old Testament picture of a personal God (Schopenhauer 1974a: 186). However, it might be maintained that Friedrich Nietzsche displays a better understanding of the genesis and tendency of mainstream German idealism when he notes that the "Protestant parson is the grandfather of German philosophy" (1976: §10). The early intellectual training of Schelling and Hegel was in theology rather than philosophy, which may account for the abiding presence of theological themes in their metaphysics and their common attempts to reconcile them with the spirit of the age.

THE SECOND SYNTHESIS UNRAVELS: AFTER GERMAN IDEALISM

For a short period in the 1820s, Hegel's system obtained official recognition in the universities and Prussian administration. However, after his death in 1831, his followers split into a number of groups, each side claiming to be his legitimate heirs and the true interpreters of his system. From the distance of history, we might designate these different factions as instances of Hegelianism rather than representatives of Hegelian philosophy proper, in so far as each tended to emphasize one aspect of Hegel's synthesis and use it as a tool for polemical assaults on their opponents. Initially the Right Hegelians enjoyed the ascendancy, since they held prominent positions in the Prussian state ministries and at the University of Berlin. The Left Hegelians were, by contrast, marginalized radicals whose views excluded them from holding positions of political or institutional power. However, in time, the Left Hegelians came to dominate the intellectual and cultural scene. Schelling may have been called to Berlin in 1841 to extirpate the "dragon's seed of Hegelian pantheism", but the intellectual apologetics of the revolutions of 1848 owed more to radical interpretations of Hegel that stressed the Spinozistic themes of his philosophy – materialism, determinism and rationalist critique of the prevailing order – while discarding those he took over from classical metaphysics.

The immediate occasion for the opposition between Left and Right Hegelians was the dispute over whether Hegel's philosophy of religion gave greater weight to a religious picture (*Vorstellung*) or a concept (*Begriff*). Irrespective of its purely abstract and epistemological nature, this dispute had decidedly political and social overtones. For the Right Hegelians, a religious picture remained a necessary part of the unfolding of the concept, so that the transition from picture to concept reinforced and secured the content of the belief without evacuating its main elements. They used this interpretation to defend the establishment of the

Lutheran church in Prussia and the rationality of state institutions. By contrast, for the Left Hegelians the concept subverted and transcended the content of a religious picture, so that the translation of picture into concept dissolved the religious belief and thereby deprived state law of the sanctity it obtained through association with Christian doctrine. The Left Hegelians were the first non-theistic interpreters of the Bible since Spinoza's *Tractatus Theologico-Politicus* of 1670, and in the 1830s and 1840s David Friedrich Strauss (1808–74), Bruno Bauer (1809–82) and Ludwig Feuerbach (1804–72) applied Hegelian method to the sources and doctrines of Christianity in defence of atheist humanism, reinterpreting its messianic themes as political pictures supporting liberalism or republicanism. They thereby prepared the way for Karl Marx's (1818–83) far more radical critique of ideology and millenarian vision of a communist society without class divisions, private property or a state. In their efforts to place in doubt the underlying sources and beliefs of the religious and political establishment, the Left Hegelians stood within a recognizable tradition of European radicalism. However, in their case, they pressed Hegel's conciliatory philosophy into the service of a materialism and political extremism that owed a greater debt to the spirit of the French Enlightenment and Revolution than to Hegel himself.

The decline of Hegelian rationalism gave rise to another assault on the bourgeois religiosity of the nineteenth century in the works of Søren Kierkegaard (1813–55), whose presuppositions and aims were otherwise diametrically opposed to those of the Left Hegelians and Marx. Hegel was to Kierkegaard what Spinoza had been to Jacobi, the embodiment and ideological prop of contemporary nihilism, and like Jacobi before him Kierkegaard set out to show that scientific theory and philosophical system are fundamentally incompatible with the existential freedom and supernaturalism of Christian faith. In Kierkegaard's pseudonymous work of 1843, *Fear and Trembling*, the 'author', Johannes de silentio, attacked Hegel's optimistic religious rationalism and its theory that Christianity leads to the realization of universal ethical life through reconciliation of the subject with the externals of nature and history. Referring to the biblical story of Abraham's attempted sacrifice of Isaac, Johannes defended an account of Christian existence in which its *telos* is shown to be individual rather than communal, consisting of an unmediated and trans-ethical relation to God. A year later Kierkegaard published a further pseudonymous work, *Philosophical Fragments*, in which a second 'author', Johannes Climacus, developed a Christian view of knowledge sharply at odds with philosophical epistemology, the purpose of which was to dispute the idealist doctrine that revelation can be validated through agreement with the subject's rational and moral notions. Climacus maintained that Christianity's revealed doctrine of the universal God's incarnation in time as a particular individual is a paradox offensive to reason, with no point of contact with the innate notions of the subject. The upshot of Kierkegaard's polemic against Hegel was that the teachings of Christianity cannot be enclosed within a rational system and must therefore be accepted in faith.

Although Kierkegaard was geographically and institutionally a marginal figure in the nineteenth century, his works were a fertile source for a variety of thinkers in the twentieth, from the dialectical theology of Karl Barth, to Jean-Paul Sartre's atheist existentialism and Martin Heidegger's critique of the central presuppositions of Western philosophy originating in Greece. However, Kierkegaard was in many ways a tragic philosopher of religion, for his works dramatized the extent to which 'Christendom' has domesticated the radical demands that primitive Christianity made on the life of natural humanity. In his view, true Christian practice is incompatible with the bourgeois and contented spirit of the modern age.

In the 1850s the philosophical and religious outlook of another anti-Hegelian, Arthur Schopenhauer (1788–1860), began to attract public attention. Unlike the thought of the Left Hegelians and Kierkegaard, Schopenhauer's philosophy was not forged in the fire of opposition to Hegel's rational synthesis of tradition and modernity, but represented an independent tributary of idealism flowing directly from Kant. The first statement of his system was published in late 1818 in *The World as Will and Representation*, the year of the ascent of Hegel's philosophical star as a consequence of his appointment to the chair in Berlin.

Schopenhauer retained Kant's distinction between phenomenon and thing-in-itself, but passed beyond Kant's limitations on metaphysical knowledge by arguing that we know the thing-in-itself as it appears within our bodies as will. This, however, is not the rational, free will of Kant's moral theology, but a blind hungry will that objectifies itself in the phenomenon in a tragic attempt to escape its inner yearning by feeding on itself. In common with Schelling and Hegel, Schopenhauer resurrected constitutive teleological judgement, but since his immanent principle of order is blind will rather than reason or spirit, his theory goes some way towards dispensing with the residue of anthropomorphism associated with final causality and the theological implications of natural order. For him teleology merely accounts for the universal suitability of organic nature and for the particular features of an organism that enable it to defend and maintain itself within a natural system that is best characterized by Hobbes' war of all against all. Consistent with this contrast between Schopenhauerian will and Schellingian and Hegelian spirit, Schopenhauer maintained that when nature obtains knowledge of itself in the medium of human consciousness, it feels no compulsion to self-congratulation, but is revolted by this revelation of its inner being and thereafter seeks to bring about its own denial.

In relation to the philosophy of religion, Schopenhauer was an atheist who concurred with the rationalist attacks on the sources and theological doctrines of Christianity formulated by Spinoza, Hume and Kant. However, his metaphysics of the will supported a pessimistic and tragic view of life that has much in common with Kierkegaard and Augustinian Christianity. The misery and wretchedness of life conditioned by will and crowned by death leave human beings in need of a metaphysical interpretation of the cosmos, as a consolation for death, explanation of morality and support for public virtue. For this reason Schopenhauer observed the decline of Christianity with foreboding, since its doctrine of the sinfulness of human nature, morality of selfless love and ethics of self-denial had raised the spiritual tendencies of Europe and kept materialism, positivism and ethical *eudaemonism* at bay. He aimed to offset the cultural and intellectual drift towards secularism by championing the cosmological doctrines of the godless religions of the East as replacements for Christian theology, but with an identical ethical and salvific tendency. In the last half of the nineteenth century Schopenhauer was one of the most famous European philosophers, and his reputation as the 'sage of Frankfurt' encouraged many Europeans dissatisfied with Christianity to turn to the doctrines and practices of Buddhism and those of the monist school of Hinduism, Advaita Vedānta.

Schopenhauer's pessimistic philosophy had a contrary effect on the intellectual development of a figure who, although also originally marginal, was to have a very great effect on the intellectual and religious culture of Europe: Friedrich Nietzsche (1844–1900). Nietzsche was at first influenced by Schopenhauer's pessimism, but soon turned against his former 'educator' and began to style Schopenhauer as his 'antipode'. However, in the development of his pessimism of strength and affirmation in opposition to Schopenhauer's pessimism of weakness and denial, Nietzsche retained the latter's image of the tragic nature of life and scorn for progressive, materialist, scientific or political solutions to its main problems. Nietzsche was also much affected by Schopenhauer's defence of Christian practice in a godless world, for in his view Christianity's ethics of selflessness and salvation through asceticism are simply nihilistic without the presuppositions of God, freedom and immortality. In Nietzsche's view the development of European culture from the Renaissance up to Schopenhauer had issued in the death of God, but this upheaval in the realm of metaphysical belief called for a correlative re-evaluation of the guiding ideals and values of Christianity. These were not, as Schopenhauer and other post-theists imagined, universal values or values-in-themselves, but merely a local system that made sense only within the framework of theistic belief. To act and value as a Christian without believing in Christian doctrine was, claimed Nietzsche, to be a consummate nihilist or 'European Buddhist', willing one's own nothingness in order to escape the abyss of not willing at all (Nietzsche 1994: III.28).

The most creative and original thinking within the philosophy of religion after the failure of Hegelian rationalism was, therefore, taking place on the margins, unsupported by institutions and for the most part completely ignored. The Left Hegelians rarely had official positions; Kierkegaard was a minor figure even in Denmark (his fame consisted of being lampooned in the local press); and, until late in their lives, Schopenhauer and Nietzsche lived in total obscurity (with Nietzsche obtaining the fame that had otherwise eluded him only after he had gone insane). They were all, as Nietzsche often said of himself, untimely. In the universities and the state administration, traditional theology retained a fairly comfortable position. But as the latter half of the nineteenth century brought new scientific theories, new cultural forms, and the outbreak of the political hostilities that led up to the First World War, these extreme and non-conciliatory positions in the philosophy of religion gradually came to the forefront.

DARWIN AND THE PHILOSOPHY OF RELIGION

The immediate challenge to the institutional privileges of theological orthodoxy came not from the previously discussed radical positions within the philosophy of religion, but from external intellectual disciplines, and most spectacularly and definitively from natural history, on the occasion of Charles Darwin's (1809–82) publication of *On the Origin of Species by Means of Natural Selection* in 1859.

Darwin himself had no grudge against Christian theology or any specific intention to undermine the privileged position in the cosmos it bestowed on human beings. However, it might be claimed that the impact of his theory of evolution single-handedly brought to an end the intellectual respectability of attempts at interpreting the natural world and the spiritual qualities of human beings as parts of a teleological pattern warranting inferences to a transcendent or immanent personal agency. Previous philosophical assaults on teleological explanation, such as those of Spinoza, Hume and Kant, were not as decisive as Darwin in refuting the argument from design. As philosophical criticisms the best they could do was to dispute the scientific status of teleology, object that the natural order admitted of explanations other than intelligent design or trace the universal tendency to interpret nature as an organism to our subjective conscious intentions and thereby protest that teleology resides on anthropomorphic projection. Although Schopenhauer had attempted to attribute the adaptation of means to ends in nature to an impersonal and blind agency, his speculative method and metaphysical premises were remote from Darwin's methodology, and, despite his efforts to the contrary, a residue of anthropomorphism still attached to his concept of the will in nature. Darwin's theory of natural selection improved on these philosophical critiques by accounting for the infinite complexity of nature and the innumerable adaptations between parts and whole *without* resorting to either chance or transcendent or immanent purposes. Instead, it explained how adaptation is the result of a vastly extended process of natural causation, involving variation and elimination of attributes. Natural selection through descent imitates intelligent design, and also, therefore, explains the almost universal subjective tendency to interpret nature as an organism. Darwin's theory of evolution presented a formidable and unprecedented challenge to the old argument from design while simultaneously inspiring new forms of metaphysical speculation: in England through the works of Herbert Spencer (1820–1903), and in France through those of Henri Bergson (1859–1941).

LAST ATTEMPT AT A SYNTHESIS: NEO-KANTIANISM

The last four decades of the nineteenth century witnessed a period of immense political, social and ideological upheaval in Europe, very little of it favourable to traditional Christian doctrine or the institutions of Christianity. Revolutions and clamour for reform destabilized nations from within, while war and political conflict destabilized them from outside. An unprecedented growth in industrialization, especially in Germany, issued in the race to compete with other European nations for colonies as sources of cheap labour and natural resources. The rise of new movements and ideologies, such as social Darwinism, communism, trade unionism and nationalism, challenged the social role of the churches, enforcing them either to retreat in the face of the mass appeal of these new creeds, or to dilute the distinctiveness of Christian doctrine by placing it in the service of their ends: an instance of the former strategy is the Vatican's withdrawal in the face of Italian unification, and of the latter the rise of Christian Socialism.

In a bid to cope with the hostile social, political and intellectual landscape of late-nineteenth-century Europe, philosophers of religion who hoped to preserve some of the central values of Christian ethics and their presupposition – the possibility of moral personhood – made use of the resurgence of neo-Kantianism in the universities to defend a Kantian-style division between fact and value. The social and political environment presented a spectacle in which Christian virtue was not evident, while Darwinian theories of human nature suggested it had never been possible. In a last attempt to preserve the idea of Christianity in a materialist and positivist age, theologians such as Albrecht Ritschl (1822–89) located it in a realm apart, the quasi-Platonic domain of interior conscience and human need. This development is also evident outside Germany, for in the works of William James (1842–1910) and John Henry Newman (1801–90) we find the tendency to ground theism on a concept of conscience that strongly resonates with Kant's doctrine of the primacy of pure practical reason. Such theories might be called Augustinian, in so far as they argue for an affective dimension within human life that eludes scientific explanation, and allow that the claims of the heart provide some sort of warrant, however attenuated, for belief in the traditional doctrines of Christianity.

This fact–value defence of Christianity was formulated not as a rejoinder to either naturalism or fideism, but to provide a basis for those who aimed to preserve as much of traditional belief and practice as possible under unsympathetic cultural and intellectual conditions. A fideist might ask whether assent to the dictates of conscience necessitates belief in a personal God or the incarnation of Jesus, while a naturalist might want to enquire after the exact location of or epistemological route to this realm of values, or whether it has any real existence apart from its claims on the hearts of those who were raised within nineteenth-century Christianity.

CONCLUSION

The resurgence of a Kantian fact–value distinction and doctrine of conscience in defence of theism at the end of the nineteenth century shows that, throughout this period, the mainstream and institutional stance in the philosophy of religion was conciliatory, consisting of attempts to adapt theistic belief and practice to present conditions. Although the fact–value distinction of neo-Kantianism, James and Newman might be deemed the reverse of the project of mainstream German idealism, in so far as Schelling and Hegel founded Christian values on systematic metaphysics, it can be considered a manifestation of the same conciliatory spirit, in so far as its aim was to safeguard as much of the Christian heritage as possible for modernity. Our account of the prevalence of theism up to the end of the nineteenth century challenges views propounded by other commentators, especially theologians, who are apt to depict the nineteenth century as the period in which religion was marginalized by the death of God, and cultural and intellectual life received its bearings from new ideologies, such as positivism, secularism and materialism. Just as Schelling and Hegel neither surrendered to nor avoided Enlightenment critiques of theism, so James and Newman aimed to re-establish the main themes of Western metaphysical reflection on the deity on alternative grounds, in order to circumvent critiques of religion inspired by Darwinism. The instinct if not the method is identical: to reconcile traditional belief to the new conditions prevailing in a changed intellectual landscape.

Not until the outbreak of the First World War do the radicals within the philosophy of religion – the successors of Left Hegelianism, Kierkegaardian fideism and the tragic atheism of Schopenhauer and Nietzsche – come to the fore, and the spirit of reconciliation retreats. The socialist and communist descendants of Left Hegelianism claimed the large-scale destruction of the war as testimony to the corruption of Christian culture; Darwinians and the heirs of Schopenhauer and Nietzsche, such as Sigmund Freud (1856–1939), interpreted it as proof of their theories that human nature is ineradicably aggressive and destructive; while Kierkegaard's fideist disciple, Karl Barth (1886–1968), proclaimed the war as divine judgement.

But even into the post-war era the prevalence of theism in European thought remained an issue for many thinkers. For Martin Heidegger (1889–1976) our thinking and valuing is largely a matter of playing with the shadows of God, for the onto-theological categories of Platonism disseminated by Christianity are the very scaffolding on which our culture is built, dominating the main lines of our thought in ways of which we are largely unaware. And on the other side of the philosophical divide, the Anglo-American critique of representationalism instituted by Ludwig Wittgenstein (1889–1951) can be interpreted as another attempt to eradicate theism from European thought, for representationalism rests on the assumption that the world is knowable because it reflects the divine ideas and the moral norms established by the will of God. The conciliatory spirit that laboured to keep the central themes of metaphysics at the forefront of philosophical debate in the nineteenth century may have been severely challenged by the spread of secularization in the twentieth, but the most important philosophers of the later period were still aware of the extent to which philosophy had only partially extricated itself from religion.

2

JOHANN GOTTLIEB FICHTE

Yolanda D. Estes

Johann Gottlieb Fichte (1762–1814) was born on 19 May 1762 in Rammenau, Saxony. His parents were farmers who supplemented their income by weaving. Young Fichte showed great intellectual promise, so Baron Ernest Haubold von Miltitz offered to sponsor his education in hope of turning the boy into a fine village parson. Fichte studied at the Universities of Jena, Wittenburg and Leipzig. As a student he was intellectually attracted (and morally repulsed) by material determinism. After von Miltitz's death, Fichte was forced to seek work, but he did not become a village parson. While tutoring a student in Immanuel Kant's philosophy, Fichte decided that transcendental idealism offered a viable theoretical and practical alternative to materialism. He set off on foot to visit his idol in Königsberg.

Fichte wrote his first book, *An Attempt at a Critique of All Revelation* (1792), in homage to Kant. The book, wherein he denied all miracles or revelation other than immediate moral consciousness, helped him secure a position at the University of Jena. By the time Fichte arrived in Jena, he had formulated his own radical interpretation of transcendental idealism, which he called the *Wissenschaftslehre* and described as the 'first philosophy of freedom'. His passionate, insightful approach to philosophy quickly won the devotion of his students, but his career was plagued by controversy. Conservative foes, both within and outside the university, suspected Fichte's political and religious views. These critics hounded him with allegations, which ranged from disrupting public worship to fomenting insurrection, based on misinterpretations of his actions, lectures and writings.

Fichte lost his position owing to accusations of atheism after the publication in 1798 of "On the Basis of Our Belief in a Divine Governance of the World" (Fichte 1994: 141–54). In 1800 he fled to Berlin, where he served briefly as professor, dean and rector at Humboldt University (1810–14). In Berlin, he published the *Vocation of Man* in 1800, presented the *Lectures on the Wissenschaftslehre* in 1804 (Fichte 2005b) and completed *The Way to a Blessed Life, or the Religionslehre* in 1806, his final statement on the philosophy of religion. Fichte died of typhoid fever on 29 January 1814, leaving behind his wife (Johanna) and their son (Immanuel Hermann).

FICHTE'S PHILOSOPHY

Fichte made unusual demands on his readers and listeners. His terminology often changed because he treated philosophical terms as representing concepts, or mental actions: isolated by deliberate abstraction, comprehended by persistent reflection and expressed by discursive communication. In so far as a philosophy is "animated by the very soul of the person who adopts it", aspiring philosophers were expected to reproduce these activities for themselves (Fichte 1994: 20; 1992: 86–7). The first activity that Fichte required of the would-be idealist was to abandon the empirical standpoint of experience and to assume the transcendental standpoint of philosophy.

According to Fichte, the *Wissenschaftslehre* must provide an account of the conditions necessary for experience (the empirical standpoint), which preserves individual freedom and thereby the possibility of social, political and moral freedom. By abstracting from the object and reflecting on the subject of consciousness (thus ascending to the transcendental standpoint), the transcendental philosopher forms the concept of the I (pure self-consciousness) and postulates it as the ground of experience (1994: 10–11; 1992: 108–11). The philosopher discovers that self-consciousness presupposes a quintuple relationship (fivefold synthesis) wherein a law of unity (the pure will) joins the rational individual, the rational world, the material object, and the material world within one act of consciousness (1992: 444; 2005b: 197–201). Thus, consciousness encompasses all being; but only individual, embodied consciousness exists.

This account would remain hypothetical except that the fivefold synthesis occurs in experience. Fichte claims that moral activity presupposes an immediate non-sensible awareness (intellectual intuition) of a (moral) law of unity and a concomitant awareness of the conditions necessary to fulfil its command: an individual will, an object affected by the will (the body), a sensible world order wherein willing becomes deed and an intelligible world order wherein willing accomplishes its goal (1992: 293–4, 337–8, 437; 2005a: 71, 157; Breazeale & Rockmore 2002: 212–19). In "On the Basis of Our Belief in a Divine Governance of the World", Fichte appeals to the intellectual intuition of the moral law to account for religious belief. In *The Way to a Blessed Life, or the Religionslehre*, he employs the fivefold synthesis to explain religious experience as a whole (Fichte 2005b: 197–201; 1910: 124).

THE BASIS OF RELIGIOUS BELIEF

According to Fichte, transcendental philosophy neither demonstrates facts nor confirms beliefs but rather explains how these convictions arise in human consciousness. Just as philosophy accounts for the beliefs of experience in general, so philosophy of religion accounts for the beliefs of religious experience in particular. Although different religions include various beliefs, all religious people believe in God. Whatever features their idea of God involves, it includes the concept of a divine governance, or an intelligible world order whereby good prevails over evil. Philosophy of religion must explain how this concept originates in consciousness (Fichte 1994: 143–4).

Fichte rejects many conventional arguments that try to infer God's existence from the sensible world. Such arguments claim that the nature or existence of the sensible world implies an intelligible cause or designer, but no concept of the sensible world provides any grounds for religious belief. Considered empirically, the world is a matter of fact or experience, which requires no causal explanation; considered transcendentally, it is derived from the I, which admits of no explanation, because it is presumed as the ground of experience (*ibid.*: 144–6).

An intelligible world order can only be derived from the concept of an intelligible world, which arises in moral activity through a conjoined immediate consciousness of the moral law (or categorical imperative) and freedom. Fichte, unlike Kant, treats moral consciousness as an intellectual intuition. Like Kant, he claims that moral action is motivated by the idea of right. Like Kant, he believes that acknowledging the moral law entails recognizing the conditions necessary to discharge moral obligations. These conditions include a sensible world governed by a sensible order whereby the moral subject accomplishes its deeds, and an intelligible world governed by an intelligible order whereby it fulfils its intended goal. According to Fichte, "Once one has resolved to obey the [ethical] law within oneself, then the assumption that this goal can be accomplished is utterly necessary. It is immediately contained within this very resolve. It is identical to it" (1994: 145–8).

The moral subject occupies the empirical standpoint wherefrom it regards both the sensible and intelligible worlds as facts that require no explanation. (In making this claim, Fichte implies that empirical consciousness includes both sensible and intelligible experience; thus he, again, differs from Kant.) The philosopher derives sensibility from intelligibility (e.g. from the I). Although both the philosopher and the moral subject acknowledge limits on the I's activity, the moral subject interprets these restrictions as defining its own particular duties or individual moral vocation. The moral subject discovers itself as an individual with certain drives, interests and constraints, which produce particular, immediately perceived obligations. Fichte argues that this immediate consciousness is the only possible religious revelation (*ibid.*: 150).

The moral subject first discovers itself through its duties, so individual moral calling is the 'absolute starting-point' of all subjective consciousness; likewise, it first discovers the sensible and intelligible worlds through the moral law, so the moral world order is the 'absolute starting-point' of all objective consciousness (*ibid.*: 151). Taken together, these convictions constitute moral consciousness, which grounds all human experience. Considered philosophically, this starting-point is 'absolute' only in so far as the transcendental philosopher postulates it; but the philosopher is also a moral subject and thus possesses an extra-philosophical justification for the philosophical starting-point. Neither the moral subject nor the philosophical subject can question this foundation without damaging its status. The moral order requires no author or creator, and presuming that there is one would subordinate the moral law to an intellect, which would be limited by the constraints on any consciousness (*ibid.*: 151–2). Consequently, Fichte claims, "We require no other God, nor can we grasp any other" (*ibid.*: 151).

By Fichte's account, religion consists in pursuing one's moral vocation without regard for sensible results: "This is the only possible confession of faith: joyfully and innocently to accomplish whatever duty commands in every circumstance, without doubting and without pettifogging over the consequences" (*ibid.*: 150). To do otherwise involves subjecting morality to one's own finite intellect and thereby assuming the status of God (*ibid.*: 150–51). For Fichte, atheism is any type of moral consequentialism, whether the anticipated results exist in the present world or another. Agnosticism, or religious scepticism, refuses to commit to any foundation and thus despairs of all knowledge and a moral world order. Considered practically, atheism and agnosticism are indistinguishable. For Fichte, God's existence is not debatable but rather the ultimate ground of all knowledge (*ibid.*: 152).

It is easy to imagine why "On the Basis of Our Belief in a Divine Governance of the World" generated controversy. The essay identifies God with the moral world order, asserting the irrationality and immorality of belief in a personal creative deity. In addition to regarding individual moral consciousness as the only legitimate source of religious authority and human moral activity as the only legitimate manifestation of religiosity, Fichte treats personal happiness and immortality as irrelevant, condemning any action performed for the sake of temporal or eternal consequences. Finally, he rejects all other philosophical positions as theologically and philosophically incoherent and ultimately as morally bankrupt examples of atheistic thinking.

THE ATHEISM DISPUTE

The atheism dispute (1798–1800) involved the social, moral and religious implications of transcendental idealism (Breazeale & Rockmore 2002: 279–8; Giovanni 1989). It began with the publication of Fichte's "On the Basis of Our Belief in a Divine Governance of the World" and F. K. Forberg's "The Development of the Concept of Religion" (Forberg [1798] 1969) in the *Philosophisches Journal einer Gesellschaft Teutscher Gelehrter*, which Fichte and F. I. Niethammer edited. The articles received little attention until a maudlin (and anonymous) pamphlet, "A Father's Letter to his Son Concerning Fichte's and Forberg's Atheism", initiated a pamphlet war between friends and foes of the *Wissenschaftslehre*.

In 1799, protests led by a few concerned parties inspired Friedrich-August, prince-elector of Saxony, to seize the *Philosophisches Journal* and to threaten to withdraw all Saxon students from the University of Jena. Duke Karl-August of Weimar, who had authority over Jena, was not troubled by the confiscation order but could ill afford the loss of revenue and reputation. The threat required a diplomatic response, so he prepared an obligatory admonition of Fichte and Niethammer. Fichte took offence, engaging in a vitriolic self-defence and offering to resign if censured. Karl-August sent the prepared reprimand with a postscript accepting Fichte's 'resignation'. Although hundreds of students signed petitions for Fichte's reinstatement, Fichte was forced out of Jena. Eventually, and with considerable difficulty, he secured refuge in Berlin.

By some accounts, the atheism dispute concerned trifling personal and theological issues. Various reactionary parties, led by (often anonymous) contributors to the journal *Eudämonia*, had long persecuted Fichte with slanderous accusations. Fichte had often responded hysterically to real and perceived insults by demanding protection from the Weimar Court, so his threat to resign was the last of many overreactions that challenged Karl-August's patience and authority. Additionally, his seeming contempt for Weimar endangered the tolerance that his colleagues enjoyed under their relatively enlightened sponsor. Finally, Fichte's impassioned public self-defence against the atheism charge alienated many influential allies, including Kant and F. H. Jacobi.

During the atheism dispute, Kant published a repudiation of Fichte, claiming that the *Wissenschaftslehre* lacked religious and philosophical significance. Jacobi, a fideist author, described it as a more thoroughgoing atheism than Spinozism, which reduced freedom to formal egoism and God to an abstract moral principle. He complained that Fichte substituted a mere human concept for a living, efficacious God (Fichte 1994: 159–60). Some less informed readers were undoubtedly shocked by Fichte's disregard for many tenets of traditional religious belief, such as a personal, creative deity, revealed texts and an afterlife. Others were perhaps delighted by the alleged pantheistic, sceptical or iconoclastic implications of the *Wissenschaftslehre*.

In fact, the atheism dispute hinged on the question of whether transcendental idealism entailed social anarchy and moral despair. As a supporter of the French Revolution and author of the 'first philosophy of freedom', Fichte tested the social and political order. By vesting ultimate moral authority in the individual, he wrested it from the hallowed powers of church and state. His vision of personal moral revelation foisted tremendous responsibilities on the frail human conscience. Although Jacobi coined the term 'nihilism' to describe the ethical anarchy that he believed Fichte's 'inverted Spinozism' implied, he was not alone in doubting the average individual's ability to support those burdens without the reinforcement of some temporal or eternal consequences (Giovanni 1989).

During the atheism dispute, many misconceived criticisms were directed towards "On the Basis of our Belief in a Divine Governance of the World". Fichte was not an iconoclast; and his profoundly anti-sceptical philosophy was certainly not pantheistic. He supported traditional organized religion as a means to spiritual development (abhorring the possibility of philosophers sermonizing from the lecterns or of ministers philosophizing from the pulpits). Likewise, he took pains to distinguish between moral subjects, moral activity and the moral order (or God). Although the intelligible world encompasses all three, the moral subject relies on an external moral order to fulfil the intentions that motivate its activity. In so far as Fichte regarded philosophical concepts as activities, he construed the concept of God as a living, efficacious order and thus never implied that the moral order was a human invention (1994: 160–61). He responded to these objections in the *Vocation of Man*, which offers a satirical portrayal of Jacobi and a poignant description of the intelligible world (1987: 61–5, 67–123; Breazeale & Rockmore 2002: 317–44).

THE WAY TO A BLESSED LIFE

"On the Basis of our Belief in a Divine Governance of the World" accounts for only the origin of religious belief, but *The Way to a Blessed Life, or the Religionslehre* explains the development of this concept in human consciousness. Anticipating Nietzsche, Fichte defines human life in terms of interests and desires, or love through which empirical subjects perceive themselves and reality. "Show me what you truly love – what you search and strive for with all your heart in hope of finding true self-satisfaction – and you have exposed your life to me. As you love, so you live" (Fichte 1910: 13). Satisfied love generates moral goodness and blessedness, but misdirected love produces evil and in turn frustration and suffering. In connecting feeling and morality, Fichte differs markedly from Kant, who regards feeling as a moral-religious temptation. Moreover, unlike Kant, he locates the 'kingdom of ends' within human experience, arguing that the empirical subject enjoys peace and contentment in exact proportion to its level of spiritual development.

Life is love, but love seeks unity, so human life is characterized by duality and yearning. Love demands merger with an infinite, eternal one-ness (God or being), but most individuals feel this drive without understanding it because their consciousness is limited. They whet their desire on the objects that constitute their meagre world until despair guides them to the proper object of love and thus to a blessed life. Human spiritual development consists in widening the scope of consciousness and thereby increasing comprehension of the self, its desires and its goals. *The Way to a Blessed Life* traces this development through five conscious standpoints (*ibid.*: 12, 16–18, 21–2, 42, 151; 1987: 24–5, 78–9).

At the standpoint of sensibility, the empirical subject discovers itself as a sensibly determined will in a material world. The sensuous individual hopes to become at one with itself by satisfying its desires for specific sensible feelings, things and goals. When it accomplishes these objectives, it feels momentarily unfettered and content; but pleasure only sharpens its need and thereby impels it towards other diversions, enslaving it to the vagaries of caprice. The life of sensibility ends in self-dissolution, which leaves the sensuous subject (like Søren Kierkegaard's jaded 'aesthete') revolted by its compulsions. Despair forces the sensuous subject to recognize the inadequacy of sensible gratification (Fichte 1910: 104–5, 126; 1987: 73, 84–5).

At the standpoint of ethics (legality or lower morality), the empirical subject perceives itself as an intelligible will besieged by sensuous desire. In order to preserve its autonomy, it submits to an internal ethical law, which demands impassive self-determination against personal inclination and external constraints. To the extent that the stoic individual resists inclination, it feels virtuous and independent; but the empty, formal imperative provides no positive aim for its virtue. Fichte identifies this attitude with Kantian morality. He claims (as Hegel reiterates in criticism of Fichte) that the ethical subject imposes ascetic servitude on itself, thus avoiding self-reproach by oppressing its individual personality. Nonetheless, in choosing obedience to the law, the subject acknowledges potential disobedience, which implies that an external categorical imperative supersedes its own will (1910: 112–18).

At the standpoint of (higher) morality, the individual regards itself as a means for executing the moral law, which it loves as its own will. The moral subject's particular internal and external limitations (Fichte's 'personality' or Jean-Paul Sartre's 'facticity') reveal its personal vocation wherein morality, individuality and desire coincide. The moral subject wants to extend this inner harmony to the external world, so it intends for its willing to achieve sensible results, particularly regarding its interaction with other individuals in the social world. In so far as the moral subject believes in its moral efficacy, it feels free, but it perceives disappointment as a source of shame. In so far as the moral subject accepts the moral world order, it feels confident, but it perceives possible failure as a source of fear. Since the moral subject acknowledges all conditions necessary for fulfilling its obligations, so it believes in the efficacy of a moral world order. Nonetheless, like Kierkegaard's 'knight of infinite resignation', Fichte's moral subject 'performs the motions' of faith in a state of moral despair. This suffering compels the subject to reflect on itself and thereby to clarify its moral goal, which consists in striving to develop the intelligible world (Fichte 1910: 131–5, 146; 1987: 90).

At the standpoint of religion, which is part of 'higher morality', the individual perceives itself as participating in the ongoing development of the intelligible world. It understands that every individual's unique contribution is eternally preserved within the intelligible world (Fichte's 'postulate of immortality'). The moral-religious subject strives without needing sensible results, because it believes in the moral world order, or God. Just as Kierkegaard's 'knight of faith' performs the elusive 'additional motions' of faith (but without a 'teleological suspension of the ethical') so Fichte's moral-religious subject achieves a subtle focus on the object of faith. The moral-religious individual recognizes that the outer consequence of its willing depends partly on other individuals' freedom, which it should promote. Its ultimate task consists in cultivating freedom in itself and others and therefore it wills a sensible result conditionally as a temporal manifestation of the divine life. In so far as the moral-religious subject is wholly devoted to its present activity, it feels neither anxiety for future results nor sorrow for past failures. Although acting within the sensible world, it loves the intelligible world. Thus, love creates the concept of God (Fichte 1910: 136–47, 162; 1987: 75, 80–81; 1994: 146–7).

In order to experience a relationship with God, human beings need only act morally, but in order to understand this relationship they must reach the transcendental standpoint of philosophy. Fichte claims that philosophy serves two main practical purposes (1910: 28). First, it reconciles the seeming conflicts between faith and knowledge that distress many individuals (*ibid.*: 61–2; 1987: 26–7; 1992: 81). Secondly, it is a vocation for (and thus necessary for the blessedness of) a few individuals who have an unusually strong drive for knowledge (1987: 114–15). At the transcendental standpoint of science, the knowing subject comprehends the relation between God, or *Sein*, and existence, or *Dasein* (1910: 83; 1987: 99).

THE RELATION BETWEEN BEING AND EXISTENCE

The *Religionslehre* provides an overview of Fichte's *Wissenschaftslehre*. According to the principles of the *Wissenschaftslehre*, consciousness encompasses all being, and thus *Sein* (being) and *Dasein* (existence) are united within consciousness. Being is an infinite unity that includes self-conscious existence, which is manifest as desire. Desire presupposes both acquaintance with and separation from the desired object, so the conscious subject perceives itself as divided (in part one with being and in part separate from being). Being includes multiplicity, which raises two questions: what introduces diversity within being; and what restores unity within being?

Being exists only in so far as it is perceived or thought by consciousness, but thinking is governed by the law of reflective opposition (or principle of diversity), which requires that every object be conceived as something determinable in opposition to something determinate. In philosophical reflection, this requirement is felt as an inexplicable limitation of consciousness (which appears in ordinary consciousness as an 'ought' or command from being) (Fichte 1910: 66–7). Thus, discursive consciousness cannot even conceive of itself 'in itself' but only 'as being' or 'as existence'.

In thinking about being, the knowing subject posits it as a determinate self-consciousness in opposition to a determinable and (in so far as thinking is unlimited) infinitely divisible manifold, or world. Thinking introduces a primary division within being, which exists as a self-consciousness that appears to itself as a world (*ibid.*: 58–71). In thinking about existence, the knowing subject must again think of itself as something determinate in opposition to something determinable. Thus, thinking introduces a secondary division within being whereby existence is divided into a determinate consciousness and five determinable standpoints of consciousness: sensibility, ethics or legality, morality, religion and knowledge or philosophy (*ibid.*: 72–86).

At the standpoint of philosophy (but still under the principle of diversity), the philosophizing subject conceives of being as assuming two main forms (results of primary and secondary divisions) of existence: the form of infinity, as the world;

28

and the form of quintuplicity, as the five standpoints of consciousness. According to Fichte, these forms "can never be eliminated or superseded by anything else in real consciousness: so, the real forms, which obtain reality through this division, can only exist in real consciousness" (*ibid.*: 70).

Each aspect of the determinable quintuple form is connected to the free activity of a determinate subject, or I, which is characterized by desire or love. In so far as the I obtains a complete comprehension of itself, it recognizes the desire for unity as love of a unifying, or moral, law. Understood from this perspective, the five standpoints become elements of a synthesis wherein the law of unity joins the rational individual, the rational world, the material object and the material world within consciousness. This synthesis could also be expressed in terms of the union of "reason as self-making, being as made, being as not made, making as primordial, and making as copied" (*ibid.*: 119–35; 1992: 444; 2005b: 197–201, 217).

OVERVIEW OF THE CONCEPT OF GOD IN FICHTE'S PHILOSOPHY

According to Fichte, any object of thought can be contemplated both transcendentally and empirically. At the transcendental standpoint, the philosophical subject postulates the concept of God (pure will or being) as the ground of experience. The philosopher conceives of this ground as an infinite self-determining unity. However, the philosopher's concept is limited by certain (inexplicable) laws of thinking. According to the principle of reflective opposition, God must be conceived as something determinate in opposition to something determinable. Thus, God must be thought as a determinate (individual) consciousness within a determinable world. Because thinking is discursive, philosophy can know God through the relations between individual consciousness and the world; but philosophy cannot know God, or anything else, 'in itself'. Moreover, since God is a philosophical hypothesis, philosophy cannot justify this postulate or demonstrate the reality of anything derived from it.

Wissenschaftslehre, or philosophy in general, explains experience by deriving it from the concept of God (pure will or being). *Religionslehre*, philosophy of religion in particular, explains religious belief by showing how the concept of God originates in experience. A complete philosophy of religion also explains religious experience by showing how the concept of God influences the empirical subject's thought and behaviour. At the transcendental standpoint, the philosophical subject shows that moral activity presumes a moral world order, or God. God influences human thought and activity through desire. Desire expands consciousness, allowing the empirical subject to find itself as a member of an intelligible law-governed world. Philosophy of religion cannot demonstrate the existence of God. Likewise, it cannot produce any feelings or actions, including religious sentiment or behaviour. According to Fichte, philosophy provides no meaning for human life unless its ground exists in human experience.

Religious belief and activity are confined to experience. At the empirical stand-point, the empirical subject lives according to drives, interests and desires that reflect its level of conscious development. At the level of sensibility, the sensuous subject's life is determined by desire, which is mainly directed towards particular sensible goals. At the level of lower morality, the ethical (stoic) subject lives according to an ethical law that addresses its desire for autonomy. At the level of higher morality, the moral-religious subject devotes its life to a moral law that generates the concept of an intelligible world order, or God, which the philosopher takes as the ground of consciousness. For the human subject, God is not a mystery but rather a simple fact: "Do you want to see God, as himself, face to face? Do not search for him in the clouds. You can find him wherever you are. Just look at his followers' lives and you see him. Give yourself to him and you find him in your own breast" (Fichte 1910: 83).

FURTHER READING

Beiser, F. 1987. *The Fate of Reason: German Philosophy from Kant to Fichte*. Cambridge, MA: Harvard University Press.

Breazeale, D. 1988. "Fichte in Jena". In *Fichte: Early Philosophical Writings*, D. Breazeale (ed. & trans.), 1–46. Ithaca, NY: Cornell University Press.

Doyé, S. (ed.) 1994. *J. G. Fichte: Bibliographie (1969–1991)*. Atlanta, GA: Rodopi.

Giovanni, G. Di 1994. *F. H. Jacobi: The Main Philosophical Writings and the Novel "Allwill"*. Montreal: McGill-Queen's University Press.

Hammacher, K., R. Schottky & W. Schrader (eds) 1995. *Fichte Studien Band 8: Religionsphilosophie*. Atlanta, GA: Rodopi.

Lauth, R., H. Jacob & H. Gliwitzky (eds) 1964– . *J. G. Fichte: Gesamtausgabe der Bayerischen Akademie der Wissenschaften*. Stuttgart: Frommann.

La Vopa, A. 2001. *Fichte: The Self and the Calling of Philosophy (1762–1799)*. Cambridge: Cambridge University Press.

Perovich, A. 1994. "Fichte and the Typology of Mysticism". In *Fichte: Historical Contexts/ Contemporary Controversies*, D. Breazeale & T. Rockmore (eds), 128–41. Atlantic Highlands, NJ: Humanities Press.

Seidel, G. 1996. "The Atheism Controversy of 1799 and the Christology of Fichte's Anweisung zum seligen Leben of 1806". In *New Perspectives on Fichte*, D. Breazeale & R. Rockmore (eds), 143–52. Atlantic Highlands, NJ: Humanities Press.

On ATHEISM see also Chs 10, 20; Vol. 3, Ch. 15; Vol. 5, Chs 6, 17. On IMMORTALITY see also Chs 6, 16; Vol. 1, Ch. 8; Vol. 2, Ch. 5. On SELF-CONSCIOUSNESS see also Chs 4, 5, 10, 13. On TRANSCENDENCE see also Vol. 5, Chs 10, 14.

3

FRIEDRICH SCHLEIERMACHER

Theodore Vial

In many ways the personal history of Friedrich Schleiermacher (1768–1834) reflects the most important changes in European philosophical, theological, political and educational history at the beginning of the nineteenth century. Schleiermacher was born as a subject of the Prussian monarch to a family that had been rationalists but had undergone a spiritual awakening and enrolled him in a Moravian boarding school to be raised as a pietist. In his *On Religion: Speeches to its Cultured Despisers* (hereafter *Speeches*), published in 1799 and commonly taken in the history of theology to mark the beginning of the era of modern liberal theology, Schleiermacher writes, "Religion was the maternal womb in whose holy darkness my young life was nourished and prepared for the world still closed to it" (1996: 8). He had, however, a sceptical streak (he and some friends smuggled into the school and discussed the forbidden works of Kant). In a painful letter to his father the eighteen-year-old confessed that he could not bring himself to believe in the vicarious atonement and the divinity of Jesus. His father disowned him, writing that he no longer knelt at the same altar with him. Yet in 1802 Schleiermacher returned to the Moravian seminary and famously claimed that it was the religion he learned there that carried him through the storms of scepticism: "I have become a Herrnhuter [Moravian] again, only of a higher order".[1]

Thus Schleiermacher lived through the crisis occasioned in the West by scientific epistemologies and the rise of historical consciousness during the Enlightenment, and he was the first major theologian to respond to this crisis and rethink the nature of religion and theology and their relation to other spheres of human endeavour. His work has tended to be under-appreciated in English-speaking countries for two reasons: in so far as he is identified primarily as a theologian (as opposed to his famous philosophical contemporary at the University of Berlin,

---

1. An extended version of this account can be found in Gerrish (1984), which is still the best and most accessible introduction to Schleiermacher's theology in English.

Hegel), scholarship has been confined to seminaries and divinity schools; and in so far as these schools fell under the towering influence of Karl Barth and neo-orthodox theology in the twentieth century (the 'neo' indicates a return to Calvin after the 'wrong turn' in nineteenth-century liberal theology initiated by Schleiermacher), Schleiermacher was avoided.[2] Recent work in many parts of the academy, in and beyond seminaries and divinity schools and departments of religious studies, to a great extent occasioned and supported by the ongoing publication beginning in the 1980s of a Critical Edition of Schleiermacher's works (*Kritische Gesamtausgabe*, published by de Gruyter), is beginning to make clear to English-speaking scholars that in managing to absorb and come through the Enlightenment, Schleiermacher's thought is foundational in modern theology, philosophy and education.

HERMENEUTICS

A convenient way into Schleiermacher's thought is through hermeneutics. He is frequently cited as the father of modern hermeneutics in textbooks. Paul Ricoeur (1977) identifies his most important contribution as conceiving of hermeneutics as a general discipline, one involved in every human act of communication, rather than as a set of specific techniques for dealing with problematic ancient texts. For Schleiermacher, thought is the inside of language, language the outside of thought (Schleiermacher 1998: 7). Even unexpressed thoughts of an individual are conceived linguistically. Producing and understanding any speech act (oral, written or thought) involves two parts: the language that makes this act possible (Schleiermacher calls this the 'grammatical' part), and the particular and individual use of this language by a person (the 'technical' part). Proper understanding is the reverse of expression, the goal being to understand in a speech act what the expresser meant to say to his or her intended audience. (Schleiermacher famously claimed that on occasion the interpreter can know this better than the expresser.)

In each speech act the very personality of the actor is expressed. Brent W. Sockness (2004) has demonstrated that Schleiermacher is best classified as an expressivist, along with Herder, Humboldt and Hegel, using Charles Taylor's schema of post-Enlightenment thinkers. Expressivism, for Taylor (the roots of this category go from Taylor back through Isaiah Berlin to Ernst Troeltsch), is an attempt to overcome the rift between nature and the human subject that one finds in the Enlightenment, including in Kant. Expressivists argued that human beings and nature are both dynamic powers (*Kräfte*). Authentic (free) human action

---

2. Gerrish (1984) reports that in the mid-twentieth century his own teacher, H. H. Farmer, remarked that things had become so bad that he felt he had to check under his bed for Schleiermacher every night before retiring.

expresses the human subject. Actions do not merely make manifest a form that is already complete; rather, the very act of expressing gives self-clarity and allows the subject to develop. Language and art, especially poetry, become the paradigmatic human activities. Human beings realize or express themselves by transforming nature. In so doing they make determinate, or clarify, their individual subjectivity. The key terms are development (*Bildung*), freedom and self-clarity. Style – what each individual does with the grammatical resources at their disposal – is key to human development (individual and communal), and to getting at the meaning of an author or speaker.

The grammatical part of interpretation means knowing the speaker's language as well as the speaker, or as close as possible. One can accomplish this only by reading everything written by the author, as well as the author's contemporaries. Of course one can read only one text at a time, and one must begin somewhere, not everywhere, so as one reads further one's facility at grammatical interpretation improves. As one then re-reads texts, one approaches them with a different under-standing and a different set of questions, and so reads them differently. This is the famous hermeneutical circle.

The language available to speakers and listeners (the grammatical part) is a cumulative product of previous speech acts (a combination of the grammatical and technical parts). It contains in it the personalities (styles) of previous speakers, to a greater or lesser extent (to profoundly alter the use of language is one of the marks of genius). Each speaker in his or her (technical) use of the language to a greater or lesser extent subtly shifts the (grammatical) tools available to others. In this way we are changed and shaped by our interactions with others. The 'tech-nical' acts (and Schleiermacher will include here not just language but gestures and facial expressions) of others affect the 'grammatical' range of ideas and expres-sions we can have, and vice versa. Note that since thinking is always in language for Schleiermacher, this makes human beings fundamentally, not secondarily, social beings. Through the history of such interactions groups with common customs (*Sitten*) form. Language forms the basis of every important community, from family to religious community to nation.

In Schleiermacher's later lectures on hermeneutics he added what he calls the psychological part of hermeneutics to the technical. There has been an unfortunate tendency in the secondary literature to see the psychological part as a replacement of the technical, rather than as an addition to it, and further to see the psycho-logical part as an effort mysteriously to get into the head of the speaker. If the task of technical interpretation as a whole is to understand a speech act (oral or written) as the product of an individual (rather than merely as the product of the language available to that individual), then we can see two different aspects of this technical task. One's personality or individuality influences one's speech acts both as an "indeterminate, fluid train of thoughts" (the way one thinks in general), and as "the completed structure of thoughts" in this speech act (why one speaks in just such a way in this act) (Schleiermacher 1998: 101–2). The first aspect

Schleiermacher calls psychological, the second technical proper (both being part of technical interpretation in general). Technical interpretation is undertaken by the comparative method (we have a sense of what people are like, and so can make educated guesses about how this author's personality influenced this text), and by the divinatory method "in which one, so to speak, transforms oneself into the other person and tries to understand the individual element directly" (*ibid.*: 92–3). Most scholars who accuse Schleiermacher of attempting direct access to other people's thoughts simply omit the important qualifier "so to speak" in citing this passage. Schleiermacher is quite clear that the comparative method is based on comparing an author to what we know of other people; the divinatory method is based on comparing an author to what we know about others by knowing ourselves. Both methods are comparative, both are used together, and both, as technical interpretation, are always used in tandem with grammatical interpretation.

CHRISTOLOGY

Schleiermacher's expressivism (used here always in Taylor's sense, not in the sense of George Lindbeck's 'experiential expressivism' in *The Nature of Doctrine* [1984], which must be counted among the most brilliant and influential misreadings of Schleiermacher) allowed him to avoid or reshape some of the challenges faced by traditional Christian belief in the modern world. In Christology, for example, Schleiermacher found himself facing two equally unappealing options. On the one side were the Enlightenment intellectuals who could no longer in good conscience believe in the miraculous accounts found in the Bible. For them the only way to remain within the Christian fold was some version of the claim that Jesus was a great moral teacher, a teacher who taught by word and example, but not by miracle. Stories of resurrections and walking on water had to be understood as the non-literal enthusiasm of an unsophisticated group of followers, or as the result of deliberate manipulation by enterprising disciples, or as naive reports of phenomena that did, in fact, follow what we now know to be natural law. On the other side were the confessionalists who maintained that, although it might be harder in modern times to believe in the miracles recounted in the Bible, that is simply unfortunate for modern times. Christian faith requires just such belief, most especially in the vicarious atonement effected by the death and resurrection of Jesus, and if such belief came into conflict with modern knowledge, it is modernity that must yield.

In *The Christian Faith* (1st edn 1820/21; 2nd edn 1830/31), Schleiermacher proposed a third alternative between the first, 'empirical' group, who cut off any way of thinking of the continuing presence of Christ and left too small a foundation for a vibrant religion, and the second, 'magical' group, who required as a condition of salvation a sacrifice of the intellect and a denial of the best recent advances of the human intellect. Schleiermacher argued that Christianity was the group that formed around the charismatic personality of Jesus. Given the social nature of human beings, it is natural for groups to form around charismatic leaders. What was so compelling about Jesus' personality was his perfect God-consciousness, a point to which I shall return below. For now it is sufficient to note that Jesus' personality was expressed in gesture and in language. New linguistic forms were created, and old ones took on new meanings and connotations. In gathering around this compelling man, his followers began to speak and gesture, and therefore think, in similar ways. One can think of Christianity as a revolution in language, which is at the same time a revolution in consciousness, found in the interactions of the community that was shaped by the personality of its founder.

This language continues in the Christian community, even after its founder is no longer physically present, in just the same way that language in other human communities continues, although some members leave or die, and others join or are born into it. In its interactions the Christian community carries the picture (*Bild*) of Jesus' personality, and when one joins the Christian community one is confronted by this personality in precisely the same way that Jesus' contemporaries were. This encounter is salvific. Thus Jesus is really present, *pace* the empirical group, and present in ways that redeem; but Jesus is not, *pace* the magical group, present in ways that require a violation of the laws of nature. What, precisely, salvation and redemption mean in Schleiermacher's system will become clearer below when we turn to Jesus' perfect God-consciousness. Schleiermacher's ability to find a third way between the theological options at hand, between natural science and Christian belief, in Christology and elsewhere, was the reason that he and those influenced by him were called mediating theologians.

BIBLICAL AUTHORITY

The way that Schleiermacher locates salvation in the Christian community allows him to take a sophisticated stance on the question, so pressing in modernity, of biblical authority. Martin Luther (*see* Vol. 3, Ch. 3) had formulated for Protestantism the principle of Scripture alone as the means to salvation, and John Calvin (*see* Vol. 3, Ch. 4) had cemented this principle with his argument that Scripture was self-authenticating. The same spirit that produced the revealed word of God convinced believers that this set of writings was in fact the revealed word of God. This pillar of Protestant authority became very shaky with the rise of historical criticism during the Enlightenment. David Hume (*see* Vol. 3, Ch. 19) asked why one would put more weight on the testimony of relatively uneducated barbarous witnesses, whose accounts were in any case self-promoting, than on the eyewitness of one's own senses. This places Scripture squarely in the past, creating a chasm of meaning between the literal sense and a modern-day reader looking for guidance or inspiration. One can see this crisis in biblical authority behind many of the most important eighteenth- and nineteenth-century intellectual movements. Kant, for example, tried to locate religious knowledge not in a text but in our moral sense. For Hegel, metaphysics could still teach divine truths, but reason is the vehicle that presents these truths, found only in picture form in Scripture.

Schleiermacher was in agreement that the Bible should be read as a historical document. Given his hermeneutics, the literal sense of a text for him is the meaning the original author intended to convey to his or her original audience. But Schleiermacher's theology does not rest on the foundation of biblical authority; rather, it rests on the authority of the experience of redemption found in the church community. It is quite instructive to compare the citations that confer authority in Schleiermacher's great systematic theology with Calvin's. Every page of Calvin's *Institutes of the Christian Religion* drips with scriptural quotation and allusion. The notes to Schleiermacher's *The Christian Faith*, in contrast, are full of quotations from the historic creeds of the Christian churches, in particular Reformed and Lutheran creeds (see Wyman 2007). And that is precisely because, as we saw in Schleiermacher's mediating Christology above, salvation is brought about by the experience of Christ found in specific Christian communities. Theology is the reflection on and articulation of the experience found in these communities. All Christians share the Bible; each community has its own particular experiences (Schleiermacher calls them the peculiar modifications of the religious affections). These will overlap, to be sure, but remain particular. A Protestant Systematics, then, is based on the experience of Protestant communities, which have found expression in the creeds of the Protestant churches.

While Schleiermacher has, in a sense, replaced the Bible with the church as sole authority for Protestants, the Bible is still normative because it is the first expression left to us of the religious experiences of the early Christian communities. But it is the experience of the Christian communities that is foundational. Schleiermacher was therefore able to avoid much of the angst generated by historical criticism of the Bible, and in fact he himself makes several lasting contributions to critical scholarship on the New Testament. When scholars argue about dating and authorship of various parts of Scripture, when they see the hands of redactors everywhere, this does not undermine the foundations of what Schleiermacher sees as the source of faith. On the contrary, the more we can learn about the historical circumstances that have given us Scripture the closer we can come to understanding the early community's expression of the same religious experiences found in contemporary churches.

I ought to note here that while this theological move of Schleiermacher's may reduce the anxiety of historical criticism for those who follow him, it does raise difficult issues. Schleiermacher's high esteem for the New Testament was the result of his taking it as the expression of the religious experiences of those profoundly moved by encounters with the personality of Jesus. He rarely preached on the Hebrew Scriptures, which cannot be seen as an expression of experiences shaped by Jesus. And despite the real contributions he made to New Testament scholarship, some of his claims have not withstood the test of time. Because of the strong authorial voice and unified narrative of the Gospel of John, he took that Gospel to be an eyewitness account of the life of Jesus, more reliable than the synoptic Gospels. More recent scholarship places John as the latest Gospel and perhaps the least useful for information on the historical Jesus.

SCHLEIERMACHER ON RELIGION

What, then, is this experience to be had in Christian communities, an experience manifested so strongly in Jesus that it forms the community of people attracted to his personality. In other words, what does Schleiermacher mean by 'religion'?

Schleiermacher offers two famous definitions of religion, one early (in the *Speeches*), one late (in *The Christian Faith*). A great deal of scholarship has focused on the question of whether or not these two definitions of religion amount to the same thing, or whether Schleiermacher's thought changes over time. It is not appropriate here to discuss technical issues of changes in Schleiermacher's choice of words. In taking up each definition in turn, I shall be making the implicit case that Schleiermacher's definition is largely consistent over time, and that the differences in the language he uses are accounted for by the different genres of the *Speeches* and *The Christian Faith*.

The *Speeches* is a work of apologetic theology. The despisers of the title are Schleiermacher's closest friends. Schleiermacher was part of the circle of early German Romantics who gathered around the Schlegel brothers, Friedrich and Wilhelm (Schleiermacher and Friedrich Schlegel were room-mates at the time the *Speeches* were written). These writers and poets, who formed the literary and cultural avant-garde of Berlin, had little use for religion. In their work together and in their literary salons (the most famous of which was convened weekly by Henriette Herz, wife of Marcus Herz, a doctor in Berlin who had been one of Kant's leading students), they found Schleiermacher to be a brilliant and gifted conversationalist, yet they had difficulty understanding how he could also be an ordained minister. At a surprise twenty-ninth birthday party for Schleiermacher, Friedrich Schlegel, Henriette Herz and Alexander Dohna (an aristocrat and progressive leader in the Prussian government whom Schleiermacher had helped educate as a house tutor before his call to Berlin) challenged Schleiermacher to explain his religious views. The *Speeches* are his response.

Schleiermacher begins the *Speeches* by saying what religion is not: religion is not "the meaningless fables of barbarous nations [or] the most refined deism"; it is not "the crude superstition of our people [or] the poorly stitched together fragments of metaphysics and morals that are called rational Christianity" (1996: 12). Drawing on a threefold division of human faculties common in the eighteenth and nineteenth centuries, Schleiermacher argues that religion is not a matter of knowing (as Calvin had argued and Hegel would soon argue), nor of doing (as

Kant and his followers had argued with their focus on morals), but of feeling. This is the new foundation for theological reflection discussed above. But here we must be very careful, for Schleiermacher's use of the word 'feeling' has led to all sorts of misreadings that continue to dominate the secondary literature in theology, religious studies and philosophy.

Schleiermacher's precise words in the *Speeches* are that the "rudiment[s]" of religion, the "[latent] spiritual material" of religious systems, is "an astonishing intuition of the infinite" (*ibid.*: 13). Religion is the "sensibility and taste for the infinite" (*ibid.*: 23). Every intuition, he argues, is "by its very nature connected with a feeling" (*ibid.*: 29). The key terms are 'intuition', 'infinite' and 'feeling' (*Gefühl*). 'Intuition', which translators use for the German word '*Anschauung*', carries with it in contemporary English the connotation of a vague sense or knowledge of something that we could not really, rationally or sensibly, know. (The German word '*Ahnung*', which is *not* an important term for Schleiermacher, comes closer to this sense.) On the discursive field on which Schleiermacher is playing, 'intuition' is a technical term of philosophy. This field is profoundly shaped by Kant. For Kant, an intuition is "a representation of the sort which would depend immediately on the presence of an object" (2004: 33). For Kant, an intuition can either be *a priori* (in which case it is "the form of sensibility", namely, space and time and the categories), or *a posteriori*, in which case it is a representation of an object of experience (which will be a combination of an experience of a thing-in-itself and the form of sensibility that makes an experience of this thing possible in the first place). Without getting sidetracked into the complexities of Kant's epistemology, I want simply to point out here that an intuition for Kant is something fairly obvious rather than mysterious (although the way this obvious thing comes about is anything but simple).

'Intuition' for Schleiermacher carries the same set of connotations: "Intuition is and always remains something individual, set apart, the immediate perception, nothing more" (1996: 26). Schleiermacher, no doubt, opens himself up to misinterpretation by philosophers through a rather flowery use of language that is intended to appeal to his artistic friends. I quote at length Schleiermacher's most famous (or infamous) epistemological passage, the so-called 'nuptial embrace' passage:

> That first mysterious moment that occurs in every sensory perception, before intuition and feeling have separated, where sense and its objects have, as it were, flowed into one another and become one, before both turn back to their original position – I know how indescribable it is and how quickly it passes away … Would that I could and might express it, at least indicate it, without having to desecrate it! It is as fleeting and transparent as the first scent with which the dew gently caresses the waking flowers, as modest and delicate as a maiden's kiss, as holy and fruitful as a nuptial embrace; indeed, not *like* these, but it *is itself* all of these.
>
> (*Ibid.*: 31–2)

Behind the poetic language we can see that Schleiermacher is trying to describe the point of contact of a subject with an object in the world. In Kantian fashion, he is asking, what are the conditions for the possibility of experience? In very non-Kantian fashion, he wants to argue that in every experience there must be a subject–object point of contact, in which we sense the infinite. We cannot know this moment of contact, because the application of our cognitive apparatus is immediate. "With the slightest trembling the holy embrace is dispersed, and now for the first time the intuition stands before me as a separate form" (*ibid.*: 32). For Schleiermacher, as for Kant, intuition is a matter of ordinary, not extraordinary, cognition. In arguing for intuition of the infinite in every experience Schleiermacher is taking on what Taylor identifies as one of the central problems facing the thinkers of Schleiermacher's generation. The problem "concerned the nature of human subjectivity and its relation to the world" (1975: 3). The entire post-Kantian generation struggled to overcome the subject–object, human–nature split imposed by the various Enlightenments, not least the German Enlightenment that culminates in Kant. In the *Speeches* Schleiermacher is arguing to his artistic friends, with whom he frequently discusses Kant in the salons, that religion is not fundamentally a matter of beliefs and actions and stultifying institutions. Rather, religion is precisely the same kind of intuitive, creative experience that they, as artists, cultivate and value so highly.

The infinite, of which religion is an intuition, could of course mean many things. Religion is "the immediate experiences of the existence and action of the universe" (1996: 26). "This infinite chaos, where of course every point represents a world, is as such actually the most suitable and highest symbol of religion" (*ibid.*: 27). In each particular experience one also experiences the world, the action of the universe. The 'infinite' for Schleiermacher is not mere endlessness, nor is it something supernatural and beyond human reason, nor is it something like Hegel's Absolute. It is the causal nexus in which each part of the universe acts on every other part. The object experienced immediately in intuition is part of this interaction, and so in experiencing one object the causal nexus is itself in a sense experienced. This is expressed more clearly, but in the same sense, in Schleiermacher's later work, *The Christian Faith*, where he has more to say about the infinite.

In the history of theology *The Christian Faith* stands among works of systematics as a work of the very first rank in brilliance, completeness and epoch-making influence, along with Aquinas' *Summa Theologiae*, Calvin's *Institutes* and Barth's *Church Dogmatics*. In proposition §4 of the Introduction, one of the propositions "borrowed from ethics" (which for Schleiermacher means from the philosophy of history), Schleiermacher argues that human self-consciousness contains both receptivity and activity.[3] In other words, we are aware that we are both acted on

---

3. All citations are to the standard English translation, Schleiermacher (1984). I follow standard practice in citing this text by section number, followed where appropriate by paragraph number and page.

by the universe and the things in it, and we act on the universe and the things in it. We have, therefore, feelings of relative dependence and relative freedom. In addition, we have a feeling of absolute dependence, because the very possibility of our being receptive or active depends on our existence as part of this causal nexus in the first place. We did not create this universe or ourselves (hence there can be no feeling of absolute freedom); we simply find ourselves, our consciousness, our receptivity and activity occurring within it. Schleiermacher argues that we never experience absolute dependence in a single moment; rather, it is "the self-consciousness which accompanies all our activity, and therefore, since that is never zero, accompanies our whole existence" (§4.3.16).

In the *Speeches* Schleiermacher had written that it was this experience of the infinite in the finite, which he defines as religion, that carried him through even "when God and immortality disappeared before my doubting eyes" (1996: 8). In *The Christian Faith*, which is not a work of apologetic theology written for religion's despisers but a work of systematic theology written for those training for ordination in the unified (Reformed and Lutheran) church of Prussia, he takes a slightly different tack. "[T]he *Whence* of our receptive and active existence, as implied in this self-consciousness, is to be designated by the word 'God,' and … this is for us the really original signification of that word" (§4.4.16). God, for Schleiermacher, designates the Whence of our feeling of absolute dependence.

In the same way as he identified the intuition of the infinite as the essence of religion in the *Speeches*, Schleiermacher here identifies the consciousness of absolute dependence as "the self-identical essence of piety" (§4.12). Note that while he is not claiming here to have accounted for every aspect of religion, he continues to maintain that this feeling is its foundation or essence. Note also that the feeling is one of being consciously aware, that is, a cognitive moment remains, as in the *Speeches*, and it is a conscious rather than subconscious awareness.

Schleiermacher positioned his concept of God among other possible concepts in his day. He was sensitive on the one hand to distinguish himself from the pantheism with which he was charged in the *Speeches*: "this 'Whence' is not the world, in the sense of the totality of temporal existence, and still less is it any single part of the world" (§4.4.16). On the other hand, he defended himself against speculative theologians following his Berlin colleague Hegel, as well as traditions of scholasticism and certain kinds of confessional theologians whose claims were based on revelation. All these interlocutors shared the idea that they know something of God, some concept, independent of feeling.

> Now our proposition is in no wise intended to dispute the existence
> of such an original knowledge, but simply to set it aside as something
> which, in a system of Christian doctrine, we could never have any
> concern, because plainly enough it has itself nothing to do directly
> with piety. If, however, word and idea are always originally one, and
> the term 'God' therefore presupposes an idea, then we shall simply

40

say that this idea, which is nothing more than the expression of the feeling of absolute dependence, is the most direct reflection upon it and the most original idea with which we are here concerned, and is quite independent of that original knowledge (properly so called), and conditioned only by our feeling of absolute dependence.   (§4.4.17)

We are now in a position to return to the perfect God-consciousness of Jesus and explicate what it was that made his personality so compelling that it gathered others around. As we have seen, the feeling of absolute dependence is not an experience isolated from others. Rather, it is a feeling that accompanies every receptivity and activity in a human life. As Schleiermacher wrote in the *Speeches*, every intuition gives rise to a feeling. One can, however, be more or less conscious of this God-consciousness. In the hectic give and take of everyday life, in fact, we tend not to be very aware, consciously, of our absolute dependence. This is a condition that Schleiermacher terms God-forgetfulness, or sin: "the only course open to us is to reckon everything as sin that has arrested the free development of the God-consciousness" (§66.271). This lack of awareness naturally afflicts all human beings. In §94 Schleiermacher identifies what it is that is so attractive about Jesus' personality: "The Redeemer, then, is like all men in virtue of the identity of human nature, but distinguished from them all by the constant potency of his God-consciousness, which was a veritable existence of God in Him" (§94.385). Note again how Schleiermacher mediates between Enlightenment views that Jesus was just a man, and traditional supernatural views that he was the God-man.

Were one able to live in awareness of the interconnected nexus of the universe in every receptivity and activity, or, in other words, were it possible to live in awareness of the presence of God, that would change one's consciousness of one's existence in the world, and perhaps also change one's very receptivity and activity. Schleiermacher calls this 'blessedness'. Jesus was the one human being with a perfect God-consciousness, and it is this God-consciousness that is still found in the community of those who were changed and shaped by their linguistic and physical interactions with him. This, for Schleiermacher, is redemption.

POLITICAL THOUGHT AND ACTIVITIES

Having laid out briefly the central tenets of Schleiermacher's theological system, I shall now turn to the ways this theology influenced his political thought and activities, and his contributions to education and, more specifically, to the way we conceive of and study religion.

Schleiermacher's theology took shape in the context of major political and social changes in the late eighteenth and early nineteenth centuries. Perhaps the greatest of these changes was occasioned by the French Revolution. Like many of the young European intellectuals of his generation, Schleiermacher enthusiastically

followed the events in France. Given what we have said above about his hermeneutics, Christology and ecclesiology, it is not hard to determine what was so
exciting to Schleiermacher about these developments. Full human flourishing
occurs best in an environment in which individuals are free to interact with one
another. It is in speaking and gesturing that one's own personality finds expression and is shaped fully by the possibilities expressed by others. Social structures
that constrain or diminish free interaction impede this process. Indeed, in the
context of the church, external constraints on the interactions of believers put
the very picture of Christ present in the community in jeopardy. The democratic
tendencies in France, where all classes of citizens (rather than subjects) began
to take on responsibility for their common governance, dovetailed nicely with
Schleiermacher's developing thought.

In 1806, however, the powerful citizen armies of France, led by Napoleon,
invaded and occupied Prussia. Napoleon shut down the University of Halle,
Prussia's flagship university, where Schleiermacher was on the theological faculty
and served as university preacher. Schleiermacher was forced to flee to Berlin,
which was also soon occupied.

Schleiermacher never wavered in his admiration for the French citizens, but
his hatred of Napoleon was unrelenting. In occupying Prussia, Napoleon was
suppressing the free expression of the Prussian people. Just as in a community
of individuals each must be allowed to speak freely and listen to others, so in
the community of states each must be allowed to contribute freely the best of its
philosophy, religion, art and character. To overrun the borders of a nation was to
diminish the wealth of human diversity, and it is only in diversity that the infinite,
of which each finite thing, person or community was but one expression, can be
most fully expressed.

Schleiermacher was associated with a secret patriotic cell in Berlin that, in
conjunction with other cells around Prussia, sought to arm Prussian citizens and
plan an uprising to overthrow the French. Schleiermacher undertook a mission to
Königsberg in August and September 1808, where King Friedrich Wilhelm III had
fled with his court, to facilitate the coordination of the uprising with the highest
powers in government. The hope of Schleiermacher and his co-conspirators
was not merely to end the French occupation, but also to imitate the French: a
popular uprising would nurture a culture of citizen participation in the governing
of Prussia that had never before occurred in its traditional monarchy, in which the
military consisted largely of mercenaries under the control of the noble class.

The uprising never occurred, although the king reluctantly formed militias in
1813 as Russia, Austria and Prussia joined forces to force the retreat of Napoleon.
Friedrich Wilhelm III made use of the reformers' nationalistic rhetoric for his
own political ends, but hesitated to embrace their methods and goals because he
feared that any popular role in governance would limit his traditional authority.
Although he promised Prussians a constitution, once Napoleon was defeated
he had no incentive to follow through, and no constitution was forthcoming.

With the Restoration and particularly the Carlsbad Decrees of 1819, the former reformers found themselves under suspicion as underminers of the government. Schleiermacher frequently had secret police sitting in on his lectures and sermons, and was once threatened with exile and the loss of his teaching and church positions.

Schleiermacher and the king were also at loggerheads on the issue of church governance. In 1814 the king, desiring a uniform liturgy across the churches of Prussia, began instituting a common liturgy that he himself created. Schleiermacher viciously attacked the new liturgy, both on the grounds that it was old fashioned and therefore too Catholic, but more importantly on the grounds that a liturgy could not be imposed from the top down, but rather had to be the organic development of the Christian community. Although the King ultimately prevailed in this struggle, Schleiermacher was personally exempted from having to follow the new liturgy. Schleiermacher's arguments for a Presbyterian form of church government also made him suspicious to the king.

THE ACADEMIC STUDY OF RELIGIONS

Turning from questions of theology, ecclesiology and politics to the academic study of religions, there are two important issues to consider: (i) Schleiermacher's role in the history of academic institutions; and (ii) the role of his definition of religion in the development of comparative religions and in efforts to wrestle with issues of religious pluralism.

At the institutional level, Schleiermacher played a significant role in creating the University of Berlin. Friedrich Wilhelm III's government needed to replace the University of Halle, and to rebuild Prussia's spirit by replacing with intellectual efforts what had been lost physically through Napoleon's invasion. Wilhelm von Humboldt was head of the Department of Worship and Public Instruction. Schleiermacher was one of three members of the commission working under Humboldt to found the university. He played two key roles. One was the submission of an essay in 1808 entitled "Occasional Thoughts on Universities in a German Sense". Many of Schleiermacher's basic ideas for a university, argued for in this essay, made their way into Humboldt's plan. Most important was the division of the university into four schools – philosophy, law, medicine, and theology – with the requirement that all students be grounded first in philosophy as a unifying discipline before specializing in their professional disciplines. Further, Schleiermacher argued that the university was located between *Gymnasien* (secondary schools), the primary function of which was to impart information, and research institutes. The university was where young people began the process of becoming researchers themselves. University faculty, therefore, are both teachers and researchers. Schleiermacher and Humboldt agreed that the goal of university education was weighted more towards the general development of the person ('*Bildung*' in German, which is related to the liberal arts tradition in English-speaking countries), and less the inculcation of immediately useful skills and information. Because of the state's interest in such well formed individuals, the state should support the university. But because of the state's temptation to demand immediately practical results from research, a strict policy of academic freedom from state control was desirable. The University of Berlin was one of the first modern research universities and became a model for others, not least in the United States, where many of the leading academics spent formative years of graduate school studying in Germany.

Secondly, as a member of Humboldt's commission, Schleiermacher was responsible for calling the first members of the university's faculty. He served as the first dean of the theology faculty (and three times thereafter), and was rector of the university in 1815–16. In setting up the theological faculty he devised what became the standard model of seminary education into the subject areas of exegetical, historical, dogmatic and practical theology (the plan he had outlined in *A Brief Outline of Theological Study*, 1811).

In addition to the role Schleiermacher played institutionally in developing modern universities and modern theological education, one of the most vexed questions in recent scholarship is his role in the history of the academic study of religion. He is frequently accused of protecting religion from rigorous study by making it into a private and ineffable affair of feeling. This reading overlooks the cognitive aspect of feeling discussed earlier, associating Schleiermacher's *Gefühl* exclusively with emotion. This reading of Schleiermacher has recently been challenged (rightfully so, in my opinion) by Andrew Dole (2004), who shows that many interpreters confuse Schleiermacher with Rudolf Otto (a mistake Otto never made) and that Schleiermacher in fact defined religion as a human phenomenon completely open to scientific enquiry.

Beyond the question of whether Schleiermacher's work moved the modern academic study of religion forwards or backwards lies a more fundamental question: what was his role in the manufacture of the modern category of religion? Tomoko Masuzawa (2005) asks why it is that the category 'religion' and the taxonomy of religions that seemed self-evident to scholars and to people on the street shifted so radically around the turn of the twentieth century. Students today enter classrooms in departments of religious studies with a sense that they know what religion is, even if they cannot define it, that it is a universal phenomenon and that there is a fairly standard list of eleven or twelve 'world religions' that can be compared. Most faculty enter the classroom with the same sense. But throughout the eighteenth century the Western taxonomy included just four religions: Christianity, Judaism, Islam and heathenism). Not infrequently, European explorers reported running across people with no religion whatsoever.

Masuzawa focuses on nineteenth-century British comparative theology as one of the sources of this conceptual shift. She does not, however, look at the role played by the German Romantics and idealists in this shift, a role that is at least as great (in my opinion, far greater than) the role of the British. It is clear that Schleiermacher is one of the most important of these German voices.

In the *Speeches* Schleiermacher argued that religion, an intuition of the infinite, is a universal aspect of human consciousness, available in every sense-perception. To be human is, in some sense, to be religious. In principle religion is not personal and ineffable, but common, and as such open to investigation by the human sciences. Any attempt to protect religion from free investigation would violate basic Reformation principles.

> [W]e have no desire to keep the leaders of science from scrutinizing and passing judgment from their own point of view upon both piety itself and the communion relating to it, and determining their proper place in the total field of human life; since piety and Church, like other things, are material for scientific knowledge. Indeed, we ourselves are here entering upon such a scrutiny.   (Schleiermacher 1984: §3.1.6)

Schleiermacher also argued that there is no such thing as generic religion; there are only concrete, 'positive', historical religious communities. There is no primordial religion that then ramifies into various specific religious forms. All religions share a form or structure in that they are centred around an intuition of the infinite. The specific content of these intuitions, though, and therefore of each religion, will be determined by the contingencies of history, language and personality. Formally alike, each religion will be particular.

In the introduction to *The Christian Faith*, prior to dogmatics proper, Schleiermacher creates a taxonomy of religions. He does so because, having defined religion as a sense of absolute dependence, he must now distinguish what is particular about the religious affections of the specific community for which he is writing a systematics, and he can only do this by marking it off from other species that share the same genus. While this taxonomy is a bit embarrassing by today's standards, it is a remarkable step on the path to our current sense of 'religion' and 'world religions'. Historical religious communities can be related to each other in two ways: "as different stages of development and as different kinds" (§7.31). Religions develop through the stages of fetishism (idol worship), polytheism and monotheism. Of the three religions that have developed into monotheism, Judaism "betrays a lingering affinity with Fetichism [*sic*]" because it is limited to one nation, and because it often vacillated towards idol worship before the Babylonian exile (§7.4.37). Islam, "with its passionate character, and the strongly sensuous content of its ideas", tends to keep its followers on the emotional level associated with Polytheism" (§7.4.37). Christianity, for Schleiermacher, is the highest form of monotheism (§7.4.37–8).

Turning from stages of development to kinds of religion, Schleiermacher distinguishes between religions that subordinate the moral to the natural in human conditions ('aesthetic religions'), and those that subordinate the natural to the moral ('teleological religions'). Islam, with its "fatalistic character", subordinates the moral to the natural, and so is an aesthetic religion. Judaism tends to the aesthetic because of its focus on divine rewards and punishments rather than a focus on moral challenge; nonetheless, because it is dominated by the divine commanding will, it is an active, although "less perfect", expression of teleological religion. Christianity, for Schleiermacher, is defined as the monotheistic religion best expressing the teleological type (§9.40–44). It is further distinguished from any other such religion in that in it "everything is related to the redemption accomplished by Jesus of Nazareth" (§11.52).

We must first note the essentializing of historical religious traditions (Schleiermacher's taxonomy seems to assume one normative type that identifies the essence of a tradition, out of the great diversity that in fact makes up what we isolate as a single religion), and the lack of knowledge of those traditions (especially Islam). To us this can only seem antediluvian. But we must also note the role that Schleiermacher's definitions and taxonomies play in the historical question posed by Masuzawa of the genealogy of our 'common-sense' contemporary taxonomy of world religions: fetishism and polytheism are not a separate religious category, but stages of development through which any religion can pass. We have a taxonomy of different expressions of God-consciousness, different religious affections, but all are God-consciousness. In other words, we have moved from true–false religion to different authentic religions (in Johann Gottfried Herder's sense), each of which express a genuine experience of the infinite.

In current theological efforts to grapple with religious pluralism, and to facilitate interfaith dialogue, Schleiermacher offers an interesting conversation partner. Just as individuals develop and grow by expressing themselves in communities with other very different individuals, so for Schleiermacher the diversity of religious expressions is important, for each will have a different, necessarily incomplete, intuition of the infinite in the finite. That said, the perfect God-consciousness was found only in Jesus, and Schleiermacher fully expects that over the full course of human history and development all religions will naturally begin to pass over into (Protestant) Christianity. Schleiermacher does not accept exclusivism, according to which religions which make competing claims cannot all be true and therefore other religions are not the equal of Christianity, nor does he accept the inclusivist view that all religions are different paths up the same mountain.

Schleiermacher is a key figure in the shaping of the categories with which modern philosophers of religion must operate. There may be much to discuss and criticize, over 170 years after the publication of *The Christian Faith*, in what Schleiermacher identified as the essence of religion, in his taxonomy of religions and in the way he reconciles religion and science. We ought not, however, misconstrue his role in the advance of the university-based study of religions.

The past thirty years have witnessed a remarkable renaissance in Schleiermacher studies, and a reconsideration of his influence beyond the traditional theological debates about his proper place in the Reformed tradition between Calvin and Barth.

In addition to more traditional theological loci, this influence is clearly important in hermeneutics, post-Kantian epistemology, education, political theory, the shape of the modern category of religion and appropriate methods for the study of that category.

FURTHER READING

Blackwell, A. 1982. *Schleiermacher's Early Philosophy of Life: Determinism, Freedom, and Phantasy.* Chico, CA: Scholars Press.
Crouter, R. 2005. *Friedrich Schleiermacher: Between Enlightenment and Romanticism.* Cambridge: Cambridge University Press.
Dole, A. (forthcoming) *Schleiermacher on Religion and the Natural Order.* New York: Oxford University Press.
Forstman, J. 1977. *A Romantic Triangle: Schleiermacher and Early German Romanticism.* Chico, CA: Scholars Press.
Mariña, J. (ed.) 2005. *The Cambridge Companion to Friedrich Schleiermacher.* Cambridge: Cambridge University Press.
Nowak, K. 2001. *Schleiermacher: Leben, Werk und Wirkung.* Göttingen: Vandenhoeck & Ruprecht.

On SCRIPTURE see also Vol. 1, Chs 9, 13, 17; Vol. 2, Ch. 19; Vol. 3, Chs 3, 4, 15; Vol. 5, Ch. 12. On CHRISTOLOGY see also Vol. 1, Ch. 10; Vol. 2, Ch. 3. On LANGUAGE see also Ch. 8; Vol. 2, Chs 4, 11, 12; Vol. 3, Ch. 14; Vol. 5, Chs 13, 20.

4

G. W. F. HEGEL

Paul Redding

It is said that reading her husband's posthumously published lectures on the philosophy of religion had caused the devout and pious widow, Marie Hegel, considerable distress (Pinkard 2000: 577). How could the man she knew to have been a good Lutheran express the heretical views that were to be found there? This anecdote captures well the apparent ambiguity that marked the attitude to religion of Georg Wilhelm Friedrich Hegel (1770–1831), an ambiguity that was at the heart of the undoing of the 'Hegelianism' of his followers in the years after his death.

As is well known, after Hegel's death in 1831, his followers soon split into 'Left' and 'Right' factions, and while this split is now remembered in terms of its political consequences (it was from the Left Hegelian faction that the doctrine of Marxism was eventually to emerge), the context of the split was a religious one. A contest over the properly 'Hegelian' philosophical attitude to religion had been sparked by the publication in 1835–6 of David Strauss' *The Life of Jesus Critically Examined*. While the conservative Right defended Hegelianism as a philosophy that reflected Christian orthodoxy, the Left came to see it as a humanistic doctrine of the historical emancipation of humanity. However, while this was the first internal breach of Hegelianism, the implications of Hegel's philosophy for religious belief had been contentious since his rise to prominence in the 1820s.

Only a few years after his appointment to the chair of philosophy at the University of Berlin in 1818, Hegel started to attract accusations of 'pantheism' and, a little later, 'atheism' from more orthodox thinkers. Here the issues seemed to centre on the consequences of Hegel's metaphysics for the traditional issues of the personality of God and the immortality of the soul. On the former, a defence of Hegel could appeal to the fact that Hegel had himself, in his first major work, the *Phenomenology of Spirit* (1808), explicitly characterized his position against Baruch Spinoza, the prototypical pantheist (*see* Vol. 3, Ch. 11): while Spinoza had conceived 'the absolute' as 'substance', Hegel had asserted that it had to be equally understood as 'subject' (Hegel 1977: §17). But exactly what was meant by this formula, and whether it amounted to the idea of a personal God, was in fact far from clear. Indeed, Hegel elsewhere clearly suggested that the existence of God was dependent on the existence of the human beings who had *thoughts about* God, and for an orthodox Christian this sounded much like pantheism. On the issue of the immortality of the soul, Hegel's defence seemed equally worrying. Hegel rarely seemed to say anything as simple as affirming or denying that the soul was immortal, but would direct his attention to the problems of the conception of time presupposed by the opposing concepts 'mortal' and 'immortal'.

Such aspects of Hegel's approach were in fact symptomatic of the general relation of Hegel's philosophy to religion that critics found objectionable. While officially declaring that philosophy and religion had the same *content* – 'God' – Hegel claimed that the *conceptual* form of philosophy dealt with this content in a more developed way than that which was achievable in the imagistic representational form of religion. Many opponents were suspicious that the concept of 'God' was emptied of its proper meaning in the process of Hegel's philosophical translations. Ultimately, then, the source of the corrosive effects of Hegel's philosophy on religion could indeed appear to be the insistence that the content of religious belief, like everything else, be grounded on rational, in fact *logical*, considerations – the logical coherence of the system of philosophy itself – rather than on anything like revelation.

Perhaps while he was alive, the possibility that religion and philosophy, faith and reason, could coexist might have seemed to have been exemplified in the person himself. After all, despite what he preached in the lecture hall, Hegel *did* seem to be the man his wife took him to be. But after his death, and with his thoughts now taken up by a number of very different individuals, the fissures emerged all too clearly. Hegel's popular lectures on religion, given four times at Berlin during his thirteen years there, were the first to be edited and published posthumously, and it was the doctrine articulated in these that showed the fault line that proved the undoing of a unified Hegelian philosophy of religion, and, more generally, of a unified Hegelian philosophy itself. Crucially, it was not so much the issues that concerned critics in the 1820s that were now central as much as the apparent tension between the systematic and more 'historicist' aspects of Hegelianism (Jaeschke 1990: 373–5).

This general tension within Hegel's philosophy is perhaps most clearly encapsulated in the well-known slogan from his *Elements of the Philosophy of Right* that philosophy is "*its own time comprehended in thoughts*" (Hegel 1991: 21). Did this not suggest that philosophy itself is to be understood as an historical product of a culture and to be accounted for by the particular conditions of its genesis? And are not cultural products so explained thereby 'explained away'? This was closer to the attitude of Karl Marx, who later wanted to replace Hegel's idealist philosophy with 'science' as it had come to be conceived in the later nineteenth century, but such a fate for philosophy itself was first enacted for religion. Were not forms of religion such as Christianity to be explained away genetically in terms of their evolution under conditions that perhaps no longer obtained? Of course, from his point of view, by grounding religion in *conceptual* truth, Hegel had thought he was *saving* it from the types of secular reductive analyses that were common during the eighteenth century. Moreover, rather than approach Christianity as just one of many possible forms taken by religious belief, he took it to be the 'absolute' or 'consummate' religion. If Hegel's 'Left' successors were bringing out the essential features of Hegelianism, then these would seem to be features at odds with the intentions of its founder.

To understand the conflicting attempts to grapple with the significance of religion within Hegel's philosophy it is necessary to review some of the major parameters of that cultural field within which Hegel's thought had developed and which had left their distinct traces in his mature philosophy: traces that Hegel believed could be integrated into his unified system if only one understood correctly the 'logic' of that conceptual unification.

SOURCES OF HEGEL'S PHILOSOPHY OF RELIGION

Kant's moral religion

Any attempt to understand Hegel cannot bypass the figure of Immanuel Kant (1724–1804), who had transformed the German-speaking intellectual world in the 1780s with his 'critical' philosophy. All three of his 'Critiques' – the *Critique of Pure Reason* (1781, 1787), the *Critique of Practical Reason* (1788) and the *Critique of Judgement* (1790) – had implications for religion, and in 1792 Kant addressed the issue directly in *Religion within the Boundaries of Mere Reason* (*see* Vol. 3, Ch. 21).

In the *Critique of Pure Reason* Kant had purportedly refuted traditional philosophical proofs for the *existence* of God. But in that work, and in a more developed form in the *Critique of Practical Reason*, Kant had suggested another way of reconciling philosophy and religion by claiming the *idea* of God to be necessary for all rational beings. While not able to be secured as an existent known through theoretical reason, God was nevertheless a necessary 'postulate' of practical, that is, *moral* reasoning, and Kant thought he had demonstrated the necessity of *that*.

Kant went on to sketch out this idea in terms of the notion that religious representations gave symbolic *exhibition* (*Darstellung*) to fundamentally *moral* ideas, and with this his attitude to religion seemed to be close to such enlightened thinkers as G. E. Lessing (*see* Vol. 3, Ch. 22), who had interpreted the Christian myths, taken to be *literally* false, as providing a metaphorical presentation of some deep *moral* truths (Allison 1966: 133–4). Thus in his *Religion Within the Boundaries of Mere Reason*, Kant sketches a view of the life of Christ as a moral exemplar. While not *denying* that Jesus was "a supernaturally begotten human being", he nevertheless points out that "from a practical point of view any such presupposition is of no benefit to us, since the prototype which we see embedded in this apparition must be sought in us as well" (Kant 1996: 106).

To orthodox believers this seemed dangerously close to reducing God to the status of a *mere* psychological or subjective idea. Indeed, the very project of interpreting the nature of religious belief from within a rationalistic philosophical perspective had been famously attacked by F. H. Jacobi, who had insisted that faith should not be exposed to the corrosive effects of reflective reason. The rationalistic philosophical attitude to such normative beliefs would always lead to 'nihilism', he claimed, because the Enlightenment demand to find rational grounds for any belief would always result in an endless regress of reason-giving. To avoid such regress one needed something like a 'leap' of faith or belief (*Glauben*), a notion to which he gave a Humean, empiricist gloss. Since ungrounded faith/belief was required in order for there to be belief in the objective world at all, one was thereby justified in maintaining an ungrounded belief in a personal God, who could be known immediately and intuitively in a type of immediately felt conviction. In fact, Jacobi's critique of Kant's rationalism appeared in the context of his critique of the doctrine of *another* philosopher whose influence would be deeply felt in Hegel's philosophy of religion: Spinoza.

Spinoza and pantheism

Jacobi's attack on Kant was made in the second (1789) edition of his book *Concerning the Doctrine of Spinoza in Letters to Herr Moses Mendelssohn*, first published in 1785, in which he had initiated within German letters what came to be known as the 'pantheism dispute'. There he related how Lessing, one of the culture's most respected figures, had professed to him his belief in pantheism not long before his death. Not only had Lessing affirmed the pantheist doctrine of '*hen kai pan*' (identifying God as the 'one and all'), but he had even claimed that Gottfried Leibniz had been "a Spinozist at heart" (Jacobi 2005: 243, 247). Jacobi had intended this as a warning: philosophical thought when practised free from the constraints of religion would lead to the 'atheistic' materialism that Spinoza was thought to exemplify, but he inadvertently succeeded in attracting many of Hegel's generation to Spinozism itself.

The 'Spinoza dispute' had raged in the years during which Hegel was a student of theology at the Tübingen seminary (1788–93). For Hegel, this was a period of close friendship with fellow seminarians Friedrich Schelling and Friedrich Hölderlin, and in the 1790s all three were clearly attracted to Spinozistic pantheism (Pinkard 2000: 31–2). Spinozist ideas would be developed by Schelling in particular in his precocious philosophical writings from the mid-1790s, but the form of Spinozism embraced there was meant to be the antithesis of the atheistic materialism of Jacobi's account. Schelling became intent on showing that Spinozism, rather than being *nihilistic*, was in fact compatible with the human freedom that Kant had put at the centre of philosophy with his insistence on the primacy of pure *practical*, not theoretical, reason. Schelling also gave to his Spinozism a *Neoplatonic* twist, and the philosophy of Schelling and especially, after him, that of Hegel, showed clear features of the type of thought found in the Platonism of late antique philosophers such as Plotinus and Proclus (Beierwaltes 2004; Vieillard-Baron 1979). Importantly, it was these Neoplatonic and especially *Proclean* features that would be central to Hegel's understanding of Christianity, particularly the doctrine of the Trinity, as well as to his criticisms of Spinoza.

Neoplatonism

The Neoplatonic thought of Plotinus and Proclus (*see* Vol. 1, Chs 15, 19) had been a recurring feature of German religious and philosophical thought since the late middle ages, having appeared in influential thinkers such as Meister Eckhart and Nicholas of Cusa (*see* Vol. 2, Ch. 18) and, later, Leibniz (*see* Vol. 3, Ch. 13) and Jacob Böhme. In the 1780s and 1790s, there seems to have been a revival of Platonist and Neoplatonist thought in the German states, and this would come to be especially influential on early 'Romanticism'. During the 1790s, the poet-philosopher Novalis (Friedrich von Hardenberg, 1772–1801) had even claimed to find similarities between the views of Plotinus on the one hand, and Kant and Fichte on the other (Beierwaltes 2004: 87–8). In retrospect, this does not seem too fanciful.

In the *Critique of Pure Reason*, Kant had interpreted Plato's 'ideas' as non-empirical ('pure', 'transcendental') concepts that, while not *constitutive* of any knowledge claims, were nevertheless essential for *regulating* all rational scientific enquiry with its drive to *unify* knowledge. The Platonic conception of the cosmos as a unified whole, he noted, expresses the goal of such explanatory unification: "only the whole of its combination in the *totality of a world* is fully adequate to its idea" (Kant 1998: A318/B374–5, emphasis added). But while Plato had thought of his 'ideas' as archetypes for things in themselves, for Kant Plato's ideas were rightly understood as demands for the unification of the understanding and, in relation to practical reason, the universalization of one's practical maxims in the categorical imperative.

In the "Transcendental Dialectic" of the first *Critique*, Kant had traced the origin of the illegitimate *metaphysical* concept of God to the desire to grasp the ultimate ground of the unified cosmos. To take the 'idea' associated with a particular form of reasoning (based on the use of the disjunctive syllogism) in a *constitutive* rather than regulative way, and to 'realize', 'hypostatize' and 'personalize' this idea, would result in the traditional theistic concept of God (Kant 1998: A583/B611n·). This was all part of Kant's critique of a metaphysical theology, but with the notion of his regulative 'idea' of a unified cosmos, Kant had opened his critical framework to Hegel's interpretation in which a quite different conception of the logical status of the 'idea' would be cashed out in distinctly Proclean ways. In his commentary on Plato's *Parmenides*, Proclus had criticized the attribution of 'being' to 'the One', an idea expressed in Christianized form in the 'negative' or '*apophatic*' theology of the roughly contemporary Pseudo-Dionysius (*see* Vol. 1, Ch 20). This type of thought was to reappear in late medieval Christian thinkers such as Meister Eckhart, who was to be rediscovered by Hegel and others of his generation, but the original idea of denying 'being' to 'the One' was *not unlike* Kant's own criticism of the 'hypostatization' of the idea of the ground of the unified cosmos. While Kant's thought might have been overtly free of the Neoplatonic ideas that permeated German forms of Christian mysticism, it is not difficult to see how post-Kantian thinkers may have made this link.

Schleiermacher and the religion of feeling

Given Jacobi's appeal to the 'leap of faith' to halt the rationalistic demand for the ground of any claim, it is not surprising that he would appeal to a type of conviction based on the raw immediate *feeling of certainty*. Jacobi himself was not a Romantic, but this appeal to felt certainty was something that the Romantic generation took seriously, and it was central to the theology of Hegel's Berlin contemporary and opponent, Friedrich Schleiermacher.

Schleiermacher, who had been a member of the Berlin circle of 'early Romantics' and friend and associate of Friedrich Schlegel and Novalis, had published the widely influential *On Religion: Speeches to its Cultural Despisers* in 1800 (Schleiermacher 1996), a text generally directed against the rationalist demand that religious belief be given a ground in *reason*. Schleiermacher's claim was that religious belief was based in neither theoretical nor moral reason, but in a type of pre-reflective consciousness closer to an aesthetic apprehension of the world. Schleiermacher *too* had been influenced by the Spinozist and Neoplatonic revival of the 1780s and 1790s, but had understood this in a more 'mystical' than rationalist way. In religious experience one grasped one's unity with the whole of existence, a unity that was ruptured by the reflective consciousness in which the thinker grasped himself or herself as a subject standing over against the world as object. What one grasped in religious feeling was a sense of one's 'absolute dependence' on the whole of which one had an immediate intuition. Schleiermacher's appeal to *feeling* here was thus a way of moving beyond Kant while agreeing with the limitations of theoretical *reason*.[1]

Hegel was consistently opposed to any such attempts to base a religious or any other orientation on the feelings of the 'heart' rather than on the conceptuality of reason, and lashed out at Schleiermacher's theology (Hegel 2002: 347–8). For Hegel, a retreat to feeling was a consequence of Kant's rejection of the idea of *rational* knowledge of God (*ibid.*: 343–5). However, he was *equally* critical of any *abstract opposing* of cognition to feeling. The immediacy of feeling was to be given a place in reason, and a proper conception of reason itself would show

---

1. Or at least this is how Schleiermacher was understood by Hegel. For a reading of Schleiermacher that challenges this account, see this volume, Chapter 3.

how such feelings could be integrated into a larger, rational whole. Thus, like his romantic contemporaries, Hegel denounced a conception of a distanced dry cognition that conceived itself as the antithesis of feeling: a stance characterized as the finite 'understanding' (*Verstand*), and identified with the approach of the empirical sciences. In contrast to this he appealed to a richer inferential concept of 'reason' (*Vernunft*) which allowed the cognition of the world in its Platonic unity: the concept of reason that Kant had restricted to merely 'regulative' status. In this way, then, his way beyond the framework within which Kant had reduced religious ideas to seeming subjective 'postulates' had elements in common with that of his romantic opponents.

The historicity of spirit

Another strand Hegel attempted to incorporate into the philosophical system within which he intended to preserve an appropriately normative significance for religion was the one that finally proved to be the undoing of the Hegelian movement after his death. This was a decidedly *genetic* and *historical* form of analysis of cultural phenomena that can be related back to the work of Johann Gottfried Herder, a seminal thinker who introduced an 'expressivist' or 'hermeneutic' philosophical approach to human existence with the idea that different historical communities had to be understood in terms of the distinct socially based forms of mentality or 'spirit' (*Geist*) that characterized their art, institutions and modes of thought (Taylor 1975: ch. 2). Such an expressivist approach was clearly incompatible with dualistic conceptions of mind and body, and Herder was correspondingly attracted to a form of Spinozist pantheism.

It is easy to see how such a conception of history might engender ambiguities that sit uneasily with Hegel's more systematic thought. Already in Herder there seems to be a tension between the more 'Enlightenment' conception of history as a narrative in which 'reason' and 'humanity' are progressively realized – a conception of history inherited by Hegel – and a more relativistic one in which history presents a panorama of distinct and incommensurable forms of human life and mentality (Forster 2002: xxvi–xxviii). Such relativistic reflection can easily lead to the idea that one's own defining culture and religion is, at best, *just another* perspectival realization of some eternal truth to which *all* rival cultures and religions give equal expression, and it can extend to the idea that one's religion is *merely* a historical product illegitimately claiming universal status. Hegel argued that such a reduction of religion to finite historical events was *itself* a result of reducing reason to the finite understanding. However, if Hegel succeeded in reconciling these distinct attitudes to history, it is clear that his followers did not.

Hegel was confident that his *logic* provided a framework within which such disparate elements could be ultimately reconciled. The key to understanding the way he purported to do this is to examine his conception of religion within the framework that he generated by generalizing Herder's account of 'spirit'.

THE PLACE OF RELIGION WITHIN HEGEL'S SYSTEM OF SPIRIT

Hegel had apparently been interested in the history of religions from his school-days, and his first writings after leaving the Tübingen seminary were concerned with the contrast between the naturalness of the folk religions of ancient Greece and the 'positivity' of the succeeding Christianity in which an 'external' doctrinal form was imposed on the religious community (Hegel 1948). While containing elements of Hegel's distinctive approach, such works belong to the pre-history of Hegel's mature philosophy commencing with the *Phenomenology of Spirit*, completed in Jena in 1807, in which the basic structure of Hegel's character-istic thought emerges. However, to get the clearest picture of the framework of 'spirit' within which religious thought is assigned its distinctive role, we must consider Hegel's systematic thought to which the *Phenomenology* was meant to be an introduction. This was the system presented in Hegel's *Encyclopaedia of the Philosophical Sciences*.

It is no coincidence that the three parts of the *Encyclopaedia* – *Logic*, *Philosophy of Nature* and *Philosophy of Spirit* – correspond to the structure of the Trinity, as in Hegel's system the myths of Christianity, the most developed form of religion, are meant to give symbolic expression to the conceptual architectonic from which Hegel's own system is constructed. It is within the *Philosophy of Spirit* that Hegel's explicit account of religion is to be found.

The triadic structure of the *Encyclopaedia* is reproduced within the structure of the *Philosophy of Spirit* itself, with spirit being divided into 'subjective', 'objective' and 'absolute' spirit (Hegel 1971). The philosophy of *subjective spirit* is effectively Hegel's philosophy of mind, while the 'spirit' of *objective spirit* is closer to that of Herderian historicist hermeneutics. The objective spirit of a culture is charac-terized by those action-guiding world interpretations and forms of life that can be sedimented and institutionalized into the 'ethical substance' (*Sittlichkeit*), into which an individual has their 'second birth' and from which they acquire their 'second nature'. That is, these normative structures form the conditions under which living individuals acquire 'self-consciousness' (or what would now be called 'intentionality'), and in turn such structures need to be embodied within the self-consciously lived lives of such individuals. Subjective and objective mind are then, we might say, mutually presupposing. Where Hegel's account of spirit departs from the more hermeneutic approaches deriving from Herder is in Hegel's notion of 'absolute spirit', and it is to *absolute* rather than objective spirit that reli-gion properly belongs.

In Hegel's mature account, 'art', 'religion' and 'philosophy' make up 'absolute spirit', and while each presents to human experience and knowledge the same *content*, which will variously be called 'God' or 'the Idea' depending on which of the realms this content is cognized from, each presents it in a different *medium*. Reflecting both historical and conceptual forms of progression, the development is one from a form of culture such as that found in ancient Greece, where the felt normativity of the aesthetic sensuous properties of perceivable things (as with the beauty of a statue of Apollo, for example) helps in securing their normative status, to modern 'enlightened' culture, where normative status is meant to be secured entirely *rationally* through argumentative, conceptual means.

'Religion' presents its content in a type of imagistic or storytelling discourse (Hegel's term *'Vorstellung'* is here generally translated as 'picture-language'), a form of representation that is located between the sort of immediately effective beauty of sensuous 'art' and the mediated nature of 'philosophy'. Under 'art' Hegel includes the types of folk religion of the ancient world in which art and religion are not conceived as separate realms as in the modern world, while the prototype of 'religion' is effectively Christianity, where the vehicle within which the divine has been revealed in the world is no longer a direct sensuous presence, but has to be actively recalled and recounted within the memory of the community. Hegel links the representational *medium* of religion thus conceived to the *mode* in which this content is maintained: that of "'faith' … something subjective, as opposed to which the knowledge of necessity is termed objective" (2006: 136). The only *ground* of faith can be that of "*authority*, the fact that others – those who matter to me, those whom I revere and in whom I have confidence that they know what is true – believe it, they are in possession of this knowledge" (*ibid.*: 137). In contrast, genuine knowledge has *objective* grounds: the conceptual medium of thought allows its contents to be mediated, and "to mediated knowledge belongs conclusion from one thing to another, dependence, conditionality of one determination upon another, i.e., the form of reflection" (*ibid.*: 156). Thus the characteristics of conceptual thought for Hegel said something about the type of community that allows its members to question established 'truths' in this way: it must have the freedoms of an enlightened community that foregoes all *unquestionable* sources of authority in the regulation of collective belief and action.

This 'reflected' or 'mediated' form of knowledge, according to Hegel, was particularly at home in modern life: modern society was undergoing radical changes such that appeals to human reason and freedom were replacing traditional appeals to authority, and this had to imply that orthodox Christianity, itself a religion that had taken this imagistic, allegorical form of thought to its limits, was by necessity transformed into a more rational form. Whether this newly emerging way of life represented the full development of Christianity or the transition to a distinctly *post-religious* form of life would be the question that divided Hegel's followers after his death. While Hegel seemed himself intent on *reconciling* faith and reason, he was unambiguous as to which form of representation was afforded ultimate authority:

> By thinking in terms of the Concept and grasping this content in thought, philosophy has this advantage over the pictorial thinking of religion, that it understands both, for it understands religion and

can do justice to it … and it understands itself too. But the reverse is not true. By taking its stand on pictorial thinking, religion as such knows itself only in thinking of that kind, not in philosophy, i.e., not in concepts, in universal categories of thought.   (Hegel 1985: 141–2)

A RELIGION OF THE PHILOSOPHERS

The dominant role played by conceptual thought in defining the status of religion means that Hegel's 'God' exemplifies that to which Pascal had referred negatively as the 'God of the philosophers', and while it is important that Hegel thought of his God as the Christian God, his version of this God can be understood only against the background of *Greek* philosophical theology. Crucially, Hegel's *Philosophy of Spirit* concludes with a quote from Aristotle's account of divine thinking in *Metaphysics* Λ.9 (Hegel 1971: §577), in which '*theos*' is characterized as a process of pure thinking that is directed to no object independent of itself, but which is, somehow, its *own* content (*see* Vol. 1, Ch. 5). Divine thinking is just the thinking *of* thinking itself: "*noesis noeseos noesis*" (Aristotle 1935: Λ.9 1074b33–5). What Aristotle's conception of the pure activity, *energia*, of divine thought had seemingly provided to Hegel was an alternative to *Plato's* static version of 'the idea', which he saw as lacking the principles of 'life' and 'subjectivity' (Hegel 1995: vol. 2, 139). "While, therefore, with Plato the main consideration is the affirmative principle, the Idea as only abstractly identical with itself, in Aristotle there is added and made conspicuous the moment of negativity, not as change, nor yet as nullity, but as difference or determination" (*ibid*.: 140). In fact, what is seen here in Aristotle's conception of God is effectively that to which Hegel had appealed in the preface to the *Phenomenology of Spirit* in criticism of Spinoza's pantheism, "the living Substance … being which is in truth *Subject* … pure, *simple negativity*" (1977: §18).

We need not concern ourselves with the interpretative adequacy of Hegel's reading of Aristotle's *noesis noeseos* doctrine, but simply note how it is this allegedly 'speculative' dimension of Aristotle that allows Hegel to link Aristotle to subsequent forms of thought. First, it is linked to what for Hegel was the most developed form of Greek philosophy, late antique Neoplatonism, which could equally be considered a form of *Neo-Aristotelianism* (Hegel 1995: vol. 2, 381), especially in its Proclean form (*ibid*.: 438), and thereby to the *trinitarianism* of the succeeding Christian theology (*ibid*.: 440–49), which Neoplatonism had influenced. Next, Aristotle is linked to *post-Kantian* views about the nature of individual subjectivity developed, especially, by Fichte, in which the thinking subject is no longer thought of as a 'substance', but as an activity in which the 'positing' of a plurality of objects of consciousness is at the same time the positing of itself as the unitary subject *for whom* those objects exist. With Proclus this dialectic of the One and the many had reached the most developed phase capable of antique thought, but with Fichte this Neoplatonic dialectic was now reproduced at the level of individual, *actual* consciousnesses.[2]

In the earliest of his post-Tübingen theological writings, Hegel had been attracted to the 'natural' folk religions of Greece in contrast to the 'positivity' of Christianity, but he soon moved to an attitude more favourable to Christianity, and the passage from Aristotle's '*theos*' to the Christian God is significant in this regard. Aristotle's *theos* is the pure activity of thinking,[3] but the *Christian* God had to forego this joyous self-sufficiency. While the Neoplatonists had developed the idea of God's self-differentiating egress and return, the Christian God had externalized himself into the painful and *finite* sphere of objectivity: he had *become man* and this, for Hegel, had enabled God *to achieve* the self-consciousness that was fitting *for* God. The thinking behind this seems to be the account of the conditions of self-consciousness that Hegel had first given in the *Phenomenology of Spirit*: "Self-consciousness exists in and for itself when, and by the fact that, it so exists for another; that is, it exists only in being acknowledged" (Hegel 1977: §178). To fully *become* God, God had to become *man* capable of *recognizing* God. As Hegel bluntly puts it in the *Philosophy of Spirit*: "God is God only in so far as he knows himself: his self-consciousness is, further, a self-consciousness in man and man's knowledge *of* God, which proceeds to man's self-knowledge *in* God" (1971: §564). But on becoming a man God is condemned to *die*, and the death of the God-man Jesus means that God can only live on as the third 'person' of the Trinity, the holy 'spirit'. But this spirit is just that which is expressed in the forms of consciousness and practices of the Christian community.

Again, here we see the ambiguity of Hegel's theology. Given the symbolic meaning of the biblical narratives, is the doctrine of the divinity of Jesus to be understood simply as affirming the conditions under which the 'divine' element of Aristotelian *nous* in human beings can historically develop? That is, is what is at issue simply Hegel's innovative theory of the *socially recognitive* conditions of self-consciousness and reason? On such a reading, the path to the Left Hegelians seems clear. On the other hand, while Hegel's God is clearly an immanent *this*-worldly one, dependent on human recognition, it is also clear that he cannot be reduced to any type of anthropocentric projection. God dwells and is made manifest within recognitive practices such as those of confession and forgiveness (Hegel 1977:

---

2. Ultimately with Proclus the process of the self-differentiation of 'the One' into the many that are then reunited with the One is such that the *independence* of the plurality of individual substances – that which is an important truth for the modern standpoint of individual consciousnesses – is lost (Hegel 1995: vol. 2, 436–7). The development of such ideas was only possible in the context of the transition to *Christianity* in which divine consciousness was given a finite individual form.

3. Hegel effectively equates Aristotle's *noesis noeseos* with the first person of the Trinity: "Thought, as the object of thought, is nothing else than the absolute Idea regarded as in itself, the Father" (Hegel 1995: vol. 2, 149).

§670), but the binding nature of those practices on the community testifies to their status as 'sacred' rather than 'profane'. That God's mind is, as it were, distributed across the minds of finite human beings, and is reliant on the acts of those finite beings, does not *disqualify* it from being a mind in its own right, nor does this reduce it to the status of a *mere* fiction. The complex and controversial interpretative questions about Hegel's philosophical theology thus become inextricably tied up with equally complex and controversial questions about the nature of Hegel's philosophy in general.[4]

FURTHER READING

Hegel, G. 2006. *Lectures on the Philosophy of Religion: One-Volume Edition, The Lectures of 1827*, R. Brown, P. Hodgson & J. Stewart (trans. with the assistance of H. Harris). Oxford: Oxford University Press.

Hodgson P. 2005. *Hegel and Christian Theology: A Reading of the Lectures on the Philosophy of Religion*. Oxford: Oxford University Press.

Jaeschke, W. 1990. *Reason in Religion: The Foundations of Hegel's Philosophy of Religion*, J. Stewart & P. Hodgson (trans.). Berkeley, CA: University of California Press.

O'Regan, C. 1994. *The Heterodox Hegel*. Albany, NY: SUNY Press.

Toews, J. 1980. *Hegelianism: The Path toward Dialectical Humanism, 1805–1841*. Cambridge: Cambridge University Press.

Wallace, R. 2005. *Hegel's Philosophy of Reality, Freedom, and God*. Cambridge: Cambridge University Press.

On MORALITY see also Chs 12, 18; Vol. 2, Ch. 12; Vol. 3, Chs 2, 8, 12, 14, 21, 22; Vol. 5, Ch. 6. On NEOPLATONISM see also Ch. 9; Vol. 1, Chs 19, 20; Vol. 2, Chs 3, 4; Vol. 3, Ch. 9. On REASON see also Ch. 8; Vol. 2, Chs 10, 11, 12, 16, 18; Vol. 3, Chs 8, 12, 16, 21. On SELF-CONSCIOUSNESS see also Chs 4, 5, 10, 13. On THE TRINITY see also Vol. 1, Chs 14, 17, 20; Vol. 2, Chs 2, 8, 15; Vol. 3, Chs 3, 9, 17; Vol. 5, Chs 12, 23.

---

4. I wish to thank Paolo Diego Bubbio for helpful discussions on Hegel's philosophy of religion.

5

FRIEDRICH SCHELLING

Michael Vater

The place of Friedrich Wilhelm Joseph Schelling (1775–1854) in the history of European philosophy is easily located: he was one of the major German thinkers who, in the wake of Kant's critical turn, elaborated the ambitious systematic philosophy know as 'absolute idealism', and the first of those thinkers to repudiate the rampant conceptualism of the idealist approach and to stress instead the priority of actuality over conceptual possibility. Woven throughout the fabric of the writings and lectures he produced over more than half a century is an enduring preoccupation with the question of God. Yet this is but one thread in Schelling's rich intellectual tapestry, one always interwoven with four counterparts: nature; the being both displayed and concealed in human reality; freedom or the peculiar moral-psychological status of 'personality', which only a free being (God included) can attain through a temporal process; and the divine actuality. These five elements – deity or godhead, nature, humankind, freedom and the historical process towards actual personhood – are not easily separated in Schelling's thinking, nor are these easily detached from the historical paradigms that Schelling used to integrate them: Platonic and Christian creation theologies; the heterodox process theologies of Jacob Böhme and earlier Christian mystics; and, finally, the audacious anthropocentrism of Kant's critical idealism, founded on the Copernican turn that finds in phenomena only such meaning as human understanding and moral reason can impute to them.

What makes Schelling a thinker difficult to access when one stands within the global culture of the twenty-first century is the one thing that he repeatedly stresses as he moves between such different conceptual approaches as philosophy of science, metaphysics, anthropology, history, and cross-cultural investigations into mythologies and religions: that human cognition forms a *system*, a single conceptual construct that elaborates the very architecture of being. That reality is in some sense one and univocal, that human concepts can figure it in a way that captures and mirrors exactly what it is, and that all the exploding domains of human endeavour and knowledge can find a ground in a single conceptual/

linguistic construct is an audacious claim. Strictly speaking, it is now an unbeliev-able claim. It was a difficult (perhaps hubristic) claim in its historical context; that the Kantian story of the efficacy of human reason in constructing the domains of scientific and moral discourse could be stretched by Fichte, Schelling and Hegel to include all human reality – social, psychological, cultural and historical – is literally 'fabulous', the stuff of fables. And the arch-fable, the *prōton pseudos*, is painful even to contemplate today: the belief that there is one universal culture, one universal history, one religion with universal validity, one logic, one epistem-ology, and one account of everything: modern, Archimedean and (of course!) European. When Schelling claims, then, at various stages of his long career, that nature, or the primacy of biology over physics, or history, or empirical studies of mythologies and religions will provide the royal road to *Wissenschaft* or system-atic philosophy, he is committing himself to the old philosophical faith in univer-sals, in univocal readings of texts, in literal meanings: to a unity believed to be found in the nature of things rather than in the activity of a cognitive interpreter. As skilled and clever a student of Kant as he was in his many detailed philosoph-ical moves, Schelling was insufficiently sceptical or Kantian to see that any cogni-tion or domain of human endeavour is an interpretation, that interpretations depend on a privileged selection of 'evidence' or 'data', and that a 'universal history' – of human science, social reality, cultures, and moral and religious ideas – is a conceptual impossibility, a social construct based on a particular social situa-tion and a very specific historical configuration of human activities and resources. What makes Schelling more than an innocent victim of sociocultural limita-tions, however, was the persistent resourcefulness he exhibited in overcoming the 'idols of his tribe': early on, that nature is dead and mechanical, with biological phenomena counting as mere anomalies, not the fundamental subject of science; and later, that conceptual completeness is not the test of truth – as post-Kantian idealism had rather wildly assumed – but actual existence. However, it was in his 'final' approach to system, in the replacement of the merely negative (concep-tual) philosophy of earlier idealisms with the method of *positive philosophy* (or 'philosophical empiricism'), that he falls into being insufficiently historical, cross-cultural and empirical. The *Philosophies of Mythology and Revelation* of his later years, elaborated only in the lecture hall and untested by publication, unabashedly commit the fallacy of assuming that social empiricism or cross-cultural study will verify the initial assumption of one universal culture of reason or provide a point of Archimedean support for the hope in a philosophy of history with a single narrative thread. Alas, God (or the gods) does not speak so plainly as once we hoped.

For the most part, I shall discuss Schelling's key contributions to philosophy of religion synchronically under the five headings mentioned above: nature, God, freedom, humankind and history or the manifestation of divine actuality. But first some historical scene-setting is needed: an account of his early life and writ-ings, and of some of the friendships, loves and enmities that formed the personal backdrop of his thinking. Until we broach the fifth theme, there is little to say on a classical topic in philosophy of religion, that is, proofs for the existence of God. For most of his life, Schelling argued that all of philosophy is the "ongoing proof of God", and that the construction of a systematic account of reality from the *idea* of an absolute being is all that is needed (see VII.424 and the extensive discussion in IV.364–9).[1]

SEMINARY STUDIES: PLATO, SPINOZA, KANT AND FICHTE

Schelling was born in 1775 to a clerical family in a Swabian village near Stuttgart. A precocious student, at the age of fifteen he found himself in the University of Tübingen's Protestant Seminary in the company of Friedrich Hölderlin and G. W. F. Hegel. There he made his first acquaintance with the writings of Kant, especially those in moral philosophy. A letter to Hegel from that period shows the student's contemptuous disrespect for the easy berth that Kant was getting in establishment Evangelical circles, where simple and 'inevitable' belief in a moral God dislodged the strenuous efforts of earlier theologians to prove the divine existence. While it is probable that Schelling and his older peers undertook careful and extensive study of Kant's first and third *Critiques* even at the time when Johann Gottlieb Fichte was working out his monumental systematization of critical philosophy, Schelling also explored other major figures of the German Enlightenment: he delved into Johann Gottfried Herder's ideas on history, language and religion, and through Friedrich Heinrich Jacobi's polemical *Letters on Spinoza's Doctrine* he encountered the model of 'dogmatic' philosophy that would serve, along with Fichtean 'Theory of Science' (*Wissenschatslehre*), as the twin foci of his early philosophical development. Just as he vacillates between Spinozistic 'realism' and Fichtean 'transcendental philosophy' in his earliest writings, Schelling struggles in his later life between the concept of a deity immersed in nature and in fact identified with natural and psychological processes, and a God of spontaneous freedom, love and self-revelation. What makes the tension between the alternatives poignant is the more basic assumption of the age and of the German intellectual culture that there is but one process at work, one mode of true cognition, one system.

Two texts from Schelling's seminary days prefigure themes of lifelong philosophical interest to him. His Masters thesis, *Attempt at a Critical and Philosophical Exegesis of Genesis III, the Oldest Philosophical Fragment Exploring the Origin of Human Evil* (1792) broaches the theme of human freedom and the origin of evil explored profoundly in the 1809 *Of Human Freedom*. It is also a first attempt to explore the sorts of truth communicated in *mythology*, understood to be a narrative

---

1. In-text references to Schelling's work are to his *Sämmtliche Werke* (1856–61), cited by volume and page numbers. All translations are mine.

fabricated within a limited historical and cultural content, and religious *revelation*, understood in the Enlightenment context as the communication of universal moral truths. The young theologian's attempt to deploy critique seem comically limited when read today – for example his insistence (I.13) that Moses learned the craft of indirect religious communication from the Egyptian priests and their hieroglyphs, and brought that to his 'authorship' of the great myths of cosmic and human origin in Genesis – but he makes bold assumptions: religious truth is universal and cross-cultural, and the stories of one cultural tradition speak truly only when set in the context of many cultures and many mythologies. The specific images of the snake, the prohibition, eating the fruit of the tree of knowledge, and the expulsion by the cherubim are to be viewed against the background of the ancient presupposition of an earlier 'golden age' of human unity and unity with nature, and of a catastrophic transition to the current human condition of lack, yearning and lost wholeness (I.17–19). And this universal mythology – elaborated in Ovid, Plato, Hesiod and Virgil – speaks timelessly of the human condition: either to ambiguously dwell in sensible nature and be led by its impulses as is any animal, or to wrench one's life away from the comfort zone of mundane satisfactions and attain the precarious happiness and unhappiness of the self-posited spontaneity of reason (I.32–8). The Enlightenment sensibilities of Herder and Kant are evident in Schelling's exegesis; both human freedom and historical existence begin with the forbidden tree, and once humankind acquires the taste for its particularly 'rational' fruit, nothing else can satisfy. A 1795 journal article, "On the Myths, Historical Sayings and Philosophical Fragments of the Ancient World", clarifies the idea of a philosophy communicated through myth. A people warrants its beliefs, values and modes of conduct by tradition; the sayings of the founders are received and repeated in an atti-tude of childlike trust. Whether what is passed down takes the shape of a historical narrative (*myth*, strictly speaking) or whether an abstract truth is embodied in such a narrative (*mythological philosophy*), the mode of communication is immediate. The ancient Greeks simply lived within the sensible (I.63–6). Human beings oper-ating in the mode of sensibility express their lives, customs and ways of action in the *image*; all of nature becomes an image of human actuality. Only later, when childish dreams and pictures are put aside, does humanity seek to explain nature on its own terms: "Previously, humankind sought its image (*Bild*) in the mirror of nature, now it seeks the archetype (*Urbild*) of nature in its understanding, which is the mirror of the All" (I.73–7)]. For the young Schelling, mythology is a crude tool, hardly the plastic vehicle for the expression of religious truth, for example the coincidence of the universal and the individual, that he sees as the essence of Greek art and religion in the 1802 *Lecture on the Philosophy of Art*. Moreover, the young Schelling seems to hold the work of the imagination in low regard. Although he copied Hegel's ideas as expressed in *The Earliest System-Program of German Idealism* in his own hand in the *Earliest German System-Program*, he is worlds away from that author's vision of religion reconfiguring itself in the guise of a 'new mythology' in order to speak to an ethically and politically awakened world.

Schelling's recently published notebooks on Plato's *Timaeus* (1794) show a preoccupation with themes that dominate not only his early philosophy of nature, but also shape his later (and not especially biblical) theological speculation on the process of creation. Plato's Demiurge shapes natural forces not only by efficient causality, but also by looking to the model of 'things that truly are' (*see* Vol. 1, Ch. 4); it thus teleologically shapes all the disparate elements and motions of pre-given natural stuff into the organic interdependence of 'the living animal': organic nature. That organic life, anthropomorphically interpreted as a nisus toward the cognitive and affective self-determination of the conscious individual, is the secret urge and goal of all natural order, the noumenal ground of its scientifically observable lawfulness, is the key insight into the philosophy of nature that the young philosopher adumbrated to such acclaim in the years 1797–1804. It is Plato brought into the age when biology begins to displace physics as the paradigmatic science, or where young Germans, at least, ardently followed Goethe's anti-mechanistic ideas of colour and life rather than confining themselves to the cold rigours of Newton's elegant mathematics. Plato's *Timaeus*, along with Kant's *Critique of the Faculty of Judgment*, advances the 'likely story' (or 'wild' surmise) of a world organized with a view to reason and freedom, but one somehow consonant with the 'rule of necessity' or predictable force. How one makes that story plausible again in the age that sees, in England and France, if not in Germany, the triumph of a reductive empirical science is the narrative thread of Schelling's lifelong philosophical struggle. And it is the foundation of Schelling's ingenious solution to the problem of rational personality, whether divine or human: there must be a ground of necessity, namely nature, *from which* the free person departs in order to live in the ambiguous realm of choice and decision.

While a student at Tübingen, Schelling embarked on the tortuous discipleship or 'alliance' with Fichte that would first bring him to public prominence, and later (1797–1802) bring him into conflict with his mentor. The 1794 *On the Possibility of a Form for Philosophy As Such* loosely follows Fichte's methodological reflections in *On the Concept of 'Theory of Science'*. If there is to be philosophy as such, its form and content cannot be unrelated but must determine each other. The very idea of a foundational, self-evident and self-certifying philosophy carries with it the idea of three principles: one absolutely unconditional or self-realizing, one conditionally established in dependence on the first and one relatively unconditional, merging the first two; these are, respectively, the self-positing I, the not-I and the relative I of empirical consciousness, which is their synthesis (I.90–101). Schelling departs from Fichte in appending an anticipatory history of 'Theory of Science' in modern philosophy. What is most interesting in this regard is a discussion of Kant's (notoriously unexplained) table of categories; when viewed through the lens of 'Theory of Science', there is only one fundamental category, *relation*, variously instantiated as totality (the I), limitation of reality (the not-I) and causal interdependence (the I in interaction with not-I) (I.104–10).

When Fichte issued the first or theoretical section of the *Foundations of the Science of Knowledge* in 1794, he did not acknowledge its incompleteness or indicate the dependence of the stuff of cognition (*presentation*) on the flow of non-conscious activities of the I (striving and counter-striving,), which give rise to *feeling* or being-affected. Hence Schelling's 1795 *On the I as Principle of Philosophy* fails to do justice to the phenomenological psychology that grounds Fichte's view of freedom: that I as I experience myself as free only in a conditioned sense, as embedded in a world not of my making and not easily reshaped by my efforts. What it does is lucidly explain Fichte's use of Karl Leonhard Reinhold's method of arguing from an absolute or self-warranting principle: philosophy's foundational truth, if it is to be unconditioned, cannot at all be conceived as a thing; it can be thought only as *absolute I*, that which can never become a thing. "*I am – because I am*"; I am unthinkable except in so far as I think myself. The I is its self-realization, or self-positing, as Fichte said (I.167–8). Note that Schelling argues as a metaphysician (or a Spinozist), not as a phenomenologist: the notion that philosophy might proceed hypothetically and aggregate conditioned or empirical truths as it progresses is not even worthy of consideration. Only idealism permits one to adopt a ground of truth that is at the same time the ground of reality (I.162–3). If one supposed that Schelling was merely imitating Fichte in this essay, or providing the crabbed *Wissenschaftslehre* a much-needed popular exposition, one would underestimate him. Only the first third of the essay closely follows Fichte. Subsequent sections transpose the idealistic vocabulary of Fichte's I and not-I into Spinoza's language: the I must be "absolutely infinite"; it is the "sole substance of which all other items are merely accidents"; its domain is eternity, not the time of empirical consciousness; its being is *power* (I.187–96). The final third of the essay projects Fichte's principles back onto the structure of Kant's Transcendental Analytic in the *Critique of Pure Reason*, finding in the modal categories (dismissed by Kant as an epiphenomenon of temporal location) the ground of all others. The same ontological cleavage that would put possibility and necessity in opposition in fact contains the clue to solving the apparent impossibility of freedom and necessity coexisting. The freedom of the absolute, of the I, is self-causation or necessity according to Spinoza; the transcendental freedom that the conditioned or empirical I must ascribe to itself is conditioned agency, elicited in the phenomenal I as a response to the object, which on its own terms can never be conceived as anything other than a product of natural necessity. Freedom and nature are of different orders: one must think that in the absolute, mechanism and teleology coincide, and for the empirical I, such an identity becomes a heuristic principle in science and the space for the projection of goals in the domain of action (I.226–42).

While the essays on the I and the form of philosophy are clear-sighted Fichtean studies, done with the historian's eye turned back to the roots of Theory of Science in Kant's texts, especially the first *Critique*, Schelling shows some originality and anticipates some of the grand themes of the 'philosophy of identity' in the 1795

Philosophical Letters on Dogmatism and Criticism (hereafter *Letters*). The main argument of the *Letters* is a defence of the strategy of Theory of Science: to provide a theoretical construct for the *freedom* that is the core of the human, which construct can only be validated practically, by will and action. Fichte's position is inserted between the letter of Kant's text – where the *weakness* of cognitive reason is made a stepping-stone to the postulation of a *moral God* and, subsequently, a weak theory of freedom – and a daring defence of Spinoza's dogmatic objectification of both the divine ground and the constrained freedom of the finite agent. Whereas Fichte's writings are of 'Kantian' derivation in that they take as the key to systematizing criticism Kant's chapter title in the second *Critique*, "The Primacy of the Practical", and argue for the superiority of criticism (now called *Wissenschaftslehre*, or 'theory of science') over dogmatism or the systematized realism of Spinoza, Schelling criticizes the mental and moral poverty of a 'criticism' confined to the texts of Kant, where a weak cognitive reason allies itself with an impulsive and ill-motivated moral reason that simply postulates an 'objective God' that it desires but cannot know, and through which it desires, rather cravenly, to reassure itself about its own 'morality' (I.284–92). The message of the *Critique of Pure Reason* is not the weakness of cognitive reason, but the antinomical nature of reason, which gives rise simultaneously and with equal plausibility to realism (the necessity of nature) *and* idealism (the purposiveness of the free agent). Realism, in its perfect form as a Spinozistic axiomatized system, is unable to prove itself because it must leave forever obscure the link between the absolute and the relative, or the "egress of the finite from the infinite" (I.294, 313–14). Idealism, which is basically a seizing of the stance of freedom, a self-ascription of absolute causality or spontaneity in the face of the explanation of phenomena through the serial causality of the objective order, is equally unable to validate itself, argues Schelling. It can do no more than prove the impossibility of dogmatic realism (I.301–2).

Schelling echoes Fichte's words that the choice between realism and idealism is made with one's feet, existentially, with one's lived commitments (I.307–8). But Fichte believed that only one of the paths carried the dignity of real human endeavour, and that a person whose life and character drew her to an unbending world of finished objectivity 'outside' was basically slavish and incapable of spontaneous activity. Schelling argues that Spinoza and Fichte face the same philosophical task: to explain the *existence of the world* or, what is the same thing, of *experience* (I.313). Each raises himself to an act of *intelligence* (not understanding), and posits an absolute: Fichte, *intellectual* (or non-objective) *intuition* of self in the self; Spinoza, annihilation of the finite self in the *intellectual love of God* (I.319). In both cases, the finite or objective disappears. Schelling seems to endorse the equivalence of the alternatives: each of the two, realism and idealism, aims at the identity of the subject and the object, which would really mean *loss* of finite self and *loss* of world – *if* the project could be carried out (I.330). In the end, the only thing that differentiates realism and idealism is that the former leaps into the absolute and abolishes the self *tout court*, while idealism or Theory of Science uses absolute identity as a postulate made for the sake of free activity, and thus approaches the absolute only as the *goal of an endless task* (I.331).

NATURE

After leaving the Tübingen seminary, Schelling spent some years as a tutor and studied the natural sciences at Stuttgart. In Robert Brown's experiments with molecular movement, Schelling detected a key that seemed to link the mechanical activity of inorganic nature and the self-organizing and self-maintaining activity of the biological order. He formulates a view of science that prizes two structural or organizing ideas: that nature is purposive or goal-oriented (the *teleological principle*), and that the lawfulness of natural phenomena derives from the repetition and clarification of but one logic, manifest in various orders as *powers* or exponents of the basic formula of identity-in-difference (the *principle of potentiation*). That nature *might be* regarded as self-organizing activity or an expression of an underlying and pervasive *telos* whose nature is finally unveiled in human consciousness is an idea whose historical antecedents lie in Plato and Kant. That different levels of phenomena – physical, biological and psychological – express the same underlying activity and thus repeat a basic logic in a progressively more explicit fashion may have been suggested by Spinoza's dictum that the order and expression of power in nature is the same as that expressed in the order of mind and its sequence of ideas. These two quite abstract principles frame the project of *Naturphilosophie*, which set out to provide a conceptual framework for organizing all natural phenomena into one 'science': quite a different project from the methodological and clarificatory reflections that we call 'philosophy of science'. The framework is *a priori* (or, less charitably, empirically unfounded) and is imposed on the findings of the 'working' empirical sciences only to the degree, as both Plato and Kant recognized, that there is a human need to fabricate a *story* that might make nature one and comprehensible.

What made the young philosopher's contributions to this sort of 'learning' interesting at the end of the eighteenth century was his solid grasp of contemporary empirical research and his skill in weaving the detailed theories of different domains into a unified picture. But the emphasis in *Naturphilosophie* is philosophical, not empirical. As Schelling expresses it in his first attempt at the subject, "It is true that chemistry has taught us to read the *elements*, physics the *syllables*, mathematics *nature* [as a whole], but one should not forget that it falls to philosophy to *explain* what was read" (II.6). And philosophy's mode of explanation is self-analysis, the transcendental question of how the world of experience is possible for consciousness, or, in the language of earlier episodes in modern philosophy, how our activity organizes a mass of cognitive content (presentations) into a world of experience, with both its physical and sociohistorical dimensions. The knot of necessity and freedom in the undertaking wherein I resolve to clarify the nature of my mind and action and end by constraining it in a world of matter and mechanical causality cannot be cut, for if *my* act is to perceive and my freedom the only explanation of that act, the necessary order of my presentation is the lawfulness that I come to recognize as the Idea of Nature (II.35). In the transcendental perspective, only mind can explain ideal factors: order, succession, lawfulness. Nature is a transcendental construct.

Subsequent explorations of the philosophy of nature (from 1798 to 1801) move away from the Fichtean transcendental framework of analysis to the core conceptual perplexity: how can one conceive the overlay of organic nature on the inorganic? For Schelling, the heart of the conundrum is metaphysical, not empirical: the conviction, inherited from Reinhold and Fichte, that since principles must be one or few and their outworking systematic or pervasive, there must be a common point of origin for *mechanism* (which traces the first causes of alteration in physical nature) and *teleology* (which reveals the final ground of activity in organic nature). As Schelling wrote in the Preface to *The World-Soul* (1798), this common point can at first only be postulated, and can be denominated only symbolically through antique terms such as the 'Idea of Nature' or 'World Soul'. One can speak of the line of mechanical causality being "interrupted and turned back upon itself" in living phenomena, but there is certainly conceptual difficulty in supposing that one force or lawfulness will manifest itself in contradictory ways (II.347–50). This metaphysical perplexity drives the development of Schelling's philosophy in the period of his so-called 'philosophy of identity' (1801–4).

That nature is the gradual unveiling of the power of consciousness and novelty within a structure dominated by automatic or homeostatic organization (physics) and mutually supporting differentiated functions (biology) is an obvious idea viewed in the context of Renaissance humanism, or a preposterous idea viewed in the context of philosophical empiricism. For us, Darwinian evolution validates the idea in a way that abolishes the difference between mechanism and teleology. What makes Schelling's (and later Hegel's) excursions into 'the metaphysics of science' both fascinating and difficult for contemporary readers is that the glue that holds the cosmos together for him comes from 'ideas' (in the full Platonic and Kantian sense), not from the history of biological adaptation. At this stage, Schelling does not give a theistic face to this post-Kantian version of the Renaissance idea of the 'great chain of being', although he will speak metaphorically of a 'World Soul' or demiurgic organizing principle. If one pressed him at this point for a further account of just why nature pointed towards consciousness as its goal and expressed its activity in graduated stages, he would fall back on Spinoza's minimalistic metaphysics: one substance, call it God or Nature, and two equal but different orders of phenomena, the physical and the mental, expressing the same logic when viewed cognitively, and expressing the same power viewed affectively.

In the 1800 *System of Transcendental Idealism*, Schelling still adheres to the genetic expository framework of Fichte's Theory of Science, but in the final three sections of the work (on history, teleology and philosophy of art) one can see him mounting to a new overall conceptual structure or metaphysics, different from Fichte's 'subjective' postulation of indemonstrable principles through an act of freedom grounded in 'intellectual self-intuition'. Schelling argues that beyond nature and the domain of human consciousness is an absolute domain, phenomenologically adumbrated in forms of higher culture – ethics, politics, history, science and art – but strictly beyond the reach of philosophy's methodology and argument. The artist becomes the surrogate of the philosopher confined in her subjectivity or the prophet/priest who can dream of an absolute order, but cannot supply objectivity or evidence to such claims. The work of art is at once a natural product and a work of freedom; the aesthetic 'genius' consciously undertakes its production, but unconsciously imbues her work with more than finite significance. It is thus the analogue of the absolute and an indication of an ultimate harmonization of the opposed order of nature and human freedom (III.624–9). While Schelling worked to develop a dialectical metaphysics of identity over the next three or so years, he continued to privilege the domain of art, where ultimate reality enters the realm of appearances in a finite shape (as in the Greek gods). Allied briefly with Hegel as a co-worker from 1801 to 1803, Schelling worked on a tripartite system of philosophy that privileges aesthetics as its capstone, while the young Hegel worked on a similar scheme culminating in philosophy of religion. They named this movement 'absolute' or 'objective' idealism to differentiate it from the Fichtean construct of transcendental philosophy that (supposedly) never left the confines of 'subjective idealism' (or psychologism).

Schelling's more technical efforts to fuse the divided realms of nature, ethics, and aesthetics resulted in several essays in 'identity philosophy' in the later years of his overall preoccupation with the Kantian domains of nature and aesthetics, chiefly the *Presentation of My System* (hereafter *Presentation*; 1801) and the dialogue *Bruno* (1802). Inspired by Spinoza's metaphysics of one substance manifested in coordinated but opposite orders of attributes, Schelling makes the radical claim that philosophy has access to the absolute through reason or intellectual intuition (IV.117–19). He thus elevates the epistemic status of philosophy over that of art, reversing claims made in 1800. What can the philosopher do that the aesthetic genius could only blindly adumbrate? She can deploy a formal mathematical model, positing the absolute as an identity of (relative) identities, or an 'identity of identity and difference', and provide a structural or quasi-mathematical model of nature as a realm of phenomena determined in all levels by a preponderance of objectivity over subjectivity, alongside a realm of consciousness or ideal phenomena where subjectivity outweighs objectivity. Key to the theory is the stipulation that although 'absolute identity' is the only entity or activity that can be imagined, it can appear only as a healing-over of a rupture of difference, seen in the way phenomena arranged themselves in realms of opposites. There is only identity, but all that appears is identity-in-difference or *indifference* (IV.127–9). The theory never defines what 'the subjective' and 'the objective' might be in themselves; its plausibility depends on a poetic approximation of *subjectivity* to human consciousness and of *objectivity* to a supposedly external order of nature. What Spinoza treated as the distinct order of attributes is the same as Kant's distinct orders of phenomena. The former's imperceptible *substance* is regarded as the same as Kant's unembodied *transcendental* or *rational unity of consciousness*, and, methodological niceties aside, the 'modern stance' of transcendentally grounded phenomenalism is assimilated to earlier forms of rational metaphysics. The conceptual gain for Schelling in these rather arid logical moves comes with the stipulation that all phenomena can be analysed as the 'quantitative difference' of factors that are qualitatively indifferent in the absolute; this allows the various stages or 'potencies' of phenomena to be arranged and displayed in a quasi-mathematical way. Thus the claim can be advanced that "absolute identity is not the cause of the universe, but the universe itself", the Romantics' *hen kai pan* (one and all).

GOD

Schelling's pursuit of a unified philosophy of nature gave way to essays and lectures in 1801–3 that attempted to recast the arid formalism of the 1801 *Presentation* in classical aesthetic, even Neoplatonic modes. The emergence of differentiated phenomena from the ground of absolute identity proved a difficult problem for Schelling: Spinoza had maintained that there is no explaining the egress of the finite from the infinite, and Kantian transcendentalism provided no model for going beyond phenomena to an existing ultimate ground. So Schelling reverts to the language of Platonism, transposing the graded identities-in-difference of the mathematical model of nature and consciousness into *absolute ideas*, of which their phenomenal counterparts are regarded as 'fallen' or self-separated individuals. Working backwards from Kant to Spinoza to Plato, Schelling finds himself in the milieu of the creation stories in Christian theology, and he thus finds himself having to think through the themes of will, individuation, and the 'fallenness of nature'. Operating off the capital of Greek aesthetics and Neoplatonic metaphysics, Schelling, a quintessentially 'modern' or contemporary thinker, hardly notices that he has returned to his theological starting-points until a contemporary mathematician and scientist, Carl Eschenmayer, points out that with his 'absolute' thus platonically construed, Schelling had entered the domain of 'God talk' whose object is commonly thought to be accessible only to faith or religious intuition (VI.18). The 1804 essay "Philosophy and Religion", written while Schelling was lecturing at Würzburg, shows Schelling's recognition of this theological turn. Henceforth, although never quite surrendering the philosopher's claim to 'systematic philosophy', the centre of Schelling's endeavour will be to philosophically situate the worldview of Christian theology in which divine creation, the 'fall' from grace or self-separation, freedom and the rupture between God and nature become the predominant themes.

The 1804 essay claims that God or the 'idea of the absolute' is grasped by the philosopher in *intellectual intuition*, but can be translated into the language of *reflection* or second-hand explanation in three ways: the categorical pronouncements of negative theology, the hypothetical reasoning of Spinoza's self-identical substance ("If there is a subject and an object, the absolute is the identical essence of both orders" [VI.23]), or the disjunctive approach of *Naturphilosophie*, wherein the absolute is seen as the 'indifference' of both. Schelling confronts the difficulties of explaining individuation or the 'fall of the finite' from the absolute in a fairly oblique way: the possibility of the individual resides in the absolute only as 'idea', the actuality thereof lies in an inexplicable 'leap', a self-willed succession from the absolute (VI.38). Eschenmayer posed a more difficult problem for Schelling's nature- or identity-philosophy by raising the question of freedom and moral responsibility (VI.40ff.). Schelling grandly declares that in God, freedom and necessity are identical, and morality and blessedness are God's intrinsic properties; this makes the return to divine being the flipside of the phenomenal individual's succession from God, but offers little explanation of how 'willing' is possible at all in an absolute system that identifies (divine) being with necessity and with a timeless mode of knowing in the philosopher. Taking the cosmic perspective where the question of human willing is not so much solved as dissolved, he advances an oracular statement that prefigures the process-theology framework of the essay on *Human Freedom* and *Ages of the World*: "History is an epic composed within God's spirit; it has two chief parts: the first depicts the departure of humanity from the center to the utmost distance from God, the second, its return. The first is the *Iliad*, as it were, of history, the second, its *Odyssey*" (VI.47). As for the supposed immortality of the human soul, Schelling briefly argues that its being (but not necessarily its duration) is *eternal*, and that the separation of the soul from the sensible world in death is its restoration to the 'eternal present' that includes past and future, where its self-centred freedom is transformed into a state of guilt or one of purification from guilt (VI.61–2). The treatment of the human soul is cursory in this essay, and lacks both the feeling and the curiosity of the dialogue *Clara* (1810), written shortly after the death of Schelling's wife, Caroline.

FREEDOM

The last of his writings that Schelling was to publish during his lifetime, the 1809 *Human Freedom*, returns to themes that Schelling had sketched in the 1804 essay on religion: the non-difference of God and nature, history as humanity's journey away from and back to its divine centre, and the problem of freedom – which were fudged in the earlier essay. Although he admits in the introduction that the presentation of these ideas was flawed in the earlier essay, Schelling now serves notice that the questions of freedom, good and evil, and the actuality of a personal God are at the core of his philosophical system, and that the apparent 'pantheism' of the Spinozistic 'nature-philosophy' that had previously stood as his system is to be replaced by a 'system of freedom' (VII.334–40). The impulse to vindicate the horizon of human *agency* is the spring or motor that drives human cognition, while the identity of reason imposes, as Kant had taught, the logical demand that all knowledge be integrated into a logical whole, a *system*. So neither science nor morality can be satisfied with a worldview that offers necessity and freedom on an either/or basis. There must, instead, be a *system of freedom*, no matter how contradictory that sounds to the unphilosophical ear.

The logical and metaphysical foundation for the earlier nature- and identity-systems had been a symmetrical and non-dynamic notion of identity: $A = A$. Schelling had massaged the bare identity concept, now construing it as an 'identity of identities', or as (under the young Hegel's influence) an 'identity of opposites', but most often as 'indifference' or the lack of actual opposition between items conceptually opposed, that is, in exclusive disjunction. But as ingenious as all these attempts to build a dynamic or developmental feature into absolute identity were, Schelling's early systems never got beyond the flat contradictions that characterized the system of earlier thinkers: the finite and infinite orders in Spinoza, the antinomy of necessity and freedom in Kant and the contraction between positing and counter-positing in Fichte's Theory of Science. Schelling was indeed able to organize levels of phenomena in inorganic and organic nature in terms of degrees of apparent freedom; this was the principle of the 'powers' or *Potenzen*. But, lacking either a conceptual or a biological principle of variation and growing complexity, the systems of nature and spirit were at best taxonomical exercises in description, possessing neither systematic unity nor a uniform principle of elaboration. We are so accustomed to explaining the relations between different phenomena in terms of the Darwinian mechanism of random mutation and inherited advantage that it is difficult to conceive the challenge that faced early-nineteenth-century *Wissenschaft*: how to account for the complexity and variation of phenomena and yet attain the unity of principle that the ideal of systematicity demanded. As Heidegger remarked in his lectures on Schelling's *Human Freedom*, we have simply abandoned the ideal of systematicity; the so-called information age has galaxies of techniques, technologies and cognitive disciplines receding from each other in a logical space marked by 'red shift' or paradigm redundancy. We do not much care that a deep unity is not to be found, or that the lawfulness of phenomena seems to be established independent of the universality of logic.

In the essay on freedom, Schelling first uses the crude objection to Spinoza's monism – that it is '*pantheism*', meaning that either finite beings as a whole or each one individually are 'identical' to God – to re-tool his notion of identity. That the finite being is 'in God' means not logical identity, but a relationship of dependence: the copula in a judgement denotes not equivalence, but a relationship of antecedent and consequent. The absolute identity required by the very concept of system thus encompasses both the flat-footed law of identity and the law of sufficient reason. If the 'creature', then, has the ground of its being in the divine and must be conceived in and through the eternal, that does not determine the nature of the dependent entity, and so does not rule out its autonomy or freedom (VII.340–46).

Secondly, Schelling clarifies his long-standing criticism of Fichte's system: that it is 'subjective idealism'. The fault is not in its idealism, but in its narrowing the scope of philosophy to the perspective of the finite I. The real-idealism of nature-philosophy requires a wholly idealistic counterpart, a philosophy of will, not of being. "Will is primordial being; all predicates apply to it alone – groundlessness, eternity, independence from time, self-affirmation" (VII.330).

Even these two moves, however, will not suffice to generate a concept of *human freedom*, that is, agency coupled with cognition of possibilities and moral responsibility. Idealism can provide only a formal definition of freedom; actual freedom implies agency with the possibility of *good and evil* outcomes. The question of the actuality of human freedom transforms into the question of theodicy; whether God is a co-author of evil. Schelling rejects the Augustinian notion of evil as mere privation, and insists instead that actual freedom must be grounded in something independent of God, if evil is not to be credited to the eternal's account. What is required for the actuality of evil or the efficacy of human freedom is a basis in God that is not Godself (VII.352–6).

The intricate argument circles back to the reinterpretation of absolute identity: sufficient reason denotes not just a logical relationship, but an ontological one – *ground and existence*. What is required for the reality of human freedom (and hence the existence of evil) and for the exculpation of the divine is "an element in God that is not God" (VII.359), a pre-personal basis for personal existence. 'Nature' is this ground of the divine existence and the stage for the actualization of the human potential for good and evil. Conceived in dynamic or volitional terms, it is a pre-rational orientation toward the rational, an inarticulate longing to give birth to God: a primal longing or imagination turning towards God, but not recognizing God (VII.358–61).

It would take us too far afield to discuss the influence of Böhme and other Protestant mystics on this notion of the divine unfolding from a pre-rational ground. That God's being can be mapped as a tripartite process of self-enclosure, decision and becoming personal (i.e. manifesting itself as spirit or love) provides an economic framework for interpreting the Trinity. What is philosophically most basic in this scheme is its dependence on anthropology: pre-rational and rational urges contend in the human domain, self-will stands in contrast to universal reason and the individual secures concrete existence only in her choice, her action, her decision. "The human's being is essentially his or her own deed" (VII.383). But it is in this dual tendency to self-enclosure and to universal community that the word of God is articulated and the possibility of spirit revealed (VII.363–4).

One should not be misled by the language of orthodox theism that Schelling employs. The creation of the human order with its opposed capacities is *morally necessary* for divine revelation, the *sine qua non* for God becoming actual and personal (VII.402). There is no person without an other, and no love without a counterpart that is both logically and ontologically independent of the lover. So God's becoming actual – love rather than the undifferentiated swell of forces in the primal godhead or *Ungrund* – depends on the human actuation of freedom. And the actuation of freedom means the whole sweep of human history, with its multifaceted instantiation of *every* possibility of good *and* evil. With the monolithic identity of mere nature left behind, the actual God, the Word in the form of humanity suffers through all of human history, while the attractive ideal force, the personal God or Spirit, presses on (as ideal) toward some final crisis, some decision, some division of good from evil.

A final section of the argument vindicates Schelling's claim that the philosopher can have both system and a lively sense of freedom and personality. What guarantees system is the prior nature of God, the *Ungrund* or indifference of ground and existence; it is undifferentiated being, the counterpart of Spinoza's substance. Only when creative decision separates nature from freedom, longing from reason, and binds the two in an utterly fragile way in humankind, is there development, process, evolution and the possibility of love as the reunification of the broken pieces (VII.409–12). Although Schelling will explore 'personal' or 'evolutionary theology' again in the many drafts of *Ages of the World* (1811–15), those fragmentary attempts to depict the 'past of God' or God without humanity lack the sheer intellectual and emotional power of the insistently anthropocentric – or incarnational – theology of the essay on *Human Freedom*. It is a darker picture of revelation than orthodox theology usually presents, and a much darker picture of human history than the Enlightenment usually suggests: "All history remains incomprehensible without the concept of a humanly suffering God", one embedded in all the sordid adventures of humankind (VII.401).

HUMAN NATURE

In the wake of his wife's death in 1809, Schelling produced two works, both somewhat cryptic and incomplete, that considered God's counterpart, humanity, and its role in the elaboration of the divine being. The *Stuttgart Private Lectures* (1810) offer a synoptic view of Schelling's new 'system of freedom', while the dialogue *Clara* explores traditional questions on the immortality of the human soul, albeit from the unusual perspective of the phenomenon of hypnosis or 'animal magnetism' as advocated by F. A. Mesmer. Both works present a view of human rationality or personality as founded on the irrational, or the natural basis of human faculties that, left on its own, manifests as madness (VII.469–70). The irrational in the human corresponds to the 'natural' element in God, or mere being (*das Seyn*), from which God distinguishes Godself as personal or actualized being (*das Seyende*). This process of divine evolution is identical with the creation of humanity, since God effects in it the evocation of consciousness out of the unconscious, or of spirit (intelligence) out of matter (VII.435–6). Humanity pertains to *non-being*, to that which *ought not* be, and from which, when wrongly posited as something in itself, disease, madness and moral evil manifest. This same force in God, self-love or *egoism*, is that whereby God is a unique or isolated particular. It is only through the counterbalancing power of *love* that God becomes infinitely communicative and expansive, the being of all beings. Creation, or evocation of the ideal from the real, begins with God's 'moral' act: the subordination of self-will to love (VII.438–9). The canvas of human history depicts the struggle between the forces of egoism and love, and the relative indecision of peoples and individuals over whether they wish to pertain to nature (*Seyn*) or to spirit (*das Seyende*). Schelling's theogony is still riveted on the spectacle of "a humanly suffering God" (VII.403; cf. IV.252).

God is absolutely free since God possesses absolute, active being, whereas the human being is free in a derivative sense: free from divine determination because she possesses a ground independent of God (namely, nature) and free from nature in having the divine fire kindled within her. The human ought to be the point where nature is transfigured into spirit and the continuity of all realms of being is established, but because the human realm has actuated the natural or egocentric principle, nature has instead become independent of spirit and taken on the aspect of temporality: the first period of life, or the antechamber to spirit (VIII.457–9). The detachment of the human realm from its proper place, the middle ground between the non-being of nature and the absolute being of God, has distorted the three powers or faculties that make up human reality: affect (*Gemüth*), mind (*Geist*) and soul (*Seele*). Each of these powers – conceived as a capacity for action, and not merely a state of being – has three aspects.

The three aspects of *affect* are: longing (which tends to manifest as melancholy), desire (hunger for being) and feeling (which has a cognitive, although not conscious, flavour to it) (VII.465–6). The second or mental level of powers is opposed to the first (affect); in general, it is the domain of consciousness. Its three aspects are: *egocentric will, understanding* and *will as such* (which, under the influence of disposition and egoistic will, tends to manifest as choice of evil) (VII.467–8). The third power (soul) is the principle of connection or continuity between the first two. Its aspects are: impersonal, unconscious and non-deliberative. Mind has knowledge, but the soul is said to be science itself; mind can be good, but soul is goodness itself. As the hidden divine spark, soul can relate itself to the emotional and egocentric element and express itself in art and poetry. Or it can relate itself to the highest element in the first two powers and express its inchoate grasp of reality as philosophy. Or it can relate itself to will and express itself as morality. Or it can act unconditionally, and then the sphere of its activity is religion (VII.471–3). Disordered relations in all three categories result in affective disorders, cognitive incapacities such as nonsense, or madness when understanding and soul miscommunicate. Madness is not a specific disorder, but a manifestation of the non-being or irrationality that lies at the basis of human reality: "In brief, it is precisely the irrational that constitutes the very ground of our understanding"

(VII.470). Schelling's psychological realism is startling: human reality, which should be solidly in the centre of things, is precarious!

The human being was supposed to be the creature of the centre, the point of continuity between nature and spirit. Instead of using her freedom to elevate nature into spirit, the human being instead reached back into nature, temporalized her existence and thus postponed the realization of spirit from the present – life within nature – to a spiritual world *after death*. Schelling conceives 'nature' and 'spirit' here as volitional modes, self-absorbed ego or communicative outreach, so that death is not so much the separation of mind and body as the separation of good and evil (VII.474–6; see also IX.32–3). Delivered to her own ideal world, but not necessarily God's, the whole person continues to exist, but consciousness functions immediately in the presence of its objects, and not as mediated through the senses. Post-death experience is akin to clairvoyance or a 'wakeful sleep' in which the good remember only the good and the evil only evil (VII.477–8: see also IX.65–6). In *Clara* he argues in detail that in the spiritual order God is directly the cause of the person's perceptions, the way the hypnotizer is the cause of the perceptions – deemed unusual by us – in the one hypnotized (IX.72). That God can in this way be the one mind of the spirit world comes from the existential disparity between God and the human creature; the former is active existence or agency (*das Seyende*), the latter mere being (*Seyn*). The objects to be encountered in the spirit world are much the same as those in the natural world, but intuitable only in a mental manner: "The world of spirit is God's poetry, while nature is God's sculpture" (VII.480). The more one has re-enacted the primordial moral act of freedom and subjected one's particular will to love, the more one is likely to be absorbed into the divine being in the spirit world; conversely, the more one has persisted in self-centred will, the more one will be separate. All of these naturalistic features that Schelling ascribes to post-mortem existence follow from "heaven's perfect worldliness" (IX.99).

THE DIVINE ACTUALITY

In 1815, Schelling delivered an address called *The Deities of Samothrace* to the Bavarian Academy of Sciences, with the aim of empirically reinforcing the highly speculative vision that *Ages of the World* advanced of there being an 'eternal past' preserved in God. In the address Schelling contends that there is a primal human wisdom that maintains, in some faulty way, memory of both human and divine origins, and which is passed down in ancient mythologies. Returning to the view of his early seminary essays on mythology, he contends that the succession of deities pictured in Greek, Phoenician and Egyptian mythologies points especially to a natural basis of longing that is the beginning of the birth of rational personality in God – and, of course, to the transition from figurative polytheism to monotheistic religion (VIII.350). Thus begins Schelling's journey towards 'positive philosophy', expounded in the lecture halls of Munich and Berlin, heard by students as different as Kierkegaard and Lenin, but never committed to print.

In *Lectures on History of Modern Philosophy* given in Munich after Hegel's death (the manuscript dates from 1833–4), Schelling repudiates the whole of his early philosophy – 'identity philosophy' being subsumed under the title *Naturphilosophie* – and the whole of Hegel's system as well as mere 'negative' or 'conceptual philosophy'. His early philosophy, admits Schelling, bore no relation to *existence* or to anything *real*, and hence when it treated the idea of God or the highest actuality it was merely playing with relationships that that idea takes on in human thought. We might say it was only conceptual analysis and totally vacant of significance since the question of God's reality was never posed. The constructions of idealistic philosophy are a grand sham, not an ontological proof writ large (X.125). This 'negative philosophy' was faulty not only in its use of *a priori* reasoning or 'construction', but also in importing a false developmental perspective into its idea of God. The point is not simply that the idea of deity undergoes development in its philosophical presentation, but that God is presented as the product of an objective process of development, as an evolution from natural force to rational love; God is thus present only in the end, as a result, and the so-called divine history (portrayed in works such as *Human Freedom* and *Ages of the World*) is everywhere confounded with human history and the path of thought pursued by the philosopher. Rightly understood, there is no becoming in God, and if one wants to picture this as God coming to grasp Godself, either the process is eternal and hence not a process, or the movement of *becoming* is personal and communicative, and the force of love in history was nothing but the movement of thought, an event in the philosopher's subjectivity (X.124–5). If these remarks repudiate the finite, developmental approach in conceptualizing the divine reality found in Schelling's philosophies of nature and freedom, they cut more radically against the dialectical style of Hegel's version of 'objective idealism', which plainly makes the divine reality a result dependent on a logical process and which moves from mere thought to reality only by a dialectic sleight of hand (X.126–8).

If Schelling in the end rejects the development or process view of deity implicit in the philosophy of nature and explicitly adopted in *Human Freedom*, how is the divine reality to be conceived? In a segment of an 1836 Munich lecture course that served as an introduction to philosophy, and which his editor-son issued under the title *Exposition of Philosophical Empiricism*, Schelling reverted to classical modes of thought to undercut the dualism inherent in modern philosophy which, focusing as it does on *presentation* or *perception*, can never get beyond the subject–object opposition. He uses the Pythagorean principles of *apeiron* and *peras*, and Plato's *monad* and *dyad*, to ascend to the idea of a 'highest cause', at once cause and substance (or self-caused), which brings together the relative pairs and overcomes the sheer relativity of the material or indefinite principle through the limitation imposed by the ideal, defining element (X.245–55). Only this independent and fully actual being (*das Seyende*) is capable of establishing the potentiality for being in the two relative or quasi-actual principles (*das Seynkönnende*), and only with all three principles together – that which ought not be, that which should be and the ultimate cause – do we philosophically come to something that corresponds to the biblical description of God as 'Lord of Being' (X.264–5). "The highest concept of God, hence the highest concept in general, is that which defines God as absolute independence, as fully real in itself and completely internally elaborated"; substance trumps causality when it comes to the divine reality (X.279).

That Schelling reverts to classical modes of thought in his final writings on philosophy of religion and turns away from the 'process' or 'historical' theology of his middle years is somewhat surprising. Nevertheless, the ontological difference between actuality, agency and freedom (denoted by *das Seyende*) and potentiality, passivity, and other-determination (denoted by *Seyn*), first introduced in *Human Freedom*, continues to play an important role in Schelling's thought, providing him with a philosophical means to re-establish the sense of divine transcendence that the negative philosophy compromised. The difference between freedom and being, or the superiority of agency over mere existence, is the enduring *idealistic* element in Schelling's philosophy of religion.

FURTHER READING

Asmuth, C., A. Denker & M. Vater (eds) 2000. *Schelling: Between Fichte and Hegel*. Amsterdam: B. R. Grüner.

Beach, E. 1994. *The Potencies of God(s): Schelling's Philosophy of Mythology*. Albany, NY: SUNY Press.

Bowie, A. 1993. *Schelling and Modern European Philosophy*. London: Routledge.

Brown, R. 1977. *The Later Philosophy of Schelling: The Influence of Boehme on the Works of 1809–1815*. Lewisburg: PA: Bucknell University Press.

Heidegger, M. 1985. *Schelling's Treatise on the Essence of Human Freedom*, J. Stambaugh (trans.). Athens, OH: Ohio University Press.

Norman, J. & A. Welchman (eds) 2004. *The New Schelling*. London: Continuum.

Schelling, F. 2002. *Clara, or, On Nature's Connection to the Spirit World*, F. Steinkamp (trans.). Albany, NY: SUNY Press.

Wirth, J. 2003. *The Conspiracy of Life: Meditations on Schelling and his Time*. Albany, NY: SUNY Press.

Žižek, S. 1997. *The Abyss of Freedom: Ages of the World*, with Schelling's *Die Weltalter* (2nd draft, 1813), J. Norman (trans.). Ann Arbor, MI: University of Michigan Press.

On IDEALISM see also Chs 16, 19. On MYTHOLOGY see also Ch. 15; Vol. 1, Ch. 2. On NATURE/NATURALISM see also Ch. 10; Vol. 3, Chs 20, 21, 22; Vol. 5, Ch. 4. On REVELATION see also Ch. 11; Vol. 1, Ch. 14; Vol. 2, Ch. 11; Vol. 3, Chs 7, 11, 16; Vol. 5, Chs 8, 23. On SELF-CONSCIOUSNESS see also Chs 2, 4, 10, 13.

6

ARTHUR SCHOPENHAUER

Robert Wicks

Arthur Schopenhauer's (1788–1860) popular reputation as a pessimistic atheist has tended to obscure the appreciation of his philosophy's religious import. An individualist he surely was, but he was not iconoclastic, and he experienced a great satisfaction in the belief that his independent philosophizing cohered with the ethical doctrines of the world's major religions. Foremost in his mind were Hinduism, Buddhism and Christianity, as he understood them to express a general outlook that elevates spiritual concerns over materialistic and worldly ones.

Schopenhauer's family was not religious in the traditional sense, and it had no history of grandfathers and great-grandfathers who served in the ministry or priesthood. Successful bankers and shipowners were his immediate ancestors, and he was surrounded by cosmopolitan, mercantile and elitist values at a young age. His father, Heinrich Floris Schopenhauer (1747–1805), was a leading citizen of Danzig (Gdansk), and his mother, Johanna Trosiener Schopenhauer (1766–1838), was the daughter of one of the city's senators. Mainly owing to his father's influence, Schopenhauer was raised to continue the family tradition as a businessman and person of worldly affairs.

The world of commerce conflicted with Schopenhauer's academic disposition, and he left his business apprenticeship to devote himself single-mindedly to scholarly activities before he reached the age of twenty. This was precipitated by Heinrich Floris' death soon after Schopenhauer had turned seventeen, which partially alleviated his sense of family duty. Schopenhauer's interest in philosophy also stemmed from his heartbreaking perceptions of wide-ranging poverty – much like the experiences of Karl Marx in England some years later – during a lengthy trip through Europe just prior to his father's death. These instilled in him a sense of profound resignation, rather than social activism and indignation.

For the first four decades of his life Schopenhauer lived in a variety of German cities – Hamburg, Weimar, Göttingen, Berlin, Dresden, Munich, Mannheim – punctuated by occasional visits to other European countries. He never settled in one place for more than a few years at a time. From age forty-five to his death at the age of seventy-two, he lived more stably in Frankfurt in a riverside apartment, alone with a succession of beloved poodles. He decorated his lodgings with a statue of the Buddha and a bust of Kant, along with portraits of Goethe and Shakespeare, which silently complemented his habit of reading Hindu literature at night before going to sleep. Schopenhauer was an independently wealthy, usually well-dressed solitary, who led a monkish life as an Anglophile in the middle of a bustling German city. Within this atmosphere he composed most of his reflections on religion, the majority of which we encounter in his later writings (1844–60).

SCHOPENHAUER'S 'PESSIMISTIC' RELIGIONS: HINDUISM, BUDDHISM AND CHRISTIANITY

Hinduism

Schopenhauer often read the Upanishads (*c*.1500–900 BCE) in Latin translation before retiring in the evening, as many people read the Bible. This practice in itself reveals a religious interest and mentality that extends back to the days when, in his later twenties, he was introduced to this classical Indian text by Friedrich Majer (1771–1818), an orientalist in Weimar, and to further Asian texts and journals a year later in Dresden, by his neighbour and philosopher Karl Christian Friedrich Krause (1781–1832). In Schopenhauer's own philosophical writings, we find him reciting the Sanskrit phrase "*tat tvam asi*" ("that, you are" or "thou art that") as an affirmative expression of his own metaphysical message that emphasizes the ultimate unity of all things and people.

Schopenhauer argued that there is a single cosmic energy – not an objectively physical energy, but an inner one that can be grasped by reflecting on how, for each of us, our own body has an inner dimension to it. We can observe our hand on the table, for instance, notice its objective similarity to the other physical objects beside it, and yet realize that, unlike the surrounding objects, we can also perceive our hand from the inside. We can feel pleasure and pain, and we can make our hand move to interact with other physical objects. Our hand, like our bodies in general, has a double aspect: it has an objective and subjective side. The rest of the objects on the table, in contrast to our hand, are like closed books.

It is natural to regard the objective, physical side of our bodies as the most fundamental, and its subjective, conscious quality as dependent on our physical condition. We watch people live and die, and when they die, their consciousness disappears while their lifeless body remains. It is a hallmark of Schopenhauer's philosophy to reverse this priority by maintaining that one's body, not to mention the physical world itself, is only the manifestation of a more universal subjective energy that exhibits itself directly in, and as, our consciousness. Schopenhauer referred to this energy as 'Will': we directly experience it as beings who are consciously aware that we can do things. This Will is everyone's ultimate substance, and it flows through each of us identically in the way individual streams of water shoot up from a fountain: each streaming line of water transiently appears to be different from the stream next to it, but as they return to their source into the same pool, it becomes clear that each stream is of essentially the same being.

Schopenhauer maintained accordingly that as each of us looks out on the world – including every person who has existed and will exist – we embody the 'single eye' that is timelessly looking out from all conscious beings. What this eye looks on, and what each of us thereby perceives, is universal being as Will in an objectified form. There is one reality called 'Will', nothing else, and through the Will's innumerable manifestations, among which are the conscious awarenesses of every human being and animal, this ultimate reality apprehends itself and knows itself as an object.

At the core of Schopenhauer's metaphysics we can consequently and coincidentally recognize the applicability of the Upanishadic phrase "*tat tvam asi*": the world's universalistic and subjective aspect (*Atman*) is identical to its universalistic and objective aspect (*Brahman*). To some extent, Schopenhauer's 'Will' compares to *Atman*; the world as representation, to *Brahman*. This marks a global, but qualified, affinity between Schopenhauer's view and that of the Upanishads, along with the Indian philosophical school of Advaita Vedanta (*c.* eighth century CE).

An important difference is that Schopenhauer's Will is metaphysically foundational and self-sufficient, rather than being a counterpart in a balanced, double-aspected metaphysical equation. The world as representation depends on the Will, but not vice versa. The Will is also irrational, aimless and essentially meaningless, and as such it immediately invites nihilistic reflections about the value of existence. Unlike the Upanishads, Schopenhauer did not celebrate the physical world as a divine overflow of life, where multitudes of living and natural beings blend wildly into each other in an overwhelming display of inspiration and power. The Schopenhauerian world is rather a sea of woe. It is an endless expanse of insatiable, bloodthirsty, deceptive and morally repulsive desires. This difference in tone between Schopenhauer's metaphysics and that of the Upanishads brings us a step closer to some affinities between his outlook and Buddhism, as we shall shortly see.

The contrast between the respective emotional atmospheres of Schopenhauer's metaphysics and the Upanishads sheds light on his critical assessment of pantheism: the view that there is only one infinite and glorious individual, namely, God. Against both theism and pantheism, he stated that if a God had made this world, then he would not want to be that God, since the world's misery and distress would break his heart (Schopenhauer 1988a: 63). Schopenhauer consequently criticized pantheism as an insensitive outlook in so far as it absorbs, obscures and subordinates the world's pain to the glory of the divine whole. As an alternative, he proposed that if we are set on equating the world with an infinite being, then we should identify it with the devil, yielding what one could call 'pandemonism', as opposed to pantheism. Views that assign a full reality to the daily, spatiotemporal world in a life-affirming way – and Schopenhauer maintained that pantheism does this – he referred to as instances of a morally objectionable 'optimism', locating his own pessimism on the side of compassion.

Buddhism

Following Immanuel Kant, Schopenhauer held that human beings are largely responsible for the structure of their experience. As human beings *per se*, we are rational beings who accordingly structure experience in terms of basic logical forms: we observe passing events, for instance, and intellectually expect that if events of one type occur (e.g. the heating of water to a certain degree) then events of a corresponding type will follow (e.g. the water will boil). He also followed Kant by adopting the latter's view that space and time are structures that, as far as we can know, reside exclusively in us. In Schopenhauer's opinion, if there were no people, then space and time would vanish.

Schopenhauer integrated the above reflections about logic, space and time into a single principle by stating that we project a 'principle of individuation' that structures our experience. There may be only one universal energy at the core of things, namely 'Will', but this Will manifests itself logically and spatiotemporally through the human perspective as a set of interacting individuals. For Schopenhauer, the daily world of causally related physical things in space and time is largely of our own making. It is like a movie projected onto a screen, where the Will is like the white light that passes through the film and the projector. He insisted that life is dreamlike, as ephemeral as a rainbow that shines beside a waterfall.

Schopenhauer's account of the daily world issues from the supposition that human experience depends on a principle of individuation that prescribes the temporal appearance of a single, timeless Will. This principle operates in the way a kaleidoscope fragments a single presentation into multiple images and "shows us a new configuration at every turn, whereas really we always have the same thing before our eyes" (Schopenhauer 1966b: 478). Since what is fragmented is the Will – a blind striving for nothing in particular – the resulting appearance is a set of objects, or 'representations', each of which is driven selfishly with insatiable desire. The originality of Schopenhauer's Kantianism resides at this point, in his warlike vision of the daily world. Within this world of representation, each individual sets itself against the others in an endless battle where, less like a dream and more like a nightmare, both ignorance and selfish desire combine to generate a world of pain. Ignorance prevails, since the battling individuals fail to realize that their own sense of individuality is illusory and that ultimately they are objectifications of the one Will that is articulating itself into an initial condition of ignorance.

Within this scenario, there are some affinities to Buddhism. Just as we find in Schopenhauer's characterization of worldly existence, Buddhism's canonical Four Noble Truths state that desire and ignorance are the main cause of suffering. In particular, Buddhism asserts that we suffer as a result of the deceptive desire to hold on permanently to impermanent things. Human bodies are perishable items, and yet many live holding on to their egos, to physical things, to other people, to social status, to an assortment of value systems, and to health, as if these were absolutely permanent. Much suffering issues from disregarding the fluctuating nature of things and by attempting to hold on to castles of sand or even to mountains of granite, as if they were imperishable.

Schopenhauer's view is more extreme than the Buddhist one, however, since Buddhism typically raises suspicions not about all desire, but about desires that are grounded on the assumption that there are absolutely permanent modes of being, located either without or within. Such deceptive desires are many and can be vexing, but Schopenhauer maintained more radically that we should extinguish all desire and adopt a rigorous asceticism. In this respect, his view compares not only with the more extreme ascetic versions of Hinduism, but also with Christian mysticism, especially of the quietist sort that was popular in the seventeenth and eighteenth centuries.

Christianity

Schopenhauer was convinced that philosophical expression surpasses religious expression in so far as objective and clear logic is preferable to mythological imagery and authority-derived doctrine. He nonetheless sympathized with the spirit of Christianity and understood himself as distilling essential Christian concepts into a purely philosophical form. Paramount among these is the emphasis on compassion towards other people and living things, which is also central to Buddhist ethics. His view of the general relationship between philosophy and religion is encapsulated well in the following remarks, which incidentally allow us to refer to Schopenhauer's philosophy as 'philosophy of religion', as he understood it:

> From time immemorial, all nations have acknowledged that the world has a moral, as well as physical, import. Everywhere nevertheless the matter was only brought to an indistinct consciousness, which, in seeking for its adequate expression, has clothed itself in various images and myths. These are the different Religions.
>
> (Schopenhauer 1891: 372)

> *Natural religion*, or as present-day custom calls it, *philosophy of religion*, means a philosophical system which in its results harmonizes with some positive religion, so that in the eyes of those who confess one of them, both in precisely this way are proved to be true.   (1988a: 16)

> Buddha, Eckhart and I teach essentially the same thing; Eckhart is shackled by his Christian mythology. In Buddhism the same ideas are to be found but not stunted by such mythology and hence simple and

clear, in so far as any religion can be clear. With me there is complete clearness. (1988b: 387)

Contrary to what Kant believed, Schopenhauer argued that moral awareness is not primarily a matter of self-consciously following logical rules inherent in oneself and being consistent in one's behaviour. It is instead a directly experiencable metaphysical condition, for as we relinquish our selfishness and become increasingly aware of our ultimate identity with the universal Will, we realize that every person is constituted literally by the same substance as our own. Within this more universalistic awareness, as the boundaries of our individuality fall away in attaining an empathy with humanity as a whole, we feel humanity itself to be our own individual body. Here, the tormentor and the tormented, the criminal and the victim, are apprehended as literally the same being. Immoral activity consequently becomes an instance of the Will that, in its objectified condition, is doing nothing more than repulsively feasting on its own. On realizing that the tormentor and tormented are identical, crimes against humanity become one's own crimes, and the goodness within humanity becomes one's own goodness. The state of awareness is terribly mixed and profoundly sublime. The person with such a moral awareness becomes a universal individual: a Christ-like figure who peacefully bears the sins of the world, but with an infinite suffering that follows from universal compassion. A community of moral individuals, as here described, would epitomize the idea of a Christian community composed of a set of insightful, Christ-like people.

Schopenhauer's account of human nature also resonates with an inborn principle of universal guilt, namely, Original Sin. As noted, he maintained that the Will appears in a differentiated form, not because the Will is differentiated in itself, but because our own principle of individuation – the 'principle of sufficient reason' – generates the illusory, and nightmarish, appearance of a world filled with conflicting individuals. Owing to this principle, the human being shows itself to be responsible for the world's total misery: if there were no human beings, there would be no principle of differentiation, and therefore no individuals and no suffering. Precisely because he aimed to overcome this pain-producing, guilt-generating and heartbreaking principle within ourselves, Schopenhauer advocated ascetic self-denial as a means to salvation.

The principle of sufficient reason states that for any fact or state of affairs, there is a reason why that fact or state of affairs is exactly how it is, and not otherwise. In so far as one accepts this principle, one accepts that everything falling within its scope has an explanation, even if we do not know what that explanation happens to be. Explaining things and events requires that we articulate their structure, and hence the principle of sufficient reason carries with it a principle of individuation necessary for the sake of knowledge.

The principle of sufficient reason within Schopenhauer's perspective thus stands as the philosophical correlate to the biblically sinful quest for knowledge: a quest that, as represented in the story of Adam and Eve, cast human beings into a punishing self-conscious awareness of death and destruction. For Schopenhauer, the very principle that governs our quest for knowledge and security is none other than the principle that introduces untold suffering into the world. This explains why he was morally repulsed by human nature in its inherent and insatiable quest for scientific knowledge.

Asceticism – the final stage of Schopenhauer's path to salvation – aspires to a complete 'denial of the will' where all egoistic desires are dissolved. The implied mode of awareness is indescribable in positive terms, and Schopenhauer is ambiguous about how we are to conceive of it. In some passages, he describes a condition compatible with Christian quietism, as well as with Hindu and Sufi mysticism. Here, one reduces one's worldly desires and sense of self in an effort to dissolve all sense of personal finitude. Once this is achieved, the expectation is that the infinite presence of God, of the Absolute, or of higher-dimensional realities, will enter one's consciousness to produce a divine experience. In other passages that are more Buddhistic, Schopenhauer describes an entirely detached state of mind, free of desires and at psychological rest. No special awareness of higher metaphysical dimensions is indicated; the daily pressures of the will are simply relieved to a point where, in outstanding tranquillity, one achieves an extraordinary state of consciousness, albeit of a wholly negative sort. In both alternatives, Schopenhauer aims to characterize a universalistic mode of consciousness that is free from the pressures of fleshly appetites and concerns. We have the following summary:

> Therefore that great fundamental truth contained in Christianity as well as in Brahmanism and Buddhism, the need for salvation from an existence given up to suffering and death, and its attainability through the denial of the will, hence by a decided opposition to nature, is beyond all comparison the most important truth there can be.   (1966b: 628)

SCHOPENHAUER'S 'OPTIMISTIC' RELIGIONS: JUDAISM, ISLAM AND ANCIENT GREEK POLYTHEISM

Judaism and Islam

Since the history of Christianity is so closely enmeshed with that of Judaism, one might expect Schopenhauer's account of Judaism to coincide with his rendition of Christianity, at least in general tone. This is interestingly not the case, and Schopenhauer criticized Judaism in the relatively few passages in which he spoke about it. His main criticism does not apply uniquely to Judaism, however, for many people share the supposition Schopenhauer associated with this religion. It is, namely, that the daily world in which we live is perfectly real and intrinsically good, and is not an illusion or dream. Schopenhauer referred to this attitude as a combination of "realism and optimism", quite disparagingly:

> Judaism has as its fundamental characteristics *realism and optimism* which are closely related and are the conditions of *theism* proper. For this regards the material world as absolutely real and life as a pleasant gift bestowed on us. Brahmanism and Buddhism, on the other hand, have as their fundamental characteristics *idealism and pessimism*, for they assign to the world only a dreamlike existence and regard life as the consequence of our guilt. (1974b: 378)

> I cannot here withhold the statement that *optimism* … seems to me to be not merely an absurd, but also a really *wicked*, way of thinking, a bitter mockery of the unspeakable sufferings of mankind. Let no one imagine that the Christian teaching is favorable to optimism; on the contrary, in the Gospels world and evil are used almost as synonymous expressions. (1966a: 326)

Schopenhauer's recognition of Judaism's optimism matches, as a rule, his views of Greek paganism and Islam. Sometimes he tempered his characterization of Judaism and stated that only Islam and Greek paganism are optimistic through and through (1966b: 605). In general, though, his writings show a limited concern with the differentiating details of Judaism and Islam, probably because he regarded them as being at odds with his own metaphysics from the very start.

Aside from the charge of optimism, the bulk of Schopenhauer's remaining remarks about Judaism and Islam involve descriptive references to particular practices that are largely independent of his metaphysical and attitudinal differences with them. Exceptions are found in his celebration of Sufi mysticism and his positive estimation of the Jewish people's social strength in so far as "no other community on earth stays so firmly together as does this" (1974b: 262).

In one instance, Schopenhauer asserted that Judaism distinguishes between human beings and animals, privileging the former and subordinating the latter to the extent that animal abuse becomes objectionably tolerable. Again, such a distinction between human beings and animals resides in other outlooks. A notable example is that of René Descartes (1596–1650), a Roman Catholic, who maintained that animals, since they lack animating souls, are nothing more than robotic mechanisms.

Schopenhauer also mentioned the Islamic practice of praying five times a day in conjunction with the Catholic practice of making the sign of the cross; both are cited as prime examples of how human beings can be arbitrarily trained (1974b: 603). For the most part, his less sympathetic comments are motivated by a desire to reveal the arbitrariness, but more importantly the hypocrisy, that can accompany religious affiliation as it is imperfectly instantiated in real life. Few groups were immune:

> Those devils in human form, the slave-owners and slave traders in the Free States of North America (they should be called the Slave States),

are, as a rule, orthodox and pious Anglicans who would regard it as a grave sin to work on Sundays and who, confident of this and of their regular attendance at church, hope for eternal happiness. The demoralizing influence of religions is, therefore, less problematical than the moralizing. *(Ibid.*: 355–6)

Schopenhauer's philosophically oriented criticism of Judaism, Islam and Greek polytheism as realistic and optimistic religions might seem foreign and counterintuitive, if only because it is natural to assume that the daily world is indeed the real world. His aversion to optimistic outlooks, however, can be understood if we appreciate, for instance, how our knowledge of other people is arguably better placed if we attend to the intangible quality of their inner character as opposed to how they happen physically to look. Similarly, it would make more sense to empathize with other people as much as we can, and attempt to feel as they feel, see as they see, hear as they hear and so on, ultimately aiming to discern humanity itself staring back at us. We may not literally experience another person's experience – although Schopenhauer's metaphysics admits this almost-magical possibility (1891: 340) – but the imaginative effort to empathize leads us to focus behind physical appearances and attend to the inner nature of things as it manifests itself in the consciousness of another individual.

With this attention to the inner nature of things, the objective 'world as representation' becomes subordinated to the subjective 'world as will'. Accordingly, the aesthetic surface of the world, sometimes so beautiful, becomes subordinated to the inner nature of the objects that appear. Rather than appreciate someone's impressive physical beauty and rest comfortably with their fortunate appearance, Schopenhauer asks us to empathize with the person's experience and quality of character, which could be truly vicious. In the same vein, rather than be repulsed by someone's physical deformity and rest uncomfortably with their unfortunate appearance, Schopenhauer asks us to empathize with the person's experience and quality of character, which could be truly saintly. The optimistic, scientific, immediately aesthetic, object-centred perspective, for Schopenhauer, overlooks the inner reality of things – one that he believes is essentially tormented – and draws a false implication about the nature of the world as a result: "An optimist tells me to open my eyes and to see how beautiful the world is with its mountains, plants, fresh air, animals and so forth. – Naturally these things are beautiful to *behold*, but to *be* them is something quite different" (1988a: 188).

Greek polytheism

Schopenhauer's official estimation of Greek polytheism (or 'Greco-Roman paganism', as he calls it) as an 'optimistic' religion parallels his views of Judaism and Islam. He regarded ancient Greek religion as virtually no religion at all, or as at least very different from what we now understand as religion. As evidence he observed how the gods were often treated with an astounding public disrespect, citing Aristophanes' *Frogs* as an example: "This is evident from the *Frogs* of Aristophanes, where Dionysus appears as the most pitiable poltroon and coxcomb imaginable and is made an object of ridicule; and this play was publicly performed at his own festival, the Dionysia" (1974b: 362). This could suggest that Greek polytheism is quite foreign to Schopenhauer's philosophy and that, as an optimistic, life-affirming religion that respected and personified nature, it is incongruous with his generally otherworldly perspective. The contrary fact is that Schopenhauer was not as alienated from Greek culture as he was from Judaic and Islamic culture. He read classical Greek texts in the original, and by his own admission was influenced significantly by Plato's philosophy. He also liberally seasoned his philosophical writings with Greek phrases, references and images, quite positively and without a critical edge. Among the images, the most memorable are Tantalus, the Danaids and Ixion, all illustrative of the never-ending torments and frustrations that life contains. On attaining salvation, Schopenhauer stated, "the wheel of Ixion stands still".

Schopenhauer displayed a reserved attitude towards ancient Greek culture and religion, not because he believed that the Greeks were fundamentally wrong-headed, but because he believed that they were only partially correct:

> Almost all [Greek tragedies] show the human race under the dreadful domination of chance and error, but not the resignation these bring about which redeems us from them. All this was because the ancients had not yet reached the summit and goal of tragedy, or indeed of the view of life generally.   (1966b: 434)

Schopenhauer set forth a compatibly deterministic account of daily life within his own philosophy: for him, our worldly actions are exclusively the result of our given character in conjunction with the environmental details in which we are situated. In this respect, he positively appreciated the ancient Greek submission to the dictates of fate. It is only that the ancient Greeks lacked the resignation he associated with Christianity.

Plato's influence also reveals an affirmative relationship between Schopenhauer's aesthetics and Greek polytheism. In Schopenhauer's theory of aesthetic experience, the primary purpose of art is to present idealized representations of timeless realities that are otherwise obscurely apprehended. Through a beautiful painting we see past the mist of contingent circumstance to apprehend beauty itself; through an idealized portrait of someone, we can apprehend that person's inner character more clearly and directly than we otherwise would. Good art allows us to apprehend perfection in the form of Platonic Ideas, in effect.

On the face of things, the contemplation of Platonic Ideas in aesthetic experience is not related to Greek polytheism, but if we recall Schopenhauer's estimate of his philosophy in relation to religion, the connection to the Greek pantheon emerges: "*My philosophy* is related to *religions* as is a straight line to several curves

running close to it, for it expresses *sensu proprio* [in the literal meaning] and consequently reaches directly what they show under disguises and reach in roundabout
ways" (1988b: 378). Plato's Ideas – those of perfect beauty, courage, wisdom, and
so on – are none other than the demythologized and rationalized images of the
Greek gods. Exactly in accord with Schopenhauer's description of how philosophy
ought to approach religion, Plato reconceived Aphrodite as the form of Beauty-
itself, Hercules as Courage-itself, and so on, contemplating exclusively their intelligible characters and setting aside their sensuous, spatiotemporal qualities in an
act of philosophical abstraction (*see* Vol. 1, Ch. 4). In this historical light, we can
see how the Platonic Ideas in Schopenhauer's aesthetics implicitly embody Greek
polytheism, in so far as this polytheism is represented in the rarefied and highly
intellectualized form that we owe to Plato. Schopenhauer's contemporary G. W. F.
Hegel characterized Greek religion as a 'religion of art', which adds some coinci-
dental credence to this association between Schopenhauer's aesthetics, Platonic
Ideas and the Greek pantheon.

CONCLUSION

Schopenhauer writes: "The fundamental difference in religions is to be found in
the question of whether they are optimistic or pessimistic, certainly not whether
they are monotheistic, polytheistic, Trimurti, Trinity, pantheistic, or atheistic (like
Buddhism)" (1974b: 388). The distinction between optimistic and pessimistic religions grounds Schopenhauer's writings on religion, and he evaluated the various
world religions along such lines. Buddhism emerges as the pre-eminent religion,
with Christianity and Hinduism in a close second place. At the lower levels reside
Greek polytheism, followed by Islam and Judaism. It is fair to say, though, that
Hinduism's recognition of a timeless substrate to the universe more closely reflects
Schopenhauer's conception of the timeless Will than does the Buddhistic doctrine
of universal flux, which Schopenhauer did not seem to appreciate as being at vari-
ance with his metaphysics.

Within Buddhism, Schopenhauer's metaphysics of the Will does nonetheless
compare to how the Yogācāra or 'consciousness-only' school (*c.* fourth century
CE) exclusively recognizes a universal consciousness at the foundation of experience. Even here, though, since the substantial nature of this consciousness is
questionable and since Schopenhauer does not ascribe consciousness to the
Will, the parallel remains qualified. As things stand, Schopenhauer's paradoxical
characterization of the Will as a timeless yet constantly striving act has the effect
of ascribing both static and dynamic qualities to the core of things, and this allows
for parallels to be drawn between both Hindu and Buddhist metaphysics.

Although the religious references in Schopenhauer's later works are rich and
numerous, he always privileged philosophical expression over religious expression and sought – as did philosophers during the Enlightenment – to distil the

conceptual essence of a variety of religions into a single, universal expression. Operating behind the scenes of this effort was his own, independently formulated, philosophical outlook. From this initial vantage point, he estimated the degree to which different religions coincided with his own position, praising or criticizing each accordingly.

As a point in supplementary favour of his philosophy, Schopenhauer appreciated the relatively close coincidence between his metaphysics of the Will and certain doctrines of Hinduism, Buddhism and Christianity. He also believed that the oldest languages, along with the religions that were expressed in their terms, harboured the deepest human wisdom. Given the coincidences between his philosophy and Hindu and Buddhist perspectives, he believed that his philosophy conveyed humanity's basic religious insights in a clear, conceptual form.

One limit to Schopenhauer's writings on religion resides in the relative lack of knowledge of ancient Egyptian and Chinese culture during the time when he lived. He studied the available literature, though, and formed a mixed opinion about Chinese religions. He favourably understood Daoism in the same spirit as Buddhism and identified strongly with the concept of *tian* (heaven), which is present in both Daoism and Confucianism. In contrast, he was neutrally descriptive about ritualistic nature worship, and for Confucianism's more worldly doctrines he had little patience:

> Secondly, we find the wisdom of Confucius, which has special attractions for Chinese *savants* and statesmen. Judging from translations, it is a rambling, commonplace, predominantly political, moral philosophy, without any metaphysical support, which has something peculiarly insipid and tiresome about it. (1891: 361)

Egyptian religion fared better, and Schopenhauer's judgement was consistently positive, partially owing to his opinion that Egyptian religion and culture originated in India and hence embodied some of the same doctrines as Hinduism. He also recognized a doctrine of immortality in Egyptian religion, not only in general coincidence with his own philosophy of the timeless Will, but in connection with what he regarded as the essence of religious consciousness in general: "Speaking generally, the really essential element in a religion as such consists in the conviction it gives that our existence proper is not limited to our life, but is infinite" (1974a: 126).

Schopenhauer observed that virtually every religion has some version of a doctrine that acknowledges survival after death, and he believed that his own philosophy captured the idea of immortality most accurately. In disagreement with many religious doctrines, Schopenhauer did not recognize the immortality of the individual person. Not only did he hold that self-centredness and moral consciousness are incompatible, but he insisted that individual existence is transient, illusory and relatively worthless. In his view, only our universal substance endures. It has no consciousness, but is that from which our individual, physical presence emerges and to which it returns.

Linked closely with his universalistic conception of immortality is Schopenhauer's advocacy of the Kantian account of space and time as mind-dependent structures. If space and time depend on human consciousness, then with the extinction of consciousness, they disappear as well. Despite this, Schopenhauer argued that since we cannot originate from nothing, we cannot transform into nothing when we die. In this respect, he believed in accord with many religions, and with some metaphysical comfort, that our true natures are timeless and are as indestructible as the universe we manifest. Philosophical consistency required him to deny that our immortal being as Will involves a conscious awareness of any sort. With noticeable confidence, he maintained nonetheless that we will always universalistically be, but that we will not consciously know this immortality after our bodily death, just as we did not know it before we were born.

FURTHER READING

Abelsen, P. 1993. "Schopenhauer and Buddhism". *Philosophy East & West* **43**: 255–78.

Copleston, F. 1946. *Arthur Schopenhauer: Philosopher of Pessimism*. London: Burns Oates & Washbourne.

Fox, M. (ed.) 1980. *Schopenhauer: His Philosophical Achievement*. Totowa, NJ: Barnes & Noble.

Luft, E. von der (ed.) 1988. *Schopenhauer: New Essays in Honor of His 200th Birthday*. Lewiston, NY: Edwin Mellen Press.

Magee, B. 1983. *The Philosophy of Schopenhauer*. Oxford: Clarendon Press.

Nicholls. M. 1999. "The Influences of Eastern Thought on Schopenhauer's Doctrine of the Thing-in-Itself". In *The Cambridge Companion to Schopenhauer*, C. Janaway (ed.), 171–212. Cambridge: Cambridge University Press.

Sedlar, J. 1982. *India in the Mind of Germany: Schelling, Schopenhauer and Their Times*. Washington, DC: University Press of America.

Young, J. 2005. *Schopenhauer*. London: Routledge.

On IMMORTALITY see also Chs 2, 16; Vol. 1, Ch. 8; Vol. 2, Ch. 5. On POLYTHEISM see also Vol. 1, Ch. 7. On SUFFERING see also Ch. 18. On WORLD RELIGIONS see also Chs 14, 18.

7

AUGUSTE COMTE

H. S. Jones

Auguste Comte (1798–1857), the founder of positivism, stood at the junction of two important traditions in European thought. One was what we might call an 'encyclopaedic' tradition, which aimed at the systematization of knowledge and the construction of a scientific understanding of society. The other consisted in the quest for a secular religion that would transcend Christianity by sacralizing humanity itself. The first tradition rejected theology as unscientific; the second embraced a renewed religion as the route to social regeneration (Wernick 2001: 18–19). Considered as belonging to the first tradition, Comte's main contributions to the philosophy of religion lay in his conjectural history of religion and of the modes of human consciousness. He developed his famous 'law of the three states', in which the theological state of consciousness gives way to the metaphysical, which in turn gives way to the positive or scientific. In fleshing out this law he made a significant contribution to the anthropology of religion by offering an account of how fetishistic forms of theological consciousness were transformed into monotheism by way of polytheism. Considered in the light of the second tradition, Comte was the inventor of the idea of a non-theistic 'religion of humanity', which occupied an important place in nineteenth-century religious thought. Scholars disagree about whether these two aspects of Comtes were incompatible, or two sides to the same coherent thinker. What is surely clear, however, is that a historical appreciation of Comte requires us to grasp why he considered it plausible to contemplate a synthesis of these two traditions.

Comte was born in Montpellier in 1798, into a bourgeois Catholic family whose politics were royalist. Educated at the local *lycée*, he moved to Paris in 1814 to enter the École Polytechnique, the elite scientific college founded two decades before. By this time he had renounced Catholicism and declared himself a republican. With the rest of the student body, he was expelled in 1816 for political dissent, but he retained a lifelong attachment to the Polytechnique and its technocratic ethos left an enduring mark on his intellectual character. He quickly found employment as secretary to the social visionary Henri de Saint-Simon (1760–1825), succeeding the future medieval historian Augustin Thierry (1795–1856), and this period too had a formative influence on his life and thought. He collaborated closely with Saint-Simon on a number of key works propounding the doctrine Saint-Simon had come to label 'industrialism': according to this doctrine, the defining character of modern society was its orientation to industrial production, rather than to war, and in the nineteenth century power was therefore destined to fall into the hands of a new elite of scientists, bankers and industrialists.

Comte broke with Saint-Simon in 1824 and, in the face of recurrent physical and mental ill health, set out to establish his own independent credentials as a philosopher, notably through some public lectures given intermittently in Paris from 1826 onwards, and published in six volumes as the *Cours de philosophie positive* (Course of positive philosophy; 1830–42). He had little regular income, except during the period he spent as Admissions Examiner at the École Polytechnique (1836–44). After he lost that post he was obliged to have recourse to subscriptions raised by his admirers at home and abroad, including John Stuart Mill. An intense but short-lived relationship with his "angelic impulse" Clotilde de Vaux, a young woman seventeen years his junior, precipitated a reorientation in his thinking, in which the emphasis on scientific rationalism that dominated his early system was supplanted, or supplemented, by a renewed appreciation of the role played by sentiment and emotion as social bonds. Clotilde died in 1846, but her influence, according to Comte's own account, precipitated the onset of his 'second career', in which he devoted himself to the transformation of philosophy into religion (Comte 1875–7: vol. 4, 460). He founded the Positivist Society in the revolutionary year of 1848, and set out to institute the Religion of Humanity, which he presented as the culmination of the positivist project in his *Système de politique positive* (System of positive polity; 1851–4). He died in 1857.

In his lifetime Comte had a significant international impact in the field of philosophy, particularly in epistemology and the history and philosophy of science. Mill's *System of Logic* (1843), for instance, was generous in its acknowledgement of Comte's influence, although Mill tempered his generosity in subsequent editions. The positivist movement, however, did not really take off until after Comte's death, and its impact probably reached its zenith in the last quarter of the century. Many of the founders of the Third Republic in France were influenced by the movement, the most important of them being Jules Ferry, the architect of the educational reforms of the late 1870s and 1880s. He helped create a chair in the History of the Sciences at the Collège de France for the positivist leader Pierre Laffitte. The impact of the positivist movement, however, reached far beyond France. It had an important influence on the creation of republics in eastern Europe (notably Czechoslovakia) and Latin America (notably Mexico and Brazil), and to this day the national flag of Brazil bears the positivist motto '*Orden e Progresso*' (Order and progress). Elsewhere positivism and the Religion of Humanity had fewer committed disciples, but they nevertheless acquired considerable cultural resonance. In Great Britain, for instance, it was an indispensable part of the mental furniture of thinkers such as Herbert Spencer, George Eliot and Beatrice Webb, to name but three.

LAW OF THE THREE STATES

Comte formulated his law of the three states, or three stages – the theological, the metaphysical and the positive – at the outset of his intellectual career, in the "Plan of the Scientific Work Necessary for the Reorganization of Society" written in 1822 and published in its definitive form in 1824. This was the essay that led to his break with his mentor, Saint-Simon, and Comte always regarded it as his 'opus-cule fondamental', chiefly because it was here that he first proposed the law that he deemed his greatest discovery. The law itself had been adumbrated by a series of earlier thinkers, including Turgot and Condorcet, and Saint-Simon himself had articulated a similar idea in his *Memoir on the Science of Man* (1813), well before he met Comte; but Comte made some important innovations, including tying it to his hierarchical classification of the sciences. He would elaborate the law at greater length in his first major work, the *Positive Philosophy*, published in six volumes between 1830 and 1842, and always regarded it as his fundamental discovery. It was the 'law of the intellectual evolution of humanity'. For Comte, all branches of knowledge pass successively from the theological state to the metaphysical state, and thence to the positive state, which is the definitive state of knowledge. He defined these states in terms of the different means they employed to explain the phenomena we observe. The theological and metaphysical states were both char-acterized by the quest for final causes: in the theological state, phenomena were explained by reference to the agency of gods or, in monotheism, of God; while in the metaphysical state, which he considered transitional, these supernatural agencies were replaced by what he called 'personified abstractions' such as 'nature' itself (Comte 1998: 81–2). Thus, for instance, Athena the goddess of wisdom was replaced by the concept of wisdom. The positive state was distinguished by the intellect's renunciation of the misconceived search for causes: instead, it limited itself to the formulation of laws governing the relations of observable phenomena. Comte was clearly indebted here, as he acknowledged, to David Hume (*see* Vol. 3, Ch. 19), who had argued that only a weak concept of causation as constant conjunction could be derived from sense-experience. Hume likewise anticipated Comte in seeing that the critique of the stronger sense of causation – according to which the cause produces the effect – had polemical uses in the sceptical critique of religion (or 'theology', in Comte's terminology). According to Comte, the quest for first causes was the very heart of theology, although he maintained that the concept of religion might intelligibly be detached from that quest.

It was particularly important to Comte to be able to demonstrate that the different sciences must follow this course of progress in a necessary order, according to their degree of abstraction. The sciences dealing with relatively simple phenomena at a high level of abstraction – mathematics, astronomy and physics, for example – would precede the more concrete sciences dealing with more complex phenomena, such as the chemical, the physiological and the social sciences. This had to be the case, since the more concrete sciences would build on the laws established by the more abstract. It followed that the fact that no one had succeeded in formulating positive laws of sociology (a term he coined) did not in the least prove that such laws were inconceivable; instead, it reflected the fact that a positive science of sociology could not emerge until the sciences preceding the social sciences in the hierarchy had themselves been firmly placed on a positive footing. The law therefore had a dual significance: on the one hand, it was the principal finding of the science of sociology, so illustrating the possibility of a positive social science; on the other, it demonstrated the necessity of that science (Comte 1998: xviii–xx).

Comte's investigations in the history and philosophy of science had a political purpose. He formulated his characteristic ideas during the French Restoration (1815–30), and especially in the 1820s, a decade that saw an extraordinary flowering of political and social thought in France. Like Saint-Simon, but also like François Guizot, Félicité de Lamennais and Joseph de Maistre, Comte was centrally preoccupied with the problem of 'closing the revolution'. For him, the negative or destructive work of the French Revolution was to be welcomed, since the feudal order it overturned had been dying for centuries; but it did not move beyond the destructive stage. The Revolution had not succeeded in instituting a new kind of social order to replace the originally feudal order it had extinguished. It had certainly sought to establish a new constitutional order, but for Comte political institutions were superstructural, and could not work in the absence of shared beliefs. Like Maistre and the early Lamennais, then, Comte traced the problem of social and political reconstruction to a more fundamental problem of intellectual reconstruction. The "Western disease", as he diagnosed it, took the form of "complete mental anarchy" and the lack of any moral discipline (*ibid.*: 196). Under the sway of this intellectual individualism, no authority was recognized but that of individual reasoning. This was what he later termed the "intellectual revolt of the individual against the race" (1875–7: vol. 4, 320). But whereas Maistre and the early Lamennais found the solution in ultramontane Catholicism (that is, they saw papal supremacy as the prerequisite for Catholic renewal), Comte was convinced that supernatural religion was being intellectually displaced and hence that Catholicism could not aspire to this role in the reconstruction of Europe. Revolutionary ideas were 'metaphysical', being based on concepts such as natural rights, and the metaphysical mode of thought, as Comte understood it, constituted a merely transitional phase and not a truly distinct stage in the development of the human mind. Hence it could not serve as the basis for reconstruction. A future consensus must rest on positive knowledge, and the scientists must acquire an authority comparable to that exercised by the clergy in medieval Europe.

The nature of Comte's political vision resists easy classification. He insisted that the positivist order should be characterized by the separation of temporal and spiritual powers, which he identified as an essential institutional feature of medieval Europe. At various times he was a trenchant advocate of 'centralization' and of 'dictatorship', but as a rule he preferred regulation by 'moral influences' to over-regulation by law. The latter kind of over-regulation he pejoratively labelled 'pedantocracy'. Positivism, as he defined it, advocated "systematically separating political from moral government": whereas the former rested on "superiority of physical force", the latter relied "exclusively on the forces of conviction and persuasion" (1865: 96–7). The thrust of his work was to portray political institutions as superstructural, and he consistently held that the work of intellectual and moral reconstruction must precede and lay the foundation for any enduring political reform. "Of all the various governments that we have had during the last two generations", he wrote, "all, except the Convention, have fallen into the vain delusion of attempting to found permanent institutions, without waiting for any intellectual or moral basis. And therefore it is that none but the Convention has left any deep traces in men's thoughts or feelings" (*ibid.*: 117).

PRIMITIVE RELIGION

Comte's account of the evolution of human consciousness is rather more complex than the straightforward account of the three states given above, for he also made some influential speculations about the development of the theological state to monotheism, which he took to be its purest form. In the eighteenth century Charles de Brosses (1709–77) had introduced the term 'fetishism' from the Portuguese to designate the most primitive form of human religion, and Comte probably picked up this usage from Benjamin Constant's massive and influential work *De la Religion* (On religion; 1824–31). The term indicated roughly what we today call 'animism'. Comte defined it as "our primitive tendency to conceive of all external bodies, natural or artificial, as animated by a life essentially analogous to our own, with differences of mere intensity" (Comte 1830–42: vol. 5, 30). In other words, its essential characteristic is that inanimate objects are personalized, and natural phenomena are explained as the products of the divine will of these inanimate objects. This primitive stage develops into polytheism, where gods are no longer identified with inanimate objects, but are held to act on them externally. Finally, polytheism gives way to monotheism, and instead of a community of gods we have one god understood as all-powerful or perfect.

Comte followed Constant in criticizing those thinkers who supposed that polytheism or even monotheism constituted the primitive religious state of humanity. His targets here probably included counter-revolutionary thinkers such as Louis de Bonald (1754–1840) who espoused the idea of a 'primitive revelation' of Christian truth. Instead, Comte insisted that religion had its roots in the crudest fetishism and cannibalism. Humanity's collective pride should not revolt at this account of its origins: on the contrary, it should take pride in the progressiveness that has enabled it to escape this wretched original condition (Comte 1830–42: vol. 5, 32). Equally, Comte distinguished his position from those who maintained that prior even to the fetishistic stage, human beings were in their most primitive stage altogether incapable of speculation.

Fetishism had a lasting importance in Comte's conceptualization of religion. As his intellectual career developed, so did his admiration for the fetishistic stage: this was the stage in the development of humanity when religious belief was at its most intense and all-embracing. As the later Comte reasserted the importance of religion, so he rehabilitated fetishism in rather surprising ways. No longer did he depict it simply as a primitive stage in the development of humanity that had long been outgrown. Instead, a resurgent fetishism would play an integral role in the positivist system: "fetishism ... alone of the series of educational states ... is destined to incorporation with Positivism" (1875–7: vol. 4, 14). This was because Comte came to believe that the objective or scientific dimension of positivism was insufficient to make it an adequate agent of social reconstruction: it required also a 'subjective' dimension that would enable it to satisfy the emotions as well as reason, thus closing the division between the intellect and the heart, which Comte identified as the root cause of the spiritual crisis of his time. Fetishism possessed an "unequalled spontaneity" (*ibid.*). This allowed it to appeal much more effectively to the emotions than did monotheism, which he considered the most arid form of theology: monotheism tended to separate God from his creation, whereas fetishism recognized no such distinction. The aspects of Catholic practice Comte most admired – the cult of the saints, for example, and in particular the cult of the Virgin Mary – were those that came closest to polytheism, if not to fetishism. In short, he envisaged the rejuvenation of emotional life under positivism by means of a return to aspects of fetishism.

THE RELIGION OF HUMANITY

Some of Comte's critics, among whom the most important were Mill and Emile Littré, argued that his work fell into two distinct phases demarcated by a volte-face on the question of religion (Littré 1863; Mill 1993). In his early work, up to and including the *Cours de philosophie positive*, his work centred on epistemology and on the history and philosophy of science, and his fundamental proposition was that the theological mode of thought was an anachronism in the contemporary world. But in his later work, and chiefly the *Système de politique positive*, he urged that emotion must hold sway over reason, and set out to propound the case for a secular 'religion of humanity'. Humanity, "the true Great Being", would supplant a supernatural deity as the object of worship. Comte prescribed in detail an ecclesiastical hierarchy, a set of nine sacraments, a liturgy and a litany of saints for his new religion, and offered himself for the role of pontiff, or "high priest of humanity". T. H. Huxley famously quipped that Comte's ideal was "Catholic organization without Catholic doctrine, or, in other words, Catholicism minus Christianity" (Pickering 1993: 17). Certainly positivism entailed a reappraisal of the institutional aspects of Christianity, and Comte himself described his efforts to give "systematic expression … to the wisdom of Theocracy and of Catholicism by the aid of all the knowledge acquired by man" (Comte 1875–7: vol. 4, 461). But he had in mind not so much a dogmatic as a moral discipline; and Mill, who recognized in Comte "a morality-intoxicated man", was perhaps more incisive than Huxley in seeing Comte as a Calvinist *malgré lui* (Mill 1993: 139–40, 144–5).

There was indeed an important shift in Comte's thinking between the 1830s and the 1850s, but it would be quite wrong to represent the Religion of Humanity as a sharp deviation from the body of positive philosophy that he expounded in his early work. Already in these early works Comte implicitly distinguished between theology and religion: the former was destined to pass away with the progress of humanity, but the latter was a permanent and irreplaceable social phenomenon. The essential object of any religion, he wrote, is "to conceive the universal order which dominates human existence in order to determine our general relation towards it" (1909: 51). He inferred that religion in the modern age must be a positive religion, founded on scientific knowledge of the order of the world. It would be a *demonstrated* rather than a *revealed* religion. But it would still rest on faith: this "fundamental virtue" he defined as "the disposition to believe spontaneously, without prior proof, in the dogmas proclaimed by competent authority" (1998: 217). This disposition he declared to be "the indispensable general condition allowing the establishment and the maintenance of true intellectual and moral communion" (*ibid.*: 217–18). In his essays of the 1820s we also find him insisting on the importance of the distinction between spiritual and temporal powers. The Religion of Humanity simply put flesh on the skeletal concept of the spiritual power that he outlined in 1825–6. He had, after all, diagnosed the political crisis of the era of the Restoration as, at root, a condition of 'spiritual anarchy'. "Positivism", writes Henri Gouhier, "is the religious answer to a religious problem that was posed by the [French] Revolution" (quoted in Voegelin 1975: 170).

It is also important to recognize that the Religion of Humanity, far from being a mere product of Comte's idiosyncrasy, was in fact a wholly characteristic manifestation of the religious sensibility and intellectual outlook of the nineteenth century. The term itself was not coined by Comte, but by Thomas Paine as far back as 1778 (in *The Crisis*, no. VII). The French Revolutionaries had recognized the role of civic festivals as social sacraments in the context of their assault on the Church, and had experimented with a variety of deistic or secular cults, from Jacques Hébert's 'Cult of Reason', through Maximilien Robespierre's 'Cult of the Supreme Being', to the rational religion of Theophilanthropy projected by the Idéologues under the Directory. They instituted a new revolutionary calendar to supplant the Christian calendar, and they generated a profusion of revolutionary catechisms. They also created a cult of great men, celebrated on the 'altar of liberty' in the Pantheon, the secularized church of Sainte-Geneviève in Paris. The quest for a rational religion owed much to Enlightenment deism, but was given a new twist by the Romantic movement in the aftermath of the Revolution. Under its influence the early socialism of the 1820s and 1830s was infused with ideas of religious as well as social regeneration. Saint-Simon – if not a socialist himself, at least one of the movement's most important and most immediate precursors – ended his career by calling for the creation of a 'new Christianity', which did not dispense with God altogether, but in practice reduced Christianity to an ethic of fraternal love. Christians were enjoined to seek "as quickly and completely as possible the moral and physical welfare of the most numerous class", for "in that and that alone consists the divine part of the Christian religion" (quoted in Kennedy 1994: 76). "Socialism", it has been well said, "began as an attempt to discover a successor, not to capitalism, but to the Christian Church" (Fourier 1996: xxvi).

From one point of view, the worship of humanity was a secular counterpart of the incarnational tendency that took hold of Christian theology in the middle of the nineteenth century: an 'enthusiasm of humanity', to use a popular phrase of the time, took hold of Christian as well as secular thinkers. Mill, despite rejecting the authoritarian stamp that Comte imparted to the Religion of Humanity, wholeheartedly embraced the idea that the altruistic virtues had to be nurtured by quasi-religious means. He defined religion as "the strong and earnest direction of the emotions and desires towards an ideal object, recognised as of the highest excellence, and as rightfully paramount over all selfish objects of desire". The need for such a religion could be met, he thought, by a 'Religion of Humanity', which would inculcate "the sense of unity of mankind, and a deep feeling for the general good" (Mill 1969b: 422). Like Mill, Eliot, Webb and a host of other progressive intellectuals, Comte – who coined the term 'altruism' (Comte 1875–7: vol 1, 500) – believed that the ideals of duty and of service to others were strengthened, not weakened, by their detachment from their theistic moorings. These ideals became less vulnerable to intellectual refutation, and they gained in ethical purity by being separated from their association with the fear of eternal damnation. The 'religion of humanity', in Christopher Kent's words, came to serve as "a 'scientific' surrogate for those torn by honest doubt from the old moorings of faith" (1978: 62). In Great Britain in the 1870s and 1880s the assertion of the possibility of a morally credible non-theistic religion was a major focus for periodicals such as the *Fortnightly Review*, the *Nineteenth-Century* and the *Contemporary Review*, and for groups such as the Metaphysical Society, which brought together most of the leading public intellectuals of the age. Indeed, in October 1888 Arthur Balfour, the future prime minister, took time off from his commitments as Chief Secretary for Ireland to address the Church Congress on precisely the topic of the religion of humanity. He gave 'religion of humanity' a broader definition than did Comtism, understanding the term to embrace "attempts to find in the 'worship of humanity', or, as some more soberly phrase it, in the 'service of man', a form of religion unpolluted by any element of the supernatural" (Balfour 1888: 2).

The 'humanitarian' enterprise has had many critics. The most important of them was Friedrich Nietzsche, who thought it typically British. He made a caustic remark on the project, in connection with George Eliot. "They have got rid of the Christian God, and now feel obliged to cling all the more firmly to Christian morality ... With us it is different. When one gives up Christian belief one thereby deprives oneself of the *right* to Christian morality" (Nietzsche 1990: 80). Comte and Nietzsche, indeed, stood at opposite ends of the spectrum of possible responses to the moral implications of the death of God. For Comte, an ethic founded on selflessness and love could be salvaged from the wreck, and indeed revitalized; whereas for Nietzsche this post-Christian humanitarianism or 'cult of philanthropy' represented a failure of intellectual integrity. Comte, he thought, was "that *cunningest* of Jesuits" who had "outchristianed Christianity" (1990: 80; 1982: 83).

FURTHER READING

Baker, K. 1989. "Closing the French Revolution: Saint-Simon and Comte". In *The French Revolution and the Creation of Modern Political Culture, Volume 3: The Transformation of Political Culture 1789–1848*, F. Furet & M. Ozouf (eds), 323–39. Oxford: Pergamon.

Comte, A. 1998. *Early Political Writings*, H. Jones (ed. & trans.). Cambridge: Cambridge University Press.

Lenzer, G. 1998. *Auguste Comte and Positivism: The Essential Writings*, 2nd edn. New Brunswick, NJ: Transaction.

Mill, J. [1865] 1993. *Auguste Comte and Positivism*. Bristol: Thoemmes.

Pickering, M. 1993. *Auguste Comte: An Intellectual Biography*, vol. 1. Cambridge: Cambridge University Press.

Reardon, B. 1985. *Religion in the Age of Romanticism*. Cambridge: Cambridge University Press.

Simon, W. 1963. *European Positivism in the Nineteenth Century: An Essay in Intellectual History*. Ithaca, NY: Cornell University Press.

Wernick, A. 2001. *Auguste Comte and the Religion of Humanity*. Cambridge: Cambridge University Press.

On FETISHISM see also Ch. 20. On PRIMITIVE RELIGION see also Ch. 21. On RELIGION OF HUMANITY see also Ch. 11. On SCIENCE see also Chs 11, 12, 15, 17, 19; Vol. 2, Ch. 12; Vol. 3, Ch. 17; Vol. 5, Chs 4, 19.

8

JOHN HENRY NEWMAN

Ian Ker

Although Newman (1801–90) was prolific as a theologian, the philosophical justification of religious belief was always the subject that most keenly concerned him throughout his life. However, it is only in recent years that his importance as a philosopher has been acknowledged. His own philosophical background was the empiricism of John Locke and David Hume (*see* Vol. 3, Chs 12, 19), but his preoccupation with religious belief meant that his philosophical thought was of no interest to the British empiricist tradition. On the other hand, his empiricism set him apart from British and continental idealists who were open to religious themes. It is important to note that Newman was not an empiricist in the sense of holding a sense-data theory or in denying the possibility of synthetic *a priori* truths, but only in the general sense of having an empirical and open, undogmatic approach to knowledge and truth, particularly in the very Humean way of emphasizing informal over against strictly formalized logic. Indeed, his criticism of Locke was that he was not empirical enough, complaining that Locke's "view of the human mind" was "theoretical and unreal … because he consults his own ideal of how the mind ought to act, instead of interrogating human nature, as an existing thing, as it is found in the world" (Newman 1985: 109).

Newman first became seriously interested in the justification of religious belief at the age of twenty when his younger brother Charles became sceptical about the truth of Christianity. The long letters he wrote to his brother during the next four years culminated in the argument that unbelief was due to "a fault of the *heart* not of the *intellect*", since a "dislike of the *contents* of Scripture is at the heart of unbelief". Arguments are useless when "there is at the bottom that secret antipathy for the doctrines of Christianity, which is quite out of the reach of argument" (Ker & Gornall 1978: 219). Already Newman sounds quite postmodern: "We survey moral and religious subjects through the glass of previous habits; and scarcely two persons use a glass of the same magnifying power" (*ibid.*: 226).

These early insights were developed in the seminal series of Oxford University sermons preached between 1839 and 1841 on the relation between faith and reason. When he later republished these sermons as a Roman Catholic in 1872, Newman admitted in the preface that they improved in accuracy and precision.

In the first of the sermons, "Faith and Reason, Contrasted as Habits of Mind", he used the term 'faith' in the popular sense of a feeling or sentiment and the term 'reason' to denote proof of a logical or scientific kind. He attacked the popular idea that faith simply followed reason as a 'moral quality' (Newman 1872: 182). On this view, faith is not an intellectual act at all. Instead, Newman drew a parallel with a judge who decides whether a person is guilty or innocent but does not make the person either. Similarly, reason was not the origin of faith, although it verified it. The latter is creative, the former critical, in the sense that the reasons we give for our actions are not the same as the motives we had for so acting. The New Testament certainly understood faith to be "an instrument of Knowledge and action, unknown to the world before … independent of what is commonly understood by Reason" (*ibid.*: 179), "a novel principle of action" (*ibid.*: 177) and not merely "a believing upon evidence, or a sort of conclusion upon a process of reasoning". Although not supported by "direct and definite proof", faith is not irrational not only because it cannot exist without some evidence but also because it is underpinned by "antecedent considerations" (*ibid.*: 187) or "probabilities" (*ibid.*: 191). Religious belief is not unique in this since, Newman claims, for all beliefs depend less on evidence than on "previously-entertained principles, views, and wishes" (*ibid.*: 188). Still anxious to distinguish faith from reason, he decides that faith is best defined as a "moral principle" in the sense that it is "created in the mind, not so much by facts, as by probabilities", which vary according to one's "moral temperament" (*ibid.*: 191), so that a "good man and a bad man will think very different things probable". A person, then, is responsible for their faith or lack thereof because they are responsible for those moral dispositions on which it depends. The gap between faith and the arguments or evidence for Christianity that fall short of proof is bridged by the antecedent probabilities, which themselves rest on moral presuppositions that make it likely that the object of belief is true. Although there must be rational arguments, still they need not "be the subject of analysis, or take a methodical form, or be complete and symmetrical, in the believing mind". And they take their "life" or "meaning" from probability, which by itself proves nothing (*ibid.*: 199–200).

In the next sermon, which is the key sermon, "The Nature of Faith in Relation to Reason", preached only a week later in 1839, Newman completely changed his strategy. Refusing now to accept the limited sense in which empiricists like Locke use the word 'reason', he crucially widens the terms of the debate by defining faith as "the reasoning of a religious mind, or of what Scripture calls a right or renewed heart, which acts upon presumptions rather than evidence; which speculates and ventures on the future when it cannot make sure of it" (*ibid.*: 203). If faith is regarded merely as "bad" reason, this is precisely "because it rests on presumption more, and on evidence less" (*ibid.*: 204). There is no doubt that an act of faith is "an exercise of Reason", in so far as it is "an acceptance of things as real, which the senses do not convey, upon certain previous grounds" (*ibid.*: 207). As such, it "is not the only exercise of Reason, which, when critically examined, would be called unreasonable, and yet is not so" (*ibid.*: 209). Reasoning is not exclusively syllogistic, and the fact that people may argue badly does not prove that they reason badly for they may not be clear about their real as opposed to their professed reasons. But even when they are clear, these reasons are not enough without the necessary antecedent probabilities to give them cogency. However, these probabilities are themselves assumed or taken for granted and not proved, for "there must ever be something assumed ultimately which is incapable of proof" (*ibid.*: 213). Whatever empiricists may say about the lack of proof in questions of religion is just as true where other beliefs are concerned that we do not doubt but cannot prove in a logical or scientific way. In all these cases, "we must assume something to prove anything", and in the case of more important beliefs the more complex and subtle is "the evidence on which it is received" (*ibid.*: 215). And so, Newman concludes, just as reason takes us beyond sense, so faith takes us beyond reason strictly understood as "a higher instrument" (*ibid.*: 216).

The next sermon preached later in 1839, "Love the Safeguard of Faith against Superstition", adds little to Newman's theory of faith. It explains that the antecedent probabilities on which faith depends are "grounds which do not reach so far as to touch precisely the desired conclusion, though they tend towards it, and may come very near it" (*ibid.*: 224). They not only affect the way we approach the evidence for religious belief, but also colour the evidence. Newman points out that all that is true of belief is also true of unbelief, which is formed in exactly the same way. The unbeliever cannot prove their unbelief, which also rests on antecedent probabilities, albeit of an opposite kind. Each is an "intellectual act", but faith is an act done on the right presuppositions arising out of the right moral disposition (*ibid.*: 239).

In 1840 Newman preached the second most important of these sermons on faith and reason, entitled "Implicit and Explicit Reason". He argues on the one hand that faith "cannot exist without grounds", that it must be susceptible to philosophical justification; but on the other hand that "it does not follow that all who have faith should recognize, and should be able to state what they believe, and why" (*ibid.*: 254). There must be rational grounds but these may not be understood or be producible by the believer. The difference, then, between implicit and explicit reasoning is the difference between the act of reasoning and the reflection on and analysis of the act. Reasoning, says Newman, is "not by rule, but by an inward faculty", it is "a living spontaneous energy within us", which the mind may subsequently "analyze" in its "various processes" (*ibid.*: 257). No one can help reasoning, but not all "reflect upon their own reasonings, much less reflect truly and accurately, so as to do justice to their own meaning" (*ibid.*: 258–9). In other words, everyone has a reason, but not everyone can give a reason. So while faith is an act of reasoning – although a particular kind of reasoning since there are different kinds of reasoning appropriate to different subjects – it is not "necessarily an investigation, argument, or proof; these processes being but the explicit form which the reasoning takes in the case of particular minds" (*ibid.*: 262). Even so, no "analysis is subtle and delicate enough to represent adequately the state of mind under which we believe, or the subjects of belief, as they are presented to our thoughts" (*ibid.*: 267). Moreover, apologists for Christianity are likely to produce as reasons for belief the kind of reasons that "best admit of being exhibited in argument" rather than the "more recondite feelings" that are generally "the real reasons" for belief; for it is these latter reasons that are not easily open to analysis and demonstration (*ibid.*: 271). And even the usual kind of apologetic arguments are only persuasive given "a number of very minute circumstances together, which the mind is quite unable to count up and methodize in an argumentative form" (*ibid.*: 274). Newman concludes on a note of caution: the "argumentative forms" that analyse or test reasoning are "critical, not creative", with the consequence that they are "useful in raising objections, and in ministering to scepticism" (*ibid.*: 276). After all, there is always the danger of "weakening the springs of action by inquiring into them".

These sermons, particularly the two most important ones, constituted Newman's most significant and substantial contribution to the philosophy of religion prior to the publication of *An Essay in Aid of a Grammar of Assent* (hereafter *Grammar*). Their originality lies, first of all, in their refusal to accept the received understanding of reason. Since the seventeenth century, philosophers had generally restricted reasoning either to Cartesian rationalism or to Lockean empiricism: knowledge was either deduced from logical *a priori* truths or derived *a posteriori* from sense-perception by induction. Newman sought to enlarge the concept of reason to allow, in an entirely empirical way, for the way in which we in fact reason not only in religious matters but in all areas apart from logic and science. We do not distrust our reason whenever we are not stating logical or demonstrative truths; nor is there any need to, whether in the area of religion or in any other. Indeed, we use informal reasoning in all matters that most concern us personally and not only in questions of religion. The great merit of the Oxford University sermons was to show that what philosophers regarded as 'irrational' was not therefore necessarily 'unreasonable'. Newman's achievement was to enlarge our concept of reasoning by arguing empirically against the Lockean concept of rationality.

With the rise of science, moreover, in the nineteenth century, scientific criteria of verification came to dominate epistemology, with the result that religious propositions were assumed to be factually meaningless. Philosophers of religion, from Immanuel Kant (*see* Vol. 3, Ch. 21) and Friedrich Schleiermacher to Søren Kierkegaard and then Rudolf Bultmann, generally fell back on an alternative account of the meaning of religious beliefs that would put them outside any application of scientific criteria. This account abandoned the view of theological propositions as saying something that could be factually true. The new interpretation held that factual propositions belonged exclusively to science, while religious propositions were concerned with emotion, imagination and existential choice. But Newman was convinced that Christianity was objectively, not merely subjectively, true, and in the Oxford University sermons he began to develop a richer and more complex concept of rationality that rejected dogmatic empiricism and consequently the exclusive claims assumed for scientific criteria of verification.

Newman himself thought that his theory of antecedent probability was his most original idea. Bishop Joseph Butler had emphasized probability in *The Analogy of Religion* (1736), which had greatly influenced Newman. But the problem with Butler's approach, which Newman later found in an amended version in John Keble's writings, was that it tended to undermine the whole idea of certainty. As he explained in his *Apologia pro vita sua* (1864), Newman tried to "complete" the theory by arguing that "absolute certitude ... was the result of an *assemblage* of concurring and converging probabilities", and that "probabilities that did not reach to logical certainty, might suffice for a mental certitude; that the certitude thus brought about might equal in measure and strength the certitude which was created by the strictest scientific demonstration" (Svaglic 1967: 31). As well as considering the conditions for certainty, Newman began to turn his thoughts to the nature of certainty itself. His analysis of the kind of reasoning involved in religious belief had provided an intellectual justification of belief as rational; but there was still the question of how far it is possible to achieve what may justifiably be called 'certainty' in this kind of reasoning, and in what way such certainty differs from logical and scientific certainty. This was the central problem that was to shape Newman's philosophical thought during the next three decades after the sermons on faith and reason. His conversion to Roman Catholicism in 1845 and his subsequent contacts with its scholastic theologians made him even more sensitive to the necessity of a rational faith. Apart from the odd remarks in his published works and in private letters, his progress can be followed in his philosophical notebook and in exploratory papers.

In 1870, just before the publication of the *Grammar*, he mentioned in a letter that he had been trying to write this book for the last thirty or forty years, ever since his first sermon on faith and reason in 1839. The breakthrough eventually came while he was on holiday in Switzerland in 1866, when he realized that he had been wrong in concentrating on certainty as opposed to the more basic act of assenting. The *Grammar* was in a very real sense the work of a lifetime.

The first part is concerned with the relation between assent and apprehension. It begins with the fundamental distinction between assent, which is unconditional, and inference, which is conditional. Apprehension of the terms of a proposition is needed for assent, but not for inference. Apprehension is something less than understanding, since it is "simply an intelligent acceptance of the idea, or of the fact which a proposition enunciates" (Newman 1985: 20). "Notional" propositions involving "common nouns ... standing for what is abstract, general, and non-existing" require notional apprehension; whereas "real" propositions, "which are composed of singular nouns, and of which the terms stand for things external to us, unit and individual", require real apprehension. Newman makes the important reservation that a proposition may have "a notional sense, as used by one man, and a real as used by another"; words that are "a mere common-place", an "expression of abstractions" to one person, may bring "a lively image" before the imagination of another person. Real apprehension, then, is "stronger" in the sense of being "more vivid and forcible", since "intellectual ideas cannot compete in effectiveness with the experience of concrete facts" (*ibid.*: 13–14). To avoid misunderstanding it is essential to realize that by "intellectual ideas" Newman means ideas that are abstract and general, as opposed to an idea of which we have personal experience and which therefore creates a "living image" of which we have a real apprehension and to which we can give a real assent. The 'things' or 'facts', then, of which we have 'images' are not necessarily experienced through the senses; intellectual ideas can grip the imagination as much as anything experienced through the senses.

A dogmatic religious proposition, therefore, can be assented to either notionally or really, the former being an assent merely of the intellect, the latter being also an assent of the imagination. As an example, Newman gives his well-known argument from conscience for the existence of God. Just as our knowledge of the external world is derived through and in the sense-phenomena we experience,

> so from the perceptive power which identifies the intimations of conscience with the reverberations or echoes … of an external admonition, we proceed on to the notion of a Supreme Ruler and Judge, and then again we image Him and His attributes in those recurring intimations, out of which, as mental phenomena, our recognition of His existence was originally gained. (*Ibid.*: 72)

Conscience itself has two aspects: "it is a moral sense, and a sense of duty; a judgment of the reason and a magisterial dictate"; it "has both a critical and judicial office". It is in the latter aspect of a "sanction" rather than "rule" of right conduct that conscience is primary, for it is as "a voice, or the echo of a voice, imperative and constraining" that conscience is unique in our experience (*ibid.*: 72–5). Newman admits that recognizing God "in the dictate of conscience" and "imaging the thought of Him in the definite impressions which conscience creates" would probably be impossible without some "extrinsic help" (*ibid.*: 76, 79). Our image of God is clarified through revelation and deepened through devotion. It is possible to assent to a personal God either as a theological truth or as a religious reality. But a dogmatic creed, far from being alien to a living, personal faith, is necessary because there is a need for facts to be expressed in language and for the exposition of "the truths on which the religious imagination has to rest" (*ibid.*: 82–3); likewise, because "knowledge must ever precede the exercise of the affections", religion cannot do without theology. Thus our apprehension of, and assent to, the Trinity as a complex whole or mystery is notional, because "though we can image the separate propositions, we cannot image them altogether" (*ibid.*: 88).

The second part of the *Grammar* is almost a different book, although it presupposes the theory of assent developed in the first half. Newman now turns to his central concern: how is one justified in believing what one cannot prove? He begins by returning to his initial distinction between assent and inference. The problem is whether, given that non-logical reasoning never rises above probability (as opposed to logical certainty), the assent then varies in degree according to the strength of the probability as in inference. In formal logical propositions the unconditional assent merely follows the logically necessary conclusions. But there are "many truths in concrete matter, which no one can demonstrate, yet every one unconditionally accepts" (*ibid.*: 106). Far from being merely the conclusion without the premises to an inference, assent does not depend on the inference any more than the strongest inference *necessarily* elicits assent. In the case of logical truths, inference immediately leads to assent, because "the correlative of ascertained truth is unreserved assent" (*ibid.*: 112) – although the assent is still distinct from the inference. A mathematician, for example, may not assent to the conclusion of their own proof until they have the support of another mathematician. However, just as there are no degrees of truth, so there are no degrees of assent. Suspicion and conjecture, for instance, are unconditional assent to the probability of a proposition. A 'half-assent' is not an assent at all, but only an inclination to assent. The argument that assent to non-logical truths must be conditional arises from a confusion between the act of assenting to a conclusion and the relation between the conclusion and its premises, for assent is related to a conclusion as sensation of cold or heat is related to the reading of a thermometer. There are apparent exceptions: assent on the authority of others is often not a true assent at all; "a *prima facie* assent is an assent to an antecedent probability of a fact, not to the fact itself"; a 'conditional' assent means an assent only under certain conditions; a deliberate or slow assent refers to the circumstance of the assenting; an uncertain assent is an assent that may be given up because it is not habitual; a strong assent refers to the emotional concomitants of the assent; a luminous assent is an assent where the arguments in its favour are numerous and strong (*ibid.*: 120).

Newman next differentiates "simple" assent, which is unconscious, from "complex" or "reflex" assent, which is conscious and deliberate (*ibid.*: 124). It is not investigation as such but enquiry that is incompatible with assent. It is true that an investigation may lead to a loss of assent, but the sense of the possibility of this loss is not the same as doubt; nor does assent imply an intention never to change one's mind, but instead the absence of any idea of ever changing. Assent to an assent is "certitude", the proposition is a "certainty" and the assenting is "knowing" (*ibid.*: 128). False certitudes are less common than is supposed. Certitude implies the confidence that even if certitude were to fail the certainty would remain, a requirement that disqualifies many so-called certitudes. There are various emotional signs that indicate a lack of real certitude, whereas a feeling of intellectual security signifies real certitude.

We have now reached the heart of the *Grammar*: the justification of religious certitude. Newman begins with the assent of faith, which, while unquestioning, is absolutely firm. Some assents of this kind may be lost in the process of trying to turn them into certitudes. The reflex assent of certitude is always notional because it is an assent to the truth of the simple assent. Just as the freshness and vigour of the original assent may be lost in the gaining of certitude, so too the reasoning prior to certitude may disturb the normal thought processes, encouraging doubt and reducing imaginative realities to notions. Certitude may not always be characterized by calm serenity because of some unexpected surprise or temptation to doubt. The "human mind is made for truth" (*ibid.*: 145), and so certitude includes the idea of indefectibility: the failure of certitude is the exception. But the truth is that there is no test for distinguishing true from false certitudes. If certitude is unfounded, then it is the prior reasoning, not the actual assent, that is at fault, since to have refused assent in the face of a conclusion would have been unnatural. The intellect is not infallible, but it is capable of being certain. For example, one must be entitled to be certain that after all one has made a mistake in being certain about something. False certitudes are faults, not because they are certitudes, but because they are false: "The sense of certitude may be called the bell of the intellect; and that it strikes when it should not is a proof that the clock is out of order, no proof that the bell will be untrustworthy and useless, when it comes to us adjusted and regulated" (*ibid.*: 152). Not all so-called certitudes, however, are true certitudes, which should only follow after examination and investigation, as well as being restricted to certain occasions and subject matter. Opinion is far more attainable than certitude, but even probability presupposes the certainty of first principles. An acceptance of a religious faith involves different kinds of assents, but a change of religion may merely mean the realization and development of one or more basic and continuing certitudes. But it is generally true that indefectibility is a negative test of certitude: to lose one's conviction is to show that one never had certitude, because certitude is impregnable against all shocks.

The discussion then turns to the question of how in fact certitude is normally attained. Newman begins by contrasting informal reasoning with formal inference, of which the most logical form is the syllogism. The perfection of strictly logical reasoning lies in the fact that words that denote things and that have innumerable implications are stripped of their concrete meanings precisely in order to be abstract and notional. But the abstract cannot reach the concrete. Logical inference cannot produce proof in concrete matters because its premises are assumed and ultimately depend on first principles, wherein lies the real problem of attaining to truth. For logic cannot prove the first principles that it assumes. Abstract arguments reach probability but not certainty in concrete matters, because they do not touch the particular. The language of logic has its obvious advantages in the pursuit of knowledge, but human thought is too personal and complex to "admit of the trammels of any language" (*ibid.*: 185).

We have now reached the heart of the book. It is, in fact, Newman argues, the cumulation of probabilities, which cannot be reduced to a syllogism, that leads to certitude in concrete matters. Many certitudes depend on informal proofs, whose reasoning is more or less implicit. As we view the objects of sense, so we grasp the proof of a concrete truth as a whole "by a sort of instinctive perception of the legitimate conclusion in and through the premises" (*ibid.*: 196). Such implicit reasoning is too personal for logic. The rays of truth stream through the medium of our moral as well as our intellectual being. As we gain a perspective of a landscape, so we personally grasp a truth with a "real ratiocination and present imagination", which reaches beyond the "methodical process of inference". Such "supra-logical judgment" is an "individual perception" under the influence of "an intellectual conscientiousness" (*ibid.*: 205–6). In religion, the "moral state" of the enquirer is also very important. But otherwise, in all subjects "the principle of concrete reasoning is parallel to the method of proof which is the foundation of modern mathematical science", in which the conclusion:

> is foreseen and predicted rather than actually attained; foreseen in the number and direction of accumulated premises, which all converge to it … yet do not touch it logically … on account of the nature of its subject-matter, and the delicate and implicit character of at least part of the reasonings on which it depends. (*Ibid.*: 207–8)

And so the mind in concrete matters progresses from probable antecedents to sufficient proof, and finally to certitude.

'Natural' inference, or the implicit, unconscious and instinctive movement from antecedent to consequent, proceeds not from propositions to propositions, but from concrete things to concrete things, without conscious recognition of the antecedent or the process of inference. This is, in fact, our natural way of reasoning, employed by both the peasant and the genius; it is an instinctive perception, although not a natural instinct, which is the one and the same in all. It may be damaged by learning rules or resorting to artificial aids. Like our taste, our reasoning is spontaneous and unselfconscious. It varies according to the subject matter and has many different forms. "Judgment then in all concrete matters is the architectonic faculty; and what may be called the illative sense, or right judgment in ratiocination, is one branch of it" (*ibid.*: 221).

Newman insists that his purpose is not metaphysical, like that of the idealists who defend the certainty of knowledge against sceptical empiricists, but is "of a practical character, such as that of Butler in his *Analogy*", namely, to ascertain the nature of inference and assent. Certitude he has shown to be "an active recognition of propositions as true" in response to a proof. And "the sole and final judgment on the validity of an inference in concrete matter is committed to the personal action of the ratiocinative faculty, the perfection or virtue of which I have called the Illative Sense, a use of the word 'sense' parallel to our use of it in 'good sense'" (*ibid.*: 222–3).

We have to accept our nature as it is, for it is "a fact not admitting of question, all things being of necessity referred to it, not it to other things"; "I cannot think … about my being, without starting from the very point which I aim at concluding" (*ibid.*: 224). Certainly, "there is no ultimate test of truth besides the testimony born to truth by the mind itself" (*ibid.*: 226). Thought is always thought, but it varies according to the subject matter, and there is no "ultimate test of truth and error" apart from the illative sense (*ibid.*: 231). The mind outstrips language, contemplating first principles without words or any process of analysis, with the illative sense determining the beginning, the middle and the end of any investigation.

Like the first part of the *Grammar*, the second part ends with an attempt to apply its conclusions to religious faith. Christianity may be held – as it was by contemporary Roman Catholic theologians – to be "demonstrably true", but it is not "true irresistibly", because truth, like light, cannot be seen by the blind. Where assumptions are needed, Newman prefers to "attempt to prove Christianity in the same informal way in which I can prove for certain that I have been born" (*ibid.*: 264). First principles are all-important, and here "belief in revealed truths depends on belief in natural" (*ibid.*: 266). Acceptance of the arguments for Christianity rests on acceptance of certain general truths. The Christian revelation is "the completion and supplement of Natural Religion, and of previous revelations" (*ibid.*: 250).

Alien both to the scholastic philosophers of his adopted church and to empiricist as well as idealist philosophers, Newman had no influence on subsequent philosophy. However, we can date his emergence (almost a hundred years after the publication of the *Grammar*) as a significant philosophical thinker to the year 1969, when the empiricist philosopher H. H. Price included a positive discussion of Newman in his book *Belief*; while Ludwig Wittgenstein's posthumous *On Certainty* published in the same year begins with an explicit reference to Newman and takes up many of the topics of the *Grammar* and draws some of the same conclusions (*see* Vol. 5, Ch. 13). In fact, there are also resemblances with the early Wittgenstein, although they are not so close.

First, Wittgenstein's "distinction between what can and what cannot be said in ordinary language and Newman's distinction between deductive and cumulative reasoning have much in common" (Barrett 1997: 92). For what can be said, in Wittgenstein's terminology, are statements of fact, whether empirical observations or logical deductions, while what cannot be said are expressions of a religious, ethical or aesthetic nature or the like. In other words, a religious proposition is completely different from a logical proposition. Secondly, Wittgenstein's later understanding of language as a living thing, quite different from the abstractions of logic, is very Newmanian. There are different kinds of what Wittgenstein calls 'language games', and they include the languages of logic, mathematics and science, but they also include other kinds of expression that must be judged on their own terms according to the rules of their own language game and not in accordance with other criteria. Thirdly, according to Wittgenstein, the justification of religious belief lies in the way "in which a number of ways of thinking and acting crystallize and come together" (*ibid.*: 94), which is what Newman meant by the accumulation of probabilities. Like Newman, Wittgenstein appreciated that what seems probable to one person may not seem so to another, and that dispassionate disinterest is not the way to arrive at truth in religion or ethics as it is in logic and science. Fourthly, Newman's first principles correspond to Wittgenstein's 'hinges' or assumptions that reasoning depends on. Fifthly, Wittgenstein agreed with Newman that "there is no independent standard of rationality" (*ibid.*: 97) to which appeal can be made by way of proof.

Newman, then, "identifies problems in epistemology which have only recently been recognized and offers the outline of a solution to them" (Mitchell 1990: 227). But there is another important factor in the rediscovery, or rather discovery, of Newman as a philosopher, and that is a change in our understanding of the nature of science. Newman had refused to accept that logical or scientific criteria should be made the test of religious truth, and this refusal had made him seem irrelevant both to empiricist philosophers and to theologians who had sought to give religious propositions an experiential rather than factual meaning that would not put them in conflict with science. But recent developments in the philosophy of science have, Basil Mitchell has pointed out, "for the first time in the modern era, cast doubt upon the credentials of science itself as an avenue to truth". Modern physics has its own "internal standards of rationality, which are different from, though not demonstrably superior to, those of Newton – or, indeed, of Aristotle". As a result, "the paradigm instance of factual knowledge, by comparison with which the claims of religion were thought to be problematic, can no longer be made to serve this purpose". Of course, the validity of scientific method is in practice taken for granted, even if its validity cannot be demonstrated. The scientist's situation, therefore, "is curiously analogous to that in which Newman found himself as he struggled to analyze the nature of reason and its relation to Christian faith". In the past, it was taken for granted that science was exempt from such problems and that its status as a rational method of achieving truth needed no justification. It is now arguable that Newtonian science has "its own internal standards of meaning and truth which are strictly incommensurable with those of Einsteinian science", and that therefore "no rational choice can be made between them" and "neither can claim to represent, or even approximate to, the truth about things". In that case, science finds itself in the same position as philosophy and other branches of knowledge (*ibid.*: 237–8).

Newman's understanding of the way our first principles and presuppositions determine our attitude to the evidence raises the question: how, if Christian faith is dependent on one's having been formed in the right way to have the right first principles and presuppositions, can Christian faith be called rational, since a Muslim, formed to have different first principles and presuppositions can equally claim truth for their faith? For Newman, as for Alvin Plantinga (*see* Vol. 5, Ch. 2), who rejects classical foundationalism – that is, the doctrine that it is only rational to accept a proposition if the proposition is self-evident or evident to the senses or if supported by other basic propositions – the problem is how to avoid circularity. Both thinkers are very aware of the kind of informal cumulative arguments we use in reasoning and the role of the illative sense or personal judgement in evaluating them, influenced as this is by the individual's own first principles and antecedent assumptions as well as by the particular tradition within which the individual stands. But by the same token, both face the objection, in Mitchell's words:

> that the body of evidence to which appeal is made only gives support to the system in favor of which it is adduced to the extent that it is interpreted in terms of that system, for it is this which supplies the presumptions or antecedent probabilities whose importance is constantly emphasized.
> (1990: 243)

In Mitchell's view, the only answer that Newman and Plantinga can make to this is to insist: "that God created in us certain tendencies or dispositions to believe, which will make themselves felt in our actual beliefs as long as the latter are not diluted or distorted by sin. This is, in effect, a theistic version of Hume's appeal to nature as a remedy for scepticism". However, this is hardly an answer to anyone who sees no reason to believe. True, some antecedent probabilities will be neutral as between systems of belief, and there will also be facts that will not be in dispute. But still there is no alternative rationality to appeal to, no possibility of a neutral standpoint from which to judge between differing systems of belief. Mitchell thinks that only one resolution remains for Newman and Plantinga, namely, that "a rational resolution of disputes between rival traditions does not depend upon the availability of such a neutral standpoint". Instead, it is always possible to re-examine and, if necessary, revise one's first principles or antecedent assumptions in the light of other theories. Given that these primary assumptions are held by the individual within a tradition, to appeal to the tradition to justify them will obviously seem a circular argument. But this is not peculiar to religious convictions. All branches of knowledge require training and the necessary ability to understand the relevant subject matter and make correct judgements. Even in science the discovery and recognition of scientific truths are dependent on the necessary training and ability to discover and recognize them. And in the case of poetry or music or wine, for example, taste and discrimination are required. If one is tone deaf and cannot appreciate music, one is not entitled to dismiss the music-lover's judgement as purely personal and subjective and without validity. Again, in order to make moral judgements one needs moral character, the result of formation and experience. Such judgements can be called rational, even though an amoral or immoral person will not agree with them. In other words, the problem of circularity – if it is a problem – is not one that only affects religion (*ibid.*: 243–4).

FURTHER READING

Barrett, C. 1997. "Newman and Wittgenstein on the Rationality of Religious Belief". In *Newman and Conversion*, I. Ker (ed.), 89–99. Edinburgh: T&T Clark.

Earnest, J. & G. Tracey (eds) 2006. *Fifteen Sermons Preached Before the University of Oxford*. Oxford: Oxford University Press.

Ferreira, J. 1980. *Doubt and Religious Commitment: The Role of the Will in Newman's Thought*. Oxford: Clarendon Press.

Ker, I. 1990. *The Achievement of John Henry*. Notre Dame, IN: University of Notre Dame Press [esp. ch. 2].

Macquarrie, J. 1997. "Newman and Kierkegaard on the Act of Faith". In *Newman and Conversion*, I. Ker (ed.), 75–88. Edinburgh: T&T Clark.

Meynell, H. 1990. "Newman's Vindication of Faith in the *Grammar of Assent*". In *Newman after a Hundred Years*, I. Ker & A. Hill (eds), 247–61. Oxford: Clarendon Press.

Mitchell, B. 1990. "Newman as a Philosopher". In *Newman after a Hundred Years*, I. Ker & A. Hill (eds), 223–46. Oxford: Clarendon Press.

Newman, J. 1985. *An Essay in Aid of a Grammar of Assent*, I. Ker (ed.). Oxford: Clarendon Press.

On EMPIRICISM see also Vol. 1, Ch. 7; Vol. 5, Ch. 17. On FAITH see also Chs 10, 13; Vol. 1, Ch. 13; Vol. 2, Chs 6, 12, 16, 18; Vol. 3, Ch. 8; Vol. 5, Chs 7, 18. On LANGUAGE see also Ch. 3; Vol. 2, Chs 4, 11, 12; Vol. 3, Ch. 14; Vol. 5, Chs 13, 20. On NATURAL RELIGION/THEOLOGY see also Ch. 12; Vol. 3, Chs 4, 6, 7, 11, 12, 13, 19, 23; Vol. 5, Ch. 23. On REASON see also Ch. 4; Vol. 2, Chs 10, 11, 12, 16, 18; Vol. 3, Chs 8, 12, 16, 21. On TRUTH see also Ch. 18; Vol. 1, Ch. 13; Vol. 2, Ch. 17; Vol. 3, Chs 3, 8, 13; Vol. 5, Ch. 4.

9

RALPH WALDO EMERSON

Russell Goodman

Ralph Waldo Emerson's (1803–82) philosophy of religion has roots in the Unitarian culture in which he was raised and his own mystical experiences, but it also draws from his reading in a vast array of philosophical, literary and religious texts. Emerson saw a 'wide world' (the title of his first journal) of religious thought and experience, and he sought both to distil that thought in his writings and to encourage in his audience what he calls 'the one thing in the world, of value': 'the active soul'. That 'soul', whether in the form of the 'intuition' cited in his "Divinity School Address", the 'eternal One' depicted in "The Over-Soul" or the Hindu conception of a supreme soul present in all creatures, lies at the centre of Emerson's philosophy of religion.

According to Emerson, the human experience of the divine is available to all people, but it is memorably and influentially expressed only in the lives and teachings of a few. The experience is ineffable, however, and all language about it is just a set of hints or thin remembrances of the original 'intuition'. The words and lives of Moses, Jesus, Plotinus and George Fox inspire religious traditions, but these traditions characteristically tend to focus, Emerson argues, on the personal, accidental features of their lives, while forgetting the 'impersonal' and universal truths to which they called attention.

The 'soul' at the centre of Emerson's account of religion is a soul within nature, a soul that recognizes its kinship to the natural world of corn and melons, animals and stars. Religion, Emerson holds, is best understood not from the perspective of a church or a book, but from that of the woods or a farm. As he puts it in "Circles", "We can never see christianity [*sic*] from the catechism: – from the pastures, from a boat in the pond, from amidst the songs of wood-birds, we possibly may" (*CW* 2.185).[1]

---

1. *The Collected Works of Ralph Waldo Emerson* (Emerson 1971–) are abbreviated *CW* throughout, and cited by volume and page numbers.

This essay proceeds first with an account of Emerson's development as a religious writer and thinker who incorporates elements of Christianity, nineteenth-century science, romantic poetry and Neoplatonic philosophy in his first book, *Nature* (1836). It then moves to an account of Emerson's mature philosophy that emphasizes his competing interpretations of the soul: as a fundamental 'Unity' or 'ONE' on the one hand, and, on the other hand, as a particular individual, journeying towards (as he puts it in "History") an "unattained but attainable self" (*CW* 2.5).

EARLY LIFE AND CAREER

Emerson was born in Boston in 1803 into a family of Unitarian ministers. He graduated from Harvard College in 1821, taught in his brother William's school for young ladies, attended the Harvard Divinity School in 1825–6 and, after a few years of preaching in Boston punctuated by bouts of ill health, took up a position as junior pastor in the Second Unitarian Church of Boston in 1829.

"The Lord's Supper"

Within two years of taking up his appointment, Emerson lost his nineteen-year-old wife, Ellen Tucker Emerson, to tuberculosis. Soon after, the seemingly conventional and popular minister resigned his position, stating his reasons in a closely reasoned sermon on "The Lord's Supper" (1832) that forecasts his critique of Christianity in the "The Divinity School Address" (1838) and his conception of the "free and brave" interpreter of literature in "The American Scholar" (1837). Emerson argues that "Jesus did not intend to establish an institution for perpetual observance when he ate the Passover with his disciples; and further … that it is not expedient to celebrate it as we do" (Myerson 2000: 69). He writes as a liberal Unitarian, who thinks that it is his duty as a Christian minister to examine the meaning of the Bible rather than to take his interpretations from someone else, and moreover to judge the expediency or usefulness of institutionalized rituals, such as the partaking of bread and wine. Even if Jesus uttered the words, "This do in remembrance of me", Emerson continues in his sermon, these words are mentioned in only one of the four Gospels, and might have been only an expression of "natural feeling" among "friends", not an instruction for a memorial feast to be imposed "upon the whole world" (*ibid.*: 70). Even if it were admitted that the immediate disciples of Jesus kept the ceremony and that the apostle Paul enjoined it, that "does not settle the question for us", Emerson continues. That question is to be settled by what is suited "to this day". The ritual as Emerson sees it practised around him is not, as it should be, an expression of gratitude to God but rather something externally "imposed by authority" (*ibid.*: 74). When a form has lost its "life and suitableness", Emerson continues, it is "as worthless … as the dead leaves that are falling around us" (*ibid.*: 76). Emerson drives home his point in the first

120

person, in a forecast of the radical individualism that characterizes his mature thought. He writes: "This mode of commemorating Christ is not suitable to me. That is reason enough why I should abandon it ... I will love him as a glorified friend after the free way of friendship and not pay him a stiff sign of respect as men do to those whom they fear" (*ibid.*: 75). Emerson thought that the original friendliness of Jesus had become perverted into a doctrine of terror and, as he was to put it in "The Divinity School Address", the words of a friend had been transformed into an "eastern monarchy of a Christianity" (*CW* 1.82). In "The Lord's Supper", Emerson takes a historical and pragmatic view of religious forms and institutions. They are to be justified not by their origins or repetitions, but by their suitability to the present age and the present person. If they no longer serve *him* – as well as others – they are to be abandoned like dead leaves. Emerson asked for but was not given permission to discontinue the administration of the Lord's Supper. He resigned his ministry in 1832 and, with the aid of an inheritance from his wife, sailed for Europe, where he stayed for almost a year.

Emerson's journey to Europe was momentous. There he met William Wordsworth and Samuel Taylor Coleridge, John Stuart Mill and Thomas Carlyle. In Paris, he saw not only the pictures in the Louvre but the rows of biological specimens in the Jardin des Plantes, which made the more profound impression on him. "The Universe is a more amazing puzzle than ever", he wrote of the *Jardin*:

> as you glance along this bewildering series of animated forms, – the hazy butterflies, the carved shells, the birds, beasts, fishes, insects, snakes, ... No form so grotesque, so savage, nor so beautiful but is an expression of some property inherent in man the observer – an occult relation between the very scorpions and man. I feel the centipede in me ... I am moved by strange sympathies, I say continually "I will be a naturalist". (*JMN* 4.200)[2]

After returning to Boston, Emerson sought to develop this vision of a nature with which we have a deep affinity in a series of lyceum lectures in the 1830s and in his first book, *Nature* (1836).

Nature

Emerson's *Nature* is both naturalistic and religious in spirit, but it is not a Christian book. Its epigraph is from a pagan philosopher, Plotinus, and it mentions Jesus only as a "virtuous man" who, like Homer, Pindar and Socrates, lived in harmony with nature (*CW* 1.16). In another move outside a strictly Christian context,

---

2. *The Journals and Miscellaneous Notebooks of Ralph Waldo Emerson* (Emerson 1960–82) are abbreviated *JMN* throughout, and cited by volume and page numbers.

Emerson suggests that all religious and philosophical traditions are engaged in a common quest for a relation to the divine, a quest, he writes, that "has exercised the wonder and the study of every fine genius since the world began; from the era of the Egyptians and the Brahmins, to that of Pythagoras, of Plato, of Leibnitz, of Swedenborg" (*CW* 1.22). Neoplatonism and Hinduism proved to be especially potent sources for Emerson's later philosophy.

In *Nature*, Emerson draws on different religious traditions but he also portrays religion as a matter of direct experience, including his own. In the opening chapter of the book, Emerson writes of the "woods" or the "wilderness" as a place of mystical experience:

> In the woods, we return to reason and faith ... Standing on the bare
> ground, – my head bathed by the blithe air, and uplifted into infinite
> space, – all mean egotism vanishes. I become a transparent eye-ball.
> I am nothing. I see all. The currents of the Universal Being circulate
> through me; I am part or particle of God. The name of the nearest
> friend sounds then foreign and accidental.   (*CW* 1.10)

These elevated moments, Emerson holds, show us possibilities of this world that are always available but rarely actualized. Borrowing language from the Kantian tradition that he assimilated through Coleridge's *Biographia Literaria*, Emerson writes that our habitual relation to nature is through "the Understanding", but that sometimes we come to nature through "Reason", a superior "instantaneous in-streaming causing power" (*CW* 1.43).

Emerson mixes religious, perceptual and naturalistic themes with an implicit emphasis on what he would come to call 'self-reliance'. For the solution to the disparate perspectives of Reason and Understanding lies just where the foundation of religion lies, in the individual soul:

> The problem of restoring to the world original and eternal beauty, is
> solved by the redemption of the soul. The ruin or the blank, that we
> see when we look at nature, is in our own eye ... The reason why the
> world lacks unity, and lies broken and in heaps, is, because man is
> disunited with himself. He cannot be a naturalist, until he satisfies all
> the demands of the spirit ... The invariable mark of wisdom is to see
> the miraculous in the common.   (*CW* 1.43–4)

Two characteristic Emersonian themes appear in this passage: the idea of unity, which the world is said to lack, and which becomes prominent in "Self-Reliance" and "The Over-Soul"; and the idea of the miraculous in the common, a central motif of the Romanticism Emerson found in Coleridge's and Wordsworth's *Lyrical Ballads* (1798). Although Emerson is known as a 'transcendentalist', he follows the English Romantics in seeking a 'natural supernaturalism' (Abrams 1971). In "The

American Scholar", an address given a year after he published *Nature*, Emerson portrays himself as part of a movement to detect "the sublime presence of the highest spiritual cause" not in things distant or foreign like "Italy or Arabia", but in what is close to home: "the meal in the firkin; the milk in the pan; the ballad in the street; the news of the boat; the glance of the eye; the form and the gait of the body" (*CW* 1.67).

"The Divinity School Address"

"The Divinity School Address", given to the graduating class of the Harvard Divinity School in 1838, does not sidestep or contextualize Christianity as *Nature* had done, but takes it on directly. Its defence of religious freedom and rejection of fear as the primary religious emotion owes much to liberal Unitarian Christianity. William Ellery Channing's "Unitarian Christianity" (1819), for example, argued that the orthodox Congregationalist doctrine of predestination tends "to pervert the moral faculty, to form a gloomy, forbidding, and servile religion, and lead men to substitute censoriousness, bitterness and persecution, for a tender and impartial charity" (quoted in Packer 1995: 335). But Emerson applies this critique to Christianity in general: "by this eastern monarchy of a Christianity, which indolence and fear have built, the friend of man is made the injurer of man ... We shrink as soon as the prayers begin, which do not uplift, but smite and offend us" (*CW* 1.82, 85). Emerson rejects a religion of fear and guilt, and, as in "The Lord's Supper", thinks of Jesus as "the friend of man".

In accord with both "The Lord's Supper" and *Nature*, Emerson looks to experience rather than to texts or institutions for religious authority. The Unitarian intelligentsia, led by Channing, saw themselves as modern empiricists in the tradition of John Locke's *A Discourse of Miracles*, which conceived of miracles as violations of natural law (*see* Vol. 3, Ch. 12). These violations of law, they held, testified to a power superior to nature. They hoped that new historical research and the new biblical criticism of Johann Gottfried Herder and Friedrich Schleiermacher would establish that the miracles attributed to Jesus actually took place. Emerson, who read David Hume's critique of miracles (in the *Enquiry Concerning Human Understanding*; *see* Vol. 3, Ch. 19) while an undergraduate at Harvard, rejected such proofs as inadequate, but also beside the point: for he held that religion's source is an experience of the world that is available always, not a divine eruption into the natural order of things. Jesus spoke of miracles, Emerson asserts in "The Divinity School Address", because "he felt that man's life was a miracle" (*CW* 1.81). In contrast, "the word Miracle, as pronounced by Christian churches, gives a false impression; it is Monster. It is not one with the blowing clover and the falling rain" (*ibid.*). The church converts the idea of miracles into something alien and threatening, and loses touch with the miracles of life all around it. The life of Jesus is not to be conceived as "peculiar", Emerson maintains, but as "part of human life, and of the landscape, and of the cheerful day" (*CW* 1.83).

Emerson's basic critique of Christianity and other institutionalized religions is that they operate at a distance from the truth, as intermediaries, when the truth with which they allegedly operate "cannot be received at second hand" (*CW* 1.80). They treat divinity as something that happened long ago, whereas, as Emerson puts it in one of his powerful, punchy phrases, "God is, not was" (*CW* 1.89). The Christians he sees around him make the mistake of speaking "of the revelation as somewhat long ago given and done, as if God were dead" (*CW* 1.84).

Emerson argues that religion originates in "the sentiment of virtue" or "religious sentiment", a response to "certain divine laws". It is "the essence of all religion", not just in Palestine, but in "Egypt, in Persia, in India, in China" (*CW* 1.80). The religious sentiment may be awakened by "the sentences of the oldest time", but only if one can find them "still fresh and fragrant". Without the sentiment in which they are grounded, these words "become false and hurtful" (*ibid.*). Whereas Jesus taught the divinity of humanity, Emerson argues, the Church teaches that only "one or two persons" are divine, and threatens to "kill you, if you say [Jesus] was a man" (*CW* 1.82).

EMERSON'S MATURE PHILOSOPHY

Unity and the over-soul

Emerson finds his mature form and his mature philosophy in his *Essays, First Series* (1841). He inherits the use of the essay from Michel de Montaigne, who is the subject of one of the essays in *Representative Men* (1850), and he uses the form to achieve a blend of the personal and the impersonal, the conclusive and the open-ended, the philosophical and the autobiographical. Emerson's philosophy, like his essays, is dialectical: or, as Emerson sometimes thinks of it, moody. "Life", he writes in "Experience", is a "train of moods, like a string of beads", with each showing "only what lies in its focus" (*CW* 3.30). Even within an essay Emerson moves from one to another view of things. "I am always insincere", he writes, "as always knowing there are other moods" (*CW* 3.145).

It is not that Emerson loses track of his insight that mystical experience – what he calls "the religious sentiment" in "The Divinity School Address" – is central to religion, but that he is unsure what this experience reveals: is it a unitary, stable, eternal "Over-Soul", or a "new yet unapproachable America", something promising and "initial" rather than already achieved? We shall follow Emerson's mature thinking about this question in four essays where religious themes are particularly prominent: "The Over-Soul", "Self-Reliance", "Circles" and "Experience".

"The Over-Soul" reveals Emerson's debt to Neoplatonism, as well as his continuing respect for Christianity. At the beginning of the essay, Emerson's list of those who have experienced "the opening of the religious sense" includes "the trances of Socrates, the 'union' of Plotinus, the vision of Porphyry, the conversion of Paul, the aurora of Behmen, the convulsions of George Fox and his Quakers, the illumination of Swedenborg" (*CW* 2.167). A common thread among them is *religious experience,* to use William James' term.[3] It is not the *doctrines* of Socrates, Plotinus, Porphyry or Fox to which Emerson calls attention, much less any institutions with which they are associated. As in "The Divinity School Address", Emerson finds an experiential core in the religious and philosophical traditions represented by these thinkers. What he had earlier described as "the religious sentiment" or "the sentiment of virtue" is now described as "an influx of the Divine mind into our mind ... an ebb of the individual rivulet before the flowing surges of the sea of life" (*CW* 2.166).

Although the metaphor of "flowing surges" suggests that the "Divine mind" is in motion and has different regions, Emerson stresses its unity, lack of division and absence of succession in the one place in the essay (apart from its title) where the term 'over-soul' appears:[4]

> The Supreme Critic on the errors of the past and the present ... is that great nature in which we rest, as the earth lies in the soft arms of the atmosphere; that Unity; that Over-Soul, within which every man's particular being is contained and made one with all other; ... We live in succession, in division, in parts, in particles. Meantime within man is the soul of the whole; the wise silence; the universal beauty, to which every part and particle is equally related; the eternal ONE. (*CW* 2.160)

The over-soul is metaphysically ultimate, and, although Emerson does not bring this point out, the absorption of the many into the great One conflicts with the separation of God and creation that is a feature of most forms of Christianity.

Emerson acknowledges that the words he employs to characterize the over-soul are simply "hints I have collected" (*CW* 2.160). He is not attached to any one form of expression, so that just in the paragraph where the 'Over-Soul' is named, he also uses the following terms, more or less equivalently: 'Supreme Critic', 'ONE', 'Wisdom', 'Highest Law', 'Unity'. He questions what purpose definitions are to serve in this case:

> An answer in words is delusive; it is really no answer to the questions you ask. Do not require a description of the countries towards

---

3. As in the title of James' *The Varieties of Religious Experience* ([1902] 1985). Cf. Emerson in "The Over-Soul": "the *revival* of the Calvinistic churches; the *experiences* of the Methodists, are varying forms of that shudder of awe and delight with which the individual soul always mingles with the universal soul" (*CW* 2.167, original emphasis).
4. The term 'over-soul' is used twice in a lecture on "Religion" that Emerson first gave in 1840, where several of the passages from "Self-Reliance" and "The Over-Soul" that are discussed in this essay appear (Emerson 1962–72: vol. 3, 271–85). The term is never used again in his published work.

which you sail. The description does not describe them to you, and
to-morrow you arrive there, and know them by inhabiting them …
The moment the doctrine of immortality is separately taught, man is
already fallen … No inspired man ever asks this question, or conde-
scends to these evidences.   (CW 2.168)

This is a mystical position, as understood by James in *The Varieties of Religious
Experience*, where the 'ineffability' of the purported knowledge is one criterion
of a mystical state. ("The subject of it immediately says that it defies expression,
that no adequate report of its contents can be given in words"; James [1902] 1985:
380.) By the logic of Emerson's argument, the Unitarians, in searching for proofs
of miraculous events to support their 'belief' or 'faith' in some doctrine, are 'fallen'
from the start. The question of the nature and existence of God is solved, Emerson
holds, not by a proof but by a realization or 'influx': "The simplest person, who in
his integrity worships God, becomes God … the influx of this better and universal
self is new and unsearchable. When we have broken our god of tradition, and
ceased from our god of rhetoric, then may God fire the heart with his presence"
(CW 2.173).

These sentences exemplify Emerson's continuing focus on the self rather than
some external being to whom we owe allegiance; his moral perfectionism, or
search for a "better and universal self"; and his hostility to the "god of tradition",
which, like an idol, is to be "broken". It might seem that without a sacred text or
a set of rituals, Emerson is not describing 'religion' at all. Indeed, although he
continues to use the terms 'religious' and 'religion', he is quite willing to dispense
with them if they do not connect with religion's living source: the soul who realizes its nature, Emerson writes, in "The Over-Soul", is "glad, young, and nimble. It
is not called religious, but it is innocent" (CW 2.175).

"Self-Reliance" is Emerson's best-known essay. It develops his concern with and
assertion of his own self, seen in "The Lord's Supper" in the claim that because the
ritual is "disagreeable to my own feelings", there is "reason enough why I should
abandon it" (Myerson 2000: 75). In the first paragraph of "Self-Reliance", Emerson
writes: "the highest merit we ascribe to Moses, Plato, and Milton, is that they set
at naught books and traditions, and spoke not what men but what they thought"
(CW 2.27). Emerson's list of heroes represents his view that original and powerful
natures are to be found equally among philosophers, poets and the founders of
the world's religions. In aligning Moses and Milton, Emerson assimilates Herder's
approach in *The Spirit of Hebrew Poetry*, which treats the Bible as a human poetic
text.

According to Emerson, self-trust or 'self-reliance' is essential to any creative
or original act, but it is at the same time trust in or reliance on something greater
than the individual self: "We lie in the lap of immense intelligence, which makes us
receivers of its truth and organs of its activity" (CW 2.37). Towards the middle of
"Self-Reliance", Emerson calls this intelligence "the ever blessed ONE", the "ultimate

fact" or "Supreme Cause" that "we reach ... on every topic" (*CW* 2.40). As in "The Over-Soul", Emerson expresses the mystic's suspicion of all language, even as he ventures his own linguistic portrayals of this "ultimate fact": "The highest truth on this subject remains unsaid; probably cannot be said; for all that we say is the far off remembering of the intuition" (*CW* 2.39).

Emerson's religiously inflected concept of self-reliance furnishes the basis for his critique of prayer, which is often little more than a form of begging. Prayer, Emerson writes, "looks abroad and asks for some foreign addition to come through some foreign virtue" (*CW* 2.44). In contrast, prayer as Emerson understands and recommends it does not look abroad, but stays at home: it is "the contemplation of the facts of life from the highest point of view. It is the soliloquy of a beholding and jubilant soul. It is the spirit of God pronouncing his works good" (*ibid.*).

Emerson increasingly sought accounts of this "soliloquy" in translations of Hindu writings, especially the *Bhagavad Gita*, *The Laws* (or as it was first translated, *The Institutes*) *of Menu* and the *Vishnu Purana*. As co-editor of the transcendentalists' journal *The Dial* in the early 1840s, Emerson published a series of "Ethnical Scriptures", where he reprinted passages from these books, such as the following from *The Laws of Menu*: "The man who perceives in his own soul the supreme soul present in all creatures, acquires equanimity toward them all, and shall be absorbed at last in the highest essence, even that of the Almighty himself" (*JMN* 6.395). It is easy to see why Emerson thought that his idea of a central oversoul, "present in all creatures", had been anticipated in India.

The *Vishnu Purana* was particularly important for Emerson. This collection of legends, ritual, and metaphysics from the seventh century CE was translated into English by H. H. Wilson in 1840 in an edition that included extensive notes on Indian philosophy. Emerson copied pages of quotations from this work into his journal, some of which make their way into *Representative Men* (1850), which contains chapters on Plato, Montaigne, Swedenborg, Shakespeare, Goethe and Napoleon. In "Plato; or the Philosopher", for example, Emerson writes of the "terrific unity" towards which speculation tends, and illustrates the point with a passage from the *Vishnu Purana*:

> The whole world is but a manifestation of Vishnu, who is identical with all things, and is to be regarded by the wise as not differing from, but as the same as, themselves. I neither am going nor coming, nor is my dwelling in any one place, nor art thou, nor are others, others; nor am I, I. (*CW* 4.29)

Emerson's Plato is as much an Asian as a European, an idea Emerson introduces biographically:

> Plato absorbed the learning of his times ... then his master Socrates; and, finding himself still capable of a larger synthesis ... he traveled

into Italy, to gain what Pythagoras had for him; then into Egypt, and perhaps still farther East, to import the other element which Europe wanted, into the European mind.   (CW 4.25)

The "other element that Europe wanted", Emerson holds, is "unity", which Plato is said to have "imbibed … in Egypt and in Eastern pilgrimages" and then to have incorporated in his philosophy (CW 4.30–31).

    Emerson does not deny that unity is a great theme in the West, for as he rightly says and as his own case illustrates, "in all nations there are minds which incline to dwell in the conception of the fundamental Unity". But he adds that this tendency towards unity "finds its highest expression in the religious writings of the East, and chiefly in the Indian scriptures, In the Vedas, the Bhagavat Geeta, and the Vishnu Purana" (CW 4.28). As there is to this day no evidence that Plato either visited India or knew any Indian texts (see Halbfass 1988), it is more appropriate to take Emerson's Plato to be a representative of Emerson himself.

Particularity and process

Emerson's Plato balances "the unity of Asia" with "the detail of Europe" (CW 4.31), and Emerson's own philosophy works towards such a balance. His conception of religion in particular is strongly attuned to what he calls "the fundamental Unity", but it is equally cognizant of the variety, multiplicity, particularity, detail and "succession" in life. These topics are major themes of "Circles", published in the Essays, First Series. The essay is a paean to change. It begins with St Augustine's notion of "God as a circle whose centre [is] everywhere, and its circumference nowhere" (CW 2.179). Each person is such a centre and so, Emerson holds, are cultures and religious institutions. Like pebbles falling in a pond, each sends it original impulse outwards with no necessary limit – "its circumference nowhere". But these circular expressions of original impulses – like the rituals Emerson opposed in "The Lord's Supper" – tend to harden with time. They must then be overcome, and according to Emerson they are overcome in a constant process of expansion and creation:

> [I]t is the inert effort of each thought having formed itself into a circular wave of circumstance, – as, for instance, an empire, rules of an art, a local usage, a religious rite, – to heap itself on that ridge, and to solidify, and hem in the life. But if the soul is quick and strong, it bursts over that boundary on all sides, and expands another orbit on the great deep …   (CW 2.180–81)

Notice that the soul's expansion is "on the great deep", not into a "lap of immense intelligence". There is no end to the expanding circles.

    From the perspective of "Circles", Jesus presents a new and powerful thought that overflows previous boundaries. But the thought has long since expended most of its life, and has become the rigid and fear-inducing institution Emerson describes in "The Divinity School Address". There, Emerson had called for the graduates to breathe new life into old forms. Now, in "Circles", he calls more radically for the abandonment of forms. No thought is finally adequate to religion, and all must be overcome. "In the thought of tomorrow", Emerson writes, "there is a power to upheave all thy creed, all the creeds, all the literatures of the nations, … Men walk as prophecies of the next age" (*CW* 2.181). In the concluding paragraphs of "Circles", Emerson describes this overcoming as "abandonment", as doing something "without knowing how or why", as "forget[ting] ourselves" (*CW* 2.190). The goal is not portrayed as realizing one's identity with the One, but as forgetting oneself, not as a return to something but as a departure, not as rest but as motion. For the "wonderful way of life" Emerson here describes, there seems nothing to hang on to but the journey itself.

The theme of life's journey is also central to "Experience", the great, tragic essay that records the death of Emerson's son Waldo and that dominates the *Essays, Second Series*. The essay begins with the claim that we "find ourselves" on a stairway whose top and bottom are out of view, and from which all objects appear indistinct and ghostly, and it ends with a tired "old heart" who has experienced "defeat" but who nevertheless urges itself onward. At its centre, however, lies an ecstatic religious vision: not of "the One" but of "the New" – or as Emerson calls it, "the newness" (*CW* 3.40). Our experience of "the newness" – what Emerson calls "the mode of our illumination" – is a glimpse, a promise, rather than a "satisfaction" or arrival. In such moments of vision we are apprised of our "vicinity to a new and excellent region of life" which he calls by many names, including "the sunbright Mecca of the desert" and "this new yet unapproachable America". "But," Emerson adds, "every insight from this realm of thought is felt as initial, and promises a sequel" (*CW* 3.41). This realm is, like America, forever new. The "One", on the other hand, does not promise a sequel, for it is everything. The secret of living in the world of sequels or succession, as we mostly do, is "to finish the moment, to find the journey's end in every step of the road, to live the greatest number of good hours" (*CW* 3.35).

The faces of reality

In the Plato essay, Emerson refuses to reduce variety to unity or unity to variety. "Two cardinal facts", he writes, "lie forever at the base [of philosophy]: the One and the two. 1. Unity or identity; and, 2. Variety" (*CW* 4.27–8). In "Nominalist and Realist", a companion piece to "Experience" that concludes the *Essays, Second Series*, Emerson states: "We are amphibious creatures, weaponed for two elements, having two sets of faculties, the particular and the catholic" (*CW* 3.135). The universe, that is to say, presents these two aspects to us, and we have two corresponding faculties for registering them. The 'nominalist' champions the particular, and the 'realist' champions unifying generalizations or ideals, but each offers an incomplete view. The universe is, in fact, "an old Two-Face", Emerson asserts, and the route to illumination lies both through the universal and through the particular. "If we cannot make voluntary and conscious steps in the admirable science of universals", Emerson advises:

> let us see the parts wisely, and infer the genius of nature from the best particulars with a becoming charity … It is commonly said by farmers, that a good pear or apple costs no more time or pains to rear, than a poor one; so I would have no work of art, no speech, or action, or thought, or friend, but the best.   (*CW* 3.143)

The two faces of reality, the particular and the general, may show us the divine, but they may not. One may find a mere meaningless jangle of particulars rather than a glimpse of "the newness" or even an exemplary pear; and one may be lost in uninspired or routine generalizations rather than apprehending the all-encompassing "One".

As we have seen, for Emerson religion at its core is a matter not of doctrine but of individual experience. While cautioning that language is inadequate to describe this experience, Emerson uses a set of terms to describe it, including "the moral sentiment" and "the religious sentiment" in "The Divinity School Address", "the wise silence" in "The Over-Soul", and being "apprised of my vicinity to a new an excellent region of life" in "Experience". These experiences reveal something for which, again, Emerson uses many names: "divine laws", "Unity", "The Over-Soul", "life, transition, the energizing spirit" (in "Circles"; *CW* 2.189), and "this new yet unapproachable America" (*CW* 3.41). Emerson was certainly drawn to the ideas of unity and the over-soul, to a great intelligence in which we lie and in which we may rest, but he was equally drawn to iconoclasm and a movement of overcoming that finds satisfaction in no term, tradition or scheme, that looks to the unstudied and spontaneous, the promising and the surprising for its "mode of illumination".

FURTHER READING

Buell, L. 2003. *Emerson*. Cambridge, MA: Harvard University Press.

Cavell, S. 1988. *In Quest of the Ordinary*. Chicago, IL: University of Chicago Press.

Cavell, S. 2003. *Emerson's Transcendental Etudes*, D. Hodge (ed.). Stanford, CA: Stanford University Press.

Clebsch, W. 1973. *American Religious Thought: A History*. Chicago, IL: University of Chicago Press.

Goodman, R. 1990. *American Philosophy and the Romantic Tradition*. Cambridge: Cambridge University Press.

Goodman, R. 1997. "Emerson's Mystical Empiricism". In *The Perennial Tradition of Neoplatonism*, J. Cleary (ed.), 456–78. Leuven: Leuven University Press.

Poirier, R. 1992. *Poetry and Pragmatism*. Cambridge, MA: Harvard University Press.
Richardson, R. 1995. *Emerson: The Mind on Fire*. Berkeley, CA: University of California Press.
Versluis, A. 1993. *American Transcendentalism and Asian Religions*. New York: Oxford University Press.

On NEOPLATONISM see also Ch. 4; Vol. 1, Chs 19, 20; Vol. 2, Chs 3, 4; Vol. 3, Ch. 9. On RITUAL see also Chs 20, 21; Vol. 1, Chs 12, 20. On THE ONE see also Vol. 1, Chs 3, 11, 14, 16, 19; Vol. 5, Ch. 15.

10

LUDWIG FEUERBACH

Van A. Harvey

Ludwig Feuerbach (1804–72) was the fourth of eight children in one of the most distinguished German families of the time. Deeply religious as a youth, he entered Heidelberg in 1823 in order to study Christian theology. But there he came under the influence of a well-known Hegelian theologian. Impressed by the intellectual grandeur of Hegelianism he decided to transfer to Berlin where Hegel taught, although he gave his father the impression that he wanted to study theology with the famous Protestant theologian Friedrich Schleiermacher. Because of financial reasons, he transferred to Erlangen in 1826 where, after completing his dissertation, he was made a Privatdozent. There he lectured on the history of modern philosophy.

In 1830 and against the advice of his father, he published anonymously a book entitled *Thoughts on Death and Immortality*, which argued that the most authentic religious faith would not contain the traditional Christian beliefs in a personal God and in personal immortality. The text, unfortunately, was accompanied by a series of derogatory epigrams directed against pietism. The book was censored by the authorities and Feuerbach was fired from the university. He married in 1837 but, unable to find academic employment, retired to a remote village near Ansbach where his wife's father owned a porcelain factory. There, in relative isolation except for trips to visit friends, he devoted his life to writing. The youngest of his two daughters died a very painful death aged three and Feuerbach never recovered from what he regarded as the senseless death of this infant.

His book *The Essence of Christianity* (hereafter *Christianity*; 1841) created a sensation, and he became one of the leaders of a group of radicals called the Young Hegelians who were dedicated to democracy and the separation of church and state. Between 1842 and 1848 he wrote several documents enunciating the principles of a new humanism, the best known of which is *Principles of the Philosophy of the Future* (1843). Regarded by the German students as a hero, he was invited in 1848 to lecture at the University of Heidelberg but was denied university facilities and forced to use the city hall. Disillusioned by the failure of the revolutions of 1848, he retreated back to his porcelain factory. When it went bankrupt in 1859, he was forced to move to a small town near Nürnberg where, ill and virtually penniless, he lived out his life with the financial aid of friends until 1872.

INTRODUCTION TO FEUERBACH'S PHILOSOPHY OF RELIGION

Perhaps no philosopher in the nineteenth century – not even Friedrich Nietzsche – developed and sustained a more systematic criticism of religion, especially Christianity, than Feuerbach. His entire life was dedicated, he once wrote, to illuminating "the obscure essence of religion with the torch of reason" (Feuerbach 1967a: 22). His first book (published in 1830) was, as mentioned earlier, a criticism of the notions of personal immortality and a personal deity, and his last book (published in 1857) was an attempt to show that religion arises when the human desire for happiness runs up against the iron necessities of nature. His aim, as he put it, was "to transform theologians into anthropologists, lovers of God into lovers of man, candidates for the next world into students of this world" (*ibid.*: 23). But unlike most vehement proponents of atheism, Feuerbach had sympathy for those human feelings and longings that find expression in religion. He wrote extraordinarily empathetic analyses of the comfort to be found in prayer and he recognized the feelings of self-worth that were derived from the belief that one was the object of divine recognition and concern. Some of his atheistic contemporaries called him a devout atheist and a mystic, appellations that Feuerbach did not reject. He claimed that he knew religion so intimately because he was himself religious.

Feuerbach's *Christianity*, the book that was to make him famous, was the first attempt to construct a projection theory of religion and to use that theory to interpret systematically the origin and persistence of religion. At least one important American philosopher, Sidney Hook, has said that this theory "still remains the most comprehensive and persuasive hypothesis available for the study of comparative religion" (1950: 221). The secret of religion, Feuerbach argued, is that human beings project their own image onto the heavens and these projected images are then converted into personal subjects for which human beings are objects. But unlike most atheistic theories of religion, Feuerbach did not dismiss these projections as mere superstition. Rather, he argued that human beings have through their history come to self-knowledge by contemplating these projections. Religion, we might say, is a mystified form of wisdom about human nature. Theology is anthropology.

Although Feuerbach is an important figure in the history of the philosophy of religion, his writings do not conform to what we now regard as the style of professional philosophers of religion. He was not primarily concerned with analysing and weighing various arguments for and against the existence of God, although he occasionally did this. His aim, rather, was to give an account of the origins and persistence of religion, especially Christianity, by means of what he called a historico-philosophical analysis of religious experience and belief. He wanted to show that beneath the explicit confessions and beliefs there was a hidden content of which religious believers were not themselves aware. To do this, one had to listen carefully to what believers themselves said and did. He was, as Marx Wartofsky (1977: 1–7) once wrote, a philosopher of the religious consciousness.

Feuerbach also differs from most atheistic philosophers because he had a very comprehensive and deep understanding of Christian theology and of the beliefs and practices of non-Christian religions. Karl Barth (1957: x), the famous Protestant theologian, once said of Feuerbach that not only has no modern philosopher been so preoccupied with theology but that his attitude was more theological than that of many theologians. Just because of his intimate knowledge of Christian theology and practice, his interpretation of that theology cannot so easily be dismissed as uninformed or superficial as can much atheistic criticism.

THE FIRST THEORY OF RELIGION

Feuerbach's philosophy of religion is difficult to summarize because he continually modified his views over time. Consequently, many commentators have categorized his development by stages. The most simple of these classifications is threefold: an early idealistic phase, a middle period in which he had rejected Hegel's idealism in favour of a naturalistic humanism, and a final materialistic phase. This rough division has some merit but is oversimplified because certain basic motifs and arguments found in one phase persist into the next. For example, although he was known for his criticism of Hegel in his so-called early middle period, in *Christianity* he is still obviously influenced by Hegel's major work, *The Phenomenology of Spirit*. And even in his so-called materialist phase he still held the view that the real essence of the human consists in the relationship between an I and a Thou.

I shall mostly be concerned with Feuerbach's so-called middle period (1841–8), with which his name is most closely associated. It was during this phase of his career that his most influential books on religion were written: *Christianity* (1841), *The Essence of Faith according to Luther* (1844), *The Essence of Religion* (1845) and *Lectures on the Essence of Religion* (hereafter *Lectures*; 1848). Feuerbach himself most valued his last book *Theogonie* (1857), but it was in *Christianity* that he developed his theory of projection that created such a sensation and with which his name is usually associated. This work is also crucial for understanding his relation to Hegelianism as well as his later thoughts on religion.

Christianity is divided into two parts. The first, which Feuerbach characterized as positive, argues that the idea of God is an involuntary projection of human predicates and that this explains not only certain specific Christian doctrines such as those of the Incarnation but also the Christian beliefs in providence and miracles. He called this section positive because he thought he had demonstrated what was true in religion. The second part, which he characterized as negative, attempts to show the contradictions that arise when the naive religious projections are taken seriously as theology.

There are three fundamental and interwoven conceptual strands that dominate the book and that need to be distinguished. The first is the Hegelian view of self-differentiation and the nature of 'spirit'; the second is the emphasis on feeling as well as anxiety and the fear of death; and the third is 'the felicity principle', the notion that the whole purpose of religion is the well-being or felicity of humankind.

The earliest chapters in which Feuerbach lays out his theory of consciousness are, as Wartofsky (1977) has shown, simply taken over from Hegel's *Phenomenology of Spirit*. This explains in part why many of his arguments are so cryptic and undeveloped. They are but the tip of an iceberg. Hegel had shown, Feuerbach assumed, that what distinguishes human beings from animals is consciousness; more specifically, self-consciousness. Animals do have a type of consciousness but not self-consciousness, which is to say they have no consciousness of being a member of a species. But it is just this consciousness of another human being that makes self-consciousness possible. The I comes into existence as a self-reflexive being only over against another Thou for which the I is itself an object. And in this process of self-differentiation, the self becomes aware that it shares its essential characteristics with this other, that it is a member of the species. In short, the self acquires species knowledge in the process of self-differentiation from others.

Feuerbach then argued that the imagination, under the pressure of feeling, seizes on this idea of the species and converts it into the notion of a single transcendent divine person. In short, the self takes all the attributes of human nature (the species characteristics) and unifies them in the notion of a perfect divine individual. "The divine being is nothing else than the human being ... freed from the limits of the human person ... and revered as a distinct being. All the attributes of the divine nature are, therefore, attributes of human nature" (Feuerbach 1957: 14).

Feuerbach was indebted to still another aspect of the Hegelian view of spirit. Hegel argued that spirit is incessantly productive, expressing itself in activities such as art, religion and philosophy. But because these 'objectifications' are external and stand over against the producer, they are alienated and must be re-appropriated. The logic of spirit, one might say, is objectification, alienation and re-appropriation. We learn who and what we are through our projections. This logic was basic to Hegel's metaphysics of spirit and his interpretation of religion. He had argued that the Infinite Spirit pours out (objectifies) its life in nature and history in the process of coming to its own absolute self-knowledge. The finite world or 'creation' is but a moment, so to speak, in the life of the Infinite. Human culture – art, religion, and philosophy – is the vehicle by which the Absolute Spirit through time comes to self-knowledge. For example, the long history of the world's religions, from animism through Buddhism, Hinduism, Judaism and Christianity, is to be seen as various stages of the revelation that the Absolute is not an impersonal substance but Subject.

This is why Hegel could consider Christianity as the absolute religion because its cultic life expresses in symbolic and imaginative form this movement or self-evolving process of the Absolute. The Christian doctrine of creation is the symbolic expression of the Infinite's objectification in the finite; the doctrine of the Fall is the symbolic expression of its alienation; and the doctrine of the Incarnation symbolizes the metaphysical truth that the Absolute is reconciling itself to its alienated creation.

Although Feuerbach adopted Hegel's notion of consciousness through self-differentiation, he turned the broader Hegelian metaphysical scheme upside down, so to speak. If Hegel had argued that the world is the self-objectification of the Absolute, Feuerbach argued that the Absolute is really the self-objectification of the human by means of which it comes to self-knowledge. To understand how Feuerbach could do this one has to have some knowledge of his prior critique of Hegel's thought, which space does not permit here. But, in short, Feuerbach had argued that Hegel inveterately and erroneously tended to treat predicates as entities. Having taken some human predicate such as 'thought' as the essence of human nature, Hegel then converted this predicate into an entity. Consequently, one could extract what was valid in Hegel's philosophy by inverting the subject and predicate and restoring their proper relationship. Instead of construing the predicate 'thought' as an entity, for example, one should invert the relationship and say that thought is the activity of existing individuals. Thought proceeds from being, not being from thought.

The consequence of this 'method of transformation' was to enable Feuerbach to argue that the gods are necessary moments in the self-knowledge of the human spirit. The various religions are not so much the self-realization of some Absolute Spirit but stages in which humanity becomes aware of its own essential nature. The gods are humanity's unconscious and indirect form of self-knowledge. Ironically, this conclusion meant that Feuerbach also viewed Christianity as the absolute religion because it expresses the most developed view of human nature as comprising reason, will and affection.

But just as for Hegel the creation is an objectified and therefore alienated moment in the life of the Absolute Spirit, so too for Feuerbach the idea of God is an alienated objectification of the human spirit. By attributing human perfections to some other divine being, the human being deprives itself of these attributes: "To enrich God, man must become poor; that God may be all, man must be nothing" (1957: 26). God, one might say, is the relinquished self of the human being. Consequently, just as the Absolute Spirit must reconcile itself with its alienated projection, Feuerbach similarly hoped to enable the reader to reconcile herself to the true meaning of the Christian religion, namely, atheism.

There was, I noted above, a second conceptual thread with which Feuerbach wove his argument, and this thread is quite un-Hegelian. Hegel basically regarded religion as the Idea wrapped in symbolism and myth. Feuerbach, by contrast, thought the religious consciousness was dominated by feeling and the imagination. His argument is that although the idea of the species arises out of self-differentiation, the imagination under the pressure of feeling converts the idea of the species into an image of a single, perfect divine being. Imagination, then, can be said to be the original organ of religion. It is original for several reasons. It is a type of representation that cloaks its abstractions in sensuous imagery that then stir the feelings, but it can also set aside all those limits that are painful to the feelings.

The imagination, however, has a deceptive power because it confuses the abstract with the concrete. It takes the abstract predicates of human nature and conceives of them as an individual being. In doing this it arouses feeling, feeling that also is unrestricted by the reality principle or the restraints of the understanding. Feeling assumes that what is longed for must be true. Since there is no deeper wish than that the Absolute be a sympathetic, loving being, the feelings find in the image of a divine person the fulfilment of all of their deepest longings and desires. Feeling longs for a personal God and the imagination provides the object for that longing.

The reason that the gods are so emotionally powerful is because religion has its psychological roots in anxiety, the longing for happiness, suffering and the fear of death. The important Christian beliefs speak to these anxieties and longings, particularly the notion of a personal God who is bent on the salvation of humankind. And this leads us to Feuerbach's third important theme: the felicity principle. Since the essential standpoint of religion is the practical, "the end of religion is the welfare, the salvation, the ultimate felicity of man" (1957: 185). This theme is most clearly exemplified in the Christian doctrine of the Incarnation, in which God sacrifices himself for the welfare of humankind. The true but often hidden implication of this doctrine, Feuerbach argued, could only be that the welfare of humankind is more important than God. This illustrates that religion is the detour by means of which humanity comes to realize its own worth.

It is, then, by means of these three interwoven strands that Feuerbach hopes to convince his readers that this is the real but hidden meaning of Christianity. The Hegelian strand of objectification explains the concept of God as the projection of the essential human predicates of reason, will and affection (love). The psychological strand composed of feeling, anxiety and the imagination together accounts for the beliefs about providence, miracles and the practice of prayer. And the felicity principle is manifested in the doctrine of the Incarnation and belief in immortality.

It is crucial to Feuerbach's interpretation of Christianity that the lay Christian sees God as personal and loving. He believed that he could show this by looking at the prayers and hymns of Christian worship. These reveal that the most important practical belief of the average lay person is that a personal God watches over and guides the life of the believer (providence); that this deity intervenes in history when necessary (miracle); but, above all, that this God will finally grant the believer what she most deeply desires – personal immortality. What underlies all these beliefs is the twofold conviction that a personal, loving divine being is concerned with human welfare and can set aside the constraints of natural necessity. This is why the Christian deity must be a creator, because only a creator possesses that power over nature that can secure the goods desired by the believer. Finally, all of these beliefs obviously call for faith because faith is just that confidence that God can and will fulfil these wishes. Hence the believers are constantly exhorted to distrust reason with its acknowledgement of necessities (thus impossibilities) and to bring their deepest longings to God in prayer with the confidence that these prayers will be answered.

The second part of *Christianity* is negative and deals with all of the contradictions that arise when the naive projections of the imagination are taken to be real; in short, when religion becomes theology. In addition to the basic criticism that informs the entire book – that the projection of a divine being involves alienation – Feuerbach devotes chapters to the contradictions in the very notion of the existence of a transcendent spiritual being as well as to contradictions in the notion of revelation, the doctrine of the Trinity and the speculative notion of God.

There are three criticisms that are worth singling out. The first is that the traditional concept of God attempts to combine two logically incompatible types of predicates: the personal on the one hand, and the metaphysical on the other. The second is that Christian faith corrupts the truth sense; and the third is that there is an inherent incompatibility between the virtues of faith and love. So far as the incompatible predicates are concerned, Christians pray to a personal deity who is concerned for them and bent on their welfare. On the other hand, their theologians argue that God is omniscient, omnipotent and impassible and hence cannot be moved by human suffering. This contradiction arises, Feuerbach believed, because the metaphysical predicates result from the objectification of the human attribute of reason while the personal predicates arise from the projection of love.

But it is in his discussion of the corruption of the truth sense and how this is related to the contradiction between the virtues of faith and love that Feuerbach's own passion is most clearly manifested. Faith, he argued, is basically a determinate judgement concerning what is true and, moreover, what saves, and when this is made the central virtue of a religion, as it is in Christianity, it makes a different religious judgement not only false but damned. The non-Christian is not merely in error but is condemned to eternal punishment. It is just this virtue of faith that puts such a premium on the evangelization of the unbeliever. But when faith is interpreted in this way, it corrupts the truth sense and stands opposed to the virtue of love. It stands opposed to the truth sense because the object of faith is a particular event in space and time that is not available to all, and it stands opposed to love because love is universal and inclusive.

THE REVISED THEORY OF RELIGION

Although *Christianity* created a sensation and was hailed as "the truth of our time" by David Friedrich Strauss, it received the expected criticisms not only from Christian theologians but also from some atheistic philosophers such as Max Stirner and Bruno Bauer. One Protestant theologian argued that Feuerbach's criticisms might apply to Roman Catholicism but not to Protestantism, and Stirner complained that despite Feuerbach's criticism of idealism, he had merely substituted another abstraction, the species idea, as the object of veneration and the basis of morality. Stung by these criticisms, Feuerbach turned first to a study of Martin Luther and then revised in important ways his theory of religion in a short book entitled *The Essence of Religion*. This book then became the basis of a series of lectures given in Heidelberg in 1848.

In his study of Luther, Feuerbach became convinced that he was correct in thinking that Christian faith was driven by the felicity principle, and, therefore, that anthropomorphism was at the core of the Christian faith. It seemed clear to him that Luther believed that God was simply the being who expresses and promises human blessedness and fulfils that promise by the resurrection of Jesus. Moreover, despite the fact that there are passages in Luther that distinguish God radically from the human, it also seemed clear to Feuerbach that Luther believed that God had in Christ presented humankind with a visible exact image of himself. God had become a human being (*see* Vol. 3, Ch. 3).

It is my view that Feuerbach's discovery of the importance Luther placed on the felicity principle and its confirmation in the resurrection permitted him to abandon the emphasis he had placed on the abstraction 'species being' in *Christianity* and to revise his theory of religion. Instead of seeing the origins of religion in the veneration of the species idea, he now proposed a dipolar model: religion arises out of the subjective wish for happiness, on the one hand, and the sensuous confrontation with nature on which human beings are dependent, on the other. It is nature, not the species idea, that "is the first, original object of religion, as is sufficiently proved by the history of all religions and nations" (Feuerbach 2004: 2).

In his *Lectures*, Feuerbach sought to give the impression that the introduction of nature as the object of religion was a minor alteration only of his previous theory. He suggested that whereas in *Christianity* his formula had been "theology is anthropology", it now became "theology is anthropology plus physiology". But this attempt to minimize the difference between the earlier and the later theory stands in tension with the actual text. In *Christianity*, the attributes of God were all derived from human consciousness alone. The metaphysical attributes of infinitude, self-subsistence, necessary being and first cause were derived from human reason. Feuerbach argued that reason was impassible, incorporeal, without limits and the source of identity, necessity and law. So, too, the moral attributes were derived from the objectification of the will. But in the new theory, the gods are composite beings, some of their attributes derived from nature and others from human consciousness. Moreover, many of the metaphysical attributes previously derived from human nature are now explicitly derived from nature. If God is regarded as self-subsistent, that is because nature is. If God is thought to be omnipresent, that is because nature is. Surprisingly, Feuerbach even says that some of the moral attributes have their origins in nature. Indeed, even the notion of God's goodness is "merely abstracted from those beings and phenomena in nature which are useful, good, and helpful to man, which give him the feeling or consciousness that life, existence, is a good thing" (Feuerbach 1967a: 111).

In this new dipolar model, then, we have at one pole the absolutely dependent self in the grip of the drive-to-happiness and, at the other pole, nature. By 'nature', Feuerbach did not simply mean external nature but "everything which man … experiences directly and sensuously as the ground and substance of his life" (*ibid.*: 91). One might say that nature is everything that is 'not-I', even a person's inner nature that operates independently of will.

> Man with his ego or consciousness stands at the brink of a bottomless abyss; that abyss is his own unconscious being, which seems alien to him and inspires him with a feeling which expresses itself in words of wonderment such as: What am I? Where have I come from? … And this feeling that I am nothing without a *not-I* which is distinct from me yet intimately related to me, something *other*, which is at the same time my *own* being, is the religious feeling. But what part of me is I and what part is not-I? (*Ibid.*: 91)

Many of the most interesting lectures are devoted to a very complex description of the subjective pole of religion. As in *Christianity*, feeling and imagination are two of the most important elements in the analysis. In the *Lectures*, however, Feuerbach emphasized the feeling of dependency on nature. He can even say that it is the foundation of religion. It is just because human beings do not relate to nature by means of abstraction that they react to the forces of nature that impinge on them in emotive terms. Objects in nature are beautiful or disturbing, harmful or beneficial. And those forces that benefit the person are regarded as 'good' and those that threaten it are 'evil'.

Although feeling is the 'foundation' of religion, the imagination is its theoretical cause. The imagination, unconstrained by the reality principle, seizes on the various objects of nature and personalizes them. It is the imagination that in ancient times fastened on the forces of nature and under the influence of desire transformed natural beings into feeling beings; and it is the imagination in more sophisticated times that unifies all the objects of nature into one being and creates monotheism. It is the imagination that treats the lifeless as living and the involuntary as voluntary, ensouled beings. This tendency to personify the forces of nature is reinforced by the changeability of nature because changeability can easily be seen by the unsophisticated mind as a sign of intention and wilfulness. Because of these changes, the naive believer thinks these powers can be cajoled or persuaded; hence the universal practice of magic, sacrifice and petitionary prayer.

Although the imagination is not restricted by the reality principle, it does not create its images out of nothing. It has certain raw material on which it can work, such as those aspects of nature that strike it as extraordinary or certain charismatic persons. In prehistoric times the imagination seized on certain natural objects and animals on which it was dependent or that impressed it. In later times the imagination was captivated by charismatic persons such as the Buddha, Jesus, or Muhammad. Sometimes, even the coherence and unity of nature could ignite the imagination, as can be seen in the way the Bible and the Koran envisage the movements of nature as movements of the Divine.

Still, it is important not to forget that although the imagination is the theoretical cause of religion, it is driven by both anxiety and desire. At every step the human being takes towards achieving its desires, Feuerbach argued, it is threatened by some harm or injury or death, and the anxiety that is aroused by this uncertainty is the root of the religious imagination. It is particularly the thought of death that is important in this regard. If human beings did not die, he wrote, there would be no religion. "That is why I say in my notes on the *Essence of Religion* that man's tomb is the sole birthplace of the gods" (*ibid.*: 311).

Feuerbach's description of the subjective pole invokes so many principles that he sought again and again for some unifying concept that would encompass them all. His first attempt to do this is somewhat unfortunate. He proposed the single term *Egoismus* (egoism). By this term he meant simply to designate the aggregate of human needs and drives: what he called "that necessary, indispensable egoism – not moral but metaphysical, i.e., grounded in man's essence without his knowledge or will" (*ibid.*: 50). Egoism, in short, is the natural self-love that drives a person to satisfy their needs.

But because the term 'egoism' as it is normally used excludes altruism and sacrifice for another, both of which are fundamental to his I–Thou philosophy, Feuerbach increasingly replaced this term with *Glückseligkeitstrieb* or the drive-to-happiness and well-being. This term is now used to name the drive to develop or realize one's potentialities. It is the drive-to-happiness confronted by the limits of nature, including death, that creates the gods. Driven by the love of life and confronted by the indifference of nature, the imagination creates those divine beings that fulfil human desire. It is to these beings that people address their prayers and wishes for providential care, the cure of illnesses, miracles of various sorts and, above all, life after death.

With these two ideas in hand, Feuerbach turns once again in the last chapters to the interpretation of Christianity. In contrast to the earlier *Christianity*, in which the projection of the idea of the species was used to explain the origins and content of specific Christian doctrines, here the whole of theology is a circle that turns around the blessedness of humankind. The basic wish and goal of the Christian is heaven. To believe there is a God is to believe that there is no more death. But the only being that can grant this wish to survive death must be sovereign over nature. It must be omnipotent and be able to create the world by pure will. Hence the Christian God does not create the world out of matter but *ex nihilo*, by his word. But this same God is also seen as human, only in the highest degree; that is, without needs and limits. God is the superhuman being; a knowing, feeling, loving being but infinitely more knowing, feeling and loving than the human being is. God is the superlative human but without defects. Consequently, he grants the Christian her highest wish: to become immortal, to become divine.

Given this description of the subjective and objective elements that constitute this dipolar view of religion, Feuerbach's overall model looks like this. The human person is an embodied consciousness in the grip of the rage to live. In the grip of this drive, the self ('I') is confronted by the limitations and the necessities of nature. The imagination, unrestrained by the reality principle and driven by wish, seizes on aspects of nature (or nature as a whole) and personifies them. One might say that religious faith is a misinterpretation of nature.

A number of the chapters of the *Lectures* are dedicated to explaining how this misinterpretation of nature arises and the intellectual contradictions to which it leads. The error of monotheism arises when all of the powers of nature, the not-I, are unified and then made into a single divine being. And it is in these chapters that Feuerbach takes up the various arguments for the existence of God. There are three with which he is most concerned: the argument for a first cause; the argument that the coherence and order of nature are the result of intelligent design; and, finally, the argument that it is inconceivable that an unconscious nature could give rise to conscious mind or spirit.

Most of his counter-arguments are not especially original except perhaps for his claim that the notion of first cause is just a pragmatic abstraction to which the mind is driven in its attempt to seek closure. But it does not follow, he argued, that because the human mind has a need for such an abbreviated fiction that a corresponding reality exists. We must not single out the necessities of thought, isolate them, and fail to recognize they arise out of subjective needs.

Just as *Christianity* concludes with a discussion of the contradictions in that religion, so too the *Lectures* closes with a series of attacks on both theism and Christianity. Feuerbach not only deals with the contradictions in the ideas of providence and miracle, but concludes with a series of powerful attacks that anticipate those of Nietzsche. Feuerbach argues that all the attempts to set aside the necessities of nature, especially death, represent a diseased Eros: a grotesque desire to overcome the limits of human finitude. The desire for immortality, especially, is an imaginary, fantastic desire. By desiring another future world, the Christian necessarily regards this one as 'fallen', as sick. Like Nietzsche, Feuerbach wanted to 'affirm the earth': to turn yearnings for the next world into an affirmation of this one. Christians should learn to accept not only their finitude and historicity but also the I–Thou structure of human life in which true happiness is realized.

THE LAST THEORY OF RELIGION

Feuerbach had no sooner completed his lectures on religion in Heidelberg than his restless mind turned once again to the explanation of the origins and persistence of religion. After five or six years of intensive work, there appeared in 1857 a very large book of forty-two chapters entitled, *Theogonie nach dem Quellen des klassischen, hebräischen und christlichen Altertums* (Theogonie according to the sources of classical, Hebraic and Christian antiquity; hereafter *Theogonie*). The first thirty chapters of the book primarily deal with the Greek gods and it is not until chapter 31 that he turns to Christianity. Feuerbach himself thought it was his finest book on religion but it is so filled with learned historical illustrations and references that it failed to get public acceptance; so much so that a later edition in 1907 by Wilhelm Bolin and Friedrich Jodl tried to make it more accessible by the dubious device of eliminating all of the illustrative materials. The book has never been translated into English.

In this book Feuerbach, while not denying his earlier view that nature plays some role as the object of religion, emphasizes almost entirely the subjective origin of religion. He argues that the gods do not arise out of some special religious feeling or some speculative interest. Rather, they arise out of the quite concrete and material wishes and needs of the drive-to-happiness (*Glückseligkeitstrieb*). The human being, one might say, is a bundle of wishes and needs arising out of the basic wish for happiness. Human beings are striving, willing, wishing beings, and the gods are those beings that can fulfil and realize those wishes. One might say that every human activity – a contest, a battle, a project, a marriage – has a wish within it as well as the anxiety that the wish may not be fulfilled. But all human wishes are accompanied by the awareness that there is a chain of events intervening between willing (*Wollen*) and being able to succeed (*Können*). The imagination seizes on a being that eliminates this intervening chain, a being that is not subject to limitation and failure, a being that can do what it wishes to do. The gods are such beings. A god, Feuerbach argues, is a being in which the distinction between willing and wish has been abolished. Faith just is the certitude that our wishes will be fulfilled. It is an objectification of the wish. Because there are a variety of cultures and because there is scarcely anything that has not at some time been the object of wishing, there are a variety of gods. But beneath this variety there are always more basic wishes: to be free from hunger and disease, for evildoers to be punished, and not to die.

There are two closely related ideas that drive the basic argument of the book. The first is that the human being is defined as driven by the wish for happiness so that all of culture may be seen in terms of that wish. Law, morality, dreams, conscience, the taking of oaths, miracles and religion are all seen here as phenomena basically aimed at gratifying the needs and wishes of human beings. One might even say that the *Theogonie* is a phenomenology of wishing. The second idea is the restatement of the theme that Feuerbach professed to find in the writings of Luther;

namely, that a god is a being who fulfils the basic wishes of humankind. People do not first believe and then wish; rather, they believe because they wish. A god is that to whom we turn in prayer to grant our wishes, above all, the wish that we live forever.

FURTHER READING

Barth, K. 1959. "Feuerbach". In his *Protestant Thought: From Rousseau to Ritschl*, B. Cozens (trans.), 355–61. New York: Harper & Row.

Brazill, W. 1970. *The Young Hegelians*. New Haven, CT: Yale University Press.

Hanfi, Z. (ed.) 1972. *The Fiery Brook: Selected Writings of Ludwig Feuerbach*. New York: Doubleday.

Harvey, V. 1997. *Feuerbach and the Interpretation of Religion*. Cambridge: Cambridge University Press.

Johnston, L. 1995. *Between Transcendence and Nihilism: Species-ontology in the Philosophy of Ludwig Feuerbach*. New York: Peter Lang.

Löwith, K. 1967. *From Hegel to Nietzsche: The Revolution in Nineteenth-Century Thought*. Garden City, NY: Doubleday.

Smart, N., J. Clayton, P. Sherry & S. Katz (eds) 1985. *Nineteenth Century Religious Thought in the West*, vol. 1. Cambridge: Cambridge University Press.

Toews, J. 1980. *Hegelianism: The Path Towards Dialectical Humanism, 1805–1841*. Cambridge: Cambridge University Press.

Wartofsky, M. 1977. *Feuerbach*. Cambridge: Cambridge University Press.

On ATHEISM see also Chs 2, 20; Vol. 3, Ch. 15; Vol. 5, Chs 6, 17. On FAITH see also Chs 8, 13; Vol. 1, Ch. 13; Vol. 2, Chs 6, 12, 16, 18; Vol. 3, Ch. 8; Vol. 5, Chs 7, 18. On HEGELIANISM see also Vol. 5, Ch. 4. On NATURE/NATURALISM see also Ch. 5; Vol. 3, Chs 20, 21, 22; Vol. 5, Ch. 4. On SELF-CONSCIOUSNESS see also Chs 2, 4, 5, 13. On THEORY OF PROJECTION see also Ch. 14.

11

JOHN STUART MILL

Chin Liew Ten

John Stuart Mill (1806–73) rejected orthodox religions on moral grounds. He was a great admirer of the moral character of Christ, but he never embraced Christianity, and was critical of some Christian doctrines. When he stood for elections as a Member of Parliament, he announced his refusal to answer any questions about his religious beliefs (*CW* 1.274).[1] In fact, he adopted what he regarded as an alternative religion, the Religion of Humanity, which eschews any belief in an afterlife and focuses entirely on improving the condition of human beings in this life. He believed that such a non-supernatural religion could provide a sound basis for morality. But he did not publish any detailed or systematic account of religion in his own lifetime.

In her introductory note to Mill's posthumously published *Three Essays on Religion*, his stepdaughter, Helen Taylor, informs us that the first two essays, "Nature" and "Utility of Religion", were written between 1850 and 1858, while the third, "Theism", was written between 1868 and 1870. She also mentions that Mill had intended to publish "Nature" in 1873, but the other two essays were not intended for publication at the same time. She believes that the views expressed in the three essays are "fundamentally consistent" (*CW* 10.371).

Mill died on 7 May 1873, and the three essays were published together under the editorship of Helen Taylor in 1874. "Theism" is the essay most sympathetic to religion. In it Mill points out that polytheism, rather than monotheism, is "more natural to the human mind", and it requires "a considerable amount of intellectual culture" before we can reach the belief in God. Monotheism arises from the belief that every event depends on many antecedents, an alteration in any one of which might have prevented its occurrence, or significantly changed its character. So an event cannot be governed by any single being unless it has control of the whole of

---

1. References to Mill's works are to the *Collected Works of John Stuart Mill* (Mill 1963–91), abbreviated *CW*, and cited by volume and page numbers.

nature, and not just one part of it. Monotheism is therefore the product of a scientific view of nature as a unified system.

SCIENTIFIC EVIDENCE OF A CREATOR

Mill asks whether it is consistent with scientific knowledge to attribute the origins of all natural phenomena to the will of a creator. These phenomena occur in accordance with general laws. If there is a creator then it must be his intention that natural events conform to fixed laws. Scientific evidence does not disprove the existence of such a creator, but is there evidence to prove it? Mill examines various types of evidence put forward.

He regards the design argument as having "a really scientific character" (*CW* 10.446). Certain effects in nature bear the marks of intelligent design. They resemble the works of human creation, but are beyond the power of human beings to make. They can therefore be treated as the work of a greater than human power. Thus the structure of the eye shows a designing mind as it conduces to the production of sight. An alternative account that connects the structure of the eye with sight is that creatures who see well have advantages over others, and hence the development of the structure of the eye can be explained in terms of "the survival of the fittest". Darwin's *On the Origin of Species* was published in 1859, and Mill was obviously alluding to it here. But Mill regarded the Darwinian account as so far a "remarkable speculation", and concluded that in the present state of our knowledge, there is "a large balance of probability in favor of creation by intelligence" (*CW* 10.450).

But what are the attributes of the designer? All the evidence, Mill argues, points to a designer who is not omnipotent. He needs to adapt means to achieve his ends, whereas an omnipotent designer could have attained his ends directly through the exercise of his will. While the evidence is against God's omnipotence, it does not rule out his omniscience and absolute freedom. But neither can we prove that he has these attributes.

What evidence is there of the purposes of the creator or designer? Much of what is created is not intended to promote any moral end, or the good of any sentient being, but only to ensure that the works created will last for some time. This applies to both animate and inanimate works. There is some evidence that benevolence is an attribute of the creator in that pleasure seems to arise from the normal working of the created machinery, whereas pain usually arises from "some external interference with it". But one is not justified in making "the inference that his sole or chief purposes are those of benevolence, and that the single end and aim of Creation was the happiness of his creatures" (*CW* 10.458).

Mill summarizes his discussion of the divine attributes:

> A Being of great but limited power, how and by what limited we
> cannot even conjecture; of great and perhaps unlimited intelligence,

but perhaps, also, more narrowly limited than his power: who desires and pays some regard to the happiness of his creatures, but who seems to have other motives of action which he cares more for, and who can hardly be supposed to have created the universe for that purpose alone. (*CW* 10.459)

REVELATION AND SCEPTICISM

As for revelation, Mill maintains that the evidence would either be external, depending on the testimony of the senses or of witnesses, or internal, in which the alleged revelation itself supports its divine origin. He quickly dismisses the internal evidence. If the doctrine of an alleged revelation is bad, then it cannot be the work of a good and wise God. On the other hand, if the doctrine is morally good, then there is no reason to attribute it to God either, because the human faculties that are capable of recognizing moral goodness would also be competent to discover the relevant moral doctrine.

So if there is to be evidence of revelation, it would have to be external, showing the existence of supernatural facts. Mill refers to David Hume's argument against miracles. Since miracles are contradicted by experience, being a breach of a law of nature, there is the strongest reason, based on experience, for disbelieving them. At the same time, we have commonly experienced the mendacity and mistakes of witnesses who report events such as alleged miracles. Mill does not accept this argument because he points out that the evidence of experience against miracles is negative, and therefore not conclusive: we often discover facts that we had not previously experienced. The evidence for miracles rests on positive evidence, which has to be balanced against the negative evidence against their occurrence.

But although Mill is less radical than Hume in his rejection of miracles, he still rules them out as evidence of revelation. A miracle is not simply the discovery of a "new and surprising fact" that depends on a newly discovered law of nature. A miracle does not depend on the supercession of one law by another. Rather, it is based on the rejection of all natural laws. The presumption against there being a miracle is therefore very much stronger than that against any new and unexpected phenomenon. The testimony for miracles in the case of every revealed religion, including Christianity, is:

the uncross-examined testimony of extremely ignorant people, credulous as such usually are, ... unaccustomed to draw the line between the perceptions of sense, and what is superinduced upon them by the suggestions of a lively imagination; unversed in the difficult art of deciding between appearance and reality; and between the natural and the supernatural. (*CW* 10.479)

Mill maintains that even the testimony of Christ has no great value because it is based on "internal conviction", and the best people are "the readiest to ascribe any honorable peculiarity in themselves" to God, "rather than to their own merits" (*CW* 10.481).

Mill concludes his discussion of theism by stating that "The rational attitude of a thinking mind towards the supernatural, whether in natural or in revealed religion, is that of skepticism as distinguished from belief on the one hand, and from atheism on the other" (*CW* 10.482). This identifies him clearly as an agnostic on religion. But although Mill maintains that there are no rational grounds or arguments based on theistic belief for immortality or eternal life, he thinks that it is appropriate to exercise our imagination, and indulge in the hope that there is a future life after death. It is not necessary to be "always brooding over death". "All *unnecessary* dwelling upon the evils of life is at best a useless expenditure of nervous force" (*CW* 10.484).

Although not himself a believer, Mill maintains that the life and character of Christ provides an exemplary moral guide. All of us, even unbelievers, would do well if we endeavoured "so to live that Christ would approve our life" (*CW* 10.488).

THE UTILITY OF RELIGION

In "Utility of Religion", Mill's focus is on the usefulness rather than the truth of religious beliefs. He considers the role of supernatural religion in sustaining social morality and in keeping individuals on the right path. He argues that when the moral duties derived from religion are effectively imposed, this is not because religion itself is effective in providing sanctions for social morality. Rather, these duties are backed by education and public opinion. Duties, however they are derived, can be successfully supported in these ways. The effective power of beliefs depends on their wide acceptance, and not on their religious origin. For example, the social morality of the Greeks did not depend on religion. On the other hand, religious requirements are not taken seriously when they are not backed by the sanction of public opinion. The threat of divine punishments, when confined to the remoteness of the afterlife, is not a very powerful deterrent to ordinary persons who are confronted with immediate strong temptations. Divine rewards and punishments, administered after death, are regarded as uncertain. They are meted out not for specific acts, but on the basis of a person's whole life. People can easily persuade themselves that the balance will in the end be in their favour. It is precisely because of the great magnitude of the threatened punishment that nobody, "except a hypochondriac here and there", believes that it will be inflicted on him. "Bad religions teach that divine vengeance may be bought off, by offerings, or personal abasement; the better religions, not to drive sinners to despair, dwell so much on the divine mercy, that hardly any one is compelled to think himself irrevocably condemned" (*CW* 10.413).

Mill goes on to invoke Jeremy Bentham on the inefficacy of purely religious obligations when they are not enforced by the sanctions of public opinion. Oaths of various kinds are, from the religious point of view, equally important. But whereas those taken in courts of justice and rigidly enforced by public opinion are taken seriously, other oaths, such as university oaths, are readily disregarded. A second case mentioned by Bentham is the practice of dueling, which, although considered sinful, continues in some Christian countries in accordance with public opinion and the personal desire to avoid humiliation. Another example is the relatively greater indulgence in illicit sexual intercourse by males than by females, even though both cases are, in religious terms, equally sinful. The difference is that public opinion does not severely condemn the conduct of males.

Mill then considers the utility of religion as a teacher, rather than as an enforcer, of social morality. Can it be argued that without religion we would not have certain useful rules of social morality? Mill grants that some of the moral precepts of Christ reach a higher level of morality than was previously known. However, once these precepts are known, as they now are, they will not be lost. On the other hand, when social morality is thought to have a supernatural origin, it is difficult to discuss, criticize or change it when it has weaknesses or ceases to be suitable to changed circumstances.

Religion also has a value to the individual in that, like poetry, it satisfies the want for "ideal conceptions grander and more beautiful than we see realized in the prose of human life" (*CW* 10.419). It is "a source of personal satisfaction and of elevated feelings" (*CW* 10.420). But for Mill the question is whether there is an alternative source apart from supernatural religion. Although an individual human life is short, the life of the human species is indefinitely long, and this provides the basis for our imagination and sympathies to satisfy their higher aspirations. We know that some have been stirred to strong sentiments by the love of country. There is no reason why the love of the whole world cannot similarly be a source of "elevated emotion" and "a principle of duty" (*CW* 10.421). We can cultivate a concern for the general good and a sense of the unity of humanity into "a sentiment and a principle capable of fulfilling every important function of religion and itself justly entitled to the name" (*CW* 10.422).

This non-supernatural religion is the Religion of Humanity. Mill argues for the superiority of the Religion of Humanity to the supernatural religions. The latter cater to a person's posthumous interests, and do not therefore strengthen the unselfish element or weaken the selfish element in human nature. Of course, the Religion of Humanity does not hold out the prospect of a life after death. But Mill believes that, as the conditions of life improve and people's lives are happier, and they are more capable of getting happiness from unselfish sources, their interest in the afterlife will diminish. Generally, those who have experienced happiness are relatively less anxious about death than those who have never been happy, for "it is hard to die without ever having lived" (*CW* 10.426). Mill alludes to the Buddhist religion rewarding a virtuous life on earth with the reward of annihilation, "the cessation, at least, of all conscious or separate existence" (*CW* 10.427). He then speculates that it is probable that:

> in a higher, and, above all a happier condition of human life, not anni-
> hilation but immortality may be the burdensome idea; and that human
> nature, though pleased with the present, and by no means impatient
> to quit it, would find comfort and not sadness in the thought that it is
> not chained through eternity to a conscious existence which it cannot
> be assured that it will always wish to preserve.   (*CW* 10.428)

NATURE AND MORALITY

In his essay on "Nature", Mill explores views that treat nature as the test of morality, of what is right or wrong, good or evil. He first distinguishes between two senses of the term 'nature'. In the first sense, 'nature' is "the aggregate of the powers and properties in the world" (*CW* 10.374). So the idea of nature includes all phenomena and all the causes of phenomena, all that happen as well as all that are capable of happening. In the second sense, 'nature' refers to all things that exist without voluntary human intervention. The natural is here opposed to the artificial, and it excludes all phenomena produced by human agency.

In the first sense, nature cannot set the standard of morality. It is unnecessary to recommend that we should act in accordance with nature, because we cannot fail to do so, no matter what we do. Some of those who use conformity to nature as the basis of morality confuse the laws of nature, which state "observed uniformities in the occurrence of phenomena", with the criminal law and the law of justice, which specify not what the case is, but what ought to be (*CW* 10.375).

Whereas we cannot but conform to nature in the first sense, we frequently act against nature in the second sense. The numerous achievements and improvements in social life involve our intervention with the spontaneous order of nature. A great deal of harm is done by the destructive power of natural calamities, and "nearly all the things which men are hanged or imprisoned for doing to one another, are nature's every day performances" (*CW* 10.385). Nature makes a "clumsy" provision for the renewal of life: "no human being ever comes into the world but another human being is literally stretched on the rack for hours or days, not infrequently issuing in death" (*CW* 10.385). The virtues that we value are acquired by cultivation, and by rising above instinct. For example, it is doubtful if any human being is naturally courageous, for fear is naturally one of the most powerful human emotions.

GOD AND EVIL

Mill's *Three Essays on Religion* received a great deal of attention in the years following its publication (see Sell 1997). Christian critics were particularly scathing
about Mill's discussion of the attributes of God. Mill had argued that the existence of evil and the nature of God's design in the world were evidence that he
lacked perfect moral goodness and that he was not omnipotent. Against this, the
critics maintain that God's purposes cannot be discovered and understood by our
limited human capacities. Thus Richard Hutton asserts that, while the attribute
of moral goodness in God must be the same kind as in human beings, it does
not follow that it must also involve the same actions. "The truth is, that we no
sooner come to try the idea of Omnipotence, than we see how utterly impossible
it is for such a creature as man to say what is, and what is not, consistent with
Omnipotence" (*ibid.*: 4). Similarly, Hutton argues that actions that are wicked in
human beings need not also be evil in God, as the motives behind the actions may
be very different. "Yet this confusion between the moral evil involved in the rash
actions of ignorant and finite beings, and the same when proceeding from utterly
different motives in an omniscient Being, pervades the whole of Mr Mill's essay
on 'Nature'" (*ibid.*: 5).

Mill had in fact confronted similar views in his lifetime. He published *An
Examination of Sir William Hamilton's Philosophy* in 1865, and there he directly
and bluntly condemned the approach to the problem of evil adopted by Hamilton's
follower Henry Mansel. Mansel had argued that what appeared to human beings
as evil was not so. God's goodness and omnipotence were to be accepted on faith
and were compatible with the appearance of evil. Mill could hardly contain his
contempt:

> Whatever power such a being may have over me, there is one thing
> which he shall not do: he shall not compel me to worship him. I will
> call no being good, who is not what I mean when I apply that epithet
> to my fellow-creatures; and if such a being can sentence me to hell for
> not so calling him, to hell I will go.   (Quoted in Packe 1954: 444)

INTERPRETING THE WILL OF GOD

This resolute belief, that a God worthy of our obedience should be held to ordinary human standards of goodness, is a point of great and wider significance.
Some religious believers justify the infliction of grave harm on innocent people
by appeals to their Holy Scriptures, which are supposed to be the word of God.
But the moral authority of God rests on his moral goodness, and not simply on
his power, and a perfectly good God, if he exists, could not possibly command
his followers to perform acts that are clearly evil. No just and good God would

endorse the conduct of Hitler or Stalin, let alone direct believers to perform acts of equivalent moral wickedness. So if we are told by a religious fanatic that his holy text supports such acts, then we would simply have to reject his interpretation of the holy text in favour of one that is compatible with widely accepted standards of good and evil that religious people themselves accept in the evaluation of human conduct. We do not need to be scholarly experts of the holy text in order to reject the proffered interpretation. We only need to be familiar with notions of good and evil that we use when we are not alluding to the will of God.

This approach to interpretation is precisely that adopted by Pierre Bayle in 1686. Christ had enjoined his followers to treat non-believers as follows: "Go out into the highways and hedges and compel them to come in, that my house may be filled" (quoted in Schneewind 1997: 6). This would seem to justify the use of coercion on non-Christians to make them come to church. But, as J. B. Schneewind has noted, such an interpretation was explicitly rejected by Bayle. It was evil to use physical violence on unbelievers, and Bayle believed that "Any literal interpretation which carries an obligation to commit iniquity is false" (*ibid.*: 6). So what Christ must have meant is that unbelievers "should be given arguments and evidence that would compel them on rational grounds to assent to the truth" (*ibid.*: 7).

Bayle's argument resembles Mill's rejection of the internal evidence for divine revelation. If the doctrine, which is supposed to be revealed, is bad, then it cannot be the word of a good God. Although Mill did not specifically address the issue of how a holy text might be used to guide or justify conduct, it is clear that the implicit principles invoked, that a good God could not command evil acts and that there are moral standards independent of God's wishes, serve as powerful constraints on what believers may do in the name of a benevolent and just deity.

But, assuming that a revealed moral doctrine passes a satisfactory independent test of not being morally evil, there is still the question of interpreting the scope and rationale of the doctrine. Elsewhere, especially in his essay *On Liberty*, Mill has much to say on the subject. One of Mill's arguments for freedom of expression is that without it we would not know the meaning and the grounds of an opinion.[2] True beliefs will lose their vitality and sink into dead dogmas. This argument provides another basis for rejecting the literal interpretation of a holy text as a source of right conduct. Even divinely inspired moral doctrines have to be applied to new and changing circumstances, and a blindly literal application would run counter to the rationale and intention of the doctrine. Legal analogues of this problem are instructive.

H. L. A. Hart (1994: 126ff.) gives the example of a rule prohibiting vehicles from entering a park. The rule clearly excludes motor cars and buses from entering, but a decision based on the purpose of the rule would have to be made on whether it

---

2. See the discussion of this and other Millian arguments for freedom of expression in Ten (1980: ch. 8).

also excludes electrically propelled toy cars and roller skates, which were not yet invented when the rule was formulated. However, as Lon Fuller (1958) has shown, a literal interpretation of the rule would be a mistake. Suppose now that there is a proposal to mount a truck used in the Second World War on a pedestal in the park.[3] In normal circumstances, a truck would clearly be a vehicle to be excluded from the park because of the noise and the risk of injuries it would cause to strollers in the park. But mounted on a pedestal, the truck should not be regarded as a vehicle according to the proper meaning of the law. (There may, of course, be other reasons for rejecting the proposal, for example, aesthetic reasons, or even a moral concern that the proposal celebrates unacceptable martial virtues.)

Fuller also gives a more striking, and perhaps a more controversial, example of a statute that makes it a misdemeanour to sleep in a railway station. Consider two cases. First, a passenger, waiting at 3am for a delayed train, was sitting in an upright position on a railway bench, but the arresting officer heard him snoring. In the second case, a man had settled down on the bench with a blanket and pillow, but had not fallen asleep when he was arrested. Fuller believes that a judge would not have misinterpreted the statute if he or she lets off the first person, but fines the second person. This is because the statute was intended to discourage tramps from using the railway benches, thereby depriving weary passengers, such as those waiting for delayed trains, of seats. Fuller is therefore recommending an interpretation of the statute that goes against the literal meaning of the term 'sleep'.

Fuller's general point, that we should interpret a statute in accordance with its purpose rather than literally, seems correct, even if his specific application of it to justify the fining of a tramp and to leave unpunished a better-off passenger might not go down well with some egalitarian lawyers. Applying the general point to the interpretation of a holy text would lead us to reject a literal interpretation in favour of one that takes account of context and circumstances. This in itself does not imply that a religious person who uses a holy text to justify his conduct would have to show that his actions also satisfy an independent moral standard, as Bayle and Mill had suggested. Just as a statute might serve purposes that are not morally acceptable, such as giving an unfair advantage to a particular religious or racial group at the expense of others, so too a doctrine in a holy text might be intended to serve an unjust religious cause. Bayle's and Mill's point will only be applicable if it is also claimed that the author of the doctrine in the holy text is a good and just God, worthy of our worship. But a religious fanatic, who invokes the literal interpretation of a holy text to justify his killing or persecution of unbelievers, might be caught in the double whammy that his proposed conduct could not possibly be authorized by a just God *and* that even if his God is not wholly just, the circumstances in which he would direct or allow such acts are much more limited.

---

3. In Ten (2007) I discuss Fuller's views in the broader context of an account of the rule of law.

CHRIST AND CHRISTIAN MORALITY

Although Mill was very firm in his view that the ultimate principles of morality must be the test of God's attributes and activities, he nonetheless held Christ up as an exemplar of moral excellence. This surprised and drew fire from some unbelievers, who in other respects admired Mill. Thus George Foote attacks what he describes as "Mill's panegyric on Christ" (Sell 1997: 224). Foote compares Christ unfavourably with "the long and glorious life of Buddha" and "the mighty genius of Muhammed" (*ibid.*: 230). Christ's teaching is not new, nor particularly helpful. Confucius had taught the golden rule long before Christ, and "without any of the absurdities" with which Christ surrounded it. Unlike Christ, Confucius did not enjoin us to love our enemies: "'No' he said, 'if I love my enemies, what should I give to my friends? To my friends I give my love, and to my enemies – justice!'" (*ibid.*: 234).

Foote also points out that elsewhere, in his essay *On Liberty*, Mill himself had "shown the evil of taking Christ, or any other man, as 'the ideal representative and guide of humanity'" (*ibid.*: 227). This is not quite correct. In *On Liberty*, Mill refers to Christ's "moral grandeur" (*CW* 18.235). There his focus is on freedom of discussion, and on the importance of allowing even beliefs widely regarded as true, such as the doctrines of Christianity, to be disputed and challenged. He directs his criticisms at those Christians who pay lip service to these doctrines, but do not in fact treat Christianity as a "living belief" that regulates their conduct. He is concerned about the limitations and incompleteness of what he calls "Christian morality", rather than the character and personality of Christ himself. Thus he explains what he means by "Christian morality":

> What is called Christian, but should rather be termed theological, morality was not the work of Christ, or the Apostles, but is of much later origin, having being gradually built up by the Catholic church of the first five centuries, and though not implicitly adopted by moderns and Protestants, has been much less modified by them than might have been expected. (*CW* 18.255)

Mill explains the respects in which Christian morality is incomplete and one-sided. It is "negative rather than positive, passive rather than active". There is "its horror of sensuality", its encouragement of "an essentially selfish character" in human morality by disconnecting our sense of duty from the interests of our fellow creatures, its inculcation of submission to all established authority, and its failure to give recognition to the idea of obligation to the public (*ibid.*). Unless Christian morality is supplemented by some secular standards, "there will result, and is even now resulting, in a low, abject, servile type of character, which, submit itself as it may to what it deems the Supreme Will, is incapable of rising to or sympathizing in the conception of Supreme Goodness" (*CW* 18.256). Christian morality alone cannot therefore lead to "the moral regeneration of mankind" (*CW* 18.257).

In his *Autobiography*, Mill claims that he is one of the very few people in the country who has "not thrown off religious belief, but never had it" (*CW* 1.45). In *On Liberty*, he concludes his discussion of the limitations of Christian morality by pointing out that "a large portion of the noblest and most valuable moral teaching has been the work, not only of men who did not know, but of men who knew and rejected, the Christian faith" (*CW* 18.25). No doubt one of the men Mill had in mind who rejected Christianity was his father James Mill. James Mill had a short career in the Scottish Presbyterian ministry, which he abandoned before the birth of his first child, John Stuart Mill, in 1806.

THE RELIGION OF HUMANITY

When Mill adopted some sort of religious belief, it was not belief in what he calls a "supernatural religion". Rather, he adopted the Comtian secular Religion of Humanity, although, as we shall see, he strongly rejected some aspects of Auguste Comte's version of it. For Mill, the necessary conditions of a religion are: "There must be a creed, or conviction, claiming authority over the whole of human life; a belief, or set of beliefs, deliberately adopted, respecting human destiny and duty, to which the believer inwardly acknowledges that his actions ought to be subordinate" (*CW* 10.332). Although the Religion of Humanity is a religion without a God, it qualifies as a religion. Indeed, in "Utility of Religion", Mill argues that the Religion of Humanity fulfils the "essence of religion" better than even the best manifestations of supernatural religion. That essence is "the strong and earnest direction of the emotions and desires towards an ideal object, recognized as the highest excellence, and as rightly paramount over all selfish objects of desire." In the case of the Religion of Humanity, that object is "the Human Race, conceived as a continuous whole, including the past, the present, and the future" (*CW* 10.333).

This point is also made in *Utilitarianism*, in which Mill argues for a form of utilitarianism as the ultimate basis for morality. But utilitarianism requires that a person be "as strictly impartial as a disinterested and benevolent spectator" between his own happiness and that of others. The power of education and public opinion should be used to establish in each person "an indissoluble association between his own happiness and the good of the whole" (*CW* 10.218). Comte had shown "the possibility of giving to the service of humanity, even without the end of belief in Providence, both the psychical power and the social efficacy of a religion" (*CW* 10.232).

But even while applauding Comte, Mill was fearful that Comte's "system of politics and morals" would exert such great pressure on individuals as "to interfere unduly with freedom and individuality" (*CW* 10.232). This apprehension is directed to the hierarchical organization and institutional structure that Comte had proposed for his Religion of Humanity. Mill's hostility to this aspect of Comte's thinking was very deep, and it was expressed not just in his published works, but also in a letter to Harriet Taylor, dated 15 January 1855, in which he confides, "opinion tends to encroach more and more on liberty, and almost all projects of social reformers of these days are really *liberticide* – Comte, particularly so" (*CW* 14.294). When the essay *On Liberty* was published in 1859, Mill accuses "modern reformers" of being no different from "churches and sects" in asserting "the right of spiritual domination", even though they were strongly opposed to past religions:

> M. Comte, in particular, whose social system, as unfolded in his *Systeme de Politique Positive*, aims at establishing (though by moral more than by legal appliances) a despotism of society over the individual, surpassing anything contemplated in the political ideal of the most rigid disciplinarian among the ancient philosophers.
>
> (*CW* 18.227)

Against all the evidence of Mill's fundamental commitment to individual liberty, there are still commentators who maintain that he regarded liberty as something of merely instrumental value. Thus Joseph Hamburger (1999) has argued that Mill wanted to promote the Religion of Humanity and to undermine Christianity, and that he regarded liberty as a means towards these ends.[4] Hamburger is wrong not only about the nature of Mill's commitment to liberty and the extent of his endorsement of the Comtian Religion of Humanity, but also about his destructive hostility towards Christianity. Mill did not wholly reject Christian doctrines. He thought, as we have seen, that their virtues were limited, and required supplementation from other sources. His continued respect for Christ as a moral exemplar was repeated in *Utilitarianism*: "In the golden rule of Jesus of Nazareth, we read the complete spirit of the ethics of utility" (*CW* 10.218).

CONCLUSION

The atheist Hume went to his grave calmly, with his views about the non-existence of an afterlife intact. He earned the admiration of his friend Adam Smith, who remarked: "Poor David Hume is dying very fast, but with great cheerfulness and good humour and with more real resignation to the necessary course of things, than any whining Christian ever dyed with pretended resignation to the will of God" (Mossner 1980: 606). The agnostic Mill also died calmly, remarking to Helen Taylor before he died, "You know that I have done my work" (Packe 1954: 507). Like Hume, he did not believe in the afterlife. But unlike Hume, he did not rule out the hope of such a life. For this, he was condemned by the unbeliever Foote

---

4. For a critical discussion of Hamburger's view, see Ten (2002).

as "sentimental and superstitious". Foote blamed this "perversion" of Mill's judgement on his love for Harriet Taylor. "He buried her at Avignon, and resided near her grave until he could lie beside her in the eternal sleep. No doubt the long vigil at his wife's tomb shows the depth of his love, but it necessarily tended to make his brain the victim of his heart" (Sell 1997: 220). Foote contrasted Mill's indulgence in the hope of immortality with his earlier view that found comfort in annihilation. But Mill himself probably saw no inconsistency in his views. Part of the work he saw himself as doing was to show the many-sidedness of various issues with which he engaged throughout his life. Perhaps here, as elsewhere, he could rightly claim to have done his work when he was attacked both by some Christians and by some anti-Christians alike.

FURTHER READING

Capaldi, N. 2004. *John Stuart Mill: A Biography*. Cambridge: Cambridge University Press.
Millar, A. 1998. "Mill on Religion". In *The Cambridge Companion to Mill*, J. Skorupski (ed.), 176–202. Cambridge: Cambridge University Press.
Ryan, A. 1974. *J. S. Mill*. London: Routledge & Kegan Paul.
Ten, C. 2002. "Hume's Racism and Miracles". *Journal of Value Inquiry* **36**: 101–7.

On INTELLIGENT DESIGN see also Ch. 12; Vol. 1, Chs 4, 8; Vol. 3, Ch. 23. On RELIGION OF HUMANITY see also Ch. 7. On REVELATION see also Ch. 5; Vol. 1, Ch. 14; Vol. 2, Ch. 11; Vol. 3, Chs 7, 11, 16; Vol. 5, Chs 8, 23. On SCEPTICISM see also Vol. 1, Ch. 12; Vol. 3 , Ch. 5. On SCIENCE see also Chs 7, 12, 15, 17, 19; Vol. 2, Ch. 12; Vol. 3, Ch. 17; Vol. 5, Chs 4, 19. On UTILITARIANISM see also Vol. 3, Ch. 23.

12

CHARLES DARWIN

Michael Ruse

Charles Robert Darwin (1809–82) is rightly known as the father of evolutionary theory. In his great book *On the Origin of Species* (hereafter *Origin*), published in 1859, he made the idea of evolution – gradual descent by law-like means from primitive beginnings – virtually commonsensical. At the same time, he offered a mechanism, natural selection, that is today recognized as the chief force driving evolution. But his work was much more than purely scientific. It had implications throughout Western culture, most especially in religion. Let us start with a brief sketch of Darwin's ideas and then turn to religious questions: revealed religion, natural religion, and humankind.

Darwin himself described the *Origin* as "one long argument", but truly it falls into three parts (Ruse 2008). First, Darwin talked about the success of animal and plant breeders, and showed how they achieve their ends by choosing or selecting and then breeding from the forms that have the features they desire. Then, secondly, Darwin argued that there is an analogous process in the natural world. This comes about because (as the Reverend Robert Malthus had pointed out at the beginning of the nineteenth century) there is a constant pressure brought on by the greater capacity of organisms to reproduce over their abilities to find food and space. Darwin wrote:

> A struggle for existence inevitably follows from the high rate at which all organic beings tend to increase. Every being, which during its natural lifetime produces several eggs or seeds, must suffer destruction during some period of its life, and during some season or occasional year, otherwise, on the principle of geometrical increase, its numbers would quickly become so inordinately great that no country could support the product. Hence, as more individuals are produced than can possibly survive, there must in every case be a struggle for existence, either one individual with another of the same species, or with the individuals of distinct species, or with the physical conditions

of life. It is the doctrine of Malthus applied with manifold force to the whole animal and vegetable kingdoms; for in this case there can be no artificial increase of food, and no prudential restraint from marriage. Although some species may be now increasing, more or less rapidly, in numbers, all cannot do so, for the world would not hold them.

(1859: 63–4)

Then, from this, Darwin went on to show that a natural form of selection will follow:

Let it be borne in mind in what an endless number of strange peculiarities our domestic productions, and, in a lesser degree, those under nature, vary; and how strong the hereditary tendency is. Under domestication, it may be truly said that the whole organisation becomes in some degree plastic. Let it be borne in mind how infinitely complex and close-fitting are the mutual relations of all organic beings to each other and to their physical conditions of life. Can it, then, be thought improbable, seeing that variations useful to man have undoubtedly occurred, that other variations useful in some way to each being in the great and complex battle of life, should sometimes occur in the course of thousands of generations? If such do occur, can we doubt (remembering that many more individuals are born than can possibly survive) that individuals having any advantage, however slight, over others, would have the best chance of surviving and of procreating their kind? On the other hand, we may feel sure that any variation in the least degree injurious would be rigidly destroyed. This preservation of favourable variations and the rejection of injurious variations, I call Natural Selection. (*Ibid.*: 80–81)

It was Darwin's claim that, given enough time, natural selection would lead to permanent change: evolution (what he normally called 'descent with modification'). In later editions of the *Origin*, Darwin introduced the alternative name 'survival of the fittest' for natural selection. He also always endorsed a secondary kind of selection, what he called 'sexual selection'. This came from a struggle within a species for mates, rather than a struggle with members of other species or with the environment. It gives rise to things such as the antlers of deer and the tail feathers of the peacock. Clearly, it too was based on Darwin's reading of the world of breeders, where much selection is for things such as pretty birds and fierce dogs.

The third part of the *Origin* is where Darwin sets out to convince the reader that the world of life really did evolve. He applied evolution through selection to the problems of the different areas of biology: instinct, paleontology, biogeography, systematics, morphology, embryology. On the one hand, therefore, he can solve problems. On the other hand, he gains support for his hypotheses. Typical is his discussion of a major feature of the distribution of organisms around the globe. The inhabitants of offshore islands are always like the inhabitants of the nearest mainland and never like the inhabitants of continents far away:

> [I]t is obvious that the Galapagos Islands would be likely to receive colonists, whether by occasional means of transport or by formerly continuous land, from America; and the Cape de Verde Islands from Africa; and that such colonists would be liable to modifications; the principle of inheritance still betraying their original birthplace.
>
> (*Ibid.*: 397–8)

Likewise in an area such as morphology. Why are the forelimbs of so many mammals, forelimbs that have such different functions, nevertheless similar in structure?

> If we suppose that the ancient progenitor, the archetype as it may be called, of all mammals, had its limbs constructed on the existing general pattern, for whatever purpose they served, we can at once perceive the plain signification of the homologous construction of the limbs throughout the whole class.   (*Ibid.*: 435)

Darwin always intended his theory to apply to our species, *Homo sapiens*. In the *Origin*, wanting as it were to get his basic ideas out on the table, he made but the briefest reference to human beings: "Light will be thrown on the origin of man and his history" (*ibid.*: 488). But no one was deceived by the brevity of this comment, and much of the subsequent discussion of the 'monkey theory', as it was known, centred on human origins. Finally, in 1871, Darwin himself entered the fray with *The Descent of Man* (hereafter *Descent*), where he made it clear that he thought we have natural origins, specifically from primates (although not from species still extant today), and that natural selection supplemented by sexual selection was the driving force in human evolution. And this is a good place to jump off into religion.

REVEALED RELIGION

As we turn to discuss Darwin and religion, two preliminary points will help our understanding. First, what of Darwin himself and his religious beliefs? He was brought up in the Church of England (Anglican, or what Americans call Episcopalian) and intended for a while to be a clergyman (Browne 1995). In his early twenties, this was sidelined when he spent five years aboard HMS *Beagle*, mainly in and around South America, functioning as the ship's naturalist. During

the voyage Darwin's beliefs moved from Christian theism – seeing God as inter-
vener and Jesus as divine – to a form of deism – seeing God as an unmoved mover
who does not get directly involved in the universe. Darwin's mother's family (her
father was Josiah Wedgwood, the potter) were Unitarians, deists, as were others
of his acquaintance, so this was no great step for him to take, especially after his
marriage in 1839 to his first cousin, Emma Wedgwood.

This lasted right through the writing of the *Origin*. Often in that work Darwin
makes reference to the creator. There is no reason to think he is being insincere. But by the time he wrote the *Descent*, he had become a non-believer: never
an atheist, but what his friend and supporter Thomas Henry Huxley called an
'agnostic'. This was a common position for late Victorian intellectuals. In Darwin's
case, it is clear that he hated much religious doctrine, especially that about eternal
punishment for non-believers. But Darwin was ever an English gentleman
and would never make a strong public case for non-belief. After his death, the
Church had no trouble embracing him and interring him in that English Valhalla,
Westminster Abbey.

Secondly, it must be recognized that Darwin was first, middle and last a scientist. Everything else was extraneous. As he came to scientific maturity in the 1830s,
under the tutelage of such deeply Christian men of science as John Henslow and
William Whewell, then respectively professors of botany and mineralogy (later of
philosophy) at the University of Cambridge, he learnt that science is science and
religion is religion. It is absolutely forbidden to bring religion – miracles especially
– into one's science. Even if one believes in miracles, this can never be a scientific
claim (Ruse 1979). Hence if Darwin, as he did, treats human beings in a purely
naturalistic way, this does not in itself imply that he thought that human beings
are purely material objects governed by unbroken natural law or, rather, even if he
himself thought they are purely natural beings, that others must necessarily think
the same.

This second point plays directly into the way that Darwin treated revealed religion – the religion of faith and revelation (especially the Bible) – in his writings.
By the time he wrote the *Origin*, he no longer believed in the miracles of Jesus
and certainly not in the resurrection. But whether he did or not, he would have
thought it totally inappropriate to bring such incidents into his science. Things
like that would have to be accepted on faith, and no amount of science for or
against would be at all relevant. To use the language of theology, Darwin would
have believed in the order of grace and the order of nature, and kept the two apart.
(Although by the time of writing the *Origin*, as a personal matter, he was no longer
accepting of the order of grace.)

Of course, if you accept the theory of the *Origin*, you can no longer accept the
literal truth of the creation story of Genesis. For Darwin and indeed for most
people, including most religious people (American Protestants of the South being
a major exception), this was no longer a major issue. From the beginning of the
nineteenth century, it had become increasingly apparent that there was no way

that one could reconcile the findings of modern geology with a limited earth history or with the traditional six days of creation (Ruse 2005). The flood also had to be interpreted in a revised or metaphorical fashion. Some – for instance, Adam Sedgwick, professor of geology at Cambridge – wanted to preserve some aspects of the Genesis story, for instance, those dealing with original sin. But, again, Darwin would have thought that as a scientist this was no business of his. It was not even something at the back of his mind as he wrote the *Origin*.

Obviously, those of us who look back at Darwin and the *Origin* from today might argue that the *Origin* was part of a general naturalizing trend in Western thinking (again, parts of America today being the obvious exception) that simply made religious belief less plausible and compelling. Or, if one wants to retain some kind of religious belief, one might argue that the *Origin* was part of a general naturalizing trend that called for a deep re-evaluation of such belief – perhaps a turn to a more metaphorical understanding of things, allied perhaps with a conviction that faith unsupported by evidence and reason is the only true way to God. So, one certainly should not underestimate the significance of the *Origin* with respect to revealed religion. But one should not overestimate its significance either, quite apart from the fact that science was only one factor in the ways that religion has had to change. Higher criticism, the turn to treating the Bible as a humanly written book, is at least as important, if not more so.

NATURAL RELIGION

Today's best-known atheist, the Oxford biologist and popular-science writer Richard Dawkins (1986), has said that only after Darwin was it possible to be an intellectually fulfilled atheist. There is truth in this, although whether there is as much truth as Dawkins would extract is another matter. The big issue is the question of design. One of the major arguments for the existence of God is the argument from design or (as it is sometimes known) 'the teleological argument' (Ruse 2003). It dates back to Plato in the *Phaedo*, where Socrates uses it to explain why he does not fear death (*see* Vol. 1, Ch. 4). It was then taken up by the great Christian theologians, especially Thomas Aquinas (*see* Vol. 2, Ch. 13). After the Reformation, it had a major role to play in England, theologically and socially. Natural theology was the route that the Anglican Church took between the tradition of Catholicism and the exclusively biblically based religion of the Puritans. Design also became a major factor in the biology of the day: people like the clergyman-naturalist John Ray, at the end of the seventeenth century, used the search for design to guide their studies of the living world. David Hume, of course, attacked the argument in his posthumously published *Dialogues Concerning Natural Religion* (1779), but even he at the end (confirming Dawkins) admitted that it really did not seem as though the living world came by chance, by blind law (*see* Vol. 3, Ch. 19). And shortly after that, Archdeacon William Paley reinforced the significance and plausibility of the argument from design in his *Natural Theology* (1802) (*see* Vol. 3, Ch. 23).

Darwin grew up with this background of natural theology, and in the 1830s this was reinforced by the publication of the *Bridgewater Treatises*, eight works that were devoted to the design argument. He always accepted the main premise of the design argument, namely, that the living world seems as if it has been designed, and right through and beyond the *Origin*, although he denied that God had designed and created miraculously, he thought that there was a designer. To his friend the Harvard-based botanist (and keen Christian) Asa Gray, Darwin wrote:

> I see no necessity in the belief that the eye was expressly designed. On the other hand I cannot anyhow be contented to view this wonderful universe & especially the nature of man, & to conclude that every-thing is the result of brute force. I am inclined to look at everything as resulting from designed laws, with the details, whether good or bad, left to the working out of what we may call chance.
>
> (Letter to Asa Gray, 22 May 1860)

Even this faded in the next decade, but the conviction that the organic world seems as if designed never did.

The important thing is that, in line with his methodology, Darwin, no matter what he believed, could never have allowed the designer to get into his science. He fought with Gray over this, for the botanist wanted a God-designed direction to the raw building blocks of evolution, the variations or what we today would call the 'mutations'. Similarly, Darwin dismissed the Duke of Argyll, amateur naturalist and well-known politician, when the latter tried his hand at mixing science and religion: "Creation by Law – Evolution by Law – Development by Law, or, as including all those kindred ideas, the Reign of Law, is nothing but the reign of Creative Force directed by Creative Knowledge, worked under the control of Creative Power, and in fulfillment of Creative Purpose" (Argyll 1867, quoted in Ruse 2005: 293–4).

How, then, did Darwin explain the design-like aspect of organisms? This was the role of natural selection. It leads not simply to change, but to change of a particular kind. It promotes features that help organisms to survive and reproduce, features such as the hand, the eye, teeth, and the nose. But these features, adaptations or (as Darwin sometimes called them) contrivances, are the very features at the centre of the design argument! It is because organisms have these features, because organisms are adapted, that we do not think them purely random, but design-like. It was Darwin's genius to show how you can get design-like features without a designer: to show how design-like features follow from natural (and sexual) selection. Often, the adaptations of the organism were likened to the machines of human beings, or to being watch-like, to borrow a famous analogy from Paley. It is for this reason that Dawkins (1986) says that Darwin led us into a world of the 'blind watchmaker'. You do not have to assume that there is a watchmaker when confronted by organic adaptation. It is possible not to believe.

But is it necessary not to believe? Darwin made it possible not to be a Christian, but did he make it obligatory to be an agnostic or an atheist? Dawkins seems to think so, but here he slips in another argument: the argument from evil. If evil exists, particularly natural evil, then how can there be an all-loving, all-powerful God? Dawkins plays on another part of the already-quoted letter from Darwin to Asa Gray:

> With respect to the theological view of the question; this is always painful to me. – I am bewildered. – I had no intention to write atheistically. But I own that I cannot see, as plainly as others do, & as I shd. wish to do, evidence of design & beneficence on all sides of us. There seems to me too much misery in the world. I cannot persuade myself that a beneficent & omnipotent God would have designedly created the Ichneumonidae with the express intention of their feeding within the living bodies of caterpillars, or that a cat should play with mice. Not believing this, I see no necessity in the belief that the eye was expressly designed.   (Letter to Asa Gray, 22 May 1860)

To this, Dawkins adds his own gloss:

> If Nature were kind, she would at least make the minor concession of anesthetizing caterpillars before they are eaten alive from within. But Nature is neither kind nor unkind. She is neither against suffering nor for it. Nature is not interested one way or the other in suffering, unless it affects the survival of DNA ... The total amount of suffering per year in the natural world is beyond all decent contemplation.   (1995: 131)

He concludes:

> As that unhappy poet A.E. Houseman put it:
>
> > For Nature, heartless, witless Nature
> > Will neither know nor care.
>
> DNA neither knows nor cares. DNA just is. And we dance to its music.   (*Ibid.*: 133)

Theologians and philosophers have standard arguments against this kind of conclusion. Most popular is that of Gottfried Wilhelm Leibniz who argued that God's power, his omnipotence, never implied that he could do the impossible (*see* Vol. 3, Ch. 13). He cannot make two and two equal five, and if he has decided to create through law – and there may be good theological reasons for this – then some bad things are bound to happen. Burning one's flesh is painful, but better this than being unaware of the effects of flame and then perishing. Paradoxically and amusingly, Dawkins (1983) himself supports this line of argument. He argues that the only way in which blind law could create design-like features – what he calls 'organized complexity' – is through natural selection. So perhaps the ill effects of selection were bound to happen.

Whatever the conclusion one wants to draw here – whether it be continued faith, agnosticism or atheism – things have changed. The argument from design no longer compels as it did. Some theologians welcome this. In 1870 (twenty-five years after he converted to Catholicism), the great John Henry Newman wrote about one of his works:

> I have not insisted on the argument from *design*, because I am writing for the 19th century, by which, as represented by its philosophers, design is not admitted as proved. And to tell the truth, though I should not wish to preach on the subject, for 40 years I have been unable to see the logical force of the argument myself. I believe in design because I believe in God; not in a God because I see design.
>
> (Newman 1973: 97)

He continued: "Design teaches me power, skill and goodness – not sanctity, not mercy, not a future judgment, which three are of the essence of religion" (*ibid.*). Newman was simply not in the business of using science to support his religion and many today would agree with him. Faith points to design, not design to faith. The German theologian Wolfhart Pannenberg (1993) speaks of the need for a "theology of nature", not a "natural theology".

HUMAN BEINGS

The big question is not so much whether human beings evolved – everyone who takes on evolution realizes that you cannot hold back when it comes to our species – but what precisely this means in the light of religion, particularly the Abrahamic religions of Judaism, Christianity and Islam. One issue is that of the soul: that which most variations on these religions think survives the body at death. Truly, there is nothing in Darwinism that speaks for or against this, and generally religious people have recognized this. The late Pope John Paul II (1998), stood at the end of a long tradition when he said that although he accepted evolution, natural selection even, he thought that souls were put into human beings miraculously by divine power. I doubt that Darwin thought this so, but he had nothing to say on the subject.

A point where there is more possibility of interaction and tension is that regarding the status of human beings judged against other animals (and plants).

Leaving aside the question of extraterrestrials, for the religious person human beings here on earth cannot simply be another organism like the rest. We are made in the image and likeness of God. Whatever that means, we are special: at the least we are going to be superior in intelligence and have a moral sense. And surely for the believer we cannot be accidental. We had to have occurred. Perhaps it would not matter if we had green skin and six fingers, but the arrival here on earth of something like human beings was a necessity.

This seems to mean that some form of progress is being presupposed. There has to be an upward rise in the line of evolution, and we human beings have to have won. We are further up the greasy pole than other species. But many think that evolution – Darwinian evolution particularly – cannot be progressive. It is relativistic. What survives is what survives. If one has predators and lives in dark surroundings, then having dark colouring is a good thing; if one lives in light surroundings, then being light is a good thing. Stephen Jay Gould was a strong critic of the notion of progress, speaking of it as "a noxious, culturally embedded, untestable, non-operational, intractable idea that must be replaced if we wish to understand the patterns of history" (Gould 1988). Making reference to the asteroid that hit the earth some 65 million years ago and killed the dinosaurs, Gould wrote:

> Since dinosaurs were not moving toward markedly larger brains, and since such a prospect may lie outside the capabilities of reptilian design …, we must assume that consciousness would not have evolved on our planet if a cosmic catastrophe had not claimed the dinosaurs as victims. In an entirely literal sense, we owe our existence, as large and reasoning mammals, to our lucky stars. (1989: 318)

Darwin disagreed. Although he was strongly against the idea that there is a necessary, upwards progression because of some kind of mystical force, he thought that progress did occur and that human beings are at the top of the tree of life. In *Descent* he wrote:

> In the class of mammals the steps are not difficult to conceive which led from the ancient Monotremata to the ancient marsupials; and from these to the early progenitors of the placental mammals. We may thus ascend to the Lemuridae; and the interval is not very wide from these to the Simiadae. The Simiadae then branched off into two great stems, the New World and Old World monkeys; and from the latter, at a remote period, Man, the wonder and glory of the Universe, proceeded. (1871: vol. 1, 213)

At times, particularly in some of his early notebooks, Darwin rather implied that progress comes as a result of the forces of nature always trying out new possibilities:

The enormous number of animals in the world depends, of their varied structure & complexity. – hence as the forms became complicated, they opened fresh, means of adding to their complexity. – but yet there is no <NECESSARY> tendency in the simple animals to become complicated although all perhaps will have done so from the new relations caused by the advancing complexity of others.

(January 1939, in Barrett *et al.* 1987: E95)[1]

Interestingly, Gould would probably have agreed to this. Although he was anti-progress, he thought that even if human beings had not appeared here on earth, something like them would appear somewhere in the universe. Moreover, the process driving the rise to human beings was a kind of random walk. A drunken man on a pavement cannot go through the wall but will eventually end up in the gutter, even though he does not intend to.

Darwin, however, also endorsed a selection-driven process leading to progress. He thought that there are what today's evolutionists call 'arms races', where one line competes against another and overall improvement occurs: the prey gets faster, so the predator gets faster. This kind of comparative improvement leads (in his opinion) to some form of absolute improvement, particularly in as much as it promotes brain power. "The inhabitants of each successive period of the world's history have beaten their predecessors in the race for life, and are, in so far, higher in the scale of nature; and this may account for that vague yet ill-defined sentiment, felt by many palæontologists, that organisation on the whole has progressed" (Darwin 1859: 345). Can this account for intelligence? It seems that it can:

If we take as the standard of high organization, the amount of differentiation and specialization of the several organs in each being when adult (and this will include the advancement of the brain for intellectual purposes), natural selection clearly leads towards this standard: for all physiologists admit that the specialization of organs, inasmuch as in this state they perform their functions better, is an advantage to each being; and hence the accumulation of variations tending towards specialization is within the scope of natural selection.

(Darwin 1959: 222)[2]

I should say that although not everyone today is convinced by this kind of argumentation, there is considerable support by professional biologists for something along these lines. America's leading evolutionist, Edward O. Wilson, writes:

---

1. Darwin inserted the 'NECESSARY' at a later time.
2. This passage was added in the third edition of *On the Origin of Species* (1861).

[T]he overall average across the history of life has moved from the simple and few to the more complex and numerous. During the past billion years, animals as a whole evolved upward in body size, feeding and defensive techniques, brain and behavioral complexity, social organization, and precision of environmental control – in each case farther from the nonliving state than their simpler antecedents did.

(1992: 187)

He adds: "Progress, then, is a property of the evolution of life as a whole by almost any conceivable intuitive standard, including the acquisition of goals and intentions in the behavior of animals" (*ibid.*).

We may be intelligent animals, but are we moral animals? Christians think that we are fallen, tainted with original sin. But we are able to fall only because of our moral nature. Beasts are not moral and cannot fall (or rise). Many think that Darwin's ideas lead to the end of morality. Social Darwinism, so-called, is usually a doctrine of bloody *laissez faire*, of the weakest to the wall, and too bad for those who lose. "Might gives the right to occupy or to conquer. Might is at once the supreme right, and the dispute as to what is right is decided by the arbitrament of war. War gives a biologically just decision, since its decision rests on the very nature of things" (Bernhardi 1912: 10).

This is not Darwin's philosophy at all. In the *Descent*, he gave a detailed and careful analysis of morality, thought it genuine and tried to show how it emerges because of selective pressures. He even went so far as to quote and endorse a purple-prose passage from the sage of Königsberg, Immanuel Kant:

Duty! Wondrous thought, that workest neither by fond insinuation, flattery, nor by any threat, but merely by holding up thy naked law in the soul, and so extorting for thyself always reverence, if not always obedience; before whom all appetites are dumb, however secretly they rebel; whence thy original? (Darwin 1871: vol. 1, 70)

Generally, however, Darwin was more in line with the utilitarianism of British empiricism. "The term, general good, may be defined as the term by which the greatest possible number of individuals can be reared in full vigour and health, with all their faculties perfect, under the conditions to which they are exposed" (*ibid.*: vol. 1, 98).

How does morality evolve, since it seems to involve sacrifice of the individual for the group? Sometimes Darwin seemed to think that it involved what evolutionists today call 'reciprocal altruism': you scratch my back and I'll scratch yours.

In the first place, as the reasoning powers and foresight of the members became improved, each man would soon learn that if he aided his fellow-men, he would commonly receive aid in return. From this low motive he might acquire the habit of aiding his fellows; and the habit of performing benevolent actions certainly strengthens the feeling of sympathy which gives the first impulse to benevolent actions. Habits, moreover, followed during many generations probably tend to be inherited. (*Ibid.*: vol. 1, 163–4)

But Darwin also inclined here to what today's evolutionists call 'group selection', where selection can promote features for the general good, even though the individual suffers.

But there is another and much more powerful stimulus to the development of the social virtues, namely, the praise and the blame of our fellow-men. The love of approbation and the dread of infamy, as well as the bestowal of praise and of blame, are primarily due ... to the instinct of sympathy; and this instinct no doubt was originally acquired, like all the other social instincts, through natural selection.

(*Ibid.*: vol. 1, 164)

It seems that this sympathy, something which is for the good of the group, can be promoted by selection because it is so important:

To do good unto others – to do unto others as ye would they should do unto you, – is the foundation-stone of morality. It is, therefore, hardly possible to exaggerate the importance during rude times of the love of praise and the dread of blame. A man who was not impelled by any deep, instinctive feeling, to sacrifice his life for the good of others, yet was roused to such actions by a sense of glory, would by his example excite the same wish for glory in other men, and would strengthen by exercise the noble feeling of admiration. He might thus do far more good to his tribe than by begetting offspring with a tendency to inherit his own high character. (*Ibid.*: vol. 1, 165)

Group selection is controversial in contemporary evolutionary circles (Ruse 2006). Some, philosopher Elliott Sober and biologist David Sloan Wilson (1997) for example, endorse it strongly. Others, Dawkins (1976) for example, are not at all keen on it. The point is that all would agree with Darwin that selection somehow makes for morality.

Does this then mean that morality is bogus, simply an adaptation put in place by natural selection, with no further meaning? People like E. O. Wilson seem to think that this is so. Speaking of the sub-branch of Darwinian theory that deals with human thought and behaviour, so-called 'sociobiology', Wilson believes that its power to explain things like morality and other aspects of religion spells the end of traditional thought. All is now to be subsumed to biology.

Most importantly, we have come to the crucial stage in the history of biology when religion itself is subject to the explanations of the natural sciences. As I have tried to show, sociobiology can account for the very origin of mythology by the principle of natural selection acting on the genetically evolving material structure of the human brain.

> If this interpretation is correct, the final decisive edge enjoyed by scientific naturalism will come from its capacity to explain traditional religion, its chief competition, as a wholly material phenomenon. Theology is not likely to survive as an independent intellectual discipline. (Wilson 1978: 192)

This does not follow at all (Ruse 2001). Because evolution might give a causal explanation, it does not imply that the thing being explained is necessarily chimerical. I can give an evolutionary explanation of why I can see a truck bearing down on me, but it does not follow that the truck does not exist. The very opposite is true, in fact. Similarly with morality and religion generally. It may indeed be the case that morality is a sham and that religion is false, but that needs to be proved independently, and then of course explanations are needed as to why we believe in things that are shams and are false. As it happens, for religion generally Darwin himself makes a stab in that direction, suggesting that it might be an illusion caused by purely animal instincts:

> The tendency in savages to imagine that natural objects and agencies are animated by spiritual or living essences, is perhaps illustrated by a little fact which I once noticed: my dog, a full-grown and very sensible animal, was lying on the lawn during a hot and still day; but at a little distance a slight breeze occasionally moved an open parasol, which would have been wholly disregarded by the dog, had any one stood near it. As it was, every time that the parasol slightly moved, the dog growled fiercely and barked. He must, I think, have reasoned to himself in a rapid and unconscious manner, that movement without any apparent cause indicated the presence of some strange living agent, and that no stranger had a right to be on his territory. (1871: vol. 1, 67)

But Darwin is quick to point out that this is not a logical disproof of religion, but simply a naturalistic explanation, which is all that he as a scientist can give. If religion is an illusion, then this might explain why we have it nevertheless. And if, after all, religion is not an illusion, there must still be a naturalistic explanation for its existence, and why not this one?

I stress again that Darwin was a scientist. He was not a theologian or a philosopher. But I trust I have now shown why his presence is so important in such a volume as this.

FURTHER READING

Browne, J. 1995. *Charles Darwin: Voyaging, Volume 1*. New York: Knopf.

Darwin, C. 1959. *The Origin of Species by Charles Darwin: A Variorum Text*, M. Peckham (ed.). Philadelphia, PA: University of Pennsylvania Press.

Dawkins, R. 1983. "Universal Darwinism". In *Evolution from Molecules to Men*, D. Bendall (ed.), 403–25. Cambridge: Cambridge University Press.

Gould, S. 1989. *Wonderful Life: The Burgess Shale and the Nature of History*. New York: W. W. Norton.

John Paul II 1997. "The Pope's Message on Evolution". *Quarterly Review of Biology* **72**: 377–83.

Ruse, M. 1999. *The Darwinian Revolution: Science Red in Tooth and Claw*, 2nd edn. Chicago, IL: University of Chicago Press.

Ruse, M. 2001. *Can a Darwinian be a Christian? The Relationship between Science and Religion*. Cambridge: Cambridge University Press.

Ruse, M. 2003. *Darwin and Design: Does Evolution Have a Purpose?* Cambridge, MA: Harvard University Press.

Ruse, M. 2005. *The Evolution–Creation Struggle*. Cambridge, MA: Harvard University Press.

Ruse, M. 2006. *Darwinism and Its Discontents*. Cambridge: Cambridge University Press.

Ruse, M. 2008. *Charles Darwin*. Oxford: Blackwell.

Sober, E. & D. Wilson 1997. *Unto Others: The Evolution of Altruism*. Cambridge, MA: Harvard University Press.

Wilson, E. O. 1978. *On Human Nature*. Cambridge: Cambridge University Press.

On ARGUMENT FROM DESIGN see also Vol. 3, Ch. 23; Vol. 5, Ch. 17. On EVIL/PROBLEM OF EVIL see also Ch. 18; Vol. 1, Chs 18, 19; Vol. 2, Ch. 16; Vol. 3, Chs 13, 18, 19; Vol. 5, Chs 19, 22, 23. On INTELLIGENT DESIGN see also Ch. 11; Vol. 1, Chs 4, 8; Vol. 3, Ch. 23. On MORALITY see also Chs 4, 18; Vol. 2, Ch. 12; Vol. 3, Chs 2, 8, 12, 14, 21, 22; Vol. 5, Ch. 6. On NATURAL RELIGION/ THEOLOGY see also Ch. 8; Vol. 3, Chs 4, 6, 7, 11, 12, 13, 19, 23; Vol. 5, Ch. 23. On REVEALED RELIGION see also Vol. 3, Ch. 22; Vol. 5, Ch. 23. On SCIENCE see also Chs 7, 11, 15, 17, 19; Vol. 2, Ch. 12; Vol. 3, Ch. 17; Vol. 5, Chs 4, 19.

13

SØREN KIERKEGAARD

William McDonald

Søren Kierkegaard (1813–55) was born into the Danish Golden Age, the remarkable cultural flourishing that occurred in Denmark in the first half of the nineteenth century. Between about 1780 and 1850 Denmark's economy changed from feudal agrarian to predominantly mercantile and capitalist, with radical social consequences (Kirmmse 1990: 9–26). The population became largely urban; education transformed peasants into potential participants in democracy; newspapers and feuilleton literature burgeoned; artistic and scientific experimentation abounded; the fixed class structure of feudalism softened to enable greater social mobility; and the authority of religion was weakened under assaults from philosophical reason, bourgeois complacency, mass communication and new forms of aesthetic diversion (Pattison 2002: chs 1–4).

Kierkegaard was both a beneficiary of, and a reactionary against, these developments. His father, Michael Pedersen Kierkegaard, had been rescued from a life of poverty as a peasant boy on the Jutland heath by being apprenticed to his uncle, a merchant in Copenhagen. By virtue of a keen business sense and some judicious investments, Michael Kierkegaard became one of Denmark's wealthiest men (Garff 2005: 3–8). This wealth enabled Søren to be educated at a leading grammar school (the School of Civic Virtue), to read philosophy, theology and literature at Copenhagen University, and eventually to pursue his vocation as a religious author without the distraction of having to earn a living. However, in addition to a substantial sum of money and an astute intellect, his father bequeathed Søren a melancholic temperament and a heavy burden of guilt. Much of Søren Kierkegaard's philosophical psychology of religion is motivated by his personal quest to transfigure this pervasive melancholy and guilt into 'eternal bliss' through the cultivation of faith, hope and love. However, he also believed that "the very mark of my genius is that Governance broadens and radicalizes whatever concerns me personally", just as one of his pseudonyms wrote of Socrates: "His whole life was personal preoccupation with himself, and then Governance comes and adds world-historical significance to it" (*KW* 22: 189–90).[1]

In his childhood, Kierkegaard was exposed to weekly meetings of the Society of Moravian Brethren as well as to the sermons of J. P. Mynster, later Bishop Primate of the Danish People's Church (Garff 2005: 10–12). The former has its roots in *Herrnhut* pietism, the latter in liberal-rationalist Lutheranism, although Mynster himself was raised by a staunchly pietistic stepfather (Kirmmse 1990: 100). The Moravian Brethren emphasized the inward deepening of religious feeling, fostered anticlerical attitudes and attacked bourgeois comforts, while the state church catered primarily to the rising middle class and in the 1830s assimilated itself to the intellectual fashion of Hegelianism. Kierkegaard's *oeuvre* traces a distinct trajectory from positive engagement with Hegel's work and its early reception in Denmark by J. L. Heiberg, through an intermediate and ironic engagement with Hegel in his dissertation *The Concept of Irony: With Continual Reference to Socrates*, through a long-running satire on the work of the Hegelian theologian H. L. Martensen, accompanied by a turn against Heiberg (Stewart 2003: 596–610), to a complex parody of Hegel's *Encyclopedia of the Philosophical Sciences* (McDonald 1997), and then to a diagnosis of the case of the Hegelian pastor Adolph Adler as an unconscious satire on Hegel (*KW* 24: 131). Alongside this negative critique of Hegelianism, Kierkegaard retained a deep devotion to his Moravian roots, especially to the edifying hymns of H. A. Brorson, and the Moravian emphasis on inward deepening through contemplation of the tension between "the conviction of sin and the joy of salvation" (Burgess 2004: 236).

Kierkegaard remained publicly loyal to Mynster until the latter's death, when his successorMartensen pronounced Mynster "a witness to the truth". Kierkegaard's long-standing resentment toward Martensen, and his repressed criticisms of Mynster, then boiled to the surface in his scathing attack on the established Church. In a series of newspaper articles, and in his own broadsheet *The Moment*, Kierkegaard lambasted the Church as a degenerate institution of Christendom that had lost touch with what it really is to be a Christian. Kierkegaard's authorship, from *The Concept of Irony* to *Concluding Unscientific Postscript*, can be characterized above all as the concern to show how to become a Christian in Christendom (*KW* 22: 8).

'AUTHORSHIP' AND COMMUNICATION

In his retrospective self-interpretation, *The Point of View for My Work as an Author: A Direct Communication, Report to History*, Kierkegaard identifies as his

---

1. *Kierkegaard's Writings* (1978–2000) are abbreviated *KW*, and cited by volume and page numbers. *Søren Kierkegaards Papirer* (1968–78) are abbreviated Pap., and cited by volume and entry numbers.

'authorship': a 'first division' of (largely aesthetic) pseudonymous writings from *Either/Or* to *Concluding Unscientific Postscript*, accompanied by a 'second division' of eighteen edifying discourses published under his own name, and a 'third division' of exclusively religious writings, accompanied by "a little aesthetic article" (*KW* 22: 29). The simultaneous publication of 'edifying discourses' with 'aesthetic works' and the calculated balancing of the three divisions, he argues, demonstrate that his intention from the outset was to be a religious author.

The Point of View was written in 1849, but only published posthumously. Kierkegaard's religious writing continued until three weeks before his death on 11 November 1855. The works written between *The Point of View* and the articles in *Fædrelandet* (The fatherland), in which he attacks Martensen and the established Church, constitute a "second literature" (Elrod 1981: xi) and comprise two books by the ideally Christian pseudonymous 'Anti-Climacus', "Two Ethical-Religious Essays" by the pseudonymous 'H.H.' and various edifying discourses published under his own name (*KW* 26: xvii–xix). They present Christian discourses to awaken, edify and give greater inner depth to readers already committed to ethical-religious life, rather than to provoke those still mired in the despair of aesthetic immediacy to a choice of *either* aestheticism *or* ethical-religious life. The direct attack on the established Church after this interlude marks a return to the increasingly urgent problem of how to become a Christian in Christendom, with special emphasis on the obstacles presented by a complacent, bourgeois clergy.

At the outset of his 'authorship' Kierkegaard devised a 'maieutic' art of communication, inspired by Socrates but ultimately differentiated from the method of that "simple wise man of old" (*KW* 15: 133). Its aim is to act as 'midwife' at the birth of the reader's subjectivity. The birth of reflective self-consciousness is a prelude to religious awakening, which can only be effected by God. In a sketch for "The Dialectic of Ethical and Ethical-Religious Communication" (Pap. VIII.2.B 79–89), Kierkegaard distinguishes 'direct' from 'indirect' methods of communication. In order to communicate cognitive information about something that can be the object of science or scholarship, direct communication is adequate. However, in order to communicate a *capability*, whose object is practical self-knowledge, the teacher needs to inculcate a dialectical relationship between teacher, pupil and the object of knowledge, which Christ as teacher demonstrates. Kierkegaard's 'authorship' is an exercise in the maieutic art of indirect communication aimed at preparing the reader for ethical-religious rebirth into the capability of practising Christian faith. While it has 'analogies' to the indirect communication embodied in the life of Christ – the God who paradoxically appears as a servant, who suffers and dies to redeem humankind from its sins – these are analogies "under erasure" (Derrida 1976: 60).

Kierkegaard's 'authorship' contains three divisions: aesthetic pseudonymous works; edifying discourses; and Christian discourses and deliberations. Works in the latter two divisions were published under his own name. Kierkegaard requests that quotes from the pseudonymous texts be attributed to the pseudonym concerned, rather than to himself (*KW* 12.1: 627). The homiletic literature in the second division, published simultaneously with the pseudonymous works, is designed both to underscore the indirect messages of the pseudonymous works and to 'build up' ethical-religious emotions, attitudes and resolutions in the reader. These include: expectancy, hope, faith, gratitude, love, inner strength, patience, courage, endurance of suffering and joy. Kierkegaard borrowed the notion of discourses (*Taler*) from the Moravian Brethren tradition of lay preaching (without authority), and uses them for edification and deliberation. 'Edifying' (*Opbyggelige*) is more literally translated in the Princeton edition of *Kierkegaard's Writings* (1978–2000) as 'upbuilding', and 'deliberations' (*Overveielser*) means more literally 'weighings-up'. Unlike a discourse, a deliberation "does not presuppose the definitions as given and understood", but must stir people to reflect, "call to them, turn their comfortable way of thinking topsy-turvy with the dialectic of truth" (*KW* 16: xi).

The aesthetic, pseudonymous works, on the other hand, are addressed to the cultivated reading public. These readers, on Kierkegaard's diagnosis, suffer from too much intellectual reflection and too little subjective passion. They assume they are Christians by virtue of having been born into Christendom and having been baptized in the state church. Their intellectual reflection is infected by diseases of modernism: Danish Hegelianism and its confidence that all existence can be construed intelligibly and without remainder in philosophical concepts; the empty irony and fantastical, hubristic self-creation characteristic of the German Romantics; the evaluation of boredom as the worst suffering and the interesting as the highest good; the flight from boredom into entertainment, pleasure and gossip; and the abrogation of responsibility as individuals through submersion in the opinions of the press and the crowd. Above all, they suffer from despair: "the sickness unto death". Kierkegaard saw his initial task as a religious writer to disabuse his readers of these illusions, as prophylaxis to the radical cure of despair with faith.

To achieve that end, he began his 'authorship' with an overtly aesthetic work, which epitomizes the sensibility of the Romantic. He sought to seduce members of 'the reading public' through their own interests, while challenging these interests with constant irony. The aesthete portrayed in *Either/Or* lives for intensity in reflective imagination, swings in the moment from mood to mood, displays brilliant pyrotechnics of wit, is totally self-interested, exploits others for the delectation of his own consciousness, revels in the arbitrary, tries paradoxically to master chance, and is unwittingly in the grip of despair. The first volume of *Either/Or* ends with "The Seducer's Diary", which is a far more shocking portrayal of seduction than is found in Friedrich Schlegel's *Lucinde*, to which it is in part an ironic response. Unfortunately for Kierkegaard, the first reviewers failed to take into account the ironic critique implicit in this portrayal, along with the import of the second volume of the book (cf. Heiberg 1843: 290–92).

The second volume of *Either/Or* consists in letters to the aesthete from his friend Judge William, a doyen of civic virtue. Its structure echoes that of Friedrich

Schleiermacher's *Confidential Letters Concerning Friedrich Schlegel's Lucinde*, although its content consists in admonition against the aesthetic life and advocacy of the ethical life. Whereas the first volume tries to manoeuvre the reader into critical self-reflection by means of internal irony, the second volume seeks to awaken the reader to the limits of the aesthetic way of life as seen from the outside. In particular, it seeks to apprise the reader of the ethical connection between individual and community, to the spiritual potential inherent in ethical-religious choice, and to the possibility of preserving elements of the aesthetic even within apparently stodgy, bourgeois institutions such as marriage. Judge William maintains that only by choosing the ethical-religious life over the aesthetic – which is a life of immersion in immediacy, fate and luck – can the individual start on the task of becoming a self with "eternal validity" (*KW* 4: 215). This choice amounts to a serious commitment to evaluate one's motives and actions under the categories of 'good' and 'evil', and to strive freely to do what is good. Judge William, as an embodiment of civic virtue, equates 'the good' with 'duty', and duty with 'the universal' (*KW* 4.263ff.). The universal, in turn, is understood to be that which is acknowledged by public reason and customary morality to be required or acceptable behaviour. In other words, the universal amounts to cognitive normative ethics. However, the choice to commit to this cognitive normative ethics must itself be non-cognitively motivated (Lübcke 1991: 93–6). There is no rationally sufficient metaethical justification for this normative ethics, nor a psychologically compelling reason to adopt it. Hence the need for indirect communication, irony, admonition, exhortation and other rhetorical or even non-discursive motivations to "awaken" the "dreaming spirit" (*KW* 8: 91) to its potential to become a new self.

Judge William, however, does not have the last word in *Either/Or*. The second volume ends with a sermon by an anonymous pastor on the theme "The Upbuilding That Lies in the Thought That in Relation to God We Are Always in the Wrong" (*KW* 4: 339–54). The judge has been rather too sanguine in his belief in the possibility of fulfilling the moral law. It is one thing to advocate serious commitment to obeying the dictates of duty, and quite another to achieve real obedience. Another problem is that duty, on this view, is limited to the jurisdiction of customary morality, where customs are relative to a particular society and epoch. The ultimate deontological commitment should be *absolute* and not (relatively) *universal*. Even the judge needs a higher perspective.

Fear and Trembling, by the pseudonymous Johannes de silentio, explores the limits of the ethical further along these lines. Its focus is the story sketched in Genesis 22 of God's command to Abraham that he sacrifice his son Isaac on Mount Moriah. Within both Jewish and Christian traditions, Abraham is taken to be 'the father of faith', so to understand his response to this divine command promises deep insight into the nature of religious faith, as well as into 'divine command' ethics. The subtitle to *Fear and Trembling*, however, is "Dialectical Lyric" and its author's *nom de plume* suggests an essential ineffability about the subject matter. The understanding of faith through the Old Testament figure of Abraham, presented by Johannes in the form of a dialectical lyric, is far from a transparent philosophical concept accessible to universal reason. Furthermore, we are warned by the epigraph taken from J. G. Hamann – "What Tarquinius Superbus said in the garden by means of the poppies, the son understood but the messenger did not" (*KW* 6: 3) – that this will be an indirect communication.

Johannes wants first to impress on the reader the enormity of the dilemma facing Abraham: on the one hand, he has a heartfelt love for his late-begotten son, and civic duties to his wife and his community to observe traditional prohibitions against murder; on the other hand, he has an absolute duty to obey God. This abysmal conflict could rend every weaker soul. Is he mad to think God has spoken in this way? Is God morally questionable for having uttered this command? Are love of children and community of ultimate or only relative importance? If, on hearing the Sunday sermon on Abraham, an insomniac were to go home and sacrifice his son, would we not think he was criminal or dangerously deluded rather than an exemplar of faith (*KW* 6: 28–9)? Yet, if we are truly to feel the passionate commitment of faith, we must not be so quick to pass judgement.

Johannes distinguishes the case of Agamemnon, the "tragic hero", from Abraham, the "knight of faith". The tragic hero belongs to the universe of civic virtue. His or her actions are intelligible and justifiable to the community. When the deity demands appeasement in the form of a human sacrifice, the nation's interests take priority over the private agony of an individual: Agamemnon must sacrifice his daughter Iphigenia for the sake of the expedition against Troy. This is intelligible to the community of Greeks, who recognize it as tragic for Agamemnon (*KW* 6: 57–8). The knight of faith, on the other hand, is condemned to silence. Abraham cannot share his dilemma with Sara or Isaac or any member of his community, since that would bring the decision back within the bounds of civic duty. Normally the individual, as a member of a moral community, is subordinate to the universal. Under the impetus of faith, however, the individual becomes superior to the universal by assuming an "absolute duty to the absolute" (*KW* 6: 56). Abraham's decision to obey God's command, against the demands of universal ethics, amounts to a "teleological suspension of the ethical" (*KW* 6: 54–7). This both condemns him to silence about justifying his decision and elevates him to the status of "knight of faith".

'The ethical' here is understood in Judge William's terms, as immanent civic duty. In *The Concept of Anxiety*, Vigilius Haufniensis introduces the notion of "second ethics" (*KW* 8: 21) – Christian ethics reconstituted on the other side of faith – epitomized by Christ's love rather than by Abraham's obedience. The notion of a "teleological suspension of the ethical" is confined to *Fear and Trembling*: there is never any question of suspending the "second ethics" of self-sacrificing Christian love. Nor is there a question of wholesale rejection of civic duty. The appeal to an absolute duty to the absolute provides a permanent fulcrum for leverage against naturalistic and relativistic ethics. It acts as a regulative ideal for immanent systems of morality, but can only ever be accessed through conscience, faith and sin-consciousness, and can never be justified in terms of the civic duty it suspends or finds exceptions to. It is a plea for the ongoing possibility of civil disobedience in the name of a higher duty. *Fear and Trembling* is not a justification of Euthyphro's claim that the holy is whatever is pleasing to the gods (Plato [1941] 1961: 174). It is the more negative claim that the duties demanded by civil obedience do not in principle exhaust our moral obligations. On this view we can never exhaustively specify our moral obligations in immanent terms. We need the possibility of appeal to a transcendent source of moral inspiration: something 'eternal', which paradoxically enters historical time; something infinite, which paradoxically requires finite acts; and something perfectly good, which paradoxically apprises us of our moral possibilities by virtue of engendering our consciousness of sin. The story of Abraham is instructive about the serious commitment required by faith, the psychological agony and spiritual trials faith risks, and the unconditional acceptance of God's authority over any earthly claims. But ultimately, on Kierkegaard's view Abraham's trial belongs to the spiritual immaturity of Judaism, which can at best be used as a dialectical springboard towards Christianity. Once the spiritual trial is over, in Judaism, the individual can enjoy life. In Christianity, on the other hand, becoming spirit entails suffering throughout one's life (Kirmmse 1994: 87–8).

TIME, TEMPORALITY, ETERNITY AND TRUTH

Whereas *Fear and Trembling* explores the psychological ramifications of serious faith, and the limits faith places on customary morality, *Philosophical Fragments* explores the problem of how a temporally existing human being can relate to eternal truth. Truth is conceived here as tenseless, atemporal and holistic. Since it always already is, it cannot come into being. This sets up a deep problem for the existing individual, who aspires not merely to know the truth intellectually, but to exist in the truth. This is the crux of 'Lessing's problem', which is articulated in the subtitle of *Philosophical Fragments* as whether there can be a "historical point of departure for an eternal consciousness", and whether "an eternal happiness [can] be built on historical knowledge" (*KW* 7: 1).

Johannes Climacus explores these questions by contrasting their Socratic solution to the paradoxical religious solution. The Socratic solution, found in Plato's *Meno*, is formulated in terms of whether the truth can be learned. The Socratic paradox of learning is that someone who knows the truth cannot seek it, since it is already known, yet someone who does not know cannot seek it, since it is not known what to look for (*KW* 7: 9). By eliciting the knowledge of Pythagoras' theorem from an ignorant slave boy, Socrates demonstrates that truth is always already known, but needs to be recollected. The role of the teacher is merely to provide an occasion for recollection, and the temporally existing individual relates to the truth 'backwards' in time. The individual already contains the condition for learning the truth, so that the teacher does not provide anything essential in order for the individual to come into conscious relation to it. Teacher and learner stand in a reciprocal relation, in which the teacher provides an occasion for the learner to learn and the learner provides an occasion for the teacher to teach (*KW* 7: 23). The teacher stands in the same relation to the truth as the learner, who remains essentially the same person before and after the occasion of 'recollection'.

In paradoxical religion, by contrast, the teacher provides both the truth and the condition for learning it, and is thereby essential for the learner. Truth is here understood to be (eternally valid) practical self-knowledge, which can be communicated only by indirect means. It transforms the learner into a new self, from one state of being into a new state of being. The teacher is essentially different from the learner, since the teacher already embodies the truth, while the learner is transformed into a new self by the truth. It is the recognition by the learner of the absolute alterity of the teacher as the embodiment of the (eternal) truth that effects the learner's self-transformation. Yet in order to provide the condition for learning this truth, the teacher needs to communicate it indirectly, so that the learner will acquire it as a practical capability that has dialectical dynamism. This is not the sort of truth that can be communicated as information, once and for all, and assimilated seamlessly into the fabric of immanence. This truth is a task, to be acquired repeatedly throughout the existing individual's life, by constant reaffirmation in faith. The task is oriented towards the future, motivated by hope, and sustained by patience and faith.

The teacher who embodies transformative truth must embody its indirect communication. Since truth is conceived as eternal, it must be embodied by a god. In order for the god to communicate indirectly, this embodiment must be incognito. Instead of appearing in the form of conceptual truth, immanent to human knowledge and assimilable as information, the god appears paradoxically as a servant, and hungers, suffers and dies like a lowly human being (*KW* 7: 32–3). This embodiment of truth is an offence to reason and to decorum. It flouts logical consistency by positing that eternity can enter time, that the immortal can die and that the infinite can become finite. It proclaims the message that, by faith in this absurd claim, the finite, temporal, mortal human being can be reborn into infinity, eternity and immortality.

The claim embodied in this purported teacher, however, cannot be assimilated to one's immediate, aesthetic self. Instead, it poses a challenge and a task: to see *how* one relates to this purported truth. Whenever the individual is tempted to relate to it through reason, it reappears as an offence. Alternatively, it can be related to with faith, which is a subjective passion. Although one can build one's faith up into an abiding disposition of character through practising prayer, patience, hope and love, offence remains as a possibility. While Christianity claims that the eternal actually entered time at a particular moment in history, in the person of the God-man, this same eternal truth enters the existing individual only in consciousness, through faith. This truth is not explicable in the form of discursive knowledge, since it is dialectically related to the learner as a possibility for self-transformation, which is accessible only in each moment that faith repeats a passionate inward commitment to belief in the God-man as the actual embodiment of eternal truth. In this way, subjectivity is truth, but also (mere) subjectivity is untruth, since only if faith is directed towards actual truth is it true faith, with the potential for radical self-transformation (*KW* 12.1: 207–10).

FREEDOM, ANXIETY AND SIN

Because there can never be objective certainty about the claim that a particular historical person is the incarnation of eternal truth, and because the claim is communicated indirectly, as a task for freedom, the individual has to take responsibility for relating to the claim. This creates anxiety. Anxiety is a category of reflection that takes *possibilities* as its intentional objects. Anxiety is essentially oriented towards the future in terms of one's possible actions, so that even when one feels anxious about the past, this is really anxiety only about the possibility of repeating it in the future. Anxiety as a psychological state is a prelude to sin-consciousness (*KW* 8: 91–2). It is a phase in developmental psychology that is required for spirit to become conscious of itself. It displaces innocence, and is first manifest in children's intimations of "the adventurous, the monstrous, and the enigmatic", and later can manifest as melancholy (*KW* 8: 42). It also appears in the awakening of sexual desire, which reflects the individual out of innocent 'immediacy' into awareness of the possibilities of freedom with respect to another person. This emerges subconsciously in bashfulness, which teeters between a fall from innocence and the simultaneous retention of innocence, generated by the dawning awareness of sexual difference (Grøn 1993: 33). Anxiety, then, emerges as a psychological relation to the possibilities of freedom opened up by self-reflection. Self-reflection is enabled by differentiating oneself from, and relating oneself to, another person. Anxiety reaches its ultimate intensity when the individual reflects on the freedom inherent in relating to the absolute other: God. In so far as self-identity is bound to our relations with others, this God-relation has the potential to transform our own identity absolutely. The more at stake, the more anxiety; the more anxiety, the more spirit (cf. *KW* 8: 42) – and spirit *is* the self (*KW* 19: 13).

On Plato's analysis of becoming, a being has to pass through a state of nonbeing to another state of being.

> The Christian view takes the position that non-being is present everywhere as the nothing from which things were created, as semblance and vanity, as sin, as sensuousness removed from spirit, as the temporal forgotten by the eternal; consequently the task is to do away with it in order to bring forth being. (*KW* 8: 83)

In the task of becoming a (Christian) self, the individual has to overcome anxiety by resolving to displace the 'non-being' of sin with 'substantial' good. By having faith that Christ was the incarnation of God, his life can be taken as a model of divine goodness as expressed in human form. Sin is understood as the falling short of this ideal in every (merely) human life. Sin-consciousness provides a negative criterion for faith, and is the condition provided by God for learning the eternal truth in time. Sin-consciousness provides a task for freedom, to repent and to strive henceforth to imitate the life of Christ more strenuously. The task of imitation requires the substantiation of the good through works of love. It also requires faith that Christ is both teacher and redeemer, and that his sacrifice signifies the forgiveness of sin.

DESPAIR, HOPE, FAITH AND LOVE

Despair is the opposite of faith (*KW* 19: 49). It is "the sickness unto death" since faith must be renewed throughout life – at every moment of consciousness of the possibility of offence or of doubt or of despair. Despair is the failure to acknowledge that God established the reflexive relation that constitutes one's self (*KW* 19: 13–14). The self is spirit, as a relation of self-consciousness, which relates the hybrid components of the human being to one another and to God. "A human being is a synthesis of the infinite and the finite, of the temporal and the eternal, of freedom and necessity" (*KW* 19: 13). But the synthesis requires (self-conscious) spirit to bring the elements into (appropriate) relation with one another in order to become a self. Spirit, in turn, is ultimately posited only through relation to God as absolute other by means of sin-consciousness – which requires faith. Therefore to be a self requires faith, which implies that one is not in despair.

Despair is a misrelation in one's potential self (*KW* 19: 15–16). In order to cure it, the individual must cultivate faith. Christian faith is both a duty of obedience to God and a happy passion, which anticipates the eternal in the constantly renewed expectancy of joy, even in the face of suffering. Faith is a relation through spirit to the eternal in time, with the seriousness of passion. Faith always has a task, and "as long as there is a task there is life, and as long as there is life there is hope" (*KW* 15: 279). Christian hope is self-fulfilling, since it is a *resolve* to expect, as certain, "eternal salvation *by the grace of God*" (*KW* 5: 268). Like faith, eternal hope is a duty: always to expect the good for all people (*KW* 16: 248). It is distinguished from earthly hope by never being ashamed, disappointed or impatient, and serves spiritual self-relation by strengthening faith against despair.

Kierkegaard conceives Christian love, too, as a duty. It is both a gift (*Gave*) and a task (*Opgave*). God's gift of love, epitomized in his self-sacrifice to atone for human sin, lies outside all economies of exchange. In emulating this love, the faithful do not expect rewards in exchange for faith or works of love, but give for the good of the other. Love is here conceived as *agape*, the love that sacrifices itself for the sake of the other, as opposed to self-regarding love, which looks first to its own. Christian love requires that the ego be annihilated, that one becomes as nothing before God, so that only God is seen as the author of works of love. The ultimate work of love is to enable another freely to enter a proper God-relationship. This requires that authors of works of love erase themselves as authors, so that gratitude to them does not bind the beneficiary in a feeling of dependence to a mere human. Kierkegaard signifies the erasure of himself as author of *Works of Love* by means of a dash, to make way for the words of God, as spoken by the Apostle John: "Beloved, let us love one another" (cf. McDonald 2003: 86). Even the pseudonymous Johannes Climacus erases himself as author in "An Understanding with the Reader" appended to *Concluding Unscientific Postscript*, when he writes that "everything is to be understood in such a way that it is revoked" (*KW* 12.1: 619), and that the importance of the pseudonyms (including himself) is "in wanting to have no importance, in wanting, at a remove that is the distance of double-reflection, once again to read through solo, if possible in a more inward way, the original text of individual human existence-relationships, the old familiar text handed down from the fathers" (*KW* 12.1: 630).

GRACE, WORKS, FAITH AND SALVATION – BEFORE GOD

Following Martin Luther (*see* Vol. 3, Ch. 3), Kierkegaard asserts that "a person is saved by faith alone" (*KW* 21: 16). But faith is dialectically qualified, and is only renewed through constant striving against sin and against offence. Nor can we forget about grace or works as paths to salvation, since sin-consciousness as the negative criterion of faith is given by virtue of God's grace as the condition for learning the eternal truth in time. Furthermore, faith is only recognizable in good works (*KW* 21: 19). Faith has the capacity to transform the human being into a new self, who strives to imitate Christ's life as the incarnation of divine love. Faith is also crucial to believing in divine forgiveness, and hence to the acceptance of Christ as redeemer and the grace such redemption implies (Barrett 2003: 83).

Above all, we are to strive to be transformed into selves by faith, hope and love "before God" (cf. *KW* 19: 77–9). This means that we are to strive in each moment of freedom to inform our intentions, acts and emotions with the consciousness of the eternal, with the knowledge of our own shortcomings but also of our redemption through forgiveness in Christ, with the constant expectancy of good for all, and with the will to work for that good in everyone we encounter. We are to erase our egos in so far as these interfere with faith, hope and love and the freedom of others to relate to God, and should serve by becoming 'transparent' in such a way that God's love shines through our works. Nevertheless, although we should recognize our affinity with God by virtue of both human beings and God being essentially spirit, we should not forget the absolute difference either, but should humbly worship God as servants. The notion of living our lives "before God" should act as a regulative ideal (cf. Pattison 1997: 79), by means of which we maintain consciousness of faith and ultimately receive eternal salvation.

FURTHER READING

Eriksen, N. 2000. *Kierkegaard's Category of Repetition: A Reconstruction*. Berlin: de Gruyter.

Evans, S. 1992. *Passionate Reason: Making Sense of Kierkegaard's "Philosophical Fragments"*. Bloomington, IN: Indiana University Press.

Ferreira, J. 2001. *Love's Grateful Striving: A Commentary on Kierkegaard's "Works of Love"*. Oxford: Oxford University Press.

Ferreira, J. 1991. *Transforming Vision: Imagination and Will in Kierkegaardian Faith*. Oxford: Clarendon Press.

Gouwens, D. 1996. *Kierkegaard as Religious Thinker*. Cambridge: Cambridge University Press.

Grøn, A. 1997. *Subjektivitet og Negativitet: Kierkegaard*. Copenhagen: Gyldendal.

Mackey, L. 1986. *Points of View: Readings of Kierkegaard*. Tallahassee, FL: Florida State University Press.

Pattison, G. 2005. *The Philosophy of Kierkegaard*. Chesham: Acumen.

Taylor, M. 1975. *Kierkegaard's Pseudonymous Authorship: A Study of Time and the Self*. Princeton, NJ: Princeton University Press.

Walsh, S. 1994. *Living Poetically: Kierkegaard's Existential Aesthetics*. University Park, PA: Pennsylvania State University Press.

On AESTHETICS see also Ch. 18; Vol. 1, Ch. 15. On ETHICS see also Ch. 19; Vol. 1, Ch. 11; Vol. 2, Chs 4, 8; Vol. 3, Ch. 9; Vol. 5, Chs 12, 15, 21. On FAITH see also Chs 8, 10; Vol. 1, Ch. 13; Vol. 2, Chs 6, 12, 16, 18; Vol. 3, Ch. 8; Vol. 5, Chs 7, 18. On LOVE see also Ch. 17; Vol. 5, Ch. 16. On SELF-CONSCIOUSNESS see also Chs 2, 4, 5, 10.

14

KARL MARX AND FRIEDRICH ENGELS

Roland Boer

Karl Marx and Friedrich Engels were born within two years of each other, Marx 1818 in Trier and Engels in 1820 in Barmen (Wuppertal). While Marx received a formal education, obtaining a doctorate from the Friedrich Wilhelm IV University in Berlin, Engels was largely self-taught, since his father put him to work in the family business the moment he matriculated from the gymnasium at the age of seventeen. Although Marx was the deeper thinker of the two, Engels was by far the better writer. Both beat their own path to historical materialism, until their meeting of minds in Paris in 1844. From then on they were collaborators, settling finally in England to escape political persecution. From here they organized the International Working Mens Association, or First International, which quickly spread to other countries. Marx died from overwork at the age of sixty-five in 1883, while Engels lived on until 1895, eventually succumbing to throat cancer from his love of fine tobacco, wines and beer.

Since Marx and Engels made their living by writing, they wrote an immense amount of material. Much of it was journalism for various newspapers and magazines in Europe and North America, but a great deal also comprised substantial studies of economics, philosophy, history, politics, military matters and, last but not least, religion. The most complete collection of their works is the fifty-volume *Marx and Engels Collected Works*, published between 1975 and 2005. The German edition, the *Marx-Engels Gesamtausgabe* remains incomplete at forty-two volumes and there is more material still turning up. Now under the guidance of the International Institute for Social History in Amsterdam, it is hoped that the German edition will finally be completed.

Most of Marx's discussions of religion appear in his earlier works, especially *The Leading Article in No. 179 of the* Kölnische Zeitung (Marx [1842] 1975d), *Proceedings of the Sixth Rhine Province Assembly. First Article: Debates on Freedom of the Press and Publication of the Proceedings of the Assembly of the Estates* ([1842] 1975e), *Contribution to the Critique of Hegel's Philosophy of Law: Introduction* ([1844] 1975b), *Contribution to the Critique of Hegel's Philosophy of Right* ([1843]

1975a) and the *Theses on Feuerbach* ([1845] 1976a). Written during his early years of journalism and research, these are only the most substantial among them. Many of his works contain comments and observations but it is impossible to list them here. Engels wrote a number of key texts on religion over his lifetime, including *Letters from Wuppertal* (Engels [1839] 1975c), observations on religious life in Bremen while he was there ([1839–42] 1975a–f,y), three essays on Schelling's lectures in Berlin ([1841–2] 1975g–i), religious satire ([1842] 1975b), extended correspondence with his friends the Graeber brothers on matters theological and biblical ([1839–41] 1975j–x) and then a series of major works: *The Peasant War in Germany* ([1850] 1978), *The Book of Revelation* ([1883] 1990a) and, towards the end of his life, the influential *On the History of Early Christianity* ([1894–5] 1990c). Two other joint texts are also steeped in religious matters, namely *The Holy Family* (Marx & Engels [1845] 1975) and *The German Ideology* ([1845–6] 1976). Some, but not all, of these works, have been gathered in various collections over time (see "Further reading").

While Marx never seems to have had any religious commitment, Engels grew up in a pious Calvinist household in Wuppertal. Through great struggle he eventually gave his Calvinism away, but not before it had left him with a deep knowledge of the Bible and a life-long interest in matters biblical and religious.

THE RELIGIOUS TURN OF GERMAN PHILOSOPHY

The most well-known and influential argument of Marx and Engels is that religion cannot be considered apart from its social and economic conditions. While Marx tended to view religion as the expression of alienation, Engels was more prepared to grant it a liberating dimension. Yet there is far more to their views on religion than this argument. It is my task to explore some of those other dimensions in what follows. In fact, religion appears in the work of Marx and Engels in three ways: the context in which they first developed historical materialism, the use they make of religion in developing their own arguments, and explicit arguments concerning religion.

Beginning with the context, for a number of historical reasons Germany and Prussia dealt with a whole range of modern issues through religion, which really means Christianity and the Bible. While France had the radical atheistic criticism of Voltaire and company and while England had the deists, in Germany the debate was restricted to the nature of the Bible. So we find in the early part of the nineteenth century the bombshell of David Strauss' *Das Leben Jesu* (The life of Jesus; 1835, 2006), where he argued that the accounts of Jesus in the Gospels are mythological, or the arguments of the biblical critic Bruno Bauer (1838, 1840, 1841, 1842) for a democratic self-consciousness, or those of Ludwig Feuerbach ([1841] 1986, 1989) that religion is actually the projection of what is best in human beings, a projection that leads us to create an entity called 'God'. Through these theological and biblical works all of the central questions were debated, such as democracy, freedom (of the press), reason, republicanism, parliamentary representation, and so on. It cannot be stressed enough that these debates took place above all on the territory of the Bible. It was there that Marx and Engels began their philosophical and political work.

AGAINST THE THEOLOGICAL HEGELIANS

In order to develop their own system of thought, Marx and Engels had to distinguish themselves from the overwhelming theological frame in which German thought operated in the 1830s and 1840s. For a time Marx counted himself as a friend of Bauer, hoping for a university appointment under his patronage. For his part, Engels identified closely with the Young Hegelians in Berlin, especially during his year of military service (1842). His works on Schelling ([1841–2] 1975g–i) and the satirical poem *The Insolently Threatened Yet Miraculously Rescued Bible* ([1842] 1975b) come from this period. However, as their collaborative work progressed, they had to come to terms with the major Young Hegelians, especially in the two rambling joint works, *The Holy Family* ([1845] 1975) and *The German Ideology* ([1845–6] 1976).

Ludwig Feuerbach's projections

Alongside Strauss' *Life of Jesus*, Feuerbach's *The Essence of Christianity* ([1841] 1986, 1989) was one of the most significant texts of the time. Marx saw the idea that religion and the gods were projections of human beings as a huge breakthrough. He used and extended what may be called the 'Feuerbachian inversion' at a number of points in his own work. Feuerbach's idea is an inversion since it argues that previous thought about religion began at the wrong point, namely in the middle. God was not a pre-existing being who determined human existence; rather, human beings determine God's existence.

Marx takes this argument and claims that it marks the end of the criticism of religion: "For Germany the *criticism of religion* is in the main complete, and criticism of religion is the premise of all criticism" (Marx [1844] 1975b: 175; [1844] 1976b: 378). He goes on to suggest that the first great phase of criticism – the criticism of religion – began with Luther and ended with Feuerbach. The next revolutionary phase begins after Feuerbach and Marx is part of that new phase.

For Marx, Feuerbach was the last word on religion. Statements such as the following are pure Feuerbach:

> Religion is the general theory of this world, its encyclopaedic compendium, its logic in popular form, its spiritual *point d'honneur*, its enthusiasm, its moral sanction, its solemn complement, and its universal

basis of consolation and justification. It is the *fantastic realization* of the human essence since the *human essence* has not acquired any true reality.   ([1844] 1975b: 175; [1844] 1976b: 378)

However, Marx also wanted to go beyond Feuerbach on two counts. First, since human beings project religion from within themselves, the place to begin analysis is not in the heavens, but here on earth with flesh-and-blood people. Secondly, the fact that people do make such projections was a signal that something was wrong here on earth. If people placed their hopes and dreams elsewhere, then that meant they could not be realized here and now. So the presence of religion becomes a sign of alienation, of economic and social oppression. *That* needs to be fixed. We find this theme very strongly in the famous *Theses on Feuerbach*, especially the fourth and eleventh theses:

> Feuerbach starts out from the fact of religious self-estrangement, of the duplication of the world into a religious world and a secular one. His work consists in resolving the religious world into its secular basis. But that the secular basis lifts off from itself and establishes itself as an independent realm in the clouds can only be explained by the inner strife and intrinsic contradictoriness of this secular basis. The latter must, therefore, itself be both understood in its contradiction and revolutionized in practice. Thus, for instance, once the earthly family is discovered to be the secret of the holy family, the former must then itself be destroyed in theory and in practice.
>
> The philosophers have only *interpreted* the world in various ways; the point is to *change* it.   (Marx [1845] 1976a: 4–5)

Marx would go on to use the 'Feuerbachian inversion' in a number of ways, not least to argue that Hegel's position on the state was exactly the same as theology: it began with abstracted ideas such as state, sovereignty, constitution and tried to make human beings fit (see Marx [1843] 1975a). Much later on, in 1886, Engels would fill this picture out in his lucid prose and show why Feuerbach was so important for the development of historical materialism (Engels [1886] 1990b).

Bruno Bauer's A-theology

Given Feuerbach's importance, it is not for nothing that the first section of *The German Ideology* should be devoted to his work. There is also a section given over to Bruno Bauer. In a number of writings Marx would come back to Bauer, initially to defend him (Marx [1842] 1975f), but then later to attack him mercilessly. Why? The basic reason is that Bauer achieved a radical republican and democratic position through his biblical criticism and theology. Marx in particular was thoroughly opposed to such a possibility: theology dealt with heaven and was not concerned with earth – *that* was the task of the new historical materialism. For Marx, Bauer was far too much under the influence of Hegel's idealist method and in many respects Marx's distancing from Bauer is an effort to come to terms with Hegel. So we find the repeated and often heavily satirical criticism (especially in *The Holy Family*) that 'Saint Bruno' Bauer left matters in the realm of theology and thereby stunted his critical work. Marx was also excising the influence of someone who had been a close friend, first as joint members of the Young Hegelian *Doktorklub* from 1837, later as a teacher of the book of Isaiah at the University of Berlin in 1839 and as one who might have gained Marx a position. The problem was that Bauer was dismissed from Berlin in 1839 for his radical theological and political positions. He argued that the church was ossified and dogmatic, for it claimed universal status for a particular person and group. In the same way that we find a struggle in the Bible between free self-consciousness and religious dogmatism, so also in Bauer's own time the religious dogmatism of the church needed to be overthrown. In its place Bauer argued for atheism, a democratic Jesus for all and republicanism.

Max Stirner's world history

So we find Marx and Engels at the point where Feuerbach's inversion has enabled them to step beyond the criticism of religion and focus on the criticism of the earthly conditions of human struggle, and Bauer's radical theology had to be negated since religion cannot provide one with a radical critique. The engagement with Max Stirner is a little different. Most do not bother with the endless pages of *The German Ideology* given over to a detailed refutation of Stirner's *The Ego and His Own* (1845, 2005), preferring to stop after the early description of the new historical materialist method.

However, the Stirner section is crucial for the following reason: Marx and Engels develop the first coherent statement of historical materialism, which really is a theory of the workings of world history, in response to Stirner's own theory of world history. The way they wrote the manuscript (which was never published in their lifetimes) is important: as they wrote sections on Stirner they found that increasingly coherent statements of an alternative position began emerging in their own thought. Some of these statements remain in the Stirner section, while others were moved to the beginning of the manuscript and placed in the Feuerbach section. What we find is that in contrast to Stirner's radical focus on the individual, Marx and Engels develop a collective focus. Instead of Stirner's valuation of spiritual religion, they sought an approach that was very much of this world. Above all, Stirner wanted to provide a schema of world history that was pitched against Hegel. The reason why Marx and Engels devote so much attention to him is that they too want a schema of world history that overturns Hegel. The catch is that the very effort at producing a theory of world history is a religious act. One only has to look at the structure of Marx and Engel's criticism, moving through the major books of the Bible and quoting the Bible *ad nauseam*, criticizing Stirner's prophetic role and theological dabbling, to see that what is at stake is religion. In the same way that the final edited form of the Bible moves from creation to the end of history and the new Jerusalem, so also does Hegel offer a theory of world history in terms of the unfolding of spirit, so also does Stirner do so in terms of the ego, and so also do Marx and Engels in terms of the march of modes of productions, each one collapsing owing to internal contradictions.

THE TWO SIDES OF OPIUM: THE AMBIVALENCE OF RELIGION

Try the following game: begin a discussion on religion and then after a while mention Marx; then ask for the first word that comes into people's heads. Invariably the answer will be 'opium'. The key passage, over which much ink has been spilled, is as follows: "*Religious* suffering is, at one and the same time, the *expression* of real suffering and a *protest* against real suffering. Religion is the sigh of the oppressed creature, the heart of a heartless world, and the soul of soulless conditions. It is the *opium* of the people" (Marx [1844] 1975b: 175; [1844] 1976b: 378). Too often we assume that Marx felt that he (or rather Feuerbach) had put the last nail in the coffin of religion. And too often we assume that he did not hear the knocking from the inside of the coffin. However, Marx was a little more astute than that, as the preceding quotation shows. Here we find a profound awareness of the ambivalence of religion. It is both expression of suffering and protest against it; it provides people with a sigh, a heart, a soul in the midst of a heartless and soulless world. Now, Marx wants to set about changing that oppressive and soulless world, but what he also recognizes is that religion is politically ambivalent. We may put this more strongly and say that here we find the possibility that religion may be both revolutionary and reactionary, that it may seek to overturn the world and build it up from scratch or it may seek to preserve the old one and its comfortable position within it. Or even that a single religion such as Christianity has this tension within it. Even the famous phrase 'opium of the people' carries this ambivalence: Marx himself, like so many of his contemporaries, used opium as a medicine to relieve his many ailments. It was regarded as a blessed relief before the days of aspirin. Yet there was increasing concern over the negative effects of opium and a growing opinion that it was more of a panacea than a cure.

IDOLS, FETISHES AND GRAVEN IMAGES

One of the most read sections of Marx's *Capital* is the one called "The Fetishism of Commodities and the Secret Thereof" (Marx [1867] 1996: 81–94; [1867] 1962: 85–98). Here Marx traces the way commodities gain a life of their own and begin to interact with one another as though they were social beings. At the same time, human social relations suffer for they have become like the relations between things. It is as though commodities and human beings have swapped roles. Yet, this is by no means the first time Marx has made such an argument. It derives ultimately from the study of religion. Marx offers the following hint at the opening of this section in *Capital*: "A commodity appears, at first sight, a very trivial thing, and easily understood. Its analysis shows that it is, in reality, a very queer thing, abounding in metaphysical subtleties and theological niceties" (Marx [1867] 1996: 81; [1867] 1962: 85).

So let us follow his hint and see where it leads. The first stop is with the emerging study of world religions, where data and studies were becoming available from Latin America. In criticizing the various decisions by the Rhine Province Assembly (a gathering of nobles) back in 1839, Marx compares the Spanish fetish of gold (in the eyes of the Cubans) to the nobles' fetish of wood, for they wished to punish the peasants who helped themselves to fallen wood (Marx [1842] 1975e: 262–3). There is also, tantalizingly, the lost manuscript *On Christian Art*, which apparently dealt with fetishism. A little later (1844) Marx would develop the argument that money as a mediator of exchange is analogous to Christ the mediator. Christ is projected by human beings as the ideal mediator, whom we must worship, from whom we have our being, without whom we are worthless, and above all as the one who mediates between us and God and enables our salvation. So also does money become a quasi-divine mediator: before it too we must kneel, we gain our worth from money, its pursuit becomes our goal in life, and it mediates between objects and us (see Marx [1844] 1975c: 212). In other words, the criticism of money and commodities has a distinctly religious angle to it.

That angle, I would suggest, is the criticism of idolatry. The logic of idolatry is as follows: a worshipper makes an object of wood, stone, metal or even plastic. She shapes it into an appealing figure, places it in a prominent place and whenever she looks at it she is reminded of her god. However, at some point the symbolic connection is broken and the figure itself becomes the object of veneration. Now it is raised to divine status, granted superhuman powers, controls one's life and so on. The term 'fetish' is merely a more neutral term for 'idol' but the logic is strikingly similar. One could argue that Marx's criticism of capital, especially its fetishism of commodities, is also a criticism of the mystical, religious air that capital acquires. The criticism of religion has become the criticism of capital.

THE BIBLICAL TEMPTATIONS OF ENGELS

As mentioned earlier, Engels grew up in a very pious Calvinist household and was clearly committed until his late teens or early twenties. In the process he came to know his Bible very well, could read the New Testament in Greek and could quote almost any verse at will. And for all his efforts to become a staunch atheist, he was never quite able to excise the Bible from his thought or the tendency to make a biblical allusion or quote a verse here and there. In his early works two features of the Bible show up that were to continue to have an influence in the way he thought: a liking for apocalyptic biblical texts and the challenge of contradictions.

I begin with the question of contradictions. The burning issue that turns up again and again in Engels' early texts is: what do we do with contradictions in the Bible? For example, how can Gideon have asked God to stop the sun in Judges if the earth revolves around the sun? Or why do we find two very different gene-alogies for Jesus, the son of God (who should not need a genealogy), in Matthew and Luke? The problem is by no means new and has taxed biblical critics for millennia. But for Engels and his Calvinist peers, a contradiction in a text that was written by an all-powerful and unchanging God was a problem. Did it mean that the Bible was not the *ipsissima verba* of God? Did he put them there deliber-ately? Is he fallible? A contradiction or three in the text raised profound questions about the nature of God and one's faith. For Engels, in his correspondence with the Graeber brothers (Engels [1839–41] 1975j–x) and in his poem *The Insolently Threatened Yet Miraculously Rescued Bible* ([1842] 1975b), the issue of contradic-tions is absolutely central. It is one of the major factors that would lead Engels, like so many other students of the Bible, to lose his faith. But in the process contradic-tion became a central feature of historical materialist analysis, albeit now between classes and above all between the forces and relation of production.

As for apocalyptic, Engels often made use of the scene of final judgement at the end of history, whether playfully, in critical satire or in order to express his own sense of the times. So we find him characterizing his close friend Friedrich Graeber (a minister in the church) playing cards oblivious to the final battle of good and evil that rages around him ([1839] 1975o). Then there are his mock depictions of the battles between the orthodox theologians and 'The Free', as the Young Hegelians of Berlin called themselves ([1841] 1975q; [1842] 1975b). And then at the close of his booklet *Schelling and Revelation* ([1842] 1975g), he makes a very different use of the book of Revelation. Flushed and excited with the new discoveries, having just read Feuerbach's *The Essence of Christianity* and feeling the shackles of his old narrow belief structure snapping open, Engels celebrates with a rousing image of the final battle between free thought and obscurantism, all of which ends with the arrival of a New Jerusalem.

Marxism is often accused of being a secular version of apocalyptic history, with its struggle between the proletariat and the bourgeoisie that will eventually lead to communism. Marx himself might have become excited at times (he was known to get red-faced and nervous before speaking in public), but this element would seem to be a legacy of Engels rather than Marx. It shows up later on, after he gave away his faith, in two respects. First, Engels became a respected military analyst and correspondent, writing a huge number of sparkling newspaper articles and books on the military. Secondly, late in life he came back to the book of Revelation to make use of the newly established historical criticism of the Bible (Engels [1883] 1990a). The purpose was to defuse the wild speculation and excitement the biblical book has generated over time by showing that the lurid imagery actually has a mundane historical reference point in the Roman Empire, for it refers to the expected return of Nero and his defeat by God's forces.

ENGELS' THEOLOGICAL ESSAYS

There is one last feature of Engels' essay on the book of Revelation that is vitally important: he points out that Christianity was actually a revolutionary movement and that the book of Revelation is an expression of that movement. This argument would become the centrepiece in two final works to be considered here, his *On the History of Early Christianity* and *The Peasant War in Germany*.

While *The Peasant War in Germany* is mostly concerned with Engels' great love, namely tracing out battle plans, troop movements and assessing tactics, it also has a curious argument concerning Thomas Müntzer. The latter was the leading theologian of the revolt and war in 1525. A reformer who was deeply influenced by Martin Luther (*see* Vol. 3, Ch. 3), he took Luther's position to its logical conclusion, threw in the need for constant contact with God through dreams and visions and predicted that the final battle of Armageddon would come soon. Needless to say he met a swift end against the heavy armour of the nobility. While many write off Müntzer as a crackpot, Engels wanted to give him his due. Müntzer was, argued Engels, expressing through theological and biblical language the grievances of class oppression and conflict. Religious language was the only way he knew to express such grievances. If he had lived in Engels' own day the language would have been very different. Indeed, Engels gives his argument a strange twist, suggesting that the closer Müntzer gets to economic and class analysis, the more atheistic he becomes. Despite this odd move, the text gained a life of its own and the better parts of the argument were expanded by the likes of Karl Kautsky (2002) and Ernst Bloch (1969). Müntzer also became a hero of the German Democratic Republic.

What Engels had managed to do with this piece on the Peasant War is point to a revolutionary side of Christianity. At this stage (1850) Engels still wanted to separate the revolutionary sharply from the religious; the twain should never meet. Forty-three years later, two years before his death, he wrote *On the History of Early Christianity*, a text that influences biblical studies to this day. The basic argument is that early Christianity was as close as one could get to a socialist movement in the ancient world. In this respect it has a number of parallels with the socialism of Engels' own day: appeal to the downtrodden masses, rapid expansion, collective cooperation and an alternative economic and social network. One reason Engels came to such a position was that it provides an answer as to why one revolutionary movement after another – such as Müntzer and the peasants, or the Bohemian Taborites, or the French communists, or Wilhelm Weitling and his communist followers in Engels' own day – drew its inspiration from Christianity.

Another reason is that with the rapid spread of socialism throughout Europe, most notably in the German Social Democratic Party (whose rise gave Engels great hope), many workers with religious commitments were joining the party. Engels wishes to reassure them that Christianity and socialism are not incompatible. A further reason lay in Engels' effort to link the relatively new critical approach to the Bible to historical materialism. Dispensing with dogmatic positions and seeking only what was historically verifiable, such critical readings of the Bible challenged many of the assumptions about the authorship, formation and nature of biblical literature. From this scholarship Engels draws on conclusions concerning the Gospels and the impossibility of knowing anything much about Jesus (here he relies on Bauer, whom Engels admired) and repeats his observations about the book of Revelation.

Above all, this booklet is the brave effort of a mature Engels to come to terms with his background. He has moved from commitment through outright rejection to a realization of how Christianity is still very much a part of him. In other words, he admits that the move from Christian commitment to a communist one is not so strange after all, for there are many elements within Christianity that have been transformed into communism. The paradox is that this text by Engels was to have an abiding influence in biblical studies, especially the argument concerning the appeal of Christianity to the lower strata of Hellenistic society.

'YOU'D DO BETTER TO READ THE PROPHETS': REVISITING THE ESCHATOLOGY OF MARX AND ENGELS

The effect of Marx and Engels on the philosophy of religion is complex. They were among the first to stress that the shape and nature of religion is heavily dependent on people's social and economic situations. They forged the historical materialist method in close response to key radical theologians such as Feuerbach, Bauer and even Stirner. Marx's hints concerning the ambivalence of religion (it is both opium and protest) is taken much further by Engels, who ended up arguing that early Christianity was a socialist movement. And one of Marx's key ideas concerning the fetishism of commodities has a complex background in the study of religions and the biblical critique of idolatry

In conclusion, let me raise an oft-made criticism of Marxism: it is merely a secularized eschatology. The criticism was first made by Leszek Kolakowski in his *Main Currents of Marxism* (1981) and has been repeated *ad nauseam* ever since: the proletariat is a collective redeemer figure and communism is the New Jerusalem after the final battle to end history. From what I have considered above, this is a crude caricature. Of course, there is influence, but it is far more complex. Marx for one was not interested in anything eschatological, and his one-time teacher Bauer was dead against it. If anyone had a liking for the apocalyptic, it was Engels: from his early fascination and use of apocalyptic themes as both satire and celebration, through his immersion in military matters and reflections on the nature of what a communist army would look like, through to his final arguments concerning the essentially socialist nature of early Christianity, Engels finds the apocalyptic an appealing literary and social tradition. The best conclusion is that the influence was mutual: religion and Marxism have actually fed into one another.

FURTHER READING

Boer, R. 2009. *Criticism of Religion: On Marxism and Theology II*. Leiden: Brill.

Marx, K. & F. Engels 1976. *On Religion*. Moscow: Progress Publishers.

McKown, D. 1975. *The Classical Marxist Critiques of Religion: Marx, Engels, Lenin, Kautsky*. The Hague: Martinus Nijhoff.

McLellan, D. 1987. *Marxism and Religion: A Description and Assessment of the Marxist Critique of Christianity*. New York: Harper & Row.

Raines, J. (ed.) 2002. *Marx on Religion*. Philadelphia, PA: Temple University Press.

On SOCIETY see also Ch. 21; Vol. 3, Ch. 2; Vol. 5, Ch. 4. On THEORY OF PROJECTION see also Ch. 10. On WORLD RELIGIONS see also Chs 6, 18.

15

WILHELM DILTHEY

Rudolf A. Makkreel

Wilhelm Dilthey was born in Biebrich on the Rhine in 1833, and died in 1911. The son of the preacher to the Count of Nassau, Dilthey followed family tradition by starting his university studies at Heidelberg in theology. There he was drawn to the philosophical systems of G. W. F. Hegel and Friedrich Schleiermacher by Kuno Fischer. In 1853 Fischer was accused of being a pantheist and his right to teach was withdrawn. As a consequence, Dilthey moved to the University of Berlin, where he came under the influence of Schleiermacher's students Friedrich von Trendelenburg and August Boeckh. Increasingly, Schleiermacher became the focus of Dilthey's interests. In 1859 he was asked to complete the editing of Schleiermacher's letters. That year the Schleiermacher Society also organized an essay competition on his hermeneutics. Dilthey submitted an essay entitled "Schleiermacher's Hermeneutical System in Relation to Earlier Protestant Hermeneutics" in 1860, which was published in part in 1893, but not fully until 1966 (see Dilthey 1996: 31). It was awarded the first prize and led to a second commission, namely, to write Schleiermacher's biography. The first volume of this biography was published in 1870 (Dilthey 1979b). It is a large volume that places Schleiermacher not only in his theological setting but also in the context of the literary and philosophical movements astir in Berlin from 1796 to 1807. The work displays Dilthey's own expanding interests in aesthetical and philosophical issues. He finally wrote his dissertation in philosophy on Schleiermacher's ethics.

Dilthey established his reputation in philosophy and history, and was eventually appointed to Hegel's chair in philosophy at Berlin. Although he gave up on the vocation to become a minister, he retained a keen interest in the nature of religious life. As a theology student, Dilthey had begun a study of many early formulations of the Christian worldview, which, although never completed, continued to influence his subsequent writings. Letters and journal entries from 1852 to 1870 also show Dilthey reflecting on the relation of religion to philosophy and searching for those states of mind where the two are still inseparable (Dilthey

1960: 30). In 1860 Dilthey writes that "it is my calling to apprehend the innermost nature of religious life in history and to bring this to the attention of our times which are moved exclusively by matters of state and science" (*ibid.*: 140). This means looking for religiosity not so much in its institutional practices and its theological doctrines as in the recesses of human experience. In a similar vein, he asserts that it is necessary to recover the "religious-philosophical worldview that is buried under the ruins of our theology and philosophy" (*ibid.*). Personally, Dilthey finds the religious dimension of life most intensely in music and writes that Bach exhibits the true religiosity of music. He is not a "religious being who gives his mood a musical expression, but one who submits his music to its divine, eternal laws" (*ibid.*: 13).

RELIGION, EXPERIENCE AND THE UNDERSTANDING OF LIFE

In book II of the *Introduction to the Human Sciences* of 1883, Dilthey asserts that "religious life is the lasting background of intellectual development rather than a passing phase of human thinking" (1979a: 138). It informs not only primitive mythical thought but also traditional metaphysics and more contemporary self-reflection. Dilthey relates religious life to inner experiences in which we possess the immediate awareness of freedom and of what it means to have a conscience or feel responsible. The religious manifests itself in all spheres of inner life that are governed by the opposition between the imperfect and the perfect, the ephemeral and the eternal (see *ibid.*: 137). Dilthey's religious experience is an extension of Schleiermacher's feeling of absolute dependence. It is a total experience that interweaves a feeling of dependence with an awareness of a higher life independent of nature. Religiosity can be said to involve an inner sense of being sustained.

Religious life is regarded as the enduring background of human intellectual development, and that development can manifest itself in mythical representation, in theological doctrine and in metaphysical conceptualization as well as in scientific theory. Myth is thus not a primitive mode of religion as is often thought, but a primitive mode of scientific theory. Whereas religious experience directly *presents* reality through feeling, myth *represents* it. Religious experience provides an immediate knowing (*Wissen*), which myth reshapes as a representational mode of cognition (*Erkenntnis*). Myth, for Dilthey, is not strictly religious because, like science, it is an attempt to explain the connectedness of natural and social phenomena.

By contrast to religious experience, which involves an intimate knowing that proceeds from the inside out, the representational cognition of myth, metaphysics and science "works from the outside towards the inside" (*ibid.*: 137). We have here an early form of Dilthey's explanation–understanding distinction. The cognition of myth, theology, metaphysics and science provides a conceptual explanation from without. The knowledge of religious experience proceeds from within, which accords with Dilthey's initial definition of understanding (*Verstehen*) as the transference of a coherence within ourselves to something outside us. In his *Ideas for a Descriptive and Analytical Psychology* of 1894, Dilthey applies this conception of understanding from religious experience to lived experience (*Erlebnis*) in general.

An experience counts as lived if it draws on the dynamic coherence of the whole psyche. A lived experience provides understanding of the self to the extent that it reflects both the depth and overall scope of the psyche. On this basis, Dilthey proposes a contrast between a psychology based on understanding from within and the more traditional psychologies based on explanation and external observation. From within, our experience constitutes a continuous nexus that psychology as a human science then needs to analyse and articulate into its basic structures. From without, our experience presents many discrete states that need to be connected. To so regard psychic life is to apply the explanatory approach of the natural sciences. In attempting to relate spatially distinct objects or states, the natural sciences necessarily appeal to causal laws, but only rarely do such explanatory uniformities need to be invoked to make sense of psychic life. Dilthey then distinguishes between the explanation that is prevalent in the natural sciences and the understanding possible in the human sciences as follows: "We explain through purely intellectual processes, but we understand through the cooperation of all the powers of the mind activated by apprehension" (1961: 172).

What defines psychological understanding is that it does not abstract from the overall characteristics of the life of consciousness in the way that the intellect does. Psychological understanding draws on the wholeness of immediate knowing while it analyses certain parts. Instead of isolating parts through abstraction, analysis foregrounds certain partial phenomena against their overall background. If analysis can provide the kind of focus and intellectual determinacy that characterizes cognition while preserving the wholeness of knowing, we can ask whether it is possible for understanding in the human sciences to bridge the gap between cognition and knowledge. Like all science, a human science like psychology will be cognitive, but can it also revive the original aura that Dilthey attributes first to religious experience and then to lived experience?

Whereas the natural sciences are cognitive in an explanatory sense that subordinates phenomena to causal laws that are universal in scope, the human sciences are cognitive in an explicatory sense that coordinates phenomena in more limited historical contexts. The natural sciences abstract from the inner aspects of our experience in order to achieve their objective results, but the human sciences cannot afford to do so. Their task is not to observe the world disinterestedly, but to critically expose our involvement in it. They can only achieve objectivity by extensive analysis of our attitudes and responses to reality. This means that understanding must articulate the structures of human interaction discursively and reflectively.

INTERPRETING OBJECTIFICATIONS OF RELIGIOUS EXPERIENCE

The early Dilthey was content with a kind of understanding that involves an immediate knowing and projects the I into the Thou. Here the task of cognition is to re-cognize in the *other* what is already known from within. As Dilthey came to appreciate the reflective aspects of understanding, he developed a less psychological and more hermeneutical approach that would also influence his conception of the religious. The first step in this direction comes in the 1900 essay "The Rise of Hermeneutics", where understanding is called the process whereby an inside is conferred on a complex of external sensory signs. Dilthey writes that the apprehension of our own states can be called understanding only in a figurative sense. Understanding must start from without rather than from within. But in this essay the move from outer to inner is still regarded as directed at a psychic reality. This finally changes in the *Formation of the Historical World in the Human Sciences* of 1910, where the transition that occurs in understanding from external signs to inner meaning is not primarily aimed at the psychological state of mind of the author. Instead, the elementary sense of inner in the realm of meaning is the intrinsic connectedness of the parts that make up the overall expression. The relation of expression to what is expressed is an inner connection due to the expression's inherent place in some public context. Expressions are intelligible because a commonality connects those expressing themselves and those attempting to understand them. This commonality constitutes a sphere that Dilthey calls 'objective spirit'. Objective spirit embodies the shared meanings that we inherit from our traditions. Whereas Hegel had used the concept of objective spirit to focus on the historical products of our socioeconomic, legal and political interactions, Dilthey also includes in objective spirit what Hegel ultimately raised to the level of absolute spirit, namely, art, religion and philosophy. It is thus clear that religion should never be conceived in an absolutist or timeless manner, but as always related to the historical ways we experience our life. Religion can become the basis for a special human science.

By contrast to how Dilthey originally located the religious in a private or inner experience, he now places it in an objective context. In the "Plan for the Continuation of the Formation of the Historical World in the Human Sciences", Dilthey writes that "because religious objects are always presupposed by lived experience, religion [exists] in a network of tradition". No longer seeing religion as a background influence on our understanding of history, he now places it more centrally in the historical itself:

> Among the lived experiences that are important for the objectification and organization of the human spirit, religiosity is especially central. History shows this, but it is also obvious from anthropological reflection. Here we are at the root where the lived experience and understanding of poets, artists, religious persons and philosophers come

together. In all of them something … emerges from the experience of life itself, that extends beyond it. The moment that leads beyond life is always embedded in life itself. The peculiar trait of religiosity is that life as experienced enters into a relation with the invisible.   (2002: 285)

Religion focuses on the invisible not as something transcendent or other-worldly, but as what is mysterious in this life itself. Religion is not about an after-life, but about the alien and unfamiliar aspects of this life that force us to better understand ourselves. Religious experience points to the shallowness of ordinary self-understanding. This is reinforced in the essay, "The Understanding of Other Persons and Their Manifestations of Life", where Dilthey goes so far as to say that when we just "experience ourselves" in the familiar contexts of everyday life, "we do not understand ourselves. Everything about ourselves is self-evident" (*ibid.*: 245–6). The fact that lived experience already provides an immediate access to ourselves may provide a kind of human intelligibility, but it does not consti-tute either understanding (*Verstehen*) or self-understanding (*Selbstverständnis*). The familiarity of lived experience is merely self-evident (*selbstverständlich*) in an uncritical way. We can only begin to understand ourselves by approaching ourselves critically as others do: from the outside. We too must interpret ourselves on the basis of our objectifications, whether in action or in language. Self-understanding involves more than the thoughtful explication of experi-ence; it also requires the critical appropriation of the objectifications of our experience.

If we are to understand ourselves, all historical objectifications, whether produced by other human beings or by ourselves, are important. Religious experi-ence, however, opens us up to an outside that is not merely of human making, but equally important for self-understanding. This is an outside that derives from some invisible source in life itself. For Dilthey the nature of religious experience is not to be found in sentimental aspirations "about otherworldiness". When life is experienced religiously "according to its true nature – full of hardship and a singular blend of suffering and happiness throughout – [it] points to something strange and unfamiliar, as if it were coming from invisible sources, something pressing in on life from outside, yet coming from its own depths" (*ibid.*: 285).

Stressing the heightened experience of life that religion provides, Dilthey speaks in almost Heideggerian tones about there being "no evasion, no yielding to the superficiality of being caught up in life, nor to the everyday forgetfulness of past and future" (*ibid.*: 285) a full seventeen years before the appearance of *Being and Time*. Religious beings surpass the everyday experience of commonality, even the ideal of community, by pursuing a more radical search for communion. Seeking to overcome their isolation from others, religious individuals transport themselves into the fundamental nature of life, uniting with other souls through a love-based understanding. Whether religious communion ultimately entails a loss of self is not made clear, but it is certainly suggested.

THE RELIGIOUS WORLDVIEW

Earlier it was pointed out that Dilthey does not place art, religion and philosophy in the ideal domain of absolute spirit. These disciplines cannot represent the ultimate truth about reality, yet they can help articulate the meaning that we search for in life. The arts, especially poetry, attempt to understand life in terms of itself on the basis of typical situations. Life is made *visible* in terms of the many ways in which human experience is expressed and acted out. As expansive as the artistic vision of the world can be, it is not as such a worldview (*Weltanschauung*). In that the religious outlook more squarely faces the enigmas of life, it brings us closer to the formation of a worldview. Religion relates the visible to the *invisible*, the familiar to the unfamiliar, life to death. Often artists appropriate religious themes as is clearly the case with sacred music and tragic literature. Finally, philosophical reflection brings *conceptualization* to the formation of worldviews and thereby attempts to stabilize them as metaphysical systems.

What provokes self-reflection and the formation of a worldview are the enigmas of life: where does life come from and why does it end in death? While alive we already know of death, but cannot understand what it signifies. In response we create imagery to help make sense of it. But a worldview is more than an aggregate of imagery. As we gather the impressions that experience offers, certain attitudes toward life are formed. In his essay "The Types of Worldview", Dilthey calls these attitudes "life-moods" (*Lebensstimmungen*). As Heidegger would later explicate these moods, they are not just psychological states, but attitudes that attune us to the world. We become aware of these attitudinal moods when we pause and suspend the way that experience ordinarily presses on. In this state of *epochē*, we abstract from the temporal–causal nexus of experience to locate an instantaneous glimpse in which everything is estimated in relation to our life concerns (*Lebensbezüge*) (1962: 81). Some things in the world are judged as furthering or expanding our life, others as oppressing or confining us. A worldview is not just cognitive, but evaluates reality in accordance with our attitudinal moods and on this basis allows for the determination of the ends and ideals of life. A worldview speaks to all aspects of our experience: the cognitive, the felt and the volitional. Together these three aspects provide a reflective knowledge.

Ultimately, knowledge (*Wissen*) is distinguished from cognition (*Erkenntnis*) by its inclusiveness and by its reflective comprehension rather than by its intimate immediacy. However, what Dilthey's early and late views about knowledge agree on is that it responds to our life concerns and can speak to our religious needs. Knowledge is not a mere intellectual achievement and cannot hope to attain the determinacy of conceptual cognition. Even the best interpretations of the meaning of life and death will be both determinate and indeterminate. Religious worldviews will always retain an obscure core that the conceptual work of theologians and metaphysicians can never fully clarify and justify. Dilthey distinguishes three main types of religious worldview: the first finds the immanence of a cosmic rationality in the order of things; the second discerns a spiritual All-One from which individual beings may be separated but must return; and the third posits a divine will who creates the world and enlists human beings in a struggle against evil (*ibid.*: 89). All three types stand in conflict with a mundane view of life best represented by one of the main metaphysical types of worldview: naturalism, or the position that human life is determined by material forces alone. The other two types of metaphysical worldview that tend to recur throughout the history of philosophy are not as such antithetical to religion. They refuse to reduce the life of nature and the human spirit to material and mechanical forces. They constitute two types of idealism: an objective idealism that seems to have some affinities with the first two types of religious worldview; and a subjective idealism or an idealism of freedom which clearly has its roots in the third religious worldview.

Each worldview type tends to assert its superiority over the others. Dilthey judges these tensions among them as unfortunate and in response highlights the importance of the universal theism that had been developed by the Italian humanists. This viewpoint, influenced by the Stoa and cultivated subsequently by Erasmus and Bodin, is characterized in the essay "Analysis of Human Life in the Fifteenth and Sixteenth Centuries" as the conviction that the divine is to be found equally in various religions and philosophies (see Dilthey 1957: 45).

Dilthey's very last essay, written during the final days of his life in 1911 while he was on holiday in the Dolomites, is entitled "The Problem of Religion". The problem to be addressed is the tension that exists between the totalizing perspective that characterizes religion and the more differentiated approaches that mark artistic, scientific and philosophical works. Religion as a human science must attempt to avoid the extremes of those who look for an abstract moral core in all religion and those who are content to describe a mere plurality of positive religions. The Enlightenment has made it increasingly difficult to acknowledge the mystical sense of communion and the mysterious profundity that lie at the heart of religiosity. From its perspective, these aspects of religion seem irrational. But according to Dilthey, Schleiermacher was able to relate these obscure aspects of religious experience to the insights of transcendental philosophy. Instead of interpreting the mystical feeling of communion as an esoteric union with God, Schleiermacher explicates it as a general awareness that is attuned to the invisible coherence of things (Dilthey 1958: 295). He gives a transcendental reading of what is intuited and felt in the religious mood by transforming it into a constant creative principle. Whereas traditionally mysticism tended to devalue our life in this world, Schleiermacher's mysticism is seen as affirming it creatively.

In addition to praising Schleiermacher's contributions for understanding religion experientially, Dilthey also looks favourably on the psychological work of William James in bringing out the varieties of religious experience in the American context where tradition was less of a constraint (*see* Vol. 5, Ch. 2, "William James"). But however much the psychological analysis of religious moods, feelings and experiences continued to interest Dilthey, he does not deviate at all from his mature standpoint that experience as such does not constitute understanding. Experience will always be subjective and must be supplemented with an understanding based on the objectifications of experience. Lived experience remains important for plumbing the depth and intensity of life, but understanding is necessary for appreciating its complexity and scope. Only by interpreting the way religious experience manifests itself objectively can we fully exhibit its richness.

The fact that Dilthey retained an interest in the subjective aspects of lived experience and in the kind of empirical research that psychologists like James brought to bear has led many to think that his hermeneutics was still too psychologistic. Paul Ricoeur, whose hermeneutical approach to the human sciences shows many similarities to Dilthey's, nevertheless criticizes him for equating understanding with psychological reconstruction. We have already seen that Dilthey does not allow our initial understanding of human objectifications to be psychological. In "The Understanding of Other Persons", elementary understanding is defined in relation to objective spirit and its fund of shared meanings. The initial framework for understanding is the medium of commonality provided by our historical tradition. Higher understanding becomes necessary when the familiar self-evident meanings of this context produce anomalies, uncover ambiguities and perhaps even confront contradictions. Then we must appeal to some other frame of reference. When we apply logical or scientific analysis to the claims found in a text, we establish a disciplinary framework to critically assess them. This is a case where higher or critical understanding shifts from the framework of commonality to universality. But higher understanding can also restrict its framework; this restriction becomes necessary when the assertions made by the same person diverge over time. Then we must consult the life course of that individual to make sense of what has happened. This is a case when understanding becomes psychological as a last resort.

Whereas experience moves forward with time, understanding is retrospective for Dilthey. But there can come a point when understanding also goes forward into what he calls *Nacherleben*, or re-experiencing. Some, like Hans-Georg Gadamer, think that Dilthey's appeal to re-experiencing makes his hermeneutics reconstructive in a positivistic sense. But this is not what Dilthey has in mind. Re-experiencing develops understanding by completing the hermeneutical circle. Whereas understanding goes back to the overall context of sense, re-experiencing goes forward by following out the parts that give focus to the whole. A re-experiencing is not a literal re-construction but produces a 'better understanding' that refines the original. One of the last things that Dilthey wrote about in his final essay is the importance of re-experiencing in religion. For someone like himself, it was difficult to attain the religious fervour of an Augustine, a Luther or a Calvin. Their situations made it possible for them to have deep and intense religious experiences that Dilthey could only approximate through the medium of music and re-experience on the basis of historical research.

In the final analysis there are two ways of accessing what it means to be religious: through lived experience and through examining the objectifications that religious life has left behind. The latter are to be found in temples, altars, grave inscriptions, hymns, icons and sacred texts that still exist in the present. They constitute an important resource for evaluating religion as a worldview. However, as a lived experience, religion "will always be subjective. Only an understanding rooted in the re-experiencing of religious creations makes possible an objective knowledge of religion" (Dilthey 1958: 304). Re-experiencing is necessary to be able to articulate the manifold shapes that religion has assumed throughout history, but the overall task of understanding is to point to the essential features that they share and thereby give religion validity as a general worldview.

While Dilthey appeals to lived experience and re-experiencing to give determinacy to our understanding of religion, he makes it clear that although religiosity may address certain human needs, it is not to be reduced to an expression of personal needs. He explicitly rejects those who think it can be "explained by the mere need for salvation ... Religion is inherent in the apprehension of the world as a life-nexus that has structure, meaning and sense" (1991: 450). True religiosity is deeply subjective but will not express idiosyncratic desires or wishes. Dilthey speaks of the religious experience as "a state of passive yielding to a real effect" stemming from the world. This real and often enduring effect is then contrasted with the artificial and sporadic effects that drugs and trances tend to have on us. The other differentiating properties of the religious experience are that it provides solace for suffering and evokes a "lasting transformation" (1958: 304).

We can conclude that for Dilthey religiosity relates such special lived experiences of solace and transformation to the world at large. Religiosity is subjective, but in an interpretive rather than expressive way. It yields to the real effects that the world has on us by interpreting at least some of them as stemming from an invisible nexus that surpasses the limit of what is cognizable but is still knowable in some mysterious way.

FURTHER READING

Crowe, B. 2005. "Dilthey's Philosophy of Religion in the 'Critique of Historical Reason'". *Journal of the History of Ideas* **66**: 265–83.

de Mul, J. 2004. *The Tragedy of Finitude: Dilthey's Hermeneutics of Life*. New Haven, CT: Yale University Press.

Dilthey, W. 1985. *Selected Works, Vol. 5: Poetry and Experience*, R. Makkreel & F. Rodi (eds). Princeton, NJ: Princeton University Press.

Dilthey, W. 1991. *Selected Works, Vol. 1: Introduction to the Human Sciences*, R. Makkreel & F. Rodi (eds). Princeton, NJ: Princeton University Press.

Dilthey, W. 1996. *Selected Works, Vol. 4: Hermeneutics and the Study of History*, R. Makkreel & F. Rodi (eds). Princeton, NJ: Princeton University Press.

Dilthey, W. 2002. *Selected Works, Vol. 3: The Formation of the Historical World in the Human Sciences*, R. Makkreel & F. Rodi (eds). Princeton, NJ: Princeton University Press.

Ermarth, M. 1978. *Wilhelm Dilthey: The Critique of Historical Reason*. Chicago, IL: University of Chicago Press.

Kluback, W. & M. Weinbaum 1957. *Dilthey's Philosophy of Existence: Introduction to Weltanschauungslehre*. New York: Bookman Associates.

Makkreel, R. 1975. *Dilthey: Philosopher of the Human Studies*. Princeton, NJ: Princeton University Press.

Owensby, J. 1994. *Dilthey and the Narrative of History*. Ithaca, NY: Cornell University Press.

Rodi, F. 2003 *Das strukturierte Ganze: Studien zum Werk von Wilhelm Dilthey*. Weilerswist: Velbrück Wissenschaft.

On MYTHOLOGY see also Ch. 5; Vol. 1, Ch. 2. On PSYCHOLOGY see also Chs 18, 20. On RELIGIOUS EXPERIENCE see also Vol. 5, Ch. 18. On SCIENCE see also Chs 7, 11, 12, 17, 19; Vol. 2, Ch. 12; Vol. 3, Ch. 17; Vol. 5, Chs 4, 19.

16

EDWARD CAIRD

Colin Tyler

Edward Caird (1835–1908) was a leading member of the British idealist movement, which flourished from the 1870s until the mid-1920s. Together with Thomas Hill Green, Caird led the mid-Victorian reaction in Britain against the empiricism of John Locke, George Berkeley and David Hume (*see* Vol. 3, Chs 12, 14, 19), the associationism of John Stuart Mill, and the crude sensationalism of Herbert Spencer (e.g. Caird 2006). He was born in Greenock, Scotland on 23 March 1835, and, after his father John's death in 1838, he was raised by his aunt Jane Caird, herself a devout and active member of the Free Kirk (Jones & Muirhead 1921). He went up to the University of Glasgow in 1855, but ill health forced him extend his time as an undergraduate and to study for a while at the University of St Andrews. He gained a Snell Exhibition in 1860, which enabled him to complete his education at Balliol College, Oxford. His tutors included Benjamin Jowett and he became lifelong friends with Green during this time. Caird graduated in 1863, with a double first. After working as a private tutor and then serving as a Fellow of Merton College, Oxford for two years from May 1864, he took up the prestigious position of Professor of Moral Philosophy at the University of Glasgow. He made his professional name during the next twenty-three years at Glasgow, particularly for his work on Immanuel Kant. In November 1893 he became Master of Balliol College, Oxford, following the death of Jowett, a position that he held until March 1907. Having already suffered a paralytic stroke in 1905, he died in Oxford from Bright's Disease, on 1 November 1908.

Throughout his career, Caird wrote as "in the main an unregenerate Hegelian", as he expressed it in a letter of 1893 to fellow British idealist F. H. Bradley (Caird 1893: 77; Tyler 2006b: ch. 3). In so doing, he shared much with his elder brother John, later Principal, Caird (see J. Caird 1880; Green 1997a). This common debt was reflected most strongly in their respective writings on religion. Edward Caird himself influenced significant church figures, including William Temple, a future Archbishop of Canterbury (Temple 1924; Iremonger 1948: 37, 39–42, 61, 163, 326, 521). One of his former pupils went so far as to call him (*c.*1921) "the prophet of the present liberal life in the Church" (anonymized letter, quoted in Jones & Muirhead 1921: 71, cf. 70–79).

Caird wrote about the philosophy of religion throughout his academic life. He gave the Gifford lectures at the University of St Andrews in the 1890–91 and 1891–2 sessions, and they were published as *The Evolution of Religion* (Caird 1893). He also gave the Gifford lectures in the 1900–1901 and 1901–2 sessions at the University of Glasgow, and they were published as *The Evolution of Theology in the Greek Philosophers* (1904). His other major books in this area were *The Social Philosophy and Religion of Comte* (1885) and particularly his *Lay Sermons and Addresses* (1907). Relevant shorter pieces include "Christianity and the Historical Christ" (1897), "Anselm's Argument for the Being of God – Its History and What It Proves" (1899) and "St Paul and the Idea of Evolution" (1903–4), as well as the more recently published "Reform and Reformation" (Caird 2005a) and "Essay on Mysticism" (2005c).

As soon as the British idealist movement began to emerge, serious doubts were expressed regarding its compatibility with orthodox Christianity. In fact, most members of the movement publicly acknowledged both their heterodoxy and their personal piety (see also Nettleship 1997: c). Hence, although the idealists tended to understand their attempts to articulate a new philosophy of religion as, in Caird's words, "an interpretation and vindication of the religious consciousness", they also wished to replace the now-defunct "external scaffolding on which religious belief formerly rested" with "a natural and rational basis" for the modern Christian faith (Caird 1893: vol. 1, 39; Jones & Muirhead 1921: 338–41). This project was influenced strongly by Hegel and German biblical criticism, particularly as developed by F. C. Baur (Sanctis 2005: ch. 2). Turning to the most significant exponent of the movement's first wave, Jowett's contribution to the 1860 *Essays and Reviews*, entitled "On the Interpretation of Scripture", was attacked by many orthodox Christian writers in the same way that his earlier theological writings had been (e.g. Conybeare 1855; Vaughan 1861; Hinchliff 1987).[1] Three years after Jowett's death, Caird quoted the observation made in Jowett's unpublished notebooks (many of which survive in the Jowett Papers, Balliol College, Oxford) that, "even if we knew exactly what came from Christ, it is in perpetual process of depravation and needs to be enlarged … There is a fallen Christianity if there is a fallen man, and man is always falling" (quoted in Caird 1897: ix).

---

1. I misidentified the anonymous author of "The Neology of the Cloister" in Tyler (2004: 4, 54).

CAIRD'S EARLY RELIGIOUS THOUGHT

Early in his own career, Caird seems to have tried to distance himself from the contributors to *Essays and Reviews* (Caird 2005a: 10, 36 n.17). Yet, his mature position was in line with that of Jowett (Caird 1903–4). He did argue in his *Evolution of Religion* that "religion involves a relation, and indeed, a conscious relation, to a being or beings whom we designate as divine", and especially for the modern Christian, to Jesus Christ and God (1893: vol. 1, 53; Jones & Muirhead 1921: 332–4). Even so, Caird agreed with the other idealists that "the development of man" is ultimately "the development of human thought", which in turn is "the marriage of the soul with the world" (Caird 1893: vol. 1, 10; cf. 26–7). Crucially, as the world changes – as the concepts and beliefs that structure the daily life of society change – so do our personal beliefs (even if they do so more as a critique of those wider cultural modifications than as an endorsement). In his review of this work, the Reverend James Iverach complained, "By all means let us … translate … [the statements of early Christianity into terms of our modern experience] if we can. But such translation must not leave out the essential facts" (Iverach 2004: 201). Iverach was most concerned by Caird's Christology, and in particular by Caird's denial of the claim that Jesus enjoyed a necessarily unique spiritual standing (see Tyler 2006a: pt 2). For Caird, in this regard:

> the utmost uniqueness which would be of any moral or spiritual value, or which is consistent with any rational conception of human development, could only be that of one in whom the different elements that had existed in the previous religious experience of man were reconciled and brought together. But this does not of itself lift him out of his place in the development of man. (1897: x)

This claim ties into another significant heresy that was characteristic of the British idealists: namely, a certain scepticism regarding the existence of an afterlife for human souls (1893: vol. 1, 31–2). Caird's contention that "all that is good in the past is immortal, and still lives with and in us" (2005a: 3) was echoed in Green's contention that "the 'immortality of the soul', as = the eternity of thought = the being of God, is the absolute first and the absolute whole … The living agent, man, … like everything else, is eternal as a determination of thought" (Green 1997b: 159). (Caird came to believe in the existence of an afterlife towards the end of his life; Caird 1907: 261–82.)

One can begin to understand Caird's theology more fully by examining his (fairly orthodox Hegelian) critique of contemporary man's spiritual condition. Caird held that the leading principle of the modern age is a vaguely articulated faith in the fundamental equality and unity of humanity (1893: vol. 1, 15, 29–30). In *Hegel*, Caird argued that the "modern spirit of subjectivity" appears at first in the modern self as a sense of "the absolute worth and dignity of the rational life which is present to each individual"; that is, as an abstract ideal of the freedom of the undetermined will (1883: 208). Soon, however, modern subjectivity has to confront "its own inward emptiness", at which point it tends to degenerate into "an abject self-despair, into a sense of infinite want". The individual may then try to escape what is in effect an existential crisis (although Caird did not use the phrase) by abdicating his inchoate capacity for self-determination, his autonomy, and seeking solace in blind obedience to "an authoritative Church". This retreat into the childlike comfort of spiritual dependence requires an almost wilful denial of the truth that destroyed the ancient Greek civilization: namely, "that man, as a rational or self-conscious being, is a law and an end to himself" (1883: 210).

Conceptually, if not in time, Caird's critique of the modern sense of subjectivity was the starting-point of his theology. His published statements of his own constructive theology appeared predominantly in the later part of his academic career. Nevertheless, his recently published essay "Reform and Reformation" (written c.1866) shows that he held a fairly developed, coherent and stable position on such matters throughout his academic career. This essay set out "the general principles of human progress, and reform", the fundamentals of which were captured in the following passage:

> Man cannot create; all his success is dependent upon his striking in with mighty agencies already at work. His highest effort is to place himself directly in the path of some irresistible law, and then let himself be borne forward by it to the certain execution of his purpose. So here ... Reform, the work of man, is dependent upon progress, the work of God, and according to the view which we take of the design which He has been and is accomplishing in the course of history, must necessarily be the nature of the efforts which *we* can make to further that design.   (2005a: 2)

As the centuries pass, theological praxis constitutes the motor for overturning epochs of consciousness and organizations of temporal life. Ecclesiastical structures are radically reformed, as are the associated religious orthodoxies, and political structures develop sometimes violently as do ideas regarding the moral rights and duties of the individual. Thus movements to reform particular attitudes and practices take on a far more profound significance: "The principle of the future spreads gradually through the old frame of things, and lo! Ere we were aware, a new world hath formed itself around us" (*ibid.*: 5).

There was an initially unsettling side to Caird's early position, which came through clearly when he claimed that "though men fail and vanish, *man* does not: though the individual is limited and sacrificed, it is to a spiritual consciousness of the race which is ever advancing" (*ibid.*: 7). He continued, a little later:

> There is a common life of humanity to which all the lives of its members
> are but means and contributions and which grows amid their decay. It
> is the strange problem of providence to which indeed almost all other
> speculative difficulties are reducible, that the Race of Man is treated
> as *the Personality*. And indeed, it would sometimes seem as the only
> Proper Person.   (*Ibid.*)

Caird insisted that the individual is not devalued in this process, however. Instead, the individual makes himself the instrument of the only power that gives any real value to his life: "the development of the image of God in man". "Can we not feel", Caird asked, "with John the Baptist, when he said, not with envy but with joy, 'He must increase, I must decrease' [John 3:30]? He had done his life-work manfully and truly" (*ibid.*: 10). This is the heterodox form of immortality referred to earlier: our contribution to the common life of the faithful and of our community more generally lives on after our individual deaths.

Yet, we do not have to seek solace merely in the hope of attaining immortality in this rather attenuated sense. Caird also characterized the individual's progress towards "everlasting blessedness in God" as the development of certain "capacities" and a certain "spiritual consciousness" (*ibid.*: 4). Caird's Aristotelianism is particularly evident in his metaphor of spiritual growth as the "unfold[ing of] the lower form of the seed – into the higher form of leaf and so on to the highest forms of flower and fruit" (*ibid.*: 4). Clearly, this is an allusion to Aristotle's doctrine of final causes (Aristotle 1996: 198a14–200a4). A further debt to Aristotle is evident in Caird's belief that the individual is drawn instinctively to realize that which is best and highest in its nature, a form of Socratic internalism that echoed Aristotle's theory of the Prime Mover (Aristotle 1935: 1072a19–1073a13; *see* Vol. 1, Ch. 5, "Aristotle"). (Similar debts are evident in other British idealists; see Tyler 1998: 176–81; Gaus 2006.)

There may seem to be some ambiguity regarding the status of Caird's early philosophy of religion, however. He referred to a temporal life without faith in a divine providence through which God is manifested as simply "a weary succession of struggles of humanity to regain its lost level, with varied success at different times, but ever more or less foiled by the same corruptive tendencies" (2005a: 2). He went on to doubt, in such a hypothetical irredeemably corrupt temporal world, whether "we had still heart for the unending struggle, after the infinite hope, which is our spur and incitement, was taken away" (*ibid.*: 2). This was Caird's version of Kant's "practico-dogmatic principle of transition to this ideal of world-perfection", whereby motivational considerations cause one "to present the course of man's life here upon earth as if it were a life in heaven" (Kant 2001: 394; Tyler 2006b: 6–9, 102–10). On this reading, it may seem that early in his career Caird conceived faith in providence as merely a comforting myth that inspires one's religious efforts (even if philosophical analysis of the latest anthropological evidence seemed to confirm the truth of that myth) (Caird 1893: 24–30, 58–60; cf. Tyler

2006b: 12–16). In his mature period, Caird offered a more familiar philosophical justification for such faith, as will become clear shortly.

It should be clear by now that, for Caird, the human race does not necessarily follow God's providential design via a path that God ordained at the beginning of time, in a manner akin to some deistic mechanism. Which path humanity follows is circumscribed by the forces of circumstance that each human being faces in their own particular lives and consciousnesses. At this early stage in Caird's intellectual life, God amends each person's possible providential path in light of their contingent free actions. The most dramatic and far-reaching example of such intervention came immediately after Adam and Eve's fall from grace.

For the early Caird, the Fall was an actual historical event: at a specific point in the real past, particular persons chose to disobey God in particular ways. If they had not, the human race could have "evolved" peacefully to a fuller and deeper appreciation of humanity's moral nature and achieved the proper subordination of human will to the will of God. Certainly, it was always "necessary" to humanity's spiritual growth that it became "conscious of moral distinctions" (Caird 2005a: 5): "to this end it was necessary that temptation should be presented – that the possibility of a course in opposition to the Divine command should be suggested to him. But it was not necessary that he should fall" (*ibid.*: 4–5). Nevertheless, Adam and Eve's choices ensured that, in order to grow in dignity, every subsequent human being has had to develop "the consciousness of good and evil" for themselves (*ibid.*: 4). We do this both "amid storm and struggle" and "by the [original] quiet process of growth", which the Fall has done so much to frustrate (*ibid.*: 4, 5).

This claim leads to the central Christian doctrine that each of us must die in order to live. Such death refers not merely to the conclusion of the individual's life of sin as a prelude to the search for atonement. It refers also to the death of innocence as a prelude to the life of moral choice and responsibility, thereby creating the possibilities both of sin and of spiritual greatness. Caird's early formulation of this claim was problematic. In "Reform and Reformation", he echoed John Milton's description of Adam and Eve's innocence prior to the Fall as "but an excrementall whiteness" (Milton [1644] 1953–82), or as Caird put it, the "the negative purity of innocence" (2005a: 3). Yet, such a phrase points to an interesting ambiguity towards the Fall. On the one hand, it has been remarked that he saw the Fall as a result of particular human being' contingent, historical sins, and the resulting stress and struggle as a modification to God's initial plan (although not to the final goal of spiritual perfection). On the other hand, the early Caird also held that, "it would be absurd to think that such a disciplined goodness [as resulted from the hardships of the fallen individual] – even though it be stained with the long conflict – were inferior to, or even on a level with the childlike stainlessness of Eden" (*ibid.*: 4). It is unclear, then, whether the early Caird believed that the Fall was actually a necessary event in humanity's spiritual development.

CAIRD'S LATER RELIGIOUS THOUGHT

Caird's later writings contained remarkably little regarding the Fall. He did not refer to it as a real historical event, and he did not claim that God intervened to amend humanity's possible paths to salvation. Instead, he conceived humanity's spiritual development as arising always from the interaction of innate and necessary transcendental principles, particular determinate, situated consciousnesses and contingent external circumstances. Yet, there remained the twin processes of peaceful conscientious self-reform on the one hand and struggle on the other, which were so important in his early phase.

The idea that human life is marked by 'storm and struggle' indicates the influence on Caird of the *Sturm und Drang* movement, which had flourished in Germany in the 1770s. Indeed, he acknowledged freely his very great debt to the movement's leader, Johann Wolfgang von Goethe. In his long study "Goethe and Philosophy", Caird argued that the proper role of philosophy was "to complete the scientific disintegration [of the world's appearances so] that, through death, it may reach a higher life" (Caird 1892: 64). This was another way in which Caird was a representative British idealist. Similarly, Bernard Bosanquet referred to our earthly life as one in which the individual develops his higher capacities through ceaseless confrontations with "the hazards and hardships of finite selfhood" (Bosanquet 1913: esp. chs 3–7; 1920: esp. chs 5 & 6; Tyler 2006b: 147–8). It was from this foundation that, in various of his writings, Caird explored the manifestations of these processes in the history of ecclesiastical, social and political institutions – or, more precisely, in the iterative reformation of increasingly more complete and nuanced articulations of a society of free and equal human beings, living both in peace and in conflict with each other and with God.

Caird's transition to a pure form of immanentism was complete by the time he published *Hegel* in 1883. In that book, he described the doctrine that one must die in order to live as an "expression of the exact truth as to the nature of spirit" (1883: 212). He went on to articulate the fundamentals of this familiar notion in the following way:

> The true interpretation of the maxim is, that the individual must die to an isolated life, – *i.e.*, a life for and in himself, a life in which the immediate satisfaction of desire as his desire is an end in itself, – in order that he may live the spiritual life, the universal life which really belongs to him as a spiritual or self-conscious being.   (*Ibid.*: 213)

It is only by living this Christian life that one could manifest one's highest potentials, and so find true and lasting satisfaction. Seeking pleasure as such is necessarily self-defeating, given that in order to avoid circularity, pleasure can only be evoked by performing actions or attaining objects whose performance or attainment one values independently of the pleasure they bring (*ibid.*: 213–18). Hence, horticulture can be pleasurable only because, say, one values independently the creation of a productive or beautiful garden. In the same sense, dancing brings pleasure only because, say, one values independently taking part in this communal activity or in showing one's skill in this area. Without these logically prior reasons to value one's activity or object, no pleasure could be gained from the successful performance or attainment.

SPIRITUALITY AND THE COMMUNITY

As a rational being with valuable potentials, however, the individual will be satisfied only with the complete and coherent realization of his highest capacities. Yet, as an inherently finite being the individual is necessarily limited in his capacity to achieve all good things to their fullest degree at the same time. Moreover, we gain a sense of our particular identity – as an 'I' in contrast to a 'you' – only via our personal interpretation of the ways in which we are treated by other persons who we simultaneously recognize as different manifestations of the single divine spirit. In practice this means that each of us gains a sense of our own respective identities by reflecting on the processes of intersubjective recognition that underpin the various social practices and purposive rational agency in which we engage. This led Caird to conclude that:

> the wider and completer the good – *i.e.*, the realization of ourselves – which we seek, the deeper and more thorough must be the negation of self on which it is based ... [I]t is only in breaking down the boundary that separates our life from the life of others, that we can at the same time break down the boundary which prevents their life from becoming ours. (*Ibid.*: 215)

Hence, each of us must orient our lives towards helping others. In practical terms, Caird held that the individual attains "the dignity of his nature" (2005a: 4) by discerning the signs of providence in the world around him and then orienting his life to chime in with a path sanctified by providence (1893: vol. 1, 14; cf. 51–3). The vitality of these continuing acts of intersubjective recognition is crucial to human development. This was yet another continuity with Caird's earlier phase. Certainly, institutional articulation of conventional values, norms and modes of action is required if the individual is to gain a relatively stable and definite sense of personal identity and of the world. Yet, institutions can perform this function only to the extent that they channel the living spirit of the people. Counterfactually, Caird (1866) attributed the decline of the Roman Empire to its ossification under a set of institutions that gradually became simply formal, empty and therefore a dead articulation of conventional mores.

Throughout, individuals should be intelligent participants in vibrant societies and institutions. Ultimately, they should look to what Caird has once called "the still small voice" of their own personal consciences "that is ever guiding them onwards" (2005a: 5). Conscientious action cannot be blind conventionalism. Entailed by this thought, for Caird, is the proposition that the divine principle can be manifested with equal purity and strength in the lives of both the laity and the clergy (1893: vol. 1, 17–18, 29–30). Consequently, the true modern Christian community is closer to being a devout and continually questioning 'kingdom of ends' than it is to being an authoritative hierarchical organization for ecclesiastical instruction and control. Consequently and despite the conflictual nature of spiritual growth, Caird – and the British idealists more generally – insisted that modern human beings develop most fully and quickly through being active and spiritually self-aware members of a true Christian community (Caird 1893: vol. 1, 45). Irrespective of its particular outward form, this community cannot be in its essence the hierarchical national organization that was found in the established church of Victorian Britain. Instead, in its purest form it would be a universal community of believers, with the whole of humanity consulting its conscience as that is manifested in the daily Christian life of every person. As Caird observed in *The Evolution of Religion*: "The belief that the best which man has it in him to do or to be, springs out of that which is common to all, and therefore that the highest good is open to all, is fatal to all systems of privilege, and it is equally fatal to all national exclusiveness" (*ibid.*: vol. 1, 16).

Remembering Caird's critique of the modern sense of subjectivity, it can be seen that those who retreat into a religion that requires implicit faith from the laity make the same mistake as the ancient Greeks and indeed modern sceptics. In their own ways, they all misunderstand what it means to be 'a law or end' to oneself. Each fails to recognize that God realizes himself in the world in and through the particular meanings and values that together constitute not just the individual's rational and conscientious consciousness, but also the praxis and communal institutions that the latter create and sustain. Lasting spiritual growth is guided not merely by "the bare idea of the unity of man", but by "the idea of that unity *as manifesting itself in an organic process of development* – first, in particular societies, and, secondly, in the life of humanity as a whole" (*ibid.*: vol. 1, 21; cf. 46). For Caird, every person has the potential to be a vehicle for the realization of God in the world. This means that retreating into a comfortable trust of the wisdom of others would require one to deny one's part in the temporal manifestation of the divine spirit. It is for this reason that "What … [each of us has] to look for [in our religious life] … is a principle which is bound up with the nature of man, and which, therefore, manifests itself in all stages of his development" (*ibid.*: vol. 1, 46–7).

In a sense then, personal salvation is achieved in the very process of battling to reform one's temporal society. The conflicts, defeats and victories that shape our lives are not purely internal, existential crises (although they may be those as well). Humanity's spiritual battles take place between individuals and social groups and, as was indicated above, concern social and economic questions as well as the organization of worship and theological debates. Informing this theory is Caird's belief that "a man's religion is the expression of his ultimate attitude to the universe, the summed-up meaning and purport of his whole consciousness of things" (*ibid.*: vol. 1, 30). This is the heart of the highest form of religion and theology that modern humanity had yet achieved. It was summarized in Caird's observation in the final chapter of *Hegel* that:

> The Christian theology is, in its essence, little more than the development of this idea [that each of us must 'die to live']; for its primary doctrine is that God – the absolute principle to which, as their unity, we must refer all things and beings – is a "Spirit," – *i.e.*, a Being whose life is self-determination and self-revelation which includes also the element of self-sacrifice. For, as we have seen, the communication or giving out of life, which is involved in the idea of such a Being, cannot stop short of the communication of *a self*, and so of *Himself* to His creatures, which are thus "made partakers of the divine nature".
>
> (1883: 218)

CONCLUSION

Such, then, are the fundamental principles of the intimately connected early and late phases of Edward Caird's philosophy of religion. He applied the later formulation to many other areas of religious belief, including the overturning of Greek paganism (Caird 1904), the correct distinction between church and state (2005b: 98–108), the development of Christian mysticism (2005c) and the duties that Christians had to 'savage' peoples (1907: 205–60; Tyler 2006b: 123–8). Moreover, they exerted a very great influence on his civic and political radicalism in securing such improvements as the extension of the franchise and educational reform, as well as gender equity (Tyler 2006b: ch. 3). Critics of Caird's philosophy of religion rarely doubted his sincerity and piety, although many found certain central elements either obscure or unconvincing (one might highlight his conception of God and his theory of providence; Iverach 2004).

Caird died shortly before British idealism fell into academic obscurity in the early 1920s, partly under the weight of philosophical criticism of its metaphysics, partly as a result of the deaths of its remaining constructive thinkers (especially F. H. Bradley and Bernard Bosanquet), partly as a result of its association with Germany, and partly as the result of changes in intellectual fashion. The decline has been reversed somewhat now, with a great deal of scholarship on British idealism being produced around the world once again. Hopefully, it is only a matter of time before Edward Caird's philosophy of religion once again receives the attention it deserves.

FURTHER READING

Caird, E. 1893. *The Evolution of Religion*, 2 vols. Glasgow: MacLehose

Caird, E. [*c.*1866] 2005. "Reform and Reformation". In *Unpublished Manuscripts in British Idealism: Political Philosophy, Theology and Social Thought*, vol. 2, C. Tyler (ed.), 1–39. Bristol: Thoemmes Continuum.

Fairburn, A. 1893. "[Review of Edward Caird's] *The Evolution of Religion*". *Critical Review of Theological and Philosophical Literature* **3**(2) (April): 198–206. Reprinted in *Early Responses to British Idealism. Volume 1: Responses to B. Jowett, T. H. Green, E. Caird and W. Wallace*, C. Tyler (ed.), 203–12 (Bristol: Thoemmes Continuum, 2004).

Haldar, H. 1927. *Neo-Hegelianism*. London: Heath Cranton.

Lewis, W. 1909. *The Fundamental Principles Involved in Dr Edward Caird's Philosophy of Religion*. Leipzig: Quelle & Meyer.

Lindsay, A. 1926. "The Idealism of Caird and Jones". *Journal of Philosophical Studies* **1**: 171–82.

Jones, H. & J. Muirhead 1921. *Life and Philosophy of Edward Caird, LLD, DCL, FBA*. Glasgow: MacLehose, Jackson.

Macquarrie, J. (ed.) 1968. *Contemporary Religious Thinkers: From Idealist Metaphysicians to Existential Theologians*. London: SCM Press.

Mander, W. 2000. "Caird's Developmental Absolutism". In *Anglo-American Idealism, 1865–1927*, W. Mander (ed.), 51–63. Westport, CT: Greenwood.

Tyler, C. 2006. *Idealist Political Philosophy: Pluralism and Conflict in the Absolute Idealist Tradition*. London: Continuum.

On IDEALISM see also Chs 5, 19. On IMMORTALITY see also Chs 2, 6; Vol. 1, Ch. 8; Vol. 2, Ch. 5. On THE FALL see also Vol. 3, Ch. 10.

17

CHARLES S. PEIRCE

Douglas Anderson

Charles S. Peirce, co-founder with William James of the American pragmatist tradition, was born in Cambridge, Massachusetts, in 1839 to Benjamin Peirce and Sarah Mills Peirce. Benjamin was a noted Harvard mathematician who also harboured a quiet affinity for experientialist religion such as that of Immanuel Swedenborg. This affinity had a lingering influence on his son's thought. Charles was raised in the cultural milieu of the Unitarian response to New England Calvinism and in his early adult life joined the Episcopal Church of America. He was also thoroughly involved with the science of his day, working in both chemistry and astronomy; this meant that, as a scientist and philosopher, Peirce was also directly involved in the dissemination of evolutionary theory. Peirce's academic career was marked by a series of difficulties. Harvard President Charles Eliot, a childhood acquaintance of Peirce, successfully prevented him from obtaining any full-time position at Harvard. He taught for four years in Johns Hopkins' developing graduate programme but was released for unspecified 'moral' reasons in 1883. Peirce also conducted gravitational research for the US Coast Survey for many years but was released from service in 1891 when the organization was overhauled. He spent the rest of his life in relative poverty and obscurity, living with his second wife, Juliette, at their home in Milford, Pennsylvania. He died there in 1914.

Peirce's tremendous influence on the American philosophical tradition is well established. His seminal papers from the 1870s, "The Fixation of Belief" and "How To Make Our Ideas Clear", laid the groundwork for what James named 'pragmatism' in 1898. Peirce also worked extensively in logic, metaphysics and epistemology. What is not as well known is that Peirce was, from his earliest years, philosophically interested in questions of religion. As Michael Raposa suggests, "Peirce's philosophy as a whole seems to have been shaped and informed by certain religious beliefs and ideas" (1989: 4). In the early years of his work, Peirce wrote sporadically on the philosophy of religion. His 1878 essay "The Order of Nature", for example, includes a brief discussion of religious outlooks that do not require the *existence* of God, foreshadowing his later claim that God can be real without being existent. In the 1890s, religious themes took a more central role in his thinking. His well-known series of 'metaphysical' or 'cosmological' essays in the *Monist* incorporated various themes from philosophy of religion: the role of 'love' in cosmic and communal development, the possibility of the reality of a 'personal god', and the practical demands of a 'gospel of love'. He also published several essays in Christian-oriented journals. In one of these, "The Marriage of Science and Religion", Peirce argued that religion was focused on the past and tradition whereas science was aimed towards the future and possibility. He suggested that the two could be held together by focusing on their different purposes. It was only late in his career, however, that Peirce tried to establish more fully the role of religion within his overall systematic outlook.

In his 1903 "An Outline of the Classification of the Sciences", he identified as the second order of metaphysical enquiry "*Psychical*, or Religious, Metaphysics, concerned chiefly with the questions of (1) God, (2) Freedom, (3) Immortality" (Peirce 1998: 260). Subsequently, he pursued this metaphysical task. As did James, Peirce reviewed studies in psychology that argued for psychical life after death, but he was not persuaded by the evidence. Not believing that consciousness was crucial to selfhood, he developed a theory of immortality by way of his semiotic system. That is, in so far as persons are essentially signs or meanings, they achieve immortality through the historical development of their meaning. In this way, for example, we can still be in conversation with Aristotle or Shakespeare. Later, his 1908 essay "A Neglected Argument for the Reality of God" addressed the question of God's reality in such a fashion as to display a sketch of his entire philosophical system. He developed his theory of categories, his inductive method of enquiry, his scholastic realism and his critical commonsensism, using them to develop the distinction between God's existence and God's reality, and to argue for the latter. Finally, in 1911 Peirce wrote several manuscript drafts of a paper on the articles of Christian faith where he again outlined the relation between religion and science. This paper's central thesis – that religion and science have different spirits but nevertheless stand in a relation of mutual dependence – provides a good framework for understanding Peirce's religious thought and I employ it here to develop an exposition of his thought.

Peirce began this essay on the articles of faith with the claim that religion and science seem to stand in opposition: "no two spirits (tendencies) not downright conflicting can well be more opposed than the spirit of science and the spirit of religion" (1963–6: MS 851). The spirit of religion, he argued, aims at guiding the conduct of life, bringing stability to one's life. A religious belief thus pervades all aspects of one's experience: "it is absurd to say that religion is a mere belief. You might as well call society a belief, or politics a belief or civilization a belief. Religion is a life, and can be identified with a belief only provided that belief be a living belief – a thing to be lived rather than said or thought" (1931–58: 6.439). Science, on the other hand, looks to enquire into truth in an ongoing historical process.

From Peirce's perspective, scientific beliefs, when first introduced as hypotheses, are not good guides to conduct. Over time, as they remain effective, these theoretical beliefs gain purchase as 'truth' and can filter down into everyday practice.

The upshot is that science and religion, although they appear antagonistic, were for Peirce reciprocally dependent. Religious belief can, for example, bring the sort of stability to a person's or a society's life that makes experimental enquiry possible. This is why in "The Fixation of Belief" Peirce maintained that other methods of fixing belief such as tenacity and authority can be useful (1992: 109–23). If religious belief establishes social conditions conducive to the possibility of theoretical enquiry, the enquirer must see this as a good. It is only when religious belief becomes inflexible and blocks the road of enquiry that problems arise. Science or theory, on its part, is problematic if it tries to govern everyday existence with untested hypotheses. However, it also stands as a mode of criticism to check the ill effects of religious dogmas that become outmoded. Peirce's 'critical commonsensism' points to this value of theoretical enquiry (1998: 346). Peirce acknowledged that most human belief arises from instinct or common sense, and that beliefs originating in this way should be respected as guides to conduct. However, when actual doubts concerning the beliefs or the particular ways they have been specified in a culture arise, the enquirer must hold them up for critique and evaluation. Thus, the pragmatic religious believer must always be open to the revision of her beliefs.

INSTINCT AND CRITICAL COMMON SENSE

Religious beliefs are, Peirce maintained, at bottom instinctive or commonsensical: all hypothetical or abductive responses we give to our basic human questions are given by "the spontaneous conjectures of instinctive reason" (1998: 443). Thus, Peirce's "neglected" argument for God's reality is "that a latent tendency toward belief in God is a fundamental ingredient of the soul, and that far from being a vicious or superstitious ingredient, it is simply the natural precipitate of meditation upon the origin of the Three Universes [of experience: quality, matter and thought]" (*ibid.*: 446). Such religious beliefs are, however, vague or indefinite; they do not appear with the trappings of specific creeds or doctrines. As Peirce wrote to James in 1905:

> The idea [of a 'living' God] is a *vague* one but is only the more irresistible for that. Subtle distinctions are out of place; the truth of common sense is that little as we can comprehend the author of all beauty and power and thought, it is really impossible, except by sophisticating the plain truth, to think otherwise than that there is a living being.
>
> (1963–6: MS L224)

For Peirce, religion is at bottom a vague sense of the world's presence:

> In each individual it is a sort of sentiment, or obscure perception, a deep recognition of something in the circumambient All, which, if he strives to express it, will clothe itself in forms more or less extravagant, more or less accidental, but ever acknowledging the first and the last … as well as the relation to that Absolute of the individual's self, as a relative being. (1931–58: 6.429)

This means that religious beliefs can be instantiated in a variety of different ways so long as they meet the generic meaning. We thus have a variety of specifications of 'God', 'the good life', 'immortality' and so forth. Our instinctive or common-sense beliefs in these ideas, as with any scientific hypothesis, have historical and cultural aspects that are fallible. Taking immortality as an example, we see that the Greek vision of shades in Hades is distinct from Christian conceptions of rebirth and from spiritualist conceptions of a ghost-like existence on earth.

The most important upshot of this view is that Peirce fully recognized that traditional churches concretized beliefs in creeds and various metaphysical world-views, or what James called 'over-beliefs'. Although these creeds and over-beliefs often enable cultural stability, they can also become impediments to the true functioning of the religious community and often sucked the life out of religious belief until "the vital spark of inspiration becomes finally quite extinct" (*ibid.*: 6.438). On this score, Peirce's thought stood in concert with that of the American transcendentalists and James. It was precisely at this juncture that, Peirce believed, the critical work of science needed to become operative. And this is why Peirce called his view '*critical* commonsensism'.

Because of their indefiniteness and their capacity for diverse specifications, instinctive and common-sense beliefs, Peirce argued, must be open to criticism. Some ideas must be modified; some may ultimately be rejected. This is what gives ideas a history, a meaning that is in transition. It is this suggestion that separates Peirce's thinking from that of the *a priorists*, intuitionists and revelationists. He agrees that religion begins experientially, but he resists their tendency to specify a definitive original belief and derive the rest of the world from it. They take the view that "religious truth having once been defined is never to be altered in the most minute particular" (*ibid.*: 1.40). On this score Peirce stood in opposition to both Augustine (*see* Vol. 1, Ch. 18) and René Descartes (*see* Vol. 3, Ch. 8). As did his transcendentalist predecessors, he saw a commitment to *a priori* specificity as the death knell of genuine religious belief: "Like a plucked flower, its destiny is to wilt and fade. The vital sentiment that gave it birth loses gradually its pristine purity and strength, till some new creed treads it down" (*ibid.*: 6.430). For Peirce, instinctive religious beliefs must live within the context of the rest of one's world of beliefs. When these come into conflict, doubt should arise and generate an enquiry to resolve it. Thus, at any given time, while remaining open to change of belief if real doubts emerge, we should conduct our lives according to the common-sense religious beliefs that seem most stable and effective. In treating Peirce's own religious beliefs, then, we must see *them* as instinctive and historical: as nearly irresistible to him in their generality, but as fully revisable in their specificity.

GOD IN THEORY AND PRACTICE

As a critical commonsensist, Peirce adhered to a belief in the *reality* of God. His emphasis on reality was underwritten by his scholastic realism, which argued that reals could be other than individual things. Indeed, to think of God as merely another existent thing was, Peirce argued, a "fetishism" (1931–58: 6.495). Peirce's God was 'personal' in the sense of a living meaning working towards as yet unspecified ends. But God was not an individual in the sense of an individuated physical person or consciousness.

For Peirce, 'God' as a vernacular term bears with it a variety of traditional Christian generic traits. God is omnipresent; God is good; God is supremely powerful; God is *Ens necessarium*. Peirce's own list of traits was decidedly Christian and included, as we shall see, the belief that God is love. Nevertheless, his point was that the history of religions reveals a cluster of generic traits that form the hypothesis of a God or gods. The religions then present us with very specific interpretations and accounts of these traits. And those who adopt a religious outlook are always in the process of modifying their specific accounts of God: the God hypothesis must be understood "as vague but as true so far as it is definite, and as continually tending to define itself more and more, and without limit" (1998: 439). In his own description of God we find Peirce himself engaged in this process of revision.

Theories of biological evolution held centre stage in the late nineteenth century and deeply influenced how people looked at the cosmos. Instead of seeing these theories as a reason for discarding religion altogether, Peirce saw them as a reason to rethink the conception of God. Within Christian traditions, God was often conceived as a creator who acted with purpose in a closed teleological structure. Peirce thought that evolutionary theory resisted such a closed teleology. Therefore, if we are evolutionists, we must ask the question whether God grows or develops. Peirce's answer was that it would be "less false to speak so" than not (*ibid.*: 440). Moreover, so far as we think of God as growing and acting with purpose, we must conceive of God as operating with a "developmental teleology": a teleology that is not closed but instead allows for growth of the *telos* itself (1992: 331).

As philosophers of religion engage in the theoretical revisions of the meaning of 'God', the vague, vernacular version remains sufficient for guiding human practice. The generic traits alone produce ends-in-view sufficient to help all persons, not just intellectuals, live worthwhile lives. If this were not true, religion could never be democratically disseminated. This is why Peirce insisted that "If God Really be, and be benign … we should naturally expect that there would be some Argument for His Reality that should be obvious to all minds, high and low alike, that should earnestly strive to find the truth of the matter" (1931–58: 6.457). The vernacular conception orients us toward truth, goodness and beauty. It is, for Peirce, the "august practicality" of God that creates the human affinity for God. We learn to create habits of conduct under God's influence in the way that long acquaintance with "a man of great character may deeply influence one's whole manner of conduct" (*ibid.*: 6.502). In so far as God is love, for example, we should likewise learn to live as loving beings.

THE CENTRALITY OF LOVE

The notion of *agape* or cherishing love played two central roles in Peirce's philosophy of religion. On the one hand, it served as the operative agent for his cosmology: for his conception of the creative evolution of the cosmos. On the other hand, as we noted, God's love served as the central model for our personal and communal conduct. Thus, both our individual religious lives and the communal actions of the church, he argued, should be governed by the principle of *agape*.

Peirce developed his Christian-oriented cosmology in an essay entitled "Evolutionary Love" (1992: 352–71). He sought to mediate between what he took to be the extreme versions of evolutionary theory that were current in the late nineteenth century. The first, which Peirce labelled 'tychasm', maintained that chance was the sole agent of evolution. The other, named 'anancasm' by Peirce, was the mechanical necessitarianism championed by Herbert Spencer, among others, that made evolution into a determinate, teleological story. Peirce offered a mediating third position, which he named 'agapasm' after the Greek word for cherishing love: this is what he meant by 'evolutionary love'. Agapasm incorporated elements of both chance and regularity but avoided the difficulties of each extreme. Tychasm had difficulty accounting for any stability or regularity in natural law, and anancasm had difficulty making sense of novelty, possibility and variety. Thus, for Peirce, agapasm made more sense of the scientific evidence available at the time.

In his theory of evolutionary love, Peirce aimed to have science and religion work in concert. Although to some the mixing of love and cosmology seemed strange, it had the descriptive advantage of making sense of the coexistence of law, variety and growth. Agapasm avoided a world of sheer contingency but at the same time resisted the closure of mechanical and theistic teleologies by defending a developmental teleology that allowed for the emergence of novel phenomena in the cosmos. Moreover, in explaining the growth of the cosmos, *agape* served equally well as a principle for human development, both individual and communal.

For the individual, being loved creates a trust in life that allows for personal growth. This agapic love of God for God's creatures, Peirce argued, should become the guide to our own religious lives. That is, we should treat each other with the same sort of cherishing concern. "An evolutionary philosophy", Peirce argued, "teaches that growth comes only from love, from – I will not say self-*sacrifice*, but from the ardent impulse to fulfill another's highest impulse" (1992: 354). On various occasions Peirce noted the practical importance of such a philosophy for teaching, for child rearing and for developing friendships.

Peirce also focused his thought on the communal dimensions of religious belief, especially a belief in love. Religion, he argued:

> cannot reside in a single individual. Like every species of reality, it is essentially a social, public affair. It is the idea of a whole church, welding all its members together in one organic, systemic perception of the Glory of the Highest – an idea having a growth from generation to generation and claiming a supremacy in the determination of all conduct, private and public. (1931–58: 6.429)

Although he did not defend any particular denomination, Peirce played up the communal role of love central to much of Christianity. However, he argued that Christian theologians in his day tended to focus on unhelpful doctrinal details and lost sight of love's efficacy. "Now", Peirce said, "the principal business of theologians is to make men feel the enormity of the slightest departure from the metaphysics they assume to be connected with the standard faith" (*ibid.*: 6.3). In response to them, he suggested that humanity create an inclusive church of love much as scientists seek to create a community of enquiry whose ideal is truth. "The *raison d'être* of a church", Peirce believed, "is to confer upon men a life broader than their narrow personalities, a life rooted in the very truth of being" (*ibid.*: 6.451). This was the sort of thinking that underwrote and inspired Josiah Royce's *The Problem of Christianity*. Peirce appropriated the common-sense or instinctive belief in love that influenced Christianity, but left it open to pragmatic testing. That is, the fruits of a church of love would reveal its success or failure.

One such test, as Peirce saw it, was the inclusivity of the church. The aim of a church of love would be, Peirce suggested, to create a self-ameliorating social group where individuals are able to realize their own possibilities. All individuals are to be included. Religion, Peirce argued, "only comes to full flower in a great church coextensive with civilization. This is true of every religion, but supereminently so of the religion of love" (*ibid.*: 6.493). When God's love is embodied in a human community, it creates the very conditions of growth and learning that we each naturally seek. If the church of love is to have any enemy, it would be egoism or what Peirce called "the gospel of greed" (1992: 357). Thus, when any church operated by aiming to exclude individuals from membership, or when a church was driven by the egoism of a few, it would fail in practice to accomplish its own projected goals.

CONCLUSION

Peirce's ideas in the philosophy of religion remained closely tied to his pragmatism, which he renamed 'pragmaticism' in 1905 (1998: 335). The import of religious beliefs was to be found in their usefulness in explaining features of the cosmos and, even more importantly, in the kinds of conduct they underwrote in human affairs. Peirce's pragmatic task was, as noted at the outset, to define the complementary roles of religion and science for human experience.

Peirce agreed with James that in the course of human conduct, we cannot often wait on the evidence of theoretical science to make practical decisions. Room had to be made for what we might call a 'working faith'. Particularly in our everyday conduct, our faith in love and a variety of generic moral principles should be our primary guide. It would be a mistake, for example, to revise our ideas on the efficacy of love or the horror of genocide on the basis of some new theory that had not been extensively tested. Nevertheless, our religious faith must always be open to revision.

Religious beliefs, when specified in particular historical contexts, cannot be allowed to trump theoretical truths that withstand experimental testing. Rather, religion must keep the avenue of enquiry open and must adapt its specifications of religious beliefs to the developing history of truth. For example, Peirce's cosmology, although named after *agape*, was essentially driven by scientific evidence suggesting both the stability of some natural species and the generation of novel species. Thus, although Peirce was a friend of religion in general, he was an opponent of what has come to be called 'fundamentalism' in any of its guises. "Owe what one may to the Church", Peirce argued, "the truth claims permanent allegiance" (1931–58: 6.450). Medieval philosophy, Peirce said, shows the ruinous effects of allowing creeds to close off enquiry. Amelioration hinges not only on the trustworthy community of love, but also on the search for truth. The upshot is that faith must remain vigilant and that reason must beware of a desire to dominate practice; each has its place in human affairs in a reciprocal relation to the other. Faith is "highly necessary in affairs", Peirce maintained, "but if it means you are not going to be alert for indications that the moment has come to change your tactics, I think it is ruinous in practice" (1963–6: MS L224).

Peirce's contemporaries, Royce and James, are both better known than Peirce for their work in the philosophy of religion (*see* Vol. 5, Ch. 2, "William James"). Peirce's extensive writings on religious issues should not, however, be overlooked. He developed a view of religion that nicely mediated between the extreme individualism of James and the communal absolutism of Royce. Indeed, when one closely examines the history of ideas, one finds traces of Peirce's philosophy of religion shot through both Royce's *The Problem of Christianity* and James' *The Varieties of Religious Experience*. Moreover, Peirce's outlook laid the groundwork for philosophies of religion as diverse as A. N. Whitehead's process thought and John Dewey's pragmatically oriented notion of a common faith (*see* Vol. 5, Ch.

4, "John Dewey" and Ch. 5, "Alfred North Whitehead and Charles Hartshorne").
Peirce's pragmatic way of going about philosophy led to his own revision of the
relation between reason and religion:

> The day has come, however, when the man whom religious experi-
> ence most devoutly moves can recognize the state of the case. While
> adhering to the essence of religion, and so far as possible to the church,
> which is all but essential, say, penessential, to it, he will cast aside that
> religious timidity that is forever prompting the church to recoil from
> the paths into which the Governor of history is leading the minds of
> men, a cowardice that has stood through the ages as the landmark and
> limit of her little faith, and will gladly go forward, sure that truth is not
> split into two warring doctrines, and that any change that knowledge
> can work in his faith can only affect the expression, but not the deep
> mystery expressed.   (1931–58: 6.432)

FURTHER READING

Anderson, D. 1995. "Peirce's God of Theory and Practice". *Revista Portuguesa de Filosofia* **51**:
    167–78.
Misak, C. 2004. "C. S. Peirce on Vital Matters". In *The Cambridge Companion to Peirce*, C. Misak
    (ed.), 150–74. Cambridge: Cambridge University Press.
Orange, D. 1984. *Peirce's Conception of God: A Developmental Study*. Bloomington, IN: Indiana
    University Press.
Pfeifer, D. 1981. "Charles Peirce's Contribution to Religious Thought". In *Proceedings of the C. S.
    Peirce Bicentennial International Congress*, K. Ketner (ed.), 367–73. Lubbock, TX: Texas Tech
    University Press.
Potter, V. 1976. "C. S. Peirce's Argument for God's Reality: A Pragmatist's View". In *The Papin
    Festschrift*, L. Armenti (ed.), 224–44. Philadelphia, PA: Villanova University Press.
Raposa, M. 1989. *Peirce's Philosophy of Religion*. Bloomington, IN: Indiana University Press.
Royce, J. 1968. *The Problem of Christianity*. Chicago, IL: University of Chicago Press.
Trammell, R. 1972. "Religion, Instinct, and Reason in the Thought of Charles S. Peirce".
    Transactions of the Charles S. Peirce Society **8**: 3–23.

On COMMON SENSE see also Vol. 3, Ch. 18. On LOVE see also Ch. 13; Vol. 5, Ch. 16. On PRAG-
MATISM see also Vol. 5, Chs 2, 4. On SCIENCE see also Chs 7, 11, 12, 15, 19; Vol. 2, Ch. 12; Vol.
3, Ch. 17; Vol. 5, Chs 4, 19.

18

FRIEDRICH NIETZSCHE

Clancy Martin

On 14 January 1880, at the beginning of his most productive period, and only eight years prior to his collapse into madness, Nietzsche wrote to his friend Malwida von Meysenbug, complaining of his deteriorating health. He tells her that he hopes for the stroke that, he believes, will put an end to his suffering. "As regards torment and self-denial, my life during these past years can match that of any ascetic of any time; nevertheless, I have wrung from these years much in the way of purification and burnishing of the soul – and I no longer need religion or art as a means to that end" (Middleton 1969: 170–71). In the same letter he goes on to say that he is proud of the fact that he has done this work "of self-help" alone; and that he has moreover "given to many an indication of how to rise above themselves, how to attain equanimity and a right mind" (*ibid.*).

For those of us who think of Friedrich Nietzsche (1844–1900) as the preeminent atheist philosopher of the nineteenth century – indeed, perhaps the pre-eminent atheist philosopher of all time – such claims should be startling. Self-transformation, purification, equanimity, a right mind: these are among the familiar goals of religion. And, indeed, in the letter Nietzsche himself says as much, even allowing that religion and art are the usual ways people accomplish such goals.

But consider also:

> *Moralizing* and *religious* literature is the most full of lies … Alongside religious wars there is always a *moral war* going on: that is, *one* impulse wants to subjugate humanity; and as religions gradually die out, this struggle will become all the more *bloody* and *visible*. We are only at the beginning! (Nietzsche 1988: 262, my trans.)

Or the famous 'madman' passage from *The Gay Science*, always worth quoting one more time:

Have you not heard of that madman who lit a lantern in the bright morning hours, ran to the market place, and cried incessantly: "I seek God! I seek God!" – As many of those who did not believe in God were standing around just then, he provoked much laughter. Has he got lost? Asked one … Is he afraid of us? Has he gone on a voyage? Emigrated? – Thus they yelled and laughed.

The madman jumped into their midst and pierced them with his eyes. "Whither is God?" he cried; "I will tell you. *We have killed him* – you and I. All of us are his murderers. But how did we do this? How could we drink up the sea?

Who gave us the sponge to wipe away the entire horizon? What were we doing when we unchained this earth from its sun? … God is dead … How shall we comfort ourselves, the murderers of all murderers? What was holiest and mightiest of all that the world has yet owned has bled to death under our knives: who will wipe this blood off us? … Is not the greatness of this deed too great for us? Must we ourselves not become gods simply to appear worthy of it? There has never been a greater deed; and whoever is born after us – for the sake of this deed he will belong to a higher history that all history hitherto …"

It has been related further that on the same day the madman forced his way into several churches and there struck up his *requiem aeternam deo*. Led out and called to account, he is said to have replied nothing but: "What are these churches now if not the tombs and sepulchers of God?"

(Nietzsche 1974: 125)

What is perhaps most striking about this passage – and many other less poetic ones like it – is Nietzsche's insistence that for us there is no God, matched with his insistence that the belief in God is the highest thing humanity has yet accomplished. To many this sounds bizarre: if we are correct that "God is dead", that there is no God, how could one hold that the (false) belief in God was also the highest thing we had achieved? But for Nietzsche, the value of a belief will be measured not against its truthfulness, but against its usefulness, against its tendency to promote life and flourishing.[1] And this is the heart of his philosophy of religion, his superficially paradoxical-seeming embracing of many of the goals of religion while attacking individual religions (especially, of course, Christianity) with a vigour and incisiveness that has never been matched. Nietzsche argues that religion was life-promoting for us for many thousands of years, but it is no longer,

---

1. So Nietzsche writes: "The falseness of a judgment is for us not necessarily an objection to a judgment; in this respect our new language may sound strangest. The question is to what extent it is life-promoting, life-preserving, species-preserving, perhaps even species-cultivating … renouncing false judgments would mean renouncing life and a denial of life" (1966a: 11).

especially because of Christianity's active promotion of a reversal of healthy values. Nevertheless he argues that many of the psychological needs previously served by religion are still pressing needs for the people of his own time. It is just that these needs must be served in new ways.[2]

In this brief survey of Nietzsche's various thoughts on the philosophy of religion – his position evolves over time – I shall begin by discussing his early notion that art may stand as a spiritual substitute for religion. Next I turn to the description of the evolution of spirituality he offers in his masterpiece *Thus Spoke Zarathustra*, in the famous passage on "The Three Metamorphoses". The centrepiece of the essay is his critique of the origins of, and the value system promoted by, Christianity, as presented chiefly in *The Genealogy of Morals*. I shall briefly remark on his discussion on the Laws of Manu, Islam and Buddhism, and I shall wrap up with his own late ideas on value, the religious impulse and spiritual transformation in *The Antichrist* and *Ecce Homo*.

SCHOPENHAUER, MAN'S HIGHEST METAPHYSICAL ACTIVITY, AND THE *ÜBERMENSCH*

Nietzsche's early writings, from his years in school at Pforta, show an unusually devout teenager and young man (cf. Hayman 1980: 29). But by the time of college, the young Nietzsche had already rejected the Christianity of his upbringing (Nietzsche's father, who was a pastor, died while Nietzsche was very young, which has led some to speculate that his attack on God had deep psychological causes) (cf. *ibid.*: 26), and his writing starts to show that he sees a tension between religious belief and the truth. In a letter to his sister he writes:

> If we had believed from youth onwards that the soul's salvation depended on someone other than Jesus – on Mahomet, say – we would no doubt have felt equally blessed. Surely it is faith alone that imparts blessedness, not the objective behind the faith … Genuine faith never fails. It fulfils whatever the believer expects from it, but it does not offer the slenderest support for a demonstration of objective truth.
>
> Here the ways of men divide. Do you want to strive for peace of mind and happiness? Then believe. Do you want to be a devotee of truth? Then seek. (*Ibid.*: 66–7)

---

2. I agree with Julian Young when he writes that Nietzsche is "*above all* a religious thinker" (2006: 201).

Nevertheless Nietzsche does not abandon the goals of religion, and the first real phase of his philosophical thinking about religion begins with Arthur Schopenhauer, the ancient Greeks and his work in *The Birth of Tragedy*.

In *The Birth of Tragedy* Nietzsche has a view of life that depends very heavily on his youthful, enthusiastic reading of Schopenhauer's *The World as Will and Representation*. Nietzsche discovered Schopenhauer when he was twenty-five years old, and he was completely captivated by Schopenhauer's pessimism and his idea that life could be redeemed through the power of art (in its opening pages he even explains that *The Birth of Tragedy* is written in the spirit of Schopenhauer and to his honour). The basic problem confronted by *The Birth of Tragedy* is the problem of Job. Life is full of suffering, and the suffering seems to be without explanation, without purpose. A further, related problem is one that Nietzsche takes from Schopenhauer's interpretation of Kant: life as we actually experience it is not 'reality', it is rather an illusion created by our minds, which necessarily structure a more fundamental chaos that, were it not structured by the mind, would make life unlivable. This establishes a dichotomy that is a staple of many religious traditions: this world we all live in is somehow less valuable or less real than the other world, the one we do not know or directly experience, which is where the truth resides. The ancient Greeks, Nietzsche argues, recognized this dichotomy, and he introduces his parallel distinction between the Apollonian and Dionysian aspects of artistic creation to show how the Greeks reconciled themselves with this unfortunate, schizophrenic fact of life.

Nietzsche's idea of the Apollonian is typified by the so-called plastic arts, especially sculpture and architecture, but also drawing and painting. Here the artist has taken formless matter and with technical skill created structure, relying on principles of harmony, balance, and order. Nietzsche compares the process to the act of dreaming, suggesting that while the structure created is importantly illusory – it is an order imposed by an active agent on more fundamentally disorderly material – it is also a great consolation to us, it makes us feel (literally, in the case of architecture) 'at home', it dignifies who we are and reassures us about existence. This is one fundamentally religious role played by religion: it makes sense of (crazy, dangerous, unpredictable, frightening) life for us, it gives us the illusion of security and stability, it dignifies us.

The notion that there is something 'illusory' about the plastic arts may be irritating to some (especially architects). The idea, when persuasive, seems to rely heavily on the illusions created by, for example, drawing and painting. The ancient Greek artist Zeuxis was said to have painted grapes so life-like that the crows would fly down and peck at them; the perspectival illusions of figural drawing – foreshortening of the limbs, and so on – were already well known in ancient Greek times, and perspectival illusions are also appealed to as a metaphor for Nietzsche, as is *trompe l'oeil* and other techniques used by artists to create visual illusions. The point, of course, is that there is something attractive and comforting about these illusions, and that the artist cannot achieve the comforting effect except as an illusion.

But there is also the other side of life. Beneath the consoling and useful illusion created by our senses and our actively artistic mind is the threatening reality of chaos, our inability to control our own destiny, the savagery of the world around us and (at least at times) our own nature, and the certainty of death. Without an awareness of these aspects of existence – which are not, for the young Nietzsche, illusory, but real or the fact of the matter – our lives become devoid of meaning and disconnected from reality. The role of the Dionysian – typified, for Nietzsche, by the art of music – is to provide, in a non-destructive way, for an intimacy with these psychologically menacing powers. Thus the art of music also provides for our release from the bonds of our individuality (here the influence of Schopenhauer, who thought that our selfhood was one more illusory creation of a mind that cannot bear to confront reality, is particularly obvious), in the familiar experience of unity with one another and with nature that comes in intense musical experience. The orgiastic festivals of Dionysus, a kind of ancient Greek rock concert, in which the drinking and dancing continued for days until the participants collapsed in exhaustion, sought to create this kind of abandon, which transports the individual beyond himself into the collective whole of nature and the universe. The Dionysian festival celebrated madness and even violence. But these are, Nietzsche insisted, crucial aspects of life, and to ignore them was to fail to understand existence and our place within it.

For the young Nietzsche, then, the highest religious experience was that which acknowledged and enhanced both these aspects of human spirituality: in the case of the ancient Greeks, this was the art of tragedy; in his own day, it was the Wagnerian opera. (At the time of *The Birth of Tragedy* Nietzsche was operating very much under the spell of his friend and sometime mentor Richard Wagner; soon his friendship with Wagner would come to an ugly end, and his view of Wagnerian opera radically changes.) In tragedy we experience and celebrate both the formal constraints (and familiar comforts) of the Apollonian, and the dangerous excesses and fatal agonies of the Dionysian. We are both beguiled by our rational minds and intoxicated by our irrational natures, and so we are reconciled with the necessary illusions of the mind while affirming the deeper meaning of life that exceeds the mind's grasp. This, for Nietzsche, is "man's highest metaphysical activity" (1966b: 18), and how we get religion.

While Nietzsche quickly abandons the neo-Kantian distinction, taken from Schopenhauer, between an illusory world of our mental lives and the real world of irrational nature (characterized, according to Schopenhauer, by "the will to life"), he continues to emphasize the importance of the Dionysian throughout his philosophical work. In fact, in what we can take as his last word on the subject of the philosophy of religion (and much else), he concludes his final work, *Ecce Homo*, with: "Have I been understood? – *Dionysus versus the Crucified*" (1968a: 101). We shall take up the interpretation of that aphorism at the end of this essay.

We should not leave the subject of Nietzsche's early Schopenhauerism without briefly addressing the influence on Nietzsche of Schopenhauer's idea of 'the saint'.

Schopenhauer had the idea that human spiritual perfection was attained not so much through the assistance of religion (although Schopenhauer thought that religion mostly assisted our spiritual efforts, he thought it would only take us so far) as through the example of greatly spiritual individuals who strove to understand the truth and embody it: the artist, the genius and the saint. The artist shows us the truth; the genius describes the truth to us or reveals it in analysis; the saint actually lives according to the truth. The saint is the ideal type of spiritual human being, who has freed himself from the narrow-minded values of his society and his time in the attempt to establish the complete freedom of mind necessary to see through the illusions of ordinary experience.

For Schopenhauer, the saint's understanding of life is inevitably pessimistic (the truth the saint sees is that life is painful and meaningless), and so his way of living conveys resignation with, and ultimately retirement from, our everyday, suffering world. Nietzsche does not follow Schopenhauer in this: soon after *The Birth of Tragedy* he begins to develop his mature view, which embraces Schopenhauer's ideal of the great spiritual type while rejecting his pessimism in favour of a life-affirming, this-world-affirming model of spirituality. Nevertheless, throughout his intellectual career we see in Nietzsche the Schopenhauerian theme that our spiritual goals can best be seen (and most likely will be achieved) through individual spiritual growth and effort, in higher types of human beings.[3] When Nietzsche invents his famous character Zarathustra and the fictional Zarathustra proposes his own fictional character, the *Übermensch*, the echoes of Schopenhauer's saint (also, certainly, Schopenhauer's artist) are audible (2005: 8–9).[4] But the *Übermensch*, who represents the loftier spiritual heights that Zarathustra believes we can attain, is, unlike Schopenhauer's saint, not a denial of this world and this life, rather just the opposite: "The *Übermensch* is the meaning of the earth" (*ibid.*: Prologue, §3).

Thus Spoke Zarathustra is a religious book through and through, offering as it does Nietzsche's excursus on the consequences and the opportunities provided by the death of God in language that deliberately parodies that of the New Testament (and many other religious texts), and the book is too rich and complex for us

---

3. Even Young, who is principally concerned to argue that Nietzsche's philosophy of religion is grounded in his thinking about what might provide the best community, agrees that Nietzsche finds the highest expression of spirituality in the exceptional individual; see Young (2006: 185). I have not argued for or against Nietzsche's "religious communitarianism" (in Young's phrase) because, unlike Young, I do not think Nietzsche conceives of his philosophy of religion in these terms. Nevertheless, Young's book is excellent, and I recommend it to anyone who wants to go deeper into Nietzsche's philosophy of religion.

4. Zarathustra meets an old saint living in the forest when he first descends his mountain to give the good news of the *Übermensch* to the world; in fact, the saint – who does not know that 'God is dead' – is the very first person Zarathustra meets.

to make much progress on its analysis here.[5] However, one passage cannot be left out: the famous discussion of "The Three Metamorphoses" at the opening of book I:

> I tell you of three metamorphoses of the spirit: how the spirit becomes a camel, the camel a lion, and the lion at last a child … What is difficult? So asks the spirit that would bear much; then it kneels down like a camel wanting to be well laden.
>
> What is the most difficult, you heroes? So asks the spirit that would bear much, that I may take it upon me and rejoice in my strength …
>
> But in the loneliest wilderness the second metamorphosis occurs: here the spirit becomes a lion who would conquer his freedom and be master in his own desert.
>
> Here he seeks his last master: he wants to fight him and his last god; for final victory he wants to fight the great dragon.
>
> Who is the great dragon that the spirit will no longer call lord and god? "Thou shalt," is the name of the great dragon. But the spirit of the lion says, "I will." …
>
> "All value has long been created, and I am all created value. Truly, there shall be no more 'I will'." Thus speaks the dragon.
>
> My brothers, why is there need of the lion in the spirit? Why is not the beast of burden, which renounces and is reverent, enough?
>
> To create new values – that, even the lion cannot accomplish: but to create freedom for oneself for new creating – that the might of the lion can do …
>
> But say, my brothers, what can the child do that even the lion could not do? Why must the preying lion still become a child?
>
> The child is innocence and forgetting, a new beginning, a game, a self-propelled wheel, a first movement, a sacred Yes-saying.
>
> Yes, for the game of creating, my brothers, a sacred Yes-saying is needed: the spirit now wills his own will, and he who had been the world's outcast now conquers his own world.   (Nietzsche 2005: 25–6)

The camel represents the Judaeo-Christian way of being in the world. The camel wants to be weighed down with a burden from outside itself, with 'The Law' or God's morality, with an externally generated understanding of the meaning of life, and it wants this because it is difficult to carry this burden, because it is strong enough to carry this load. It is a proof of the strength and virtue of the camel that

---

5. Interested readers should see Loeb (2009). Some helpful discussion of Nietzsche's philosophy of religion is also contained in the introduction and endnotes to my own translation of *Thus Spoke Zarathustra* (Nietzsche 2005).

the load it carries is not too heavy for it to bear. The camel yearns for what is diffi-cult: and what could be more difficult than satisfying the law of God?

But, Zarathustra teaches, the spirit changes: and next we see the lion, which represents the Renaissance and Enlightenment insistence on freedom and self-determination. This is where we find ourselves today, Nietzsche thinks: confronting the dragon of 'thou shalt', of Judaeo-Christian morality (portrayed in its philo-sophical form, Nietzsche thinks, in the morality of Immanuel Kant; *see* Vol. 3, Ch. 21), and even more the notion that all value has already been created, that there is no more value for humanity to discover or create. The idea represented by the dragon is that value is a function of our being told what we ought to do, rather than ourselves deciding what is valuable; and though the lion cannot itself create value, it is necessary so that we may be in a position to create value. The lion, who represents human freedom, can overcome the dragon of our past ideas of value and create the spiritual space necessary for the emergence of the child. It is the lion, then, that kills God.

The child lives in the land of spiritual opportunity that Zarathustra believes the future will bring, the country of the *Übermensch*. The spirit has not become the child yet: we are still overcoming the 'thou shalt' of our spiritual past. For the creation of new values, Zarathustra suggests, we need the freedom to forget the past, we need innocence, we need the creative spirit acting entirely on its own, out of the pure pleasure of creating (thus, "the game of creating"). This is a very optimistic view of history and human nature, and it is offered by Zarathustra only after he considers, in "The Prologue", the other alternative: the nihilism that is represented by what he calls "the last man" (Nietzsche 2005: 12–14). Zarathustra is not naive: he argues that we are at a turning point, that the freedom created by the lion could plunge us into the confusion and self-destruction that is nihilism and the radical loss of all real value, or we may find that this freedom allows us to begin the process of value creation all over again, that our culture may be refreshed by, or even reborn in, an entirely new way (or ways) of understanding our spiritual place in the universe.

As I have charted it, then, the evolution of the first stage of Nietzsche's philosophy of religion is from an early, ardent Christianity, to his quasi-Schopenhauerian idea that we can achieve our spiritual ideals in aesthetic (and especially Dionysian) experience, and then to his invention of the *Übermensch*, the saint-like, child-like ideal for the future of humanity, who has the freedom and the power to create new values. By the time of *Thus Spoke Zarathustra*, the central idea of Nietzsche's phil-osophy of religion is clear: the primary spiritual function of humanity is to create value. We now move to the next stage of his thinking, in which he provides a more detailed analysis of the kinds of value-creation humanity can pursue. For his next great thesis is that human beings have (and have pursued) one of two options: to create values that promote our flourishing, or to create values that interfere with the same. We have created gods that have helped us on our way, but we have also created gods – like, he thinks, the Judaeo-Christian god – who have hindered us:

There are *nobler* ways of making use of the invention of gods than man's self-crucifixion and self-abuse … this can fortunately be deduced from any glance at the *Greek gods*, these reflections of noble and proud men in whom the *animal* in man felt deified, did *not* tear itself apart and did *not* rage against itself.   (Nietzsche 1968b: 94)

WHAT IS IGNOBLE? THE BIRTH OF CHRISTIANITY

Nietzsche's analysis of the Judaeo-Christian value system is, by his own lights, nothing less than a historical account of man's self-crucifixion and self-abuse. We do not want to address the minutiae of Nietzsche's account of the development of Judaeo-Christian morality: that is a subject for ethicists. For the purposes of his philosophy of religion, we need to understand the larger forces in human psychology and the social structure that allow the Judaeo-Christian way of looking at the world to take such vigorous hold of Western civilization.

In *The Genealogy of Morals* Nietzsche tells a kind of state of nature story. Imagine human beings before the pressures of the environment sent them into communities and villages. These human beings were closer to non-human animals, and they could freely express their natural drives, including the drive to cruelty. As people began to band together, the drive to cruelty was modified: it was expressed in attacks on other human communities. There were, Nietzsche tells us, "terrible outbreaks" of cruelty among these small tribes, and indeed if we look at the literature of war in early human civilization we find chronicles of these frightening explosions of cruelty, which however are viewed by their perpetrators (and, as Nietzsche points out, even their victims) as entirely legitimate. But as communities begin to live increasingly near to one another, as trade emerges and population growth necessitates more and more shared borders, the drive to cruelty becomes increasingly difficult to express. People have to get along with one another. But this repression of the drive to cruelty does not eliminate the drive; rather, Nietzsche argues, in an idea he takes from Schopenhauer (and which is put to great use by Freud), the drive turns inward. This is when, according to Nietzsche, a new kind of consciousness emerges: a divided consciousness, which is both aware and aware of itself as aware. This divided consciousness is a manifestation of the drive to cruelty: that drive, turned inward, has found its expression in allowing one part of consciousness to inflict pain on the other. This is the development of what Nietzsche calls "the bad conscience", and it is experienced by consciousness as a kind of psychic pain.

Enter the priest. Once this divided consciousness and psychic pain are established, an explanation or an answer to these questions is called for: why am I in pain? Why do I suffer this mental distress? This is fertile ground, Nietzsche argues, for the flourishing of the type of religious leader that he calls, generally, "the priest", or "the priestly class". The priest can give reasons for the pain of the divided consciousness, and that reason is "guilt".

> You will have guessed what has really happened here, *beneath* all this: that will to self-tormenting, that repressed cruelty of the animal-man made inward and scared back into himself, the creature imprisoned in the "state" so as to be tamed, who invented bad conscience in order to hurt himself after the *more natural* vent for this desire to hurt had been blocked – this man of the bad conscience has seized upon the presupposition of religion so as to drive his self-torture to its most gruesome pitch of severity and rigor. Guilt before *God*: this thought becomes an instrument of torture to him. He apprehends in "God" the ultimate antithesis of his own ineluctable animal instincts; he reinterprets these animal instincts themselves as a form of guilt before God (as hostility, rebellion, insurrection against the "lord," the "father," the primal ancestor and origin of the world): he ejects from himself all his denial of himself, of his nature, naturalness, and actuality, in the form of an affirmation, as something existent, corporeal, real, as God, as the holiness of God, as God the Judge, as God the hangman, as the beyond, as eternity, as torment without end, as hell, as the immeasurability of punishment and guilt.   (Nietzsche 1968b: 92)

The priest provides the sufferer with an explanation for his suffering (Nietzsche writes: "For every sufferer instinctively seeks a cause for his suffering" [*ibid*.: 94]) and, in Nietzsche's account of the development of Christianity, he does so in an historical context that also vindicates the sufferer's undesirable social position. For along with his invention of "guilt before God" to explain psychic pain, the priest brings a new value system that will show the sufferer how to escape his pain.

> Human beings, suffering from themselves in one way or other …, uncertain why or wherefore, thirsting for reasons – reasons relieve – thirsting, too, for remedies and narcotics, at last take counsel with one who knows hidden things, too – and behold! They receive a hint, they receive from their sorcerer, the ascetic priest, the *first* hint as to the 'cause' of their suffering; they must seek it in *themselves*, in some *guilt*, in a piece of the past, they must understand their suffering as a *punishment*.   (*Ibid*.: 101)

Human beings suffer, so the story goes, because they fail to live up to what God requires of them. But now the question naturally arises: what does God require of us? How can we escape this suffering? Thus an odd, natural psychological fact – that we cannot express our drive for cruelty when we are in society together – creates the opportunity for the priest to transform the way we think about ourselves and our society. The sufferer will no longer need to feel painful guilt before God if only he subscribes to the value system taught by the priest.

Nietzsche provides some evidence for his speculative historical thesis by pointing out that, in German, the word *Schuld* means both 'guilt' and 'debt'.[6] According to Nietzsche, the priest takes our consciousness of mental suffering and explains it in terms of a debt that we have to God: the pain is the nagging of an unsatisfied creditor, it is the awareness of something that we have not yet, but ought to have, repaid. Thus when, in the hands of the priest, bad conscience becomes guilt we realize that we have only ourselves to blame; it is on account of our own, individual failure to pay a debt to God that we suffer. And how do we pay our debt to God, so as to free ourselves from this debt/guilt (*Schuld*)? The priest will show us.[7]

The priest uses guilt to accomplish what Nietzsche takes to be one of the most profound and ultimately disastrous creative acts of human history: the inversion of the value system of Western civilization. Here Nietzsche introduces his well-known distinction between the moralities of 'good versus bad' and 'good versus evil', between 'master morality' and 'slave morality'. At the heart of the value system of 'good versus bad' is the notion that what is good is that which is good for me and people like me, that which we consider to be noble, elevated, worthy; what is bad is that which is beneath us, that for which we have contempt, that which is ignoble, debased, cheap. The list of virtues and goods for master morality includes wealth, friendship, sex, strength, pride, physical health, above all the goods and virtues of 'this world', the sorts of things and activities the human animal is naturally drawn towards. The list of vices and things to be avoided is easy to anticipate: poverty, solitude, denial of the body, sickness and so on. But here is the opportunity for the priest. If he can convince the slaves – who, of course, far outnumber the masters – that the masters subscribe to what is in fact an ungodly value system, and that what the slaves themselves already possess, how they already live, is truly the more valuable in the eyes of God, then he will have a large and eager audience.

So the priest turns the old value system of the masters on its head, and invents slave morality and with it the value pair 'good and evil'. Everything the masters possess and do is not merely bad, but evil, condemned by God himself: property, pride, sex, even food. And what the slaves have, and of necessity practise, is not merely good in the sense of good-for-me-and-mine, but good in a more exalted sense, blessed, good in the eyes of God: poverty, weakness, humility, denial of the body, chastity. These reversed values of the good–bad morality are, of course, the traditional Christian virtues. The old 'good' is the good of this world; the new 'good' is the good of the next world. The old 'bad' is what we all recognize as bad

---

6. Nietzsche's thesis that Christianity has such a hold over us because of the psychological condition of guilt goes all the way back to *Human, All Too Human*, where he argues that we feel guilty because we cannot live up to the example of Christ's "unegoism", because egoism and selfishness is hard-wired into human nature. See Nietzsche (1986: bk I, §§132–3).

7. Simon May (1999) is especially helpful on the question of bad conscience and guilt (see esp. *ibid.*: 77–8). On this subject I also recommend Christopher Janaway (2007), esp. ch. 8.

in this world; the new 'evil' is what was counted good in this world, and will be the cause of eternal punishment in the next.

The psychological motive power behind this inversion of values is what Nietzsche calls *ressentiment*, usually translated simply as 'resentment'. The (individual or class) consciousness that operates according to resentment defines itself entirely in terms of what it is not: it does not create anything new, but only insists that it *is not that*, it is the opposite of that. Thus it remains psychologically and creatively derivative of the value system that it defines itself against, and this, Nietzsche argues, prevents it from growing and flourishing. Its self-definition and its goals are entirely negative. Like the fox and the sour grapes in Aesop's fable, the resentful consciousness finds satisfaction solely in terms of denying the value of that which it knows it could not possess, and for the reason that it knows – although never admits to itself – it could not possess what it truly desired.

Thus God and the afterlife, the traditional foundations of Western religion, are merely a kind of sales pitch employed by the greatest salesmen in the history of the West, the priests, who are trying to convince us to buy a new morality. The truth of the matter is, as Nietzsche tells it, that it is not God who has given us morality, but morality that has given us God. And we have bought the pitch because – at one point in our history, at least – we knew we could not have what we most desired: power, wealth, health, and so on. As slaves we resented the masters, and the priests exploited this resentment and the pain of consciousness to convince us of the merits of a new value system that depended entirely on, and reflected, the misery of our condition.

But the story does not end here. The denial of life that is crucial to the priest's new morality – the asceticism of the priest – brings with it another principle that is itself hostile to the invention of God: the will to truth. Nietzsche writes:

> All great things bring about their own destruction through an act of self-overcoming: thus the law of life will have it … In this way Christianity *as a dogma* was destroyed by its own morality; in the same way Christianity *as morality* must now perish, too: we stand at the threshold of *this* event. After Christian truthfulness has drawn one inference after another, it must end by drawing *its most striking* inference, its inference *against* itself; this will happen, however, when it poses the question *What is the meaning of all will to truth?*   (1968b: III, §27)

Christianity has created the will to truth (as opposed, for example, to the will to art and beauty, or the will to mythology), which is precisely what has led to the death of Christianity as a system of belief. When the 'madman' in *The Gay Science* passage quoted at the outset of this chapter wildly shouts that "God is dead", this is what he is proclaiming: because we have sought the truth, operating with a Christian value system that emphasizes the importance of truth, we have indeed uncovered the truth that there is no God. But things will get worse still, when the impulse toward truth turns its gaze back on itself and asks: and what value is expressed here? Then, Nietzsche thinks, even the moral system that Christianity has created and supported will be undermined.

> The most fateful act of two thousand years of discipline for truth …
> in the end forbids itself the *lie* of faith in God. You see what it was that
> really triumphed over the Christian god: the concept of truthfulness
> that was understood ever more rigorously, the father confessor's refine-
> ment of the Christian conscience, translated and sublimated into scien-
> tific conscience, into intellectual cleanliness at any price.   (1974: 307)

Ultimately, Christianity espouses the value of asceticism, that is, the good of a way of thinking that denies the importance of one's own particular well-being. When the gaze is turned outward in the manner of the ascetic, so that one finds value even in those things that run contrary to one's own interest – when indeed the fact that an enquiry stands contrary to one's interest may serve as a proof of the validity of that enquiry – then it is not long before one discovers that the truth of the matter may no longer agree with what one wants to believe is the case. That is, even if Christianity was serving the interests of humanity, the asceticism that it champions would eventually have uncovered that the Christian value system was based on a false-hood: the existence of God and the afterlife. And given that, on Nietzsche's account, Christianity is both based on a falsehood and stands in opposition to human flour-ishing, it is hardly surprising that we who have learned, because of Christianity, to love the truth, are now moving beyond it. We are no longer camels who want to carry the law as a proof of our strength: part of the burden we carried was the pursuit of truth, and that pursuit has made us happily and perhaps unexpectedly into free, defiant lions. It remains to be seen whether we can become creative children.

DIONYSUS VERSUS THE CRUCIFIED

In 1888, the last year of his intellectual life, Nietzsche's philosophy of religion becomes deeply polarized. On the one side, his attack against Christianity could not be more ruthless. On the other, his naturalist-mystical tendencies – present in subtle ways throughout his writing (much as these same tendencies are always evident beneath the surface of the work of one of his favourite ancient Greek phil-osophers, Heraclitus) – now become unmistakable. The two works that express these two superficially contradictory but genuinely complementary positions are *The Antichrist* and *Ecce Homo*.[8]

---

8. The other two works of his great year, 1888, were *Twilight of the Idols*, which offered his
   closing opinions on the questions of truth and the classic philosophical problems, and *The*

Nietzsche's polemic against Christianity begins early. In his 1874 essay on "Schopenhauer as Educator", in a remark that reminds one of many of Kierkegaard's complaints about "Christendom",[9] Nietzsche is already attacking Christianity in so far as it has been used as tool by the state:

> One should only recall what has gradually become of Christianity under the selfishness of the State. Christianity is certainly one of the purest revelations of this urge for culture and especially for the ever renewed generation of the saint; as it has been used hundreds of times, however, to turn the mills of the State's forces, it has gradually become diseased to the very marrow, hypocritical and full of lies, and has degenerated to the point where it contradicts its original aim. (1983: 72)

Here Nietzsche offers a political explanation for what is one clear theme of what we have seen thus far: although Christianity has served a great spiritual purpose, creating, among many other desirable things, an entire structure of value that includes (and champions) the value of truth, now it serves only to interfere with what is good for humanity. By the time of *Beyond Good and Evil* and *The Genealogy of Morality* he is feeling less generous towards Christianity: he argues that there is something sick and dangerous at the core of the Christian way of seeing things, that resentment was the driving force of Christianity from the outset, and so it was bound to interfere with our long-term flourishing.

When he gets to *The Antichrist*, in 1888, he is no longer pulling any punches. In his discussion of the idea of a 'holy lie' and the Hindu Laws of Manu, for example, he writes that it is not the fact that Christianity tells lies (he takes this as a given) that he objects to; his complaint against Christianity depends on the ends to which it puts its lies.

> That 'holy' ends are lacking in Christianity is *my* objection to its means. Only *bad* ends: the poisoning, slandering, denying of life, contempt for the body ... It is with the opposite feeling that I read the Law-book of Manu, an incomparably spiritual and superior work such that to *name* it in the same breath as the Bible would be a sin against the spirit.
> (1954a: 183)

Or, from the same year, in *Ecce Homo*: "Christian morality – the most malicious form of the will to lie, the actual Circe of mankind: that which has ruined it"

Case of Wagner, which is a last exercise in aesthetics (providing a nice closing bracket to a career that opened with *The Birth of Tragedy*).

9. Nietzsche (1986: 124), in another distinctly Kierkegaardian formulation, suggests that to be a Christian is just to be born into a Christian country, in much the way that one becomes a drinker of wine because one is born into a nation of wine drinkers.

(Nietzsche 1968a: "Why I am a Destiny", §7). In the same passage he even suggests that what defines him as a philosopher is that he has unmasked the lie that is Christian morality, showing that it runs counter to those basic human drives and needs that are essential to our well-being.

But one might reply to Nietzsche that Judaeo-Christian morality and Judaeo-Christian spirituality are not the same thing (Nietzsche himself writes that "religions are destroyed by belief in morality" [1968c: §151]), and that, for example, the basic spiritual lesson of Christ himself, that God is love, also stands at the heart of much Jewish thinking about the spiritual life. Nietzsche recognizes this, and many of his remarks about Christ and about certain strains of the Jewish tradition are sympathetic.[10] (So, for example, in a note from 1888: "What did Christ *deny*? Everything that today is called Christian" [Nietzsche 1968c: §158].) And Nietzsche does not argue that religion itself necessarily runs counter to the goals of human flourishing: in a discussion of Hinduism, Islam, Judaism, Christianity and Buddhism, for example, he divides the five according to whether they are affirmative of human worth or essentially negative in their view of humanity. Hinduism (and the Laws of Manu) and "Mohammedanism [and] the older parts of the Old Testament" turn out to be affirmative religions, products of a ruling class that actually advance humanity (Nietzsche 1968c: §145); Christianity and Buddhism are negative religions, because they deny the value of (at least, ordinary everyday) existence. But Buddhism still wins out over Christianity, because its negativism is a kind of philosophical acceptance, where the negativity of Christianity is merely frustration and impotence:

> Among the nihilistic religions, one may always clearly distinguish the Christian from the Buddhist. The Buddhist religion is the expression of a fine evening, a perfect sweetness and mildness – it is gratitude toward all that lies behind, and also for what is lacking: bitterness, disillusionment, rancor; finally, a lofty, spiritual love; the subtleties of philosophical contradiction are behind it, even from these it is resting: but from these it still derives its spiritual glory and sunset glow. (– Origin in the highest castes –)
>
> The Christian movement is a degeneracy movement composed of reject and refuse elements of every kind: it is not the expression of the decline of a race, it is from the first an agglomeration of forms of morbidity crowding together and seeking one another out … It also stands in opposition to every spiritual movement, to all philosophy: it

---

10. See, for example, the positive view of Jesus' spirituality in Nietzsche (1968c: §160, November 1887–March 1888), where he argues that the central view of Jesus is that "sin is of no account". Nietzsche's arguments supporting many aspects of Jewish culture and spirituality are throughout his literature: his ire with Judaism is generally reserved for when it becomes Christianity.

takes the side of idiots and utters a curse on the spirit. Rancor against the gifted, learned, spiritually independent: it detects in them the well-constituted, the masterful. (Nietzsche 1968c: §154)

The analysis here depends on Nietzsche's by now familiar idea that the merit of a system of value depends on the outlook of those who invented it: when it comes from the higher classes or castes, from the noble or master classes, it tends to reflect the empowered, confident position of those creators; when it comes, however, from the poor, the weak, the dispossessed, the base or ignoble (in Nietzsche's language), it tends to reflect the bitterness and impotence of those (for Nietzsche, reactive and resentful) creators. Thus Buddhism and Christianity, while both expressions of nihilism, express that nihilism in different ways: for the Buddhist nihilism is a positive expression of power and control, of strength and self-assertion; for the Christian nihilism is a negative expression of weakness and confusion, of impotence and the need to pity and be pitied.

The fact that the origins of a value system certainly do not entirely determine the evolution and products of that value system is a fair complaint to advance against Nietzsche's analysis. One expects that he would reply by insisting that, if anything, Christianity has evolved into something still worse than what we find at its origins, and here reasonable minds can clearly disagree (more than once Nietzsche has been defensibly asked: 'Can we really have too much pity in the world?'[11]). And there is an obvious danger of supposing that one can stand outside of a value system – of all value systems – in order to evaluate the relative merits and demerits of any particular value system. The question of how one might rank value systems – a subject that obsessed the late Nietzsche – is fraught with difficulties. But the more interesting point for us is that he does not, as we might naively suppose, dismiss religion *tout court* (even while hanging on to strong views of the importance of spirituality); rather, he encourages us to recognize the dependence of spirituality on systems of religion, and to judge those religions on the basis of their resulting moralities and the impact of those moralities on human flourishing.

Nietzsche does not offer us only critiques of past religions: he has his own positive theory of spirituality. We have already gestured toward it with the discussion from *Thus Spoke Zarathustra*, and indeed in the late work he repeatedly refers to *Zarathustra* as the key text for understanding his spiritual views. Nietzsche accepts as a premise what seems to be a view shared by all of the major world religions and the ancient Greek tragic view, as he understands it: life is full of suffering. The most important spiritual question, Nietzsche thinks, is how one responds to the fact of suffering life presents us with. Nietzsche sees something redemptive

---

11. The attack is first advanced in Philippa Foot's famous essay on Nietzsche's ethics, "Nietzsche: The Revaluation of Values" (1973), reprinted in Richardson & Leiter (2001).

about suffering, but, unlike the Christian view, he does not suppose that we are redeemed by suffering: he insists that we do not need redemption, that life does not need redemption. It is our view of suffering, rather, that stands in need of redemption; that is, we must understand suffering not as an indictment of life and our living of it, but as an essential aspect of life that constitutes part of what makes life worth living. To put his view into a simple slogan, Nietzsche advocates redemption *of* suffering as a celebration and affirmation of human beings and this life, rather than redemption *by* suffering as a protest and an accusation against human beings and this life.

But this is strong medicine, and difficult to take. Suffering is awful. How can one not merely (as we usually do) do our best to avoid suffering, nor even (as we struggle to do) attempt to be resigned to it or reconciled with it, but actually embrace suffering, truly be as grateful for the suffering in our lives as we are for the joy?

> My formula for greatness in a human being is *amor fati*: that one wants nothing to be other than it is, not in the future, not in the past, not in all eternity. Not merely to endure that which happens of necessity, still less to dissemble it – all idealism is untruthfulness in the face of necessity – but to *love* it ... (Nietzsche 1968a: "Why I am so Clever", §10)

Elsewhere in developing the same thesis he refers to the great German poet Goethe's "joyful and trusting fatalism" in which, Nietzsche writes, the "totality of everything is redeemed and affirmed ... Such a faith is the highest of all possible faiths; I have baptized it with the name *Dionysus*" (Nietzsche 1954b: 55).

It is a bit hard to know what to make of this. It seems like a kind of psychological imperative about how to guide one's emotional and spiritual – even, perhaps, intellectual – disposition toward the world and one's life within it. Elsewhere Nietzsche introduces his idea of "the eternal recurrence", and the thought experiment he proposes is very much in line with the fatalism he describes here: that is, how would one have to view oneself and one's own life in order to be able to earnestly and enthusiastically desire that every single event in one's life not only occur exactly as it had, but over and over again, throughout eternity? It seems to require a kind of revolution in one's mental states that reminds us of the profound psychological changes frequently referred to in the literature on mysticism; it is hard not to imagine Nietzsche, here, as a kind of Zen monk rapping the rest of us with a stick until we break through to *satori* and the truth.

But elsewhere in *Ecce Homo* he is less grand in his psychological ambitions, and more helpful. He writes: "*What is the seal of liberation?* – No longer being ashamed before oneself" (Nietzsche 1974: bk 3, §275). Here he goes on to suggest that to understand what it means to love one's destiny is simply to escape from shamefulness oneself and to refuse to put others to shame. This certainly does not solve the problem of human suffering writ large, but at the least it might eliminate an awful lot of the psychological suffering we inflict on one another and on ourselves, and it gives us some idea of what he means by his endorsement of thorough and joyful fatalism. The emphasis on freedom from shame also captures much of what he wants to insist on most of all, spiritually speaking: that we should be grateful for what we are and how we live, rather than view ourselves, one another and our lives on earth as something to be escaped. His last word on the subject, at the close of *Ecce Homo*, is characteristically pithy, incisive and brilliant: "Have I been understood? – *Dionysus versus the Crucified ...*" (Nietzsche 1968a: 101).

FURTHER READING

Fraser, G. 2002. *Redeeming Nietzsche: On the Piety of Unbelief*. New York: Routledge.
Golomb, J. (ed.) 1997. *Nietzsche and Jewish Culture*. New York: Routledge.
Jaspers, K. 1961. *Nietzsche and Christianity*. Chicago, IL: Regnery.
Lippitt, J. & J. Urpeth (eds) 2000. *Nietzsche and the Divine*. Manchester: Clinamen.
Mandel, S. 1998. *Nietzsche and the Jews: Exaltation and Denigration*. Amherst, NY: Prometheus.
Mistry, F. 1981. *Nietzsche and Buddhism: Prolegomenon to a Comparative Study*. Berlin: de Gruyter.
Morrison, R. 1997. *Nietzsche and Buddhism: A Study in Nihilism and Ironic Affinities*. Oxford: Oxford University Press.
Murphy, T. 2001. *Nietzsche, Metaphor, Religion*. Albany, NY: SUNY Press.
Natoli, C. 1985. *Nietzsche and Pascal on Christianity*. New York: Peter Lang.
Roberts, T. 1998. *Contesting Spirit: Nietzsche, Affirmation, Religion*. Princeton, NJ: Princeton University Press.
Young, J. 2006. *Nietzsche's Philosophy of Religion*. Cambridge: Cambridge University Press.

On AESTHETICS see also Ch. 13; Vol. 1, Ch. 15. On MORALITY see also Chs 4, 12; Vol. 2, Ch. 12; Vol. 3, Chs 2, 8, 12, 14, 21, 22; Vol. 5, Ch. 6. On PSYCHOLOGY see also Chs 15, 20. On suffering see also Ch. 6. On TRUTH see also Ch. 8; Vol. 1, Ch. 13; Vol. 2, Ch. 17; Vol. 3, Chs 3, 8, 13; Vol. 5, Ch. 4. On WORLD RELIGIONS see also Chs 6, 14.

19

JOSIAH ROYCE

Kelly A. Parker

Josiah Royce (1855–1916) was a central figure in late-nineteenth- and early-twentieth-century American philosophy. He is primarily known for his advocacy of a form of idealist metaphysics. His metaphysical interests led him to a fundamental reconsideration of topics in the philosophy of religion, ethics, the philosophy of science and logic. Royce spent his entire career as a professor at Harvard University. This position brought him into regular contact not only with William James (*see* Vol. 5, Ch. 2), Charles S. Peirce and other figures who shaped the dynamic 'Golden Age' of pragmatism, but also with the vibrant personalist movement led by Borden Parker Bowne. Both of these movements had significant influence on Royce's philosophy, particularly in the areas of ethics and religion.

Royce's work in the philosophy of religion is characterized by several important factors besides his post-Hegelian idealism and his propensity for systematic philosophy. First, Royce's childhood education in the remote mining town of Grass Valley, California – where he was born in 1855 – was heavily flavoured by his family's evangelical Christian beliefs and practices. Protestant theism and religious life were basic facts of experience for Royce, as is evidenced by the frequent and comfortable references to Scripture that appear in his writings. Secondly, Royce's undergraduate education at the University of California was in classics rather than in philosophy or divinity. In keeping with this training, he was always cognizant of the literary and historical significance of the problems of philosophy. This classicist orientation may also explain Royce's willingness to undertake comparative studies of non-Western philosophy and religion, especially Hinduism and Buddhism.[1]

---

1. For the results of Royce's studies of Eastern thought, see Royce (1976: Lecture 4; 2001a; 2001b: 189–96) and Oppenheim (2007). Royce was no dilettante in comparative philosophy and religion: he began to study Sanskrit in 1875 during his travels in Germany, and maintained his interest via a lifelong friendship with the Harvard scholar Charles Lanman, whom he had befriended in graduate school at the Johns Hopkins University (Clendenning 1999: 62–6).

Thirdly, Royce was keenly interested in the implications of science for philosophy and religion. He devoted considerable effort to remain well informed about the latest scientific discoveries. Thus, although Royce ultimately defended a form of supernaturalism, he did so in full awareness of the claims and methods of such sciences as evolutionary biology, physics and archeology. Moreover, he was actively involved in working out the implications of the revolutionary discoveries of his day in logic and mathematics. Both of these enquiries informed his conception of the individual's relation to a whole, that is, to the Absolute or, as he later conceived it, to the infinite community that constitutes reality. Finally, Royce spent his career at the very nexus of North American innovation in philosophy and psychology. He interacted with the major philosophical figures of the era, including travelling scholars from around the world, both in person and in print; he taught both philosophy and psychology at Harvard (he served as President of the American Psychological Association in 1902 and of the American Philosophical Association in 1903); he regularly reviewed manuscripts for journals and publishers; and he travelled and lectured constantly both in the United States and abroad. All of these factors ensured that Royce was well aware of new developments in philosophy, whether it be the rise of pragmatism, the reception of Nietzsche's work in Europe, the development of modern logic, or the arrival of Eastern thinkers to North America in connection with the 1893 Columbian Exposition in Chicago. As a teacher Royce influenced a number of notable students, including T. S. Eliot, George Santayana, W. E. B. Du Bois, Mary Calkins and Gabriel Marcel. His philosophical works likewise exerted a considerable influence on such intellectuals and leaders as William Ernest Hocking, C. I. Lewis, H. Richard Niebuhr and Martin Luther King, Jr.

Royce's Christianity, his classical training, his scientific literacy and his close engagement with late-nineteenth- and early-twentieth-century philosophical movements all inform his systematic philosophy. He embraced absolute idealism after completing his graduate studies in Kant (*see* Vol. 3, Ch. 21) and German idealism. He defended this metaphysical position consistently (although with significant adjustments) throughout the four decades of his career as a philosopher. Royce's writings present a highly developed, systematic cultural-historical approach to the philosophy of religion. This orientation, not to mention Royce's work itself, was largely eclipsed in English-speaking countries by twentieth-century analytic philosophy, which tended to favour more positivist and ahistorical approaches.

Religious scholars and philosophers have shown a renewed interest in Royce in recent years. Much of this interest is due to his historical position as a pre-analytic Christian philosopher who assimilated the challenges of late-nineteenth-century science and philosophy, and who developed original positions on central issues. Like Peirce, his friend and frequent interlocutor, Royce maintained the realist view that the discovery of truth is the goal of enquiry. In Royce's view truth is finally determined by an independent and objective reality, but any possible knowledge of truth is contingent on the historically situated efforts of human communities.

In this way, Royce avoided the kind of epistemological foundationalism that has rendered modern philosophy untenable in the view of many. At the same time, though, he did not embrace the kind of anti-foundationalism that many find to be equally problematic in postmodernist responses. In addition to this appeal, Royce's philosophy, and particularly his philosophy of religion, is what Cornel West has called a *prophetic* philosophy (West 1999: 186; see also West 1989: ch. 11; 1999: chs 8, 9). Royce recognizes the realities of human life, our limitations and sorrows. He also recognizes the shortcomings that are so evident in the histories of actual human communities, perhaps especially including religious communities. In his ethics and philosophy of religion he thus charges his audience to make a better world in the image of a model discovered by philosophy. In this prophetic mode, Royce instructed his audience: "Since you cannot *find* the universal and beloved community, – *create* it" (2001b: 200).

Frank M. Oppenheim (1987, 1993) has identified three distinct periods in the development of Royce's philosophy, each commencing with a significant 'insight' concerning a fundamental issue. These periods comprise those marked by Royce's initial religious insight (1883–95), by his ethical insight (1896–1912), and by his insight into the importance of Peircean semiotics (1912–16). Our present survey of Royce's philosophy and religious thought shows Royce's development across these three periods.

ABSOLUTE IDEALISM

Royce's first decisive insight, which occurred in January 1883, was explicitly religious in nature. He was already a Christian theist; the insight rendered him a lifelong idealist in metaphysics. Whereas Kant had ushered in an era of scepticism in metaphysics by asking how knowledge is possible, Royce's own metaphysical certainty about absolute idealism arose by asking how *error* is possible. Briefly, to hold an erroneous belief is to have an idea that does not connect with its intended object. But to thus miss an idea's proper object implies that the idea *is* related to its object in some mind other than my own. Further, to say that all ideas have a proper object that can be sought (as appears necessary if rational thought is to be possible at all) implies that there is some mind that maintains, or knows, all objects of true ideas. Royce summarized the resulting religious insight in *The Religious Aspect of Philosophy*:

> all the many Beyonds, which single significant judgments seem vaguely and separately to postulate, are present as fully realized intended objects to the unity of an all-inclusive, absolutely clear, universal, and conscious thought, of which all judgments, true or false, are but fragments, the whole being at once Absolute Truth and Absolute Knowledge.
>
> (1965: 423)

The very possibility of truth and error, of reason and knowledge, thus depends on the actual existence of an infinite Absolute Mind; conversely, for Royce, the actual occurrence of error establishes the existence of such a being.

INDIVIDUALS

The second insight, which Royce had formulated by March of 1896, entailed a new understanding of individuation. This insight expanded on and reinforced the first, but it introduced pronounced ethical implications. Royce detailed this "startlingly 'original' (let us say 'American') theory of individuality" (Clendenning 1970: 347) in the long "Supplementary Essay" to *The Conception of God*. A common view suggests that we first encounter fully discrete individuals in experience, then discover that these individuals are members of classes that share common characteristics, and thus arrive by a process of abstraction at the knowledge of universals. Royce went beyond the traditional realism-nominalism controversy by challenging this common understanding of how we actually encounter discrete individuals in experience. For one thing, we always distinguish an individual by reference to another individual: this individual hat is distinguished in experience by virtue of its *not* being identical to any other hat, or watch, or chair, and so on, but this process clearly relies on "the presupposed individuality of other individuals" (Royce 1897: 258). For another, we never experience any individual in all its defining relations to other individuals: of the things we encounter as individuals, we actually possess only very general knowledge. Thus "the concept of an individual in the full sense is a limiting concept, not corresponding to any fact of our conscious experience" (Clendenning 1970: 341). More complete knowledge of the individual would require much time – infinite time – to establish, and would entail knowledge of the entire world of individuals in their relations to one another. Thus, Royce realized, "Our goal is the envisagement of the one real individual, viz., the whole universe" (*ibid.*). While we can certainly pick out individuals in experience, the question concerns how this is possible without such complete knowledge. Royce concluded that acts of individuation operate through the power of particular attention, which he identified as the will or (equivalently) love (1897: 259). Only an absolute being could attend to the whole universe at once through an act of will or an expression of love, give every individual its unique defining place in that universe, and somehow relate to our own limited being so that we too can begin to apprehend the real universe of individuals-in-relation. "It is the Divine love which individuates the real world wherein the Divine Omniscience is fulfilled" (*ibid.*).

This new principle of individuation introduces a fundamentally ethical concept. If my own individuality is not fully disclosed to me or others, but must be discovered progressively over time, and if it cannot be fulfilled except in light of divine love and divine will, then the very being of my life is dependent on finding and fulfilling my own proper and unique relation to the absolute that exercises such a will and such love. The metaphysical and ethical import of this second insight informed Royce's Gifford Lectures, delivered in 1899–1900 at the University of Aberdeen and published in the two-volume work *The World and the Individual* (1976). There he examined and rejected three metaphysical positions: *mysticism*, or the world as immediately experienced unity; *realism*, or the world as comprising fully independent objects; and *critical rationalism*, or the world as constituted in infinite discrete consciousnesses. Royce advocated in favour of a teleological 'fourth conception of being' that enlists individuals to express their own wills and act so as to fulfil their purposes. These purposes can derive their full significance only from the perspective of an actual infinite consciousness.

ETHICS AND LOYALTY

In the first works of his second period Royce explored, in very abstract terms, the new notion of the individual and of the universal order of will and ideas in which all individuals find their full personality and belonging. He may have been stung by criticisms, from Peirce and others, that his conception of the divine was as yet too abstract, too much the God of a philosopher or mathematician, a far cry from the personal God of Christianity. In his 1908 *The Philosophy of Loyalty*, he began to personalize his metaphysical absolute by exploring the ethical implications of his new conception of individuality. The paradox is clear: each person has a definite unique purpose in the overall structure of the real universe, and that purpose is to will and act so as to disclose that very purpose and in doing so become a fully realized or 'genuine' individual. But of course no finite being trapped in the perspective of time can possibly know what that ultimate achievement, the individual's life itself, will be. Our actual lives are rife with uncertainty, chance, discouragement and deep ambiguity about our own motives and those of others. Moreover, even if one did know the grand purpose of the universe, we are apparently so limited as individuals that no one could do anything effective to realize that purpose.

Royce's solution to this impossible situation lies in his novel application of the virtue of loyalty. In choosing a course of action I embrace a cause; in embracing a cause I promote an ideal; in that moment I join in spirit or in fact with all others who promote that same ideal. In pursuing any action whatsoever I thus find myself bound in loyalty to my ideal and to those other people. The first step towards ethical action, then, is to promote some ideal by embracing some cause as my own. But of course some actions, causes and ideals are bad or wrong: both ordinary experience and Royce's metaphysics insist that we may be in error, the ideals we adopt may violate the proper universal order, our cause may be evil and our loyalty may be misplaced. Royce proposed an interesting variation on Kant's universalizability principle to help us determine whether this is the case in a given situation. Loyalty intrinsically wants to spread and grow in a community: it is "contagious" (1995: 65). So causes that merit my loyalty tend to increase the loyalty of others. The mark of a good cause is thus that it is essentially a "loyalty to loyalty", as well as to my more immediately visible cause. Now:

> suppose that my cause … lives by the destruction of other families, or of its own community, or other communities. Then, indeed, I get a good for myself and for my fellow-servants by our common loyalty; but I war against this very spirit of loyalty as it appears in our opponent's loyalty to his own cause. (*Ibid.*: 56)

Any predatory cause, whose pursuit *destroys* the loyalty of others, is suspect and most likely bad. To deliberately seek the destruction of loyalty in the world seems to be very close to a Roycean definition of active evil.

THE FAITH OF THE LOYAL

This conception of the causes to which we ought to be loyal leads us, at last, to the matter of faith. The ideal of universal loyalty can never be realized in fact. No finite person can comprehend the universal purpose, the ultimate cause that encompasses all others and merits every person's loyalty. Much less can any person *accomplish* this purpose. Yet, as Royce had argued earlier, there must in fact be such a universal, all-encompassing purpose. In all loyal action, Royce suggests, we demonstrate our faith in the ultimate ideal of universal loyalty to an all-encompassing purpose. Any genuinely loyal action, then, is an expression of faith and a commitment of will to a superhuman order. While relatively few people might describe even their highest ideals in this way, there is one class of causes that are especially compelling illustrations of the central role of faith. These are the admirable 'lost causes' that some among us embrace. One may think of heroic rebellion against political tyranny, or of dutiful service to protect the public in an overwhelming natural disaster as admirable instances of loyalty to a lost cause. In such cases, Royce notes, "If we believe in the lost cause, we become directly aware that we are seeking a city out of sight" (1995: 179). Indeed, those who maintain their station in the face of certain defeat do starkly demonstrate what is meant by the potentially trite-sounding formula "loyalty to loyalty". But the appeal to a transcendent ideal is not confined to these heroic situations.

In a passage that remarkably anticipates mid-century existentialist observations about angst and humanity's 'being unto death', Royce wrote: "Human life taken merely as it flows, viewed merely as it passes by in time and is gone, is indeed a lost river of experience that plunges down the mountains of youth and sinks in the deserts of age" (1995: 179–80). A single human life, however satisfying, ultimately means nothing in itself. But Royce's metaphysical and logical commitment to the necessity of an actual superhuman perspective on things saved him from existential despair: such a single life's "significance comes solely through its relations to the air and the ocean and the great deeps of universal experience" (*ibid.*: 180). Because there *are* such deeps of universal experience, according to Royce, we may be assured that such a life does have real significance: that life is, after all, willed and intended as an object of the divine mind itself. Moreover, this ultimate realization of one's genuine individuality in relation to the divine mind is what is meant by immortality of the soul: we possess a life "that in its meaning, though not at all necessarily in time or in space, is continuous with the fragmentary and flickering existence wherein we now see through a glass darkly our relations to God and to the final truth" (Royce 1900: 80). Royce still needed one more key insight, however, before he could address the question of how, from our limited perspective on a fragment of the universe, we can find existential assurance that faith in the highest cause of the universe is justified.

A GENERAL SCIENCE OF ORDER AND THE LOGIC OF ACTION

While he was publicly working out the ethical implications of his insight concerning individuals in the practical and accessible form of *The Philosophy of Loyalty*, Royce was engaged privately in a monumental effort to describe the formal structure of individual action and its relation to the absolute (Oppenheim 1987: chs 3–5). In a supplementary essay to *The World and the Individual* entitled "The One, the Many, and the Infinite", Royce had first undertaken to develop such a formal description. Following that effort, at Peirce's urging, Royce had taken up advanced studies in logic (*ibid.*: 43). The problem in his sights was precisely the paradox of the one and the many: how are we to understand the being of infinitely many distinct individuals that are all, each of them, bound together as indispensable parts of a completed whole? And how are we to understand the structure of the absolute, which Royce seems to have regarded as an actual infinite consciousness comprising the totality of all individuals *and their relations*? As Bruce Kuklick (1985: 152) has pointed out, this conception of the absolute in logical terms as 'the class of all classes' is doomed to precisely the incoherence that was revealed by Bertrand Russell in Cantor's paradox.

While Royce appears to have been unaware of the precise problems that beset his early attempts at formal description of the absolute, he was aware that the then-new 'logic of relatives' in the form promoted by Russell would not suffice for his metaphysical needs (*see* Vol. 5, Ch. 6, "Bertrand Russell"). As an example, Russell's system simplifies actions: all acts of negation are equivalent, so that a negation of a negation can be cancelled out of the expression. Royce needed a logical system that preserved the differences among actions, one more able to reflect that a left turn and its opposite, a right turn, for example, will only rarely put one back at the starting-point. Royce therefore set to work to create a logical system that could accommodate his key metaphysical and ethical principles: the being of individuals, their complex modes of internal and external relation within a singular totality, the fundamental fact of order, and the effects of action in time. By 1905 Royce had extended A. B. Kempe's work to develop his own logical system, which he called Σ (sigma) (Kuklick 1985: 194). These results were published as "The Relation of the Principles of Logic to the Foundations of Geometry" (Robinson 1951: ch. 17). His essay "Principles of Logic", which presents further developments to Σ, was published in German in 1910 and in English in 1913 (*ibid.*: ch. 16). This system avoided the problems that gave rise to Cantor's paradox in his concept of the actual infiniteness of the absolute, but Royce was still left with two apparently irreconcilable formal conceptions of the absolute (Kuklick 1985: 205–9). Research into Royce's logical works is presently incomplete. We cannot say with certainty that Royce could never resolve the problems he encountered in his formalization of metaphysics. Much less can we determine whether or not those problems could be resolved given the logical tools now available. What must be stressed is that Royce's logical work is eminently deserving of attention, both for the light it sheds on his other work, and for the potential it holds as an alternative to logical systems currently in use. Royce concluded "The Principles of Logic" with another prophetic assertion: "The Theory of Order [i.e. as described in Σ] will be a fundamental science in the philosophy of the future" (Robinson 1951: 378).

SALVATION, THE UNITY OF THE SPIRIT, AND THE CHURCH VISIBLE AND INVISIBLE

Royce's most fully developed consideration of religion, presaged in the final chapter of *The Philosophy of Loyalty*, appeared in his final two major works. *The Sources of Religious Insight*,[2] where he treated religion in general terms, is based on the 1911 Bross Lectures at Lake Forest, Illinois. *The Problem of Christianity*, which directly addresses the challenges to Christian faith in the modern age and outlines a sophisticated vision of religious community that accommodates those challenges, is based on the 1913 Hibbert Lectures at Manchester College, Oxford. At the outset of his enquiry, Royce identified the need for salvation as the central religious problem. In *The Sources of Religious Insight* he made a clear connection between the problem of salvation and the paradoxes and doubts ('the One and the Many', the problem of the justification of faith) that he had explored on so many previous occasions. In *The Problem of Christianity* he endeavoured to show how finite beings seeking salvation are united in supernatural spirit.

---

2. Royce's frequent critical references to his recently deceased friend William James, as well as the similarity of scope and the mild parallelism of the works' titles, indicate that *The Sources of Religious Insight* should be read, at least in part, as a direct response to James' enormously influential *The Varieties of Religious Experience* of 1902.

Royce described the precarious state of human existence, humanity's over-whelming need for salvation, as being defined by two universal ideas:

> The first is the idea that there is some end or aim of human life which is more important than all other aims, so that, by comparison with this aim all else is secondary and subsidiary, and perhaps relatively unimportant, or even vain and empty. The other idea is this: That man as he now is, or as he naturally is, is in great danger of so missing this highest aim as to render his whole life a senseless failure by virtue of thus coming short of his goal. (Royce 2001a: 12)

These ideas are of course precisely the ethical implications of Royce's 1896 insight, which he had developed in *The Philosophy of Loyalty*. The aim of his last works was to show how religion may allow us to escape the paradox of finite beings who strive to fulfil an infinite task (2001a: 25), and to describe what religion must be in order for such beings as ourselves to fully participate in its fulfilment.

Notably, Royce adopted new terminology for this extended enquiry into religion. He set aside both his accustomed metaphysical vocabulary and the formal language of System Σ. The Absolute Mind and its logical correlate, Σ, are here replaced by the infinite community and, in part two of *The Problem of Christianity*, by the language of Peircean semiotics or sign theory. Royce's answer to the question of how it is possible for a finite, ignorant being "to get into touch with anything divine" is that anyone may glean certain religious insights from ordinary life (*ibid.*: 25). Royce explicitly framed his insistence on the importance of community as an alternative to the individualistic philosophies of both Nietzsche and James (2001a: 58–65). Royce devoted a chapter of the book to each of seven sources of religious insight. The first is the individual's occasional awareness of an incompleteness, perhaps loneliness or a sense that higher purpose is lacking in one's life, that attends being an *individual*. The second is the sense of personal connection and support we may experience as a member of ordinary society, living with the support and companionship of other persons. The third is a discovery of reason: it is precisely Royce's own first great religious insight, that the fact of error implies there is an actual infinite perspective on the universe. The fourth is an ethical variant on the argument from error. Royce here argued that in our acts of the will we may hit or miss the proper target, just as we may do with our concepts. Against James' pragmatism and his doctrine of 'the will to believe', Royce insisted that there is, at the end of all possible future experience we can envisage, a limit-perspective in light of which our will and acts may be judged to have been right or wrong; this limit-perspective is of course the actual absolute perspective.[3] The fifth source

---

3. In presenting the third and fourth insights Royce came very close to Peirce's long-held realist 'pragmaticist' view that there is such a thing as objective truth, and that 'truth' is defined precisely as what would be maintained as true at the end of infinite inquiry. Like

of religious insight is the now familiar life of genuine loyalty to a cause, which puts us in touch with something beyond our own limited concerns. The sixth source occasioned some of Royce's most moving prose. In a chapter entitled "The Religious Mission of Sorrow", Royce turned an unflinching eye on the depths of human suffering. He offered no theodicy, but only considered what is to be done in the face of the suffering and evil that so often overwhelm individuals. In such cases, the community must patiently, painfully, put time and their own wills to work to assimilate the harm. That such assimilation is possible, and that it is often possible for the community where it is not possible for the wronged individual alone, indicates that there is a saving higher perspective. Without rationalizing their occurrence, Royce merely observes how sorrowful experiences may affect the spiritual life: "They reveal to us some of the deepest truths about what loyalty, and spiritual triumph, and the good really are. They make for salvation" (*ibid.*: 239). Finally, there is the insight derived from a life dedicated to causes that genuinely advance the universal cause of loyalty to loyalty, and which, in their dedication, connect finite individuals to that infinite cause. Persons who are bound together in this way constitute a special kind of community, and they experience a unity of spirit that transcends the merely human. The community thus formed constitutes a superhuman and conscious personality: this is the Absolute Mind, but personalized.

This unity of persons in the spirit of loyalty constitutes the true church: "I call the community of all who have sought for salvation through loyalty the Invisible Church" (*ibid.*: 280). In Royce's view, an atheistic scientist who is dedicated to the increase of knowledge, who works sincerely and loyally for that cause, is as fully a member of the invisible church as is the Christian saint or Buddhist monk who consciously follows a religious imperative. All alike are in communion with the spirit of the universal community, dedicated to seeking truth and to aligning their own wills with the universal will. In Royce's view, then, there is virtually no basis for genuine conflict between science and religion. What conflict arises is due to superficial (although undoubtedly real and often quite serious) differences based on dogmatism, misunderstanding or fear.

Royce's recognition of the invisible church obviously implies a place for 'visible churches', comprising consciously religious persons, as well. Where such a church is true to the highest ideals, that "church is as precious as it is because it is indeed devoted to the unity of the spirit, that is, because it is a part and an organ of the invisible church" (*ibid.*: 293). As an organ of the invisible church, it is specially charged to promote genuine loyalty as the means of salvation. Doctrines, traditions and parochial practices of course define a church, but Royce apparently put little stock in them. When he occasionally attended services, in the Episcopal

---

Royce, Peirce saw himself as opposed to James on this point; at the same time, however, he never agreed with Royce's view that this ultimate perspective must be actual.

Church, he found the experience stifling (Oppenheim 1987: 16). He seemed to regard much of what people take to be definitive of their actual churches and denominations to be about power, pride or other divisive concerns, which are not only irrelevant but contrary to the genuine religion of spiritual unity. Indeed, his test for distinguishing between genuine and predatory loyalty would seem to be especially important for churches, which wield considerable power in the world and unfortunately do sometimes fall short of their own ideals.

RELIGION AND PHILOSOPHY

Royce's sense of his own role in the universal order no doubt also limited his involvement in church life. While he did apparently have an active private, largely internal, Christian spiritual life (Oppenheim 1987: 15–19), he felt a strong loyalty to his humble calling as a philosopher, teacher and historian of thought. He saw a very definite role for philosophy in promoting religion. There are two main things the teacher of philosophy can contribute to the "gradual improvement of the religious life" of others. The first is "Clearness of thought about religious issues" and the second is "a judicial spirit in comparison, in the historical estimate, and in the formation of religious opinions" (Royce 1903: 282). This latter can best be cultivated, he says, by teaching the history of thought (*ibid*.: 283). This account of the role of philosophy is a valuable hermeneutic clue for Royce scholars, as these two aims are manifest throughout Royce's writings.

As for affiliation with a church, Royce advised that:

> the philosopher, by holding aloof from the visible church, helps himself to maintain in himself and to display to his students, that judicial spirit which I have insisted upon as his especial possession … To the invisible church the philosopher, if loyal to his task, inevitably belongs, whatever be his opinions. And it is to the invisible church of all the faithful that his loyalty is due. (*Ibid*.: 285)

THE WORLD AS WILL AND INTERPRETATION

Royce's third insight came in 1912, while writing *The Problem of Christianity*, apparently between the composition of parts I and II.[4] This philosophical insight into Peirce's semiotic theory allowed Royce to reframe his metaphysics and philosophy of community in new terms. The key that Royce found in Peirce was that

---

4. Royce explicitly describes the circumstances of his Peircean insight in chapter 11 of the *Problem*, though as we have seen he had already begun to strike explicitly Peircean themes in the *Sources*.

any temporal process can be described and analysed as a succession of transformations of signs, following a general triadic pattern of representation and interpretation. The notion of a sharp difference in kind between *dyadic* (two-termed) and *triadic* (three-termed) relations was fundamental to Peirce's theory of signs, and indeed to his entire philosophy.

Peirce realized that only triadic relations can define relationships of connection or transfer. To illustrate, suppose Alice sets a coin on a table, and Bob picks it up. Merely observing this sequence of two events (i.e. Alice releases the coin, Bob grasps the coin) one cannot tell what transaction has just occurred: Alice may have paid Bob, or Bob may have stolen from Alice. The two events must be brought into relation to one another in a triadic relation such as 'Alice paid the coin to Bob' or 'Bob stole the coin from Alice'. In this case, the coin is the token of a third term, the mark or sign of the intent that mediates a transaction between us. Peirce realized that such relationships constitute a realm of being beyond mere possibilities and mere existent facts. This realm of generals, of relations, is the realm of meaning that makes the world experienceable and, to a degree, rational. It is the realm of signs endlessly interpreting themselves to and for one another.

In general, this process of mediation by an intervening third is called 'interpretation'. Royce identified it as the source of a third kind of knowledge, which goes beyond that provided by perception and conception (Royce 2001b: ch. 11).[5] It essentially involves two or more minds being brought into relation with one another. Interpretation is thus the fundamental structure of community as such. With this Peircean insight, Royce now saw that the notion of community he had introduced as an alternative to the Absolute Mind was in fact a community of interpretation, and that its dynamic, ongoing formative activity constituted an order of being beyond possibility and facticity: that of general reality. The universe we know, that of the irreversible time process and the generation of novel meanings, wherein the past is present as memory and the future as hope, just *is* the universal community of interpretation; all its members themselves may be conceived as triadic signs. "The World is the Community. The world contains its own interpreter. Its processes are infinite in their temporal varieties. But their interpreter, the spirit of this universal community – never absorbing varieties or permitting them to blend – compares and, through a real life, interprets them all" (*ibid.*: 362). The *telos* of this process of interpretation is the ultimate representation of all the individual beings in the universe in their relations, a complete self-representing sign: the absolute perspective in which truth is realized.[6] With this insight Royce glimpsed the resolution of the paradoxes he had wrestled with for decades: "In such an interpreter, and in his community, the problem of the

---

5. The distinction between 'perception' and 'conception' is roughly the same as that between empiricism and rationalism.

6. Michael Raposa has coined the term 'theosemiotic' to name this approach to understanding the divine.

One and the Many would find its ideally complete expression and solution" (*ibid.*: 318). Note that, since semiosis is a dynamic and unending affair of transformation, Royce may be considered a process philosopher and theologian.

Royce saw Christianity (i.e. his own prophetic vision of it) as the very model and motivating organ of the universal process: "the general form of any such community ... is that of the ideal Pauline Church" (*ibid.*: 333). The kingdom of heaven, to which this temporal community aspires, which fosters genuine loyalty or what Paul termed "charity" (*ibid.*: 362), and whose development is guided by the love of the universal spirit of interpretation, is the Beloved Community. Membership depends on the personal choice to make its universal cause the object of one's own loyal dedication. One might adopt another attitude of the will, that of the assertion of power and the raw will to live, or that of resignation, but Royce insists that salvation lies in developing the loyal will to interpret. Because of this volitional element, Royce referred to his philosophy as "Absolute Voluntarism" (*ibid.*: 349).

ATONEMENT

The pinnacle of Royce's philosophy of religion is his account of atonement. Salvation consists in reconciliation of the detached individual to the Beloved Community. Where individuals err or sin, there is separation from the divine purpose.[7] The most dramatic instances of sin are those involving knowing betrayal of the ideals of the community and of its members for individual gain. Such treason or infidelity represents a grave spiritual crisis that demands atonement. Royce rejects the accounts of atonement that regard it as a matter of extracting an appropriate penalty, of bringing about moral repentance on the part of the sinner, or even of a community's capacity to forgive the transgression (2001b: 170–79). Atonement in the community of interpretation is "not so much a mere compensation for what has been lost, as a transfiguration of the very loss into a gain that, without this very loss, could never have been won" (*ibid.*: 181).

Atonement is an act of the community. As such it does not require any particular attitude or action of the one who has done the harm. What is needed is a creative, healing act of interpretation that moves the community, and if possible the transgressor, forwards towards spiritual unity. Under the guidance of a wise and gifted leader, a deed of atonement may be found that, once accomplished, actually strengthens the community with unimagined new relationships of loyalty. The original betrayal is not to be celebrated on this account, of course, but in the best

---

7. As in his discussion of sorrow and the problem of evil, Royce did not enter into a full account of the nature and origin of sin. His concern was to discover what we are to do when sin appears in the community. He does, however, suggest that inherited habits of thought and action may account for the persistence of sin, and for the notion of an 'original' sin (2001b: 104–6).

instances the community may be able to look back and see that through tribulations it has matured to a new level of well-being. This process is ultimately mysterious; Jesus is Royce's paradigm of the wise leader guided by the divine Interpreter Spirit who founds a community, the church, through his atoning act. Royce writes that "after Christ's work was done, the world as a whole was a nobler and richer and worthier creation than it would have been if Adam had not sinned" (*ibid*.: 185). Thus, for Royce, the Christian mystery of redemption and salvation in Christ literally defines the highest possibilities of human life.

FURTHER READING

McDermott, J. (ed.) 2005. *The Basic Writings of Josiah Royce*, 2 vols. New York: Fordham University Press.

Oppenheim, F. 2005. *Reverence for the Relations of Life: Re-imagining Pragmatism via Josiah Royce's Interactions with Peirce, James, and Dewey*. Notre Dame, IN: University of Notre Dame Press.

Oppenheim, F. 2007. "Royce's Windows to the East". *Transactions of the Charles S. Peirce Society* **43**: 288–318.

Skrupskelis, I. 2005. "Annotated Bibliography of the Published Works of Josiah Royce". In *The Basic Writings of Josiah Royce*, vol. 2, J. McDermott (ed.), 1167–226. New York: Fordham University Press.

Smith, J. 1969. *Royce's Social Infinite: The Community of Interpretation*. Hamden, CT: Archon Books.

Trotter, G. 2001. *On Royce*. Belmont, CA: Wadsworth.

On ETHICS see also Chs 13; Vol. 1, Ch. 11; Vol. 2, Chs 4, 8; Vol. 3, Ch. 9; Vol. 5, Chs 12, 15, 21. On IDEALISM see also Chs 5, 16. On LOGIC see also Vol. 2, Chs 2, 4, 17; Vol. 3, Ch. 3. On SALVATION see also Vol. 1, Chs 10, 13; Vol. 2, Ch. 3. On SCIENCE see also Chs 7, 11, 12, 15, 17; Vol. 2, Ch. 12; Vol. 3, Ch. 17; Vol. 5, Chs 4, 19.

20

SIGMUND FREUD

Adolf Grünbaum

Sigmund Freud was born in Freiberg, Moravia, then part of the Austro-Hungarian Empire, in 1856. When he was three years old his family moved to Vienna, where he entered the University of Vienna in 1873 to study medicine. He lived there until he was expelled by the Nazis, whereupon he moved to London, where he died in 1939.[1]

In his early days as a student in Vienna, Freud studied with the philosopher Franz Brentano, a Roman Catholic ex-priest and a theist, under whose sway Freud engaged in a passing flirtation with philosophical theology, but only to become a "godless medical man and an empiricist" (Gay 1987: 38). This espousal of atheism became a lifetime commitment for the father of psychoanalysis, who told us a year before he died, "Neither in my private life nor in my writings have I ever made a secret of being an out-and-out unbeliever" (Gay 1988: 526). And Peter Gay comments helpfully: "All his life he [Freud] thought that it was not atheism that needed explaining [i.e. justification] but religious belief" (*ibid.*: 526).

On the opening page of his 1925 "Autobiographical Study", Freud spoke in a sociocultural but not a religious vein when he declared: "My parents were Jews, and I have remained a Jew myself" (SE 1925, 20.7),[2] rather than having converted opportunistically to Christianity. And he elaborated: "What bound me to Jewry was (I am ashamed to admit) neither faith nor national pride, for I have always been an unbeliever and was brought up without any religion though not without respect for what are called the 'ethical' standards of human civilization" (SE 1926, 20.273).

---

1. This chapter is a revised and augmented version of the author's "Psychoanalysis and Theism" (Grünbaum 1993: ch. 7).
2. All citations of Freud's writings in English will be from *The Standard Edition of the Complete Psychological Works of Sigmund Freud*. In direct citations from this text, each reference will use the abbreviation SE, followed by the year of first appearance, volume number, and page number(s).

In this sense, he coupled his sociocultural self-identification as a Jew with a tenacious atheistic rejection of theological and ritualistic Judaism. Therefore, Gay properly emphasizes "Freud's repeated assertions that he was an atheist, an infidel Jew, all his life" (1987: 33–4). The relentlessness of that uncompromising, militant irreligiosity was epitomized by his prohibition, as the authoritarian *pater familias* in his family life, of his wife's ceremonial lighting of the Sabbath candles on Friday nights, an observance dear to her from her Orthodox Jewish upbringing. Accordingly, Gay wrote:

> Freud was not just an indifferent unbeliever but a principled atheist determined to win his bride away from all that superstitious nonsense. He was unyielding, quite imperious, in his repeated, often angry demand that she abandon what she had not questioned for a moment so far.
> (1988: 38)

Yet, despite his efforts, he failed: on her husband's death she promptly defiantly resumed the Friday night ritual!

Oskar Pfister, born in 1873 outside Zürich, was an able liberal Protestant Swiss clergyman, urgently dedicated to the alleviation of the emotional disturbances of his parishioners. Early in 1909, Pfister was electrified by his intellectual discovery of Freud, thus becoming his ardent admirer and personal friend for the rest of Freud's life. Moreover, Pfister turned into a lay psychoanalyst in his pastoral work, having received his first psychoanalytic instruction from his fellow Swiss national, Carl Gustav Jung.

But, in a 1918 letter, Freud good-naturedly though pointedly challenged his loyal champion Pfister, asking him, "Quite by the way, why did none of the devout create psychoanalysis? Why did one have to wait for *a completely godless Jew*?" (Gay 1987: viii, my emphasis). Deeming Jesus to have been one of Freud's great precursors, Pfister parried this provocative question in a 1918 reply by extolling Freud: "A better Christian never was" – a retort that Freud's psychoanalyst daughter Anna found rather bewildering (Gay 1988: 82 & n.27). Indeed, the themes of her father's two rhetorical questions became the central plank of Gay's short 1987 book, which features, we learn, three propositions: "it was as an atheist that Freud developed psychoanalysis; it was from his atheist vantage point that he could dismiss as well-meaning but futile gestures all attempts to find common ground between faith and unbelief; it was, finally, as a particular kind of atheist, a Jewish atheist, that he was enabled to make his momentous discoveries" (1987: 37).

But, it seems, the first and third of these three propositions lend themselves to two different, although not incompatible, construals as follows:

(A) unless Freud, the sociocultural Jew, had believed in atheism, he would not have been intellectually equipped to propound the core 'psychoanalytic' hypotheses credited to him; or

(B) the truth of atheism is logically necessary for the truth of the core psychoanalytic doctrines.

Construal A is apparently suggested by Gay's confident claim that "it is certain … that if Freud had been a believer like [William] James, he would not have developed psychoanalysis" (*ibid.*: 30–31). And presumably Gay intended to assert A, although perhaps without excluding avowal B. Alas, he is unclear on this point.

It would take us too far afield from the critical exposition of Freud's psychology and philosophy of religion in this chapter to appraise the substance of reading A of Gay's trio. Suffice it to say here that the substance of construal B is untenable, since it asserts that the core psychoanalytic propositions *entail* atheism, which they demonstrably do not: Freud's cornerstone theory of repression "on which the whole structure of psycho-analysis rests" (SE 1914, 14.16) is logically compatible with theism, and hence cannot entail atheism. This conclusion is a caveat against the temptation to endorse the substance of construal B.

At age forty-five, in Freud's 1901 book *The Psychopathology of Everyday Life* (SE 1901, 6.1–279), he offered his first psychiatric diagnosis of religion (theism) as an obsessional neurosis. In this way, he illustrated his psychological account of superstition (SE 1901, 6.258–9). And, over a quarter century later, partly to challenge Pfister, Freud published his short 1927 book *The Future of an Illusion* (SE 1927, 21.1–56), the 'illusion' being belief in God. Oddly, in his recent book *The God Delusion* (2006), Richard Dawkins does not mention Freud's account of religion as an illusion and indeed a delusion in Freud's technical senses of these terms. In *The Future of an Illusion*, Freud announced to his pastor friend that this essay expressed "my absolutely negative attitude toward religion, in every form and dilution" (Gay 1988: 526). As Gay aptly notes succinctly concerning the book's pre-history: "Decades of principled atheism and of psychoanalytic thinking [as illustrated by Freud's 1907 article "Obsessive Actions and Religious Practices" (SE 1907, 9.115–27)] had prepared him for it. He had been a consistent militant atheist since his school days, mocking God and religion, not sparing the God and the religion of his family" (Gay 1988: 526).

On the penultimate page of *The Future of an Illusion*, Freud notes that "an attempt has been made to discredit scientific endeavour in a radical [epistemologically sceptical] way" (SE 1927, 21.55). But, after adducing five reasons to undermine the specifics of this objection, he concludes his monograph ringingly: "No, our science is no illusion. But an illusion it would be to suppose that what science cannot give us we can [cogently] get elsewhere" (SE 1927, 21.56).

What is the import, if any, of psychology and, in particular, psychoanalysis, for the truth or falsity of theism ('religion')?

It must be borne in mind that *psychological* explanations of any sort as to why people believe in God are subject to an important caveat. Even if they are true, such explanations are not entitled to beg the following *different* question: is religious belief *justified* by pertinent evidence or argument, whatever its motivational inspiration? Freud's usage, as well as stylistic reasons of my own, prompt me to use the terms 'religion' and 'theism' more or less interchangeably, although in other contexts the notion of religion is, of course, more inclusive.

Commendably, when Freud offered his psychological account of religious allegiances, he did *not* succumb to the temptation of arguing for atheism by begging the question. He understood that a purely psychological explanation – however unflattering – of why people embrace Judaism, Christianity or Islam does not itself suffice to discredit theism. Therefore, I claim, he did *not* fall prey to the well-known genetic fallacy, which is often called 'the reductionism of nothing but'.

As he himself pointed out, those who commit this error overlook the fact that the validity or invalidity of a doctrine as well as its truth or falsity are still left open by the psychological causes of its espousal. Thus, in a section on "The Philosophical Interest of Psychoanalysis", Freud wrote:

> psycho-analysis can indicate the subjective and individual motives behind philosophical theories which have ostensibly sprung from impartial logical work. ... It is not the business of psycho-analysis [itself], however, to undertake ... criticism [of these theories] ... for ... the fact that [the acceptance of] a theory is psychologically determined does not in the least invalidate its scientific truth.
>
> (SE 1913b, 13.179)

As for the credibility of theism, he had reached a dismal verdict: "it is precisely the elements ... which have the task of solving the riddles of the universe and of reconciling us to the sufferings of life – it is precisely those elements that are the least well authenticated of any" (SE 1927, 21.27). But note how careful he was to stress the logical priority of his atheism *vis-à-vis* his psychology of theism:

> Nothing that I have said here against the truth-value of religions needed the support of psycho-analysis; it had been said by others long before analysis came into existence. If the application of the psycho-analytic method makes it possible to find a new argument against the truths of religion, *tant pis* [so much the worse] for religion; but defenders of religion will by the same right make use of psycho-analysis in order to give full value to the affective significance of religious doctrines.
>
> (SE 1927, 21.37)

In the same vein, he declared: "All I have done – and this is the only thing that is new in my exposition – is to add some psychological foundation to the [evidential] criticisms of my great predecessors" (SE 1927, 21.35).

Apparently, Freud was walking a tightrope. On the one hand, he was well aware that it is one thing to provide a *psychogenesis* of religious belief, and quite another to appraise that belief epistemologically, with a view to estimating its truth-value.

Yet, as he just told us, he also claimed that, after all, the *psychogenesis* of theism can have a *supplementary* philosophical bearing on the question of the truth or falsity of religion. And he sees his own contribution to the debate as being one of elucidating precisely that supplementary import.

Hence, if we are to examine the philosophical case that Freud tries to make for atheism, we must first consider the evidential merit of the explanatory psychological hypotheses on which his psychogenetic portrait of religion relies.

My task will be to develop and appraise the purely psychological content of Freud's theory of religion, with a view to passing an epistemological judgement on its major psychological assumptions. These pivotal hypotheses are of three main sorts. Yet, only *two* of these sorts are *psychoanalytic* in the technical sense. Thus, only two-thirds of Freud's psychology of religion depends on the epistemic fortunes of his psychoanalytic enterprise. Later, I shall comment on his effort to harness his psychogenetic account of theism in the service of his irreligious philosophical agenda.

FREUD'S PSYCHOGENESIS OF RELIGION

Just what claims did Freud make about belief in God by characterizing it as an 'illusion'? As he tells us, "we call a belief an illusion when a wish-fulfilment is a prominent factor in its motivation, and in doing so we disregard its relation to reality, just as the illusion itself sets no store by verification" (SE 1927, 21.31). Thus, this sense of the term 'illusion' is both psychogenetic and epistemological. It requires that the wish-fulfilling character of the belief content be an important motivating factor in its acceptance, whereas the availability of supporting evidence played no such psychogenetic role. In brief, Freud calls a belief an illusion just when it is inspired by wishes *rather than* by awareness of some evidential warrant for it. Hence, as he uses the label, it is psychologically descriptive but epistemologically derogatory.

Clearly, however, it remains an empirical question of actual fact whether any given illusion, thus defined, is true or false. In the vast majority of cases, middle-class girls who have believed that a prince charming will come and marry them were concocting mere fantasies. Yet, in a few instances, this hope was not dashed. Hence Freud points out that an illusion is not necessarily false (SE 1927, 21.30–31). Nor is a false belief necessarily illusory. For example, the belief that the earth is flat may be induced by inadequate observations rather than by wishes.

But, as Rosemarie Sand has pointed out,[3] Freud *impoverished* the classical notion of illusion by restricting the motives of illusory beliefs to wishes: unlike the traditional concept, which goes back to Aristotle, Freud's characterization

---

3. Private communication, 3 March 2007.

of illusory beliefs excludes other emotions (e.g. fear, anger and amorous feelings) from being causes of illusions, whereas Aristotle had countenanced sundry emotions or "states of appetite" (*On Dreams* 460b5) as motives of distorted (illusory) sense-perceptions.

In Freud's view, there is an important subclass of *false* illusions whose generating wishes are complex enough to include unconscious desires. For example, according to Freud's theory of paranoia, the false notions of persecution entertained by a paranoiac are held to be inspired by strongly repressed homosexual wishes and by the operation of unconscious defence mechanisms. Freud uses the term 'delusion' to refer to such psychogenetically complex *false* illusions (SE 1927, 21.31; 1930, 21.81; 1911, 12.59–65; 1915a, 14.263–72; 1922, 18.223–32). Thus, he also speaks of delusions of jealousy, delusions of grandeur, and the delusions associated with heterosexual erotomania.

In brief, every delusion is a false illusion, generated by requisitely complex wishes. Thus, for Freud, a false illusion can fail to qualify as a delusion, if the desires that inspire it lack the stated psychogenetic complexity. But how do both illusions and delusions matter in Freud's philosophy of religion? They do because the nub of his own philosophical argument for atheism is the attempt to demonstrate the following: *the theistic religions are delusions, rather than just illusions; in fact, they are mass delusions in important parts of the world.*

It is to be borne in mind that these two Freudian technical notions differ importantly from the senses of 'illusion' and 'delusion' found in the *Psychiatric Dictionary* published by the Oxford University Press (Campbell 1981: 307–8). By contrast to Freud's wish-laden notion of 'illusion', the Oxford *Psychiatric Dictionary* uses the same term to denote a false *sense-perception* produced by a real external stimulus, as in the case of some mirages. For example, when a straight pencil or glass tube is partially immersed in water, we have the so-called visual illusion that the submerged portion has bent and forms an angle with its free upper part, although in actual fact it is straight. In virtue of thus being induced by a real stimulus, an illusion in this sense differs from a *hallucinatory* sensation, which has no source in the subject's environment but is produced endogenously. Evidently, this sense of 'illusion' requires that the perceptually induced belief be false, whereas Freud's wish-laden notion does *not* insist on a generic attribution of falsity. And instead of requiring a particular external physical object to be the eliciting cause, his concept calls for a psychological state as the eliciting cause. Furthermore, the definition of 'delusion' in the Oxford *Psychiatric Dictionary* (Campbell 1981: 157), as with its definition of illusion, seriously diverges from that given by Freud.

THE BRIDGE FROM ILLUSION TO DELUSION

Recall that Freud labels as a 'delusion' a *false* illusion produced by wishes that are complex enough to include repressed desires or defence mechanisms. As he reminds us: "In the case of delusions, we emphasize as essential their being in contradiction with reality", that is, their falsity, whereas "Illusions need not necessarily be false" (SE 1927, 21.31). Moreover, Freud's psychogenetic, epistemological and semantic concept of delusion allows that delusional beliefs be either idiosyncratic or socially shared. In fact, as he explains in *Civilization and Its Discontents*, he sees religion as an infantilizing mass delusion:

> [O]ne can try to re-create the world, to build up in its stead another world in which its most unbearable features are eliminated and replaced by others that are in conformity with one's own wishes. But whoever, in desperate defiance, sets out upon this path to happiness will as a rule attain nothing. Reality is too strong for him … A special importance attaches to the case in which this attempt to procure a certainty of happiness and a protection against suffering through a delusional remoulding of reality is made by a considerable number of people in common. The religions of mankind must be classed among the mass-delusions of this kind. No one, needless to say, who shares a delusion ever recognizes it as such.   (SE 1930, 21.81)

> [B]y forcibly fixing them [people] in a state of psychical infantilism and by drawing them into a mass-delusion, religion succeeds in sparing many people an individual neurosis.   (SE 1930, 21.84–5)

Freud's concept of a *mass* delusion is strongly at odds with the notion of delusion encountered in the 1970 and 1981 editions of the Oxford *Psychiatric Dictionary*. First let us note the points of agreement between them. In its fourth edition of 1970, the Oxford *Psychiatric Dictionary* states, under the rubric of 'hallucination', that the belief associated with a hallucinatory sensation is a "delusion" in the sense of being "obviously contrary to demonstrable fact". And the stated reason is that a hallucination is defined as "a *sense perception* to which there is no external stimulus" (Campbell 1970: 333). Also, the fourth edition speaks of a delusion as "a belief engendered without appropriate external stimulation and maintained by one in spite of what to normal beings constitutes incontrovertible and 'plain-as-day' proof or evidence to the contrary" (*ibid.*). So far, there is no conflict with Freud's concept of delusion.

But then comes the Oxford *Psychiatric Dictionary*'s sociological demurrer: "Further, the belief held is not one which is ordinarily accepted by other members of the patient's culture or subculture [i.e. it is not a commonly believed superstition]" (*ibid.*: 191). Indeed, the fifth edition (1981: 182) repudiates Freud's *supra*cultural notion of a 'mass delusion' altogether, in favour of an entirely *intra*cultural concept of delusion. Thus, the later Oxford definition allows a false belief to qualify as a delusion *only* if it is held idiosyncratically, and it makes social consensus the *sole* arbiter of reality. It appears that the later Oxford edition *politicized* its definition of 'delusion', much as the American Psychiatric Association – under political pressure to repudiate *homophobia* – abandoned its wholesale characterization of homosexuality as a disorder (or 'perversion') in favour of innocuously being a mere sexual 'orientation'. The 1981 Oxford definition reads:

> A false belief that is firmly maintained even though it is contradicted by social reality. While it is true that some superstitions and religious beliefs are held despite the lack of confirmatory evidence, such culturally engendered concepts are not considered delusions. What is characteristic of the delusion is that it is *not* shared by others; rather, it is an idiosyncratic and individual misconception or misinterpretation. Further, it is a thinking disorder of enough import to interfere with the subject's functioning, since in the area of his delusion he no longer shares a consensually validated reality with other people.   (*Ibid.*)

Evidently, no matter how inordinately primitive, superstitious or anthropomorphic the belief, it does not earn the Oxford label 'delusion' if it is *shared* in its cultural milieu! Thus, even the paranoid beliefs of a hysterical lynch mob cannot count as deluded if they are shared by the mob's community. But we are not told how many others in a given society need to share an idea, if it is to be part of what that dictionary entry calls 'social reality'. Does it have to be a majority? And, according to the definition, what counts as 'social reality' in a highly pluralistic society such as the United States, in which there are subcultures holding radically different, incompatible beliefs? The secular humanists and the late Jerry Falwell's self-styled 'moral majoritarians' extolled by the then President Bush senior are only two such subcultures.

To avoid misunderstanding, let me emphasize that to object to social reality as the sole arbiter of warranted belief is *not* to deny that consensus among independent observers does play some role in evidential corroboration. After all, the chances that five or more experimental physicists will hallucinate *in unison* are much smaller than that only one physicist will hallucinate.

Alas, the conformist Oxford *Psychiatric Dictionary* notion of socially deviant thought as being delusional seems to be akin to the view of some Soviet psychiatrists that individual political dissent should be seen as a psychiatric problem. Non-conforming *innovative* thinkers are seen as deluded cranks. Furthermore, like the psychoanalyst E. R. Wallace, the 1981 edition of the Oxford *Psychiatric Dictionary* limits the concept of delusion to idiosyncratic thinking disorders that are socially maladaptive *within* a culture. Thus, it makes no psychiatric allowance for shared beliefs that may turn out to be highly maladaptive for the group as a whole, even biologically, such as the beliefs that issued in the Jonestown mass suicide. And what of internecine religious wars, either civil or external, as between Hindu India and Muslim Pakistan? Also, there is the Ayatollah Khomeini's theological diagnosis of President Carter as 'Satan', which was undoubtedly *shared* by his mullahs and by some of the population in Iran. According to the Oxford *Psychiatric Dictionary* definition, that belief is not delusional in Iran. By contrast, Freud depicted the belief in Satan as "nothing but a mass fantasy, constructed along the lines of a paranoid delusion" (Wallace 1983: 271).

By saying that Freud's psychogenetic portrait of theism depicts it as a collection of 'illusions', we have so far merely scratched its surface. That portrayal has at least two other major features.

(i) The relevant illusions pertain to the fulfilment of those time-honoured and widely shared human yearnings that the theologian Paul Tillich (*see* Vol. 5, Ch. 11) dubbed 'ultimate concerns'. Thus, in this context, Freud's emphasis was not on illusions – however strong – that are entertained only temporarily or by only a relatively small number of people, let alone on more or less idiosyncratic ones. A purely wish-inspired belief that your favourite team will win the Super Bowl does qualify as an illusion in the Freudian sense, but this illusion is both demographically and temporally parochial. By contrast, Freud's theory of religion claims importance for evidentially ill-founded beliefs that envisage actual "fulfilments of the oldest, strongest and most urgent wishes of mankind" (SE 1927, 21.30). As he tells us, these beliefs, although still widespread today, were already held by "our wretched, ignorant, and downtrodden ancestors" (SE 1927, 21.33). We can refer to the sort of illusion already entertained by our primitive ancestors as "archaic", although not as venerable.

(ii) A further and even more important psychological earmark of theism, in Freud's view, is that this doctrine is engendered by the cooperation or synergism of three significantly different sorts of powerful, relentless wishes. And for each wish in this trio he offers a distinct scenario that specifies its content and mode of operation. Hence let us consider the relevant triad of hypotheses in turn.

As Freud points out, the first set of these psychogenetic assumptions features wish-motives that are largely conscious or 'manifest', instead of being the repressed wishes postulated by psychoanalytic theory (SE 1927, 21.33). Accordingly, this component of Freud's triadic psychology of religion does not rely on any of his technical psychoanalytic teachings. But what are the relevant archaic conscious wishes? He explains eloquently:

> [T]he terrifying impression of helplessness in childhood aroused the need for protection – for protection through love – which was provided by the father; and the recognition that this helplessness lasts throughout life made it necessary to cling to the existence of a father, but this time a more powerful one. Thus the benevolent rule of a divine Providence allays our fear of the dangers of life; the establishment of a moral world-order ensures the fulfilment of the demands of justice,

which have so often remained unfulfilled in human civilization; and the prolongation of earthly existence in a future life provides the local and temporal framework in which these wish-fulfilments shall take place. Answers to the riddles that tempt the curiosity of man, such as how the universe began or what the relation is between body and mind, are developed in conformity with the underlying assumptions of this system. (SE 1927, 21.30)

Understandably, therefore, the protector, creator *and* lawgiver are all rolled into one. No wonder, says Freud (SE 1933, 22.163–4), that in one and the same breath Immanuel Kant (*see* Vol. 3, Ch. 21) coupled the starry heavens above and the moral law within as both being awe-inspiring. After all, Freud asks rhetorically, "what have the heavenly bodies to do with the question of whether one human creature loves another or kills him?" And he answers: "The same father (or parental agency) which gave the child life and guarded him against its perils, taught him as well what he might do and what he must leave undone" (SE 1933, 22.164).

Therefore, Freud deems it to be quite natural that human beings are receptive to the psychological subordination inherent in compliance with authority, especially authority that is claimed to derive from God. In this vein, Freud would presumably say that the Roman Catholic clergy astutely potentiates the religious fealty of its faithful by requiring them to call its priests 'Father', to refer to the Pope as 'the Holy Father', and to the Church itself as 'Holy Mother Church'. Again, Freud might adduce that when parents are asked by their children to give a reason for their commands, many an exasperated, if not authoritarian, mother or father will answer with finality, 'Because *I* say so!'

No wonder, then, that religious systems can secure the acquiescence of their believers if they teach that the will of God is mysterious or inscrutable and that some of their tenets transcend human understanding, although such avowed unintelligibility turns them into mere mumbo-jumbo. In sum, it is one of Freud's recurrent psychological contentions that theism *infantilizes* adults by reinforcing the childish residues in their minds (SE 1927, 21.49; 1930, 21.85). Even the liberal Catholic theologian Hans Küng goes so far as to say: "All religions have in common the periodical *childlike* surrender to a Provider or providers who dispense earthly fortune as well as spiritual health" (1979: 120, my emphasis).

The motivational account cited from Freud thus far is not predicated on psychoanalytic theory, and it is therefore not surprising that it was largely anticipated by earlier thinkers. Freud had been exposed to the ideas of the early-nineteenth-century German atheist-theologian, Ludwig Feuerbach,[4] whose writings made a lasting impression on him. According to Feuerbach's psychological projection

---

4. Reported in Stepansky (1986: 231–2).

theory, it was human beings who created God in their own image, rather than conversely.[5] Being dependent on external nature, and beset by the slings and arrows of outrageous fortune, human beings project their cravings and fantasies outwards onto the cosmos into a figment of their own imagination.

Feuerbach took it to be the task of his atheistic theology to *demystify* religious beliefs by showing in detail how God was an object "of the heart's necessity, not of the mind's freedom" (quoted in Stepansky 1986: 223). Freud (SE 1927, 21.35, 37) used psychoanalysis to yield a further demystification by specifying additional, repressed feelings of human dependency on a father figure that would enhance the substance and credibility of Feuerbach's psychological reconstruction of religious history. Likewise strongly influenced by Feuerbach, Karl Marx wrote: "Religion ... is ... the *protest* against real distress. Religion is the sigh of the oppressed creature, the heart of a heartless world, just as it is the spirit of an unspiritual situation. It is the *opium* of the people" (quoted in Feuer 1959: 523). In Marx's time, opium was the most available painkiller and could be bought without any prescription. Thus, in speaking of this drug, Marx is being largely descriptive and explanatory rather than pejorative (*see* this vol., Ch. 14). But Marx appreciated insufficiently that an impoverished nineteenth-century industrial proletariat and peasantry are not the only groups in society that crave supernatural consolation for the trials and tribulations of life. Freud took into account, much more than Marx did, that a good many of the rich and privileged in society also seek religious refuge from the blows of existence. At least to this extent, Freud was closer to Feuerbach's view than was Marx.

Sidney Hook drew a germane comparison between Feuerbach and Marx, declaring Feuerbach to have been "more profound":

> [W]hen Marx says, "Religion is the opium of the people," he is really echoing Feuerbach. In Feuerbach's day it wasn't a disgrace to take opium. It was a medicine, an anodyne. It was the only thing people had to relieve their pain. Feuerbach was really implying that under any system there will be tragedy, heartache, failure, and frustration. Religion, for him (he regarded humanism and even atheism as a religion), serves that function [of relieving distress] in every society. Marx ridiculed this view because he was more optimistic than Feuerbach. He believed that science would solve not only the problem of economic scarcity but all human problems that arise from it. He ignored other human problems. Feuerbach seems to me to be more realistic about most human beings. (Hook 1985: 33)

---

5. In Grünbaum (2004) I have argued in detail against divine creation *ex nihilo* by reference to Leibniz's ill-conceived question, 'Why is there anything at all, rather than just nothing?'.

In so far as Freud's psychogenetic portrayal of religion depicts it as the product of *conscious* wishes, his account draws not only on Feuerbach but also on common-sense psychology. After all, at least *prima facie*, it is a commonplace that people seek to avoid anxiety and that they therefore tend to welcome the replacement of threatening beliefs by reassuring ones. Hence, for brevity, we can refer to this component of Freud's triadic psychology of religion as 'the common-sense hypothesis', which is not to say, however, that it is obviously true.

Each of the other two components of his trinity is a set of *psychoanalytic* claims asserting the operation of repressed motives. And yet they differ from each other, since one of them relies on Freud's theory of the psychosexual development of the human individual, while the other consists of speculative *ethnopsychological* and psychohistorical claims pertaining to the evolution of our species as a whole. Accordingly, we shall label the psychoanalytic assumptions relating to the individual as 'ontogenetic', but refer to the ethnopsychological ones as 'phylogenetic'.

As previously emphasized, the legitimacy of any psychogenetic portrait of religious creeds depends on the *evidential merit* of the explanatory psychological hypotheses adduced by it. Even the common-sense component of Freud's triad is subject to this caveat. Invoking the criticisms of his great predecessors, he took it for granted that there is no cogency in any of the arguments for the existence of God offered by believers. But he coupled this philosophical judgement with the daring motivational claim that the faithful who nonetheless adduce such proofs had not, in fact, themselves been decisively moved by them when giving assent to theism. Instead, he maintained, psychologically this assent is emotional or affective in origin:

> Where questions of religion are concerned, people are guilty of every possible sort of dishonesty and intellectual misdemeanour. Philosophers stretch the meaning of words until they retain scarcely anything of their original sense. They give the name of 'God' to some vague abstraction which they have created for themselves; having done so ... they can even boast that they have recognized a higher, purer concept of God, notwithstanding that their God is now nothing more than an insubstantial shadow and no longer the mighty personality of religious doctrines. (SE 1927, 21.32)

In brief, Freud holds that, motivationally, the dialectical excogitations offered as proofs are *post hoc* rationalizations in which an elaborate intellectual façade takes the place of the deep-seated wishes that actually persuaded the theologians. Speaking epigrammatically about rationalizations in another context, Freud aptly quotes Falstaff as saying that reasons are "as plenty as blackberries" (SE 1914, 14.24).

It would seem to be basically a matter of empirical psychological fact whether the common-sense constituent of Freud's psychogenetic portrait of religion is sound. But it is not clear how to design a cogent test even of this hypothesis. For

note that the required design needs to have the following two epistemic capabili-
ties: (i) it needs to yield evidence bearing on the validity of the functional explanation of religious belief as being anxiety-reducing (presumably this explanation
postulates some kind of stabilizing psychic servomechanism that reacts homeo-
statically to psychological threat); and (ii) the required test needs at least to able
to rank the intensity of the wish to escape from anxiety, as compared to the motivational persuasiveness of the theological proofs.

Perhaps the oscillating anxieties of believers who went through cycles of doubt
and belief have already gone some way towards meeting the first condition in
accord with John Stuart Mill's method of concomitant variations, a *quantitative*
method of causal inference which he set forth in his classic *A System of Logic*
(III.8.6). In any case, it would seem that an explicitly *fideist* belief in the existence
of God – which avowedly is *not* based on any arguments – calls for *psychological*
explanation in terms of wish motives or other desires (e.g. fears)!

The second requirement, however, seems to be a tall order indeed, although it
does not warrant putting a cap on the ingenuity of potential empirical investiga-
tors. It too must be met, because of Freud's bold hypothetical claim that even the
best of the arguments for the existence of God would not have convinced the great
minds who advanced them, unless stronger tacit wishes had carried the day or had
prompted these intellects to prevaricate. But note that, so far, Freud's portrayal of
the motives for religious belief has studiously refrained from claiming that such
beliefs are false.

Hence, whatever the empirical difficulties of validating Freud's psychogenetic
portrait, they are hardly tantamount to his commission of the hackneyed genetic
fallacy, a mode of inference that he explicitly rejected by means of disclaimers
and qualifications, as we saw. Yet this state of affairs is completely overlooked in
the late Philip Rieff's unfortunately very influential book, *Freud: The Mind of the
Moralist* (1959). There Rieff offers a combination of purported intellectual history,
sociology of knowledge, and philosophy of culture. As he would solemnly have it,
Freud's psychology of religion refurbishes the inveterate genetic fallacy "by which
animus is sanctified as science" (*ibid.*: 292) with the aid of some "scientistic name
calling" (*ibid.*: 268). Moreover, as indicated by the title of Rieff's book, he sees the
huge psychoanalytic corpus as a thinly veiled system of moralisms.

To be sure, Freud deemed religion an undesirably arrestive childish fixation.
And avowedly, he did *advocate* – as an "experiment" worth making – that children
be given an irreligious education (SE 1927, 21.48). But he took pains to say at once:
"Should the experiment prove unsatisfactory I am ready to give up the reform and
to return to my earlier, purely descriptive judgement that man is a creature of
weak intelligence who is ruled by his instinctual wishes" (SE 1927, 21.48–9). How,
then, does Rieff reason that, throughout his theoretical system, Freud "can always
get from description to judgment in a single step" (1959: 293), such that *all* of
psychoanalytic theory is moralistic? Rieff explains very misleadingly and indeed
uninformedly: "because in his case histories Freud never *reported* the facts but

interpreted them, what passes for description in the Freudian method is already judgment" (*ibid.*: 293).

But when Freud spoke of possibly having to retract his reformist plea for an atheistic education in favour of returning to his "earlier, purely descriptive judgement" of human nature, he was using the term 'descriptive' in contrast to 'normative' to characterize a claim as being devoid of *moral* advocacy. And he was alert to the *truism* – which Rieff touts ignorantly as his own exposé – that the psychoanalytic method generated theory-laden *interpretations* or inferred descriptive judgements. Indeed, Freud had emphasized, in a Kantian vein, that even a purportedly observational description of phenomena is already theory-laden (SE 1915b, 14.117). Yet when Rieff uses the term 'judgement' to refer to an interpretation, he fallaciously *slides* from the fact that the latter is *theory-laden* to its also necessarily being *value-laden*. Thus, Rieff rashly infers that all psycho-analytic interpretations, simply because they are theory-laden, are tantamount to moral judgements. Hence the misbegotten title of his book, *Freud: The Mind of the Moralist*.

But the egregious lack of epistemological sophistication vitiating this charge derives from its simplistic reliance on a dichotomy between fact (observation) and interpretation (theory). Even quotidian reports of supposed raw perceptual facts are already interpretive or theory-laden, as when a sweet-tasting substance on a dinner table is identified chemically *tout court* as sugar. The same epistemic complexity is illustrated by cases of mistaken identity in eyewitness testimony in courts of law, and by conflicting accounts of automobile accidents from bystanders, no less than when someone's smile in Western culture is construed as benevolent rather than hypocritical or mischievous.

To Rieff's complete detriment, it is widely recognized that even common-sense statements of purported fact inherently feature *fallible* interpretations of percep-tual experience, much as the diagnostic readings of an X-ray by a radiologist. Hence it is an idle red herring for Rieff to animadvert that in Freud's case histories Freud never confined himself to the reportage of raw data, if such there be, from the verbal productions of his patients.

The mere compilation of uninterpreted, theory-free facts is altogether *explan-atorily* sterile. If theoreticians in any field of enquiry had heeded the untutored epistemic injunction that Rieff issued to Freud, we would never have heard of any of them. And if the father of psychoanalysis had been minded to comply with Rieff's stultifying parsimony, his enterprise too would have been aborted at the outset, or nipped in the bud. Contrary to Rieff, Freud's pervasive inferential vulnerability derives not from his alleged moralisms, but from his often reckless postulational abandon in the manner of a self-styled conjectural conquistador (cf. Grünbaum 1984, 1993, 2002). In sum, Rieff's entire case against Freud is just a house of cards.

But the imperative to avoid the genetic fallacy cuts both ways. Just as the psychogenesis of religious belief cannot itself refute theism, so also the emotional gratifications such belief affords cannot support it *epistemically*. The dissident psychoanalysts Carl Jung and Alfred Adler appreciated this point, although they did claim *psychological* value or even emotional necessity for belief in God (Küng 1979: 62–3). Jung saw God as a human projection, manufactured from human emotions and from archetypes that Jung believed to have excavated psychoanalytically from an untamed collective unconscious. But, as a therapist, he thought that we court psychological disaster if we do not give conscious expression to our presumed unconscious religious feelings. All the same, he stressed that the purportedly necessary psychological function of the idea of God has "nothing whatever to do with the question of God's existence" (Stepansky 1986: 227).

FREUD'S PSYCHOANALYTIC THEORY OF RELIGION

Turning to the two psychoanalytic ingredients of Freud's triad, consisting of his ontogeny and phylogeny of theism, we must ask whether there is any good evidence for the existence of the postulated repressed wishes. In so far as even the very existence of these hidden desires is questionable, one remains less than convinced when told that these desires have contributed significantly to the initial genesis and later persistence of religious creeds.

It is a major tenet of Freudian theory that psychopathology is rooted in the psychic conflict created by unsuccessfully repressed desires. Guided by this model of mental disorder, Freud's ontogeny and phylogeny diagnose religion as a mixture of syndromes, featuring oedipal, paranoid and obsessional elements. Yet Freud explicitly allowed that there are several interesting differences between, say, the illusions of a paranoiac and religious beliefs. For example, the specifics of the former are idiosyncratic, while the latter are usually shared, sometimes even widely (SE 1907, 9.119–20; 1927, 21.44). Let us now consider, in turn, some of the highlights of Freud's ontogeny and phylogeny of religion.

In 1901, in his *Psychopathology of Everyday Life*, Freud traced superstitions to unconscious causes (SE 1901, 6.258–60). The psychological mechanism operative here, we are told, is that of transmuting feelings and impulses into external agencies by *projection* or displacement (SE 1913a, 13.92).

> [P]sycho-analysis can also say something new about the *quality* of the unconscious motives that find expression in superstition. It can be recognized most clearly in neurotics suffering from obsessional thinking or obsessional ... states – people who are often of high intelligence – that superstition derives from suppressed hostile and cruel impulses. Superstition is in large part the expectation of trouble; and a person who has harboured frequent evil wishes against others, but has been brought up to be good and has therefore repressed such wishes into the unconscious, will be especially ready to expect punishment

for his unconscious wickedness in the form of trouble threatening him
from without.   (SE 1901, 6.260)

Obsessional neurosis features relentlessly intrusive, anxiety-producing thoughts,
rumination, doubt and scruples as well as *repetitive* impulses to perform such acts
as ceremonials, counting, hand-washing, checking and so on.

The hypothesized causes of a disorder are said to be the 'etiology' of the disorder.
Derivatively, the term 'etiology' is also used to refer to the pertinent causal
hypothesis, rather than to the presumed causes themselves. In Freud's 1907 paper,
"Obsessive Actions and Religious Practices", he employed his etiology of obsessional neurosis to diagnose religious *rituals*, no less than obsessive-compulsive
non-religious acts. According to his etiologic hypothesis, these repetitive acts
result from the conflict between a repressed forbidden instinct and the repressing
forces of consciousness. As a species of obsessive-compulsive acts, religious rites
are seen etiologically as *exorcistic defences* against evil wishes and against the disas-
ters that such forbidden desires are feared to engender by sheer magic.

Precisely by fearing that *mere* desires or thoughts can magically produce calamities, the obsessive's overvaluation of the power of mental processes betrays the
mindset of savages, who believe in just such an omnipotence of thoughts (see
Freud's case history of the Rat-Man: SE 1909, 10.229ff.; 1913a, 13.86). And by
performing the supposedly protective rituals, the obsessive wards off a crescendo
of anxiety, the qualms of conscience brought on by their neglect (SE 1907, 9.119).
Here, then, Freud's psychogenetic accent is on religious ceremonials or sacra-
mental *acts*, rather than on theoretical religious doctrine.

But what of the important differences between religious practices or doctrine,
on the one hand, and obsessive-compulsive acts or thoughts, on the other? Freud
addresses these differences head on, only to proceed to neutralize them diagnostically by psychoanalytic argument. Speaking of the "obvious" differences, he
declares:

> [A] few of them are so glaring that they make the comparison a sacri-
> lege: the greater individual variability of [neurotic] ceremonial actions
> in contrast to the stereotyped character of rituals (prayer, turning
> to the East, etc.), their private nature as opposed to the public and
> communal character of religious observances, above all, however, the
> fact that, while the minutiae of religious ceremonial are full of signifi-
> cance and have a symbolic meaning, those of neurotics seem foolish
> and senseless. In this respect an obsessional neurosis presents a trav-
> esty, half comic and half tragic, of a private religion. But it is precisely
> this sharpest difference between neurotic and religious ceremonial,
> which disappears when, with the help of the psycho-analytic tech-
> nique of investigation, one penetrates to the true meaning of obses-
> sive actions.   (SE 1907, 9.119–20)

Diagnostically, therefore, Freud rejects the objection that he has ridden rough-shod over the differences between neurosis and religion when he 'psychopatholo-gized' religion. This charge was levelled in 1983 by Wallace. According to Wallace, Freud "overlooked an important distinction between symptom and ritual: the *ego-dystonic* nature of the former versus the *ego-syntonic* [nature] of the latter" (1983: 277; for his most recent account, see Wallace 1984). Wallace means that, subjectively, the compulsive hand-washer finds his repetitive need disagreeable, whereas the religious worshipper finds his observances congenial. It is less than clear, however, that Roman Catholics, for example, typically find it ego-syntonic when they are asked to say so many Hail Marys or Lord's Prayers for penance, even though these repetitive acts may relieve the anxiety induced by the priest's admonition.

But let us grant for the sake of argument that all religious observances are ego-syntonic. Even then, according to standard psychoanalytic theory, which Wallace accepts (1983: 276), the ego-syntonic character of feelings and behaviour does not necessarily militate against their etiologic status as a neurotic manifesta-tion: the so-called 'character neuroses' are distinguished, within the theory, from the 'symptom neuroses' by precisely the fact that the former neuroses are ego-syntonic, while the latter dysfunctions are not (Laplanche & Pontalis 1973: 67–8). Thus, having the narcissistic personality syndrome need not militate against the self-satisfaction of its exemplar, and the paranoiac afflicted by delusions of gran-deur need not find them ego-dystonic or unconvincing.

Qua neurotic manifestations, religious rituals are viewed by Freud as typically conducing to psychological intimidation, uniformity and dependence, if not to outright infantilization. He does emphasize, however, that sharing in the glori-fied, enlarged obsessional neurosis of religion with other people can obviate an idiosyncratic one: "Devout believers are safeguarded in a high degree against the risk of certain neurotic illnesses; their acceptance of the universal neurosis spares them the task of constructing a personal one" (SE 1927, 21.44). This sort of trade-off is a theme that Freud returns to time and again, starting in 1907 and ending with his *Moses and Monotheism,* which appeared in 1939, the year of his death (see SE 1907; 1910, 11.123, 146; 1921, 18.142; 1930, 21.84–5, 144; 1939, 23.72–80).

It would seem that within the ranks of religious psychoanalysts, Wallace's critique of Freud's psychopathology of religion has failed to carry conviction. A notable case in point is the Roman Catholic Jesuit priest William Meissner, who is a practising psychoanalyst and professor of psychiatry at Boston College. In his 1984 book, *Psychoanalysis and Religious Experience,* he paints a sobering psycho-logical picture of religion. Meissner tells us that religious experience can occur at different levels of development, and can include at its apex "mature, integrated, and adaptive levels of psychic functioning". And, if so, then "Freud was able to envision only a segment of the broader developmental spectrum" (1984: 14). But unlike Wallace, Meissner makes the following significant concession: "the psychology of religious experience ... overlaps, and to a significant degree is intertwined with mental processes that, from a clinical perspective, can be described as patholog-ical" (*ibid.*: 9–10). Referring to one of Freud's famous case histories, Meissner says: "the Wolf Man's obsessive religiosity was a vehicle for his instinctual pathology" (*ibid.*: 60). Indeed, Meissner's verdict is rather dismal:

> A caricature of [ideal] religion, which Freud himself employed as an analogy to obsessional states, is not infrequently found among religious people in whom blind adherence to ritual and scrupulous conscientiousness, as well as conscience, dominate religious life. In fact, we can safely say that the great mass of believers lend credence to Freud's formulations.
>
> More mature and integrated forms of religious experience are modestly distributed among the people of God. Those who reach the highest level of religious experience and achieve the maximum expres-sion of religious ideals are very rare indeed ... Unfortunately, to study the religious experience of those more advanced and saintly souls who have gained a high level of religious maturity, we must rely on the secondhand historical accounts that leave many questions unan-swered and unapproachable ... the theologian directs his attention to a more or less idealized, rarely attained level of religious maturity.
>
> (*Ibid.*: 15)

Freud's psychopathological ontogeny of theism is not confined to obsessional neurosis. He thought that the Oedipus complex "constitutes the nucleus of all neuroses" (SE 1913c, 13.157, 129). Thus, we learn that the pathogens of obses-sional neurosis are interwoven with those of the Oedipus complex. In its so-called 'complete' form of ambivalence toward each parent, that complex is produced by the conflict between affectionate sexual feelings, on the one hand, and hostile aggressive feelings of rivalry, on the other, attitudes that are entertained toward both parents in the psyche of all children between the ages of three and six (Laplanche & Pontalis 1973: 282–6).

The special focus of these affects is the powerful, protective and yet threat-ening father, who has replaced the mother in her initial role of providing food and protection (SE 1927, 21.24). Being too disturbing to be entertained consciously, these emotions are repressed (Fenichel 1945: 91–8). It may be asked at once how the Oedipal conflict can be deemed pathogenically relevant, if *all* people experi-ence it in childhood while only *some* become strikingly neurotic. The Freudian answer is that people do differ in regard to their success in *resolving* the infantile Oedipus complex (SE 1925, 20.55–6), even if some ambivalence toward the father figure lingers on into adulthood.

The cosmic projection and exaltation of this authority figure as a deity in publicly approved fashion therefore has great appeal. As Freud puts it: "It is an enormous relief to the individual psyche if the conflicts of its childhood arising from the father-complex – conflicts which it has never wholly overcome – are removed from it and brought to a solution which is universally accepted" (SE 1927, 21.30). By the same token, a true child–father relationship is achieved once polytheism yields to monotheism after man "creates for himself the gods whom he dreads, whom he seeks to propitiate, and whom he nevertheless entrusts with his own protection" (SE 1927, 21.24).

Indeed, the psychoanalytically fathomed unconscious wishes of the adult's residual Oedipus complex are held to combine *synergistically* with the urgent desire for relief from the *conscious* fears of enduring vulnerability, fears that are lifelong intensifications of the child's dread of helplessness (SE 1927, 21.23–4). The product is the belief in an omnipotent God, who is thought to love each of us, even if no one else does.

Apparently, the apotheosis of the father does fit Judaism, Christianity and Islam. But Freud seems to have neglected Hinduism, Buddhism and Taoism. And at least one writer (Erdelyi 1985: 207) has claimed that as between the two parents, the mother seems to be the more important figure in these Eastern religions. Yet Freud noted that "the creator is usually a man, though there is far from being a lack of indications of female deities; and some mythologies actually make the creation begin with a male God getting rid of a female deity, who is degraded into being a monster" (SE 1933, 22.162).

Roman Catholic writers Küng (1979) and Meissner (1984) regard psychoanalytic ontogeny as a viable and illuminating part of the psychology of religious belief. More generally, the Protestant theologian Tillich opted for the use of psychoanalysis, along with Marxism, to offer unflattering motivational explanations of what he regarded as much false consciousness in Western society (see Shinn 1986).

But what are the actual empirical credentials of Freud's sexual etiology of obsessional neurosis, and of his Oedipal ontogeny of theism? In the context of the conjugal family, this Oedipal plot calls for not only an erotic love–hate triangle prior to the age of six, but also a redemptive denouement of the guilt-laden parricidal wish by projective exaltation of the father into God. It is a clear moral of Grünbaum (1984) that, far from having good empirical support, these obsessional and Oedipal hypotheses have yet to be adequately tested, even prior to their use in a psychology of religion. A *fortiori*, the psychoanalytic ontogeny of theism still lacks evidential warrant, with the possible exception of the psychogenesis of the doctrine of the virgin birth of Jesus (Grünbaum 1993: 295–8). Until and unless there is more warrant for the ontogeny, it is surely at least the better part of wisdom to place little, if any, explanatory reliance on it.

But, in his psychology of religious belief, Freud was not content to confine himself to the explanatory use of the conscious quest for anxiety reduction and of his ontogeny of theism. Rather, he went on to develop a psychoanalytic *phylogeny* of theism (SE 1913c, 13, pt IV). In his view, this historical ethnopsychology is a valid extension of psychoanalysis. He reasoned as follows:

The obscure sense of guilt to which mankind has been subject since prehistoric times, and which in some religions has been condensed into the doctrine of primal guilt, or original sin, is probably the outcome of a blood-guilt incurred by prehistoric man. In my book *Totem and Taboo* (1912–13) I have, following clues given by Robertson Smith, Atkinson and Charles Darwin, tried to guess the nature of this primal guilt, and I believe, too, that the Christian doctrine of today enables us to deduce it. If the Son of God was obliged to sacrifice his life to redeem mankind from original sin, then by the [Mosaic] law of talion, the requital of like by like, that sin must have been a killing, a murder. Nothing else could call for the sacrifice of a life for its expiation. And if the original sin was an offence against God the Father, the primal crime of mankind must have been a parricide, the killing of the primal father of the primitive human horde, whose mnemic image was later transfigured into a deity.

(SE 1915c, 14.292–3; see also SE 1939, 23.130–31)

There remains the question of how Freud conjectured the *motive* for the inferred parricide. As he tells us: "Darwin deduced from the habits of the higher apes that men, too, originally lived in comparatively small groups or hordes within which the jealousy of the oldest and strongest male prevented sexual promiscuity" (SE 1913c, 13.125). In each of these hordes or families, the dominant male imposed erotic restraints on his younger and subordinate male rivals by controlling their sexual access to the women of the clan. But this prohibition did not sit well with these rivals. Freud speculates that, driven by their ensuing hostility, and being cannibals, the rivals banded together into a brother clan to *kill and eat* their own father (SE 1913c, 13.141–2). Yet they soon began to quarrel over the sexual spoils of the father's harem, and they became highly ambivalent about their parricidal achievement. The memory of the homicide itself was repressed, and thereby generated guilt.

The resulting filial remorse, in turn, issued in two major developments: (i) the delayed enforcement of the father's original edict against incestuous sex within the clan made exogamy mandatory, thereby generating the incest taboo (SE 1913c, 13.5–6); and (ii) the prohibition of parricide turned into the expiatory *deification* of the slain parent. As Freud put it: "the primal father, at once feared and hated, revered and envied, became the prototype of God himself" (SE 1925, 20.68).

Freud assumed that, over the millennia, our primitive ancestors re-enacted the parricidal scenario countless times (SE 1939, 23.81). And, as a convinced Lamarckian, he believed that racial memories of it, cumulatively registered by our primitive ancestors – but subsequently repressed by them – were transmitted to us by the inheritance of acquired characteristics (Sulloway 1977: 274–5, 439–42). Thus, at least each male has supposedly stored this phylogenetic legacy in his unconscious, including the resulting sense of collective guilt over the primal crime (SE 1939, 23.132).

Shortly before his death, Freud confidently announced that "men have always known (in this special [Lamarckian] way) that they once possessed a primal father and killed him" (SE 1939, 23.101). He explicitly credits the Scottish biblical scholar William Robertson Smith and the anthropologist J. G. Frazer with the recognition that the Christian sacrament of communion is a residue of the eating of the sacred totem animal, which in turn appeared to Freud to hark back to the eating of the slain primal father (SE 1925, 20.68).

By combining ethnography with psychoanalysis, Freud believes he has discerned a third set of strong wishes that unite synergistically with the other two classes of his triad, and make the psychogenesis of belief in God the Father the more impera- tive. He therefore stated: "We now observe that the store of religious ideas includes not only wish-fulfilments but important historical recollections. This concurrent influence of past and present must give religion a truly incomparable wealth of [psychological] power" (SE 1927, 21.42). Moreover, the ontogeny of the Oedipus complex is, at least in its earlier stages, developmentally similar to its conjectured phylogeny. And this psychogenetic parallelism seemed all the more credible to Freud, because he saw it as the psychological counterpart of Ernst Haeckel's biogenetic law. According to Haeckel, the embryonic ontogeny of each animal, including human beings, *recapitulates* the morphological changes undergone by the successive ancestors of the species during its phylogeny. No wonder that Freud felt entitled to regard the early ontogenetic development of moral dispositions like remorse and guilt in each of us as both a replica and a phylogenetic residue of the primal father complex of early human beings (SE 1923, 19.37).

At this point, standing at the portal of his own death in 1939, Freud is ready to deploy his repression-etiology of neurosis, together with his ethnopsychological retrodictions. And he joins them to explain the frequently characteristic irration- ality of traditional theism as follows:

> A tradition that was based only on communication could not lead to the compulsive character that attaches to religious phenomena. It would be listened to, judged, and perhaps dismissed, like any other piece of information from outside; it would never attain the privilege of being liberated from the constraint of logical thought. It must have undergone the fate of being repressed, the condition of lingering in the unconscious, before it is able to display such powerful effects on its return, to bring the masses under its spell, as we have seen with aston- ishment and hitherto without comprehension in the case of religious tradition.   (SE 1939, 23.101)

As we learn on the same page, the "return" of the religious tradition refers to the *reawakening* of the repressed memory of ancestral totemistic parricide.

This reanimation was supposedly effected by two epoch-making episodes, each of which Freud claimed to be historically authentic: first, the murder of Moses by the ancient Hebrews, who rebelled against his tyrannical imposition of the intolerable prescriptions of monotheism; thereafter, "the supposed judicial murder of Christ".

But Freud's all-too-speculative psychoanalytic phylogeny of theism is dubious, if only because it assumes a Lamarckian inheritance of repressed racial memories. Also, where is Freud's *historical* evidence for his claims concerning Moses? Furthermore, contrary to the uniform evolution of religions required by his account, more recent historical scholarship seems to call for developmental pluriformity (Küng 1979: 67). And if there are such differences of religious history, it becomes more difficult to sustain the historical authenticity of the common parricidal scenario postulated by Freud's phylogeny. As Küng emphasizes, no primordial religion has hitherto been found, and indeed "the sources necessary for a historical explanation of the origin of religion are simply not available" (*ibid.*: 70–71).

Meissner (1984: ch. 5) too examines Freud's psychoanalytic phylogeny of Mosaic monotheism, and writing from the standpoint of biblical archeology, exegesis and anthropology, he reaches the following verdict: "Subsequent years have subjected the whole area of biblical studies and criticism to a radical revision that makes it clear that the fundamental points of view on which Freud based his synthetic reconstruction were themselves faulty and misleading" (*ibid.*: ix).

FREUD'S ARGUMENT FOR ATHEISM

Having maintained that, psychogenetically, theistic beliefs are illusions, Freud deploys a dialectical strategy on behalf of atheism. He aims to show that religious illusions, in particular, are very probably *false, also being delusions* in his stated technical sense.[6]

FURTHER READING

Gay, P. 1987. *A Godless Jew: Freud, Atheism, and the Making of Psychoanalysis*. New Haven, CT: Yale University Press.
Gay, P. 1988. *Freud: A Life for Our Time*. New York: W. W. Norton.
Grünbaum, A. 1993. "Psychoanalysis and Theism". In his *Validation in the Clinical Theory of Psychoanalysis: A Study in the Philosophy of Psychoanalysis*, 257–309. Madison, CT: International Universities Press.
Küng, H. 1979. *Freud and the Problem of God*. New Haven, CT: Yale University Press.

---

6. Owing to space limitations, I refer the reader to my book on psychoanalysis (Grünbaum 1993: 279–95) for an exposition and critique of Freud's argument for atheism.

Meissner, W. 1984. *Psychoanalysis and Religious Experience*. New Haven, CT: Yale University Press.

On ATHEISM see also Chs 2, 10; Vol. 3, Ch. 15; Vol. 5, Chs 6, 17. On FETISHISM see also Ch. 7. On PSYCHOLOGY see also Chs 15, 18. On RITUAL see also Chs 9, 21; Vol. 1, Chs 12, 20.

21

ÉMILE DURKHEIM

Philip A. Mellor

Émile Durkheim (1858–1917) is, along with Max Weber, unquestionably one of the two most important 'founding figures' of sociology, as well as a major influence on contemporary sociologies of religion, culture and society. Outside sociology, however, he also had a huge impact on anthropology, social psychology and criminology, as well as various branches of philosophy. Born in Épinal, France, he grew up in the Jewish community of Alsace-Lorraine and, coming from a long line of rabbis, initially seemed destined for the rabbinate, although he soon determined to abandon the family tradition. Following studies at the College d'Épinal, he was admitted to the École Normale Supérieure in Paris in 1879, studying philosophy and history (Lukes 1973: 39–43). It was here that his interest in the social implications and applications of philosophical thought started to emerge and, after a period as a philosophy teacher at a lycèe, this interest started to take a distinctively social scientific form following his first academic appointment at Bordeaux University (1887). Employed to teach social science and pedagogy, the philosophy of education, in 1895 he was given a chair in social science. This period at Bordeaux also saw the publication of his books *The Division of Labor in Society* ([1893] 1984), *The Rules of Sociological Method* ([1895] 1982) and *Suicide: A Study in Sociology* ([1897] 1952), as well as the establishment of the new, immensely influential, periodical *L'Année Sociologique*, through which Durkheim gathered together a new generation of scholars working within a sociological tradition of his own design (Poggi 2000: 3). In 1902, Durkheim moved to the Sorbonne in Paris, where his national and international influence continued to grow, and where he produced arguably his finest and most important book, *The Elementary Forms of Religious Life*, in 1912 (1995). The First World War, however, brought a great deal of misfortune and despair to Durkheim: not only did many of the most promising young Durkheimians, including Robert Hertz, lose their lives, but also Durkheim's son, Paul, was killed in action in 1915. Durkheim died, a broken man, two years later.

These are the undisputed facts of Durkheim's life, but when we attempt to clarify the nature of Durkheim's thought we are immediately faced with a paradox: on the one hand, it is universally acknowledged that Durkheim had a clearly defined vision of what sociology was and that he sought to establish its pre-eminence through his own publications and the work of the *Année Sociologique* group; on the other hand, the various accounts of Durkheim we encounter in sociology, anthropology, psychology and philosophy are so strikingly diverse that the exact nature of his thought is often much disputed, and has given rise to debates about whether he was a materialist or an idealist, a Kantian or an anti-Kantian, a conservative or a radical, as well as heated arguments about whether his philosophy of religion, culture and society is an essentially functionalist one (Shilling & Mellor 2001: 40). Periodic attempts to rescue Durkheim from his interpreters (e.g. Stedman Jones 2001) often merely exacerbate these disputes. Nonetheless, a key feature of Durkheim's work, that is not only agreed on by a broad range of his interpreters but also marks him out as a person of his time, is his profound interest in the non-rational dimensions of human life.

Durkheim, like Sigmund Freud, saw himself as a rationalist but centred his work on the analysis of what he saw as non-rational, if rationally explainable, phenomena. In this, he followed the example of Auguste Comte, the philosopher who first offered a distinctive vision of 'sociology', but this interest in the non-rational was also a key part of late-nineteenth-century sociological writings more generally. Georg Simmel, Vilfredo Pareto and even Weber, *the* theorist of modern rationalization processes, were all interested in the religious, emotional, sensual and aesthetic dimensions of human life and how these underpinned, challenged or were dominated by the more rational, institutional and structural components of modern societies. However, where in the work of Simmel and Weber this interest in the non-rational tended to be part of a somewhat bleak picture of an increasingly dominant instrumental rationality that was steadily eliminating all forms of religious enchantment, for Durkheim such pessimism was unfounded. Indeed, there are two features of Durkheim's thought that not only indicate the profound sociological, philosophical and psychological significance of non-rational phenomena, but which are also of paramount importance in terms of understanding his sociological project as a whole.

The first of these is his focus on society as a *sui generis* reality, transcendent of the individuals who constitute it. Indeed, the conventional view of sociology as the study of 'society' reflects a great debt to Durkheim: he, more than any of the 'founding figures', was concerned with the establishment of sociology as a discipline centred on the study of society as a distinct reality. The second key feature concerns the *fundamental* and *permanent* importance he attributes to the religious dimensions of society through his notion of the 'sacred'. His analysis of religions as collective representations of the emotional and moral dynamics of group life has not only had a significant impact on nineteenth- and twentieth-century sociology and anthropology but also remains a key influence on some of the more creative and interesting areas of social and cultural theory in the twenty-first century. These two key features should be understood to be linked inseparably.

ÉMILE DURKHEIM

SOCIETY AS A *SUI GENERIS* REALITY

Although Durkheim explores a number of different aspects of 'society' and, conse-quently, uses the term in a number of different ways, his primary interest is in what can be called the 'supra-individual' elements in social life relating to social actions, feelings, beliefs, values and ideals (Lukes 1973: 115). As Robert Bellah suggests, for Durkheim, "Not only is a society not identical with an external 'material entity', it is something deeply inner" (1973: ix). His critique of empiricism is significant in this regard, since he argues that reducing reality to experience inevitably results in a denial of the truth, meaning or value of anything outside the specific individual or social constructions placed on phenomena: in other words, the deepest strata of human, social and natural forms of life are simply argued away (Durkheim [1912] 1995: 12–18). Contrary to such reductions, he identifies society with "an immense cooperation that extends not only through space but also through time", combining ideas and feelings in a rich and complex set of processes through which we become "truly human" (*ibid.*: 15–16).

Central to his account of this "cooperation" is the role of *collective represen-tations* in expressing the common ideas, beliefs, concepts and symbols through which we make sense of ourselves, others and the world. Durkheim talks of the "stimulating action of society" as an embodied experience affecting nearly every instant of our lives (*ibid.*: 213). He emphasizes that collective representa-tions, "which form the network of social life", arise from the interactions between individuals but that they are not simply products, or aggregate outcomes, of "the psychic life of individuals" ([1898] 1974b: 24–5). On the contrary, he argues that "private sentiments do not become social except by combination under the action of the *sui generis* forces developed in association" (*ibid.*: 26). Thus, "individual representations", the mental forms particular to individuals, are surpassed by the collective, which add to and transform personal experiences in the light of know-ledge, sentiments and symbols developed over large tracts of time ([1912] 1995: 437). Furthermore, he suggests that this relationship between the individual and the collective is analogous to the relationship between biological mental processes within individual minds (nervous energy, neural pathways, brain functions) and those representations that constitute the "psychic life" or "spirituality" of the indi-vidual ([1898] 1974b: 27–8). Individual representations are the result of *sui generis* forces arising from the association of diverse elements within the mind, while collective representations are the dynamic outcomes of social interactions char-acterized by a "hyper-spirituality" (*ibid.*: 34). In short, the emergent, *sui generis* phenomenon that is society, although constituted by individuals, has a reality transcendent of them. This takes us right to the heart of what Durkheim under-stands society to be.

In arguing that a society has its own specific hyper-spirituality, and that this represents the distinctive object of sociological study, Durkheim is firmly rejecting reductive accounts of society and seeking to build a nuanced account of its ontological characteristics ([1906] 1974a: 27–8, 34). It is in the context of this rejection that he emphasizes the *homo duplex* character of human beings in two senses: first, human identities have individual and collective sources; secondly, their rational dimensions arise out of a non-rational stimulation and circulation of social energies within the *sui generis* reality of society ([1905] 1973). The causal significance of hyper-spirituality is manifest in this power of society to suggest and indeed impose certain ways of acting and thinking on individuals ([1895] 1982: 248). Throughout Durkheim's work, though particularly so with regard to his final major study ([1912] 1995), his understanding of the relationship between humanity's *homo duplex* character and the emergent, hyper-spiritual reality of social life is developed most systematically with regard to his stress on the foundational role of religious phenomena for society and culture.

THE SACRED

Although, in the twentieth century, the 'sociology of religion' developed as a subdisciplinary field rather than a core focus of sociological thought, this marginalization of religion as a subject matter was quite alien to much nineteenth-century sociological thought, and certainly to that of Durkheim, who emphasized the absolute centrality of religion to the study of society and culture. Indeed, for him, the fundamental processes through which social life is constituted have a religious character: the emergence of society as a *sui generis* phenomenon is a process marked by a contagious circulation of emotional energies that produce distinctive experiences and collective representations of what he calls the 'sacred'. Defining the sacred as those "things set apart and forbidden" from the profane world of everyday life, and which not only represent a community to itself but which also serve to bind individuals into a powerful sense of moral community, he argues that there can be no society without a sense of the sacred, and that the sacred–profane polarity has been an absolutely central feature of human thought and culture throughout history ([1912] 1995: 34–6, 44).

It should be noted that this emphasis on the fundamental and permanent significance of religion in human history does not constitute any kind of endorsement of religions in their own terms. Indeed, his account of religion is a sociologically reductive one, in that he does not view it as a phenomenon of divine origin or as something with a capacity for expressing fundamental truths about human beings and the universe in terms of religious beliefs or doctrines. On the contrary, religious belief systems express the hallucinatory and delirious capacities of minds to fabricate collective fantasies: whatever 'truth' religions express has to do with the reality of those collective forces that constitute them, not the 'delirium' of religious philosophy, theology or mythology (*ibid*.: 228). In emphasizing the delirious quality of *all* collective representations, however, he is not marking out religion as a particularly non-rational phenomenon: rather, he is stressing that *all* social and cultural phenomena, including scientific thought, have their origins in the non-rational processes through which societies become structured around the distinction between the sacred and the profane (*ibid.*: 239-40). Consequently, if religion is explainable as a purely social phenomenon, it is also possible to describe society as, in essence, a purely religious phenomenon.

This close intertwining of the notions of the 'social' and the 'religious' is a consistent feature of Durkheim's thought, although there are also noticeable stages in the development of the mature arguments of *The Elementary Forms*. In his first major work, *The Division of Labor in Society*, he associates religion with those collective emotions and beliefs that provide the pre-contractual foundations for the contractual dimensions of social orders, although there is some ambiguity about whether the foundational role of religion can be confined to pre-modern societies characterized by patterns of 'mechanical solidarity', in contrast to the 'organic solidarity' of modernity ([1893] 1984). After this work, however, Durkheim never again used this mechanical–organic distinction, and in *Suicide* ([1897] 1952) the role of modern religious forms is examined as being of fundamental importance in relation to certain types of suicide, specifically with regard to different Protestant and Catholic suicide rates in Europe. Shortly afterwards, however, a landmark essay on the obligatory beliefs and practices associated with religious phenomena firmly established, for him, the idea that collective emotions stimulate within individuals a sense of the moral power of society which can be identified as the 'sacred', and that therefore every act of socialization is, in effect, an initiation into the religious ([1899] 1975). By the time of *The Elementary Forms*, this interest in socialization, with its functionalist overtones, had developed into a more dynamic and fluid conception of the spread of social feelings, ideas and beliefs. Here, the sacred has a virus-like quality, spreading contagiously and contaminating everything it comes into contact with as it imbues all phenomena with the emotional energies stimulated by collective life ([1912] 1995: 327–8).

The primary means through which this sacred contagion is initially unleashed is a state of 'collective effervescence'; this refers to the emotionally stimulating effects of the congregation as a community, where for gathered individuals "a sort of electricity is generated from their closeness and quickly launches them to an extraordinary height of exaltation" (*ibid.*: 217). The anthropologist E. E. Evans-Pritchard's dismissal of the notion as a euphemism for "a sort of crowd hysteria", recalls the work of Gustave Le Bon, whose social psychological study of crowds ([1895] 1975) has sometimes been seen as an unacknowledged source of Durkheim's theory of religion, and certainly influenced Freud's thought quite significantly. While Le Bon's focus on the collective, emotional energies of crowds is indeed suggestive of Durkheim's arguments, their views on the social consequences of collective emotions could not be more different: Durkheim resolutely emphasizes their creativity and, in general, their positive social effects; for Le Bon, in contrast, crowds are thoroughly dangerous phenomena, overcoming moral reasoning and intellectual culture in their dark irrationality. While even some of Durkheim's admirers have dismissed the notion of collective effervescence as "not only crude but highly implausible" (Lukes 1973: 17), it is an absolutely indispensable part of his theory of religion and society: it is this that offers an embodied and experiential basis for his stress on the *sui generis* character of society, the *homo duplex* character of human beings, and the sacred qualities of those collective representations that reshape the consciousnesses of individuals. It is also the foundation on which he is able to offer his distinctive account of the social significance of *rituals* and *symbols*.

If collective effervescence is the raw emotional phenomena out of which solidarity experienced as the sacred is able to emerge, ritual provides the means through which emotional energy can be intensified, regulated and systematically replenished. For Durkheim, 'cults', systems of rituals, can be distinguished into 'positive' and 'negative' types: the former are focused on the potentially sacrilegious encounter with the sacred, such as in the Christian Eucharist where God is eaten symbolically/sacramentally; the latter serve to maintain the separation between sacred and profane through, among other things, taboos. Consequently, at the heart of religious life is the tension between coming into contact/not coming into contact with the sacred, mediated through a ritual process where this tension is kept 'charged' with a sort of emotional electricity. Furthermore, different types of rituals channel emotional energies in ways that are directly related to the cyclical pattern of social life, so that some deal with profusions of energy, such as we find at feasts, while others deal with depletions of social energy, such as 'piacular' rites, where the aim is to "restore to the group the energy that the events [e.g. deaths] threatened to take away" (Durkheim [1912] 1995: 415–16).

Symbols constitute a potent outcome of ritually mediated effervescence for two main reasons: first, they express the transfigured world of sensed realities brought about by emotional contagion, and express an experience of moral community; secondly, they are not simply abstract representations of collective experiences and identifications, but retain the emotional charge that created them (*ibid.*: 239, 221). Thus, the flag of a country is often treated as sacred, and a soldier will struggle to defend it on the battlefield because the symbol carries the emotional charge that binds that soldier to the community he seeks to defend: "the soldier who dies for his flag dies for his country" (*ibid.*: 222). Thus, the development of a symbolic order in a society is a product of those processes through which collective feeling becomes conscious of itself, but is also a further means of ensuring that this consciousness, the *conscience collective* as Durkheim expressed it, retains its emotional power in the hearts and minds of individuals. In short, although Durkheim's arguments about religion have often been understood in narrowly 'functionalist' terms, in the sense that religion is explained as a source for and reflection of social solidarity, in reality emotion, ritual and symbol are intimately connected in what is a highly dynamic theory of religion and society.

THE RECEPTION OF DURKHEIM'S IDEAS

The major influences on Durkheim's arguments concerning religion are well known: Numa Denis Fustel de Coulanges had a direct and long-term influence, ethnographers such as Herbert Spencer and Francis James Gillen gave him the raw data on which to construct his theory of religion, and his reading of William Robertson Smith's *Lectures on the Religion of the Semites* ([1889] 1927), with its focus on the mutual solidarity of gods and their worshippers, also had a profound effect on the development of his arguments. A unique feature of Durkheim's view of religion by the time of *The Elementary Forms*, however, is his claim to offer a universally valid model of its genesis, character and function in human culture and society. Here, his decision to develop his arguments on the basis of ethnographic data on forms of 'totemism' in indigenous groups in America and, principally, Australia, has often been seen as highly problematic: although the text refers briefly to a number of Christian beliefs and practices, to Buddhism and to the 'religious' characteristics of apparently secular phenomena such as the French Revolution, the bulk of the book uses this 'primitive' religious form to establish a general theory of all forms of religious life, including the most complex (i.e. religions such as Christianity).

Although the ambiguities in Durkheim's use of the word 'primitive' have often been commented on, he appears to mean 'simple': he believed that, since all religions are "species within the same genus", the essential nature of more complex forms could be determined by studying the most simple ([1912] 1995: 4–5). Leaving aside the heated disputes that followed about whether totemism could, in fact, be classed as a 'religion', the more fundamental problem for many was whether all religions are indeed the same sort of thing: in a European cultural context that generally assumed the superiority of the Judaeo-Christian tradition over other forms, Durkheim's focus on "the common basis of religious life" proved highly controversial. Even in sociology, other influential figures disputed the idea that all religions are essentially alike: Weber, writing at the same time as Durkheim, took precisely the opposite view to him. Nonetheless, sociological studies of a range of religious phenomena, including various forms of Christianity and Hinduism, and the religions of the people as diverse as the Eskimos and ancient Romans, allowed early followers of Durkheim such as Marcel Mauss, Henri Hubert and Robert Hertz to demonstrate the theoretical fruitfulness of this general account of religion, while its stress on the potency of emotions, rituals and symbols in both 'primitive' and 'complex' settings allowed the notorious Collège de Sociologie of Georges Bataille, Roger Caillois and Michel Leiris to develop their revolutionary 'sacred sociology'.

Durkheim certainly had many contemporary critics: his work was challenged on several points by Gabriel Tarde, while many others sympathetic to aspects of his work, such as Henri Delacroix, Alponse Darlu, Edouard Le Roy, Jules Lachelier, Gustave Belot and Georges Matisse, objected to a number of his key assumptions and arguments (Lukes 1973: 506–11). These objections covered a range of issues, from doubts about his *homo duplex* model of human beings to concerns about his insufficient attentiveness to the truth claims of religious belief systems. Also, his stress on the collective and non-rational character of religion meant that his work was received very critically by those who favoured more rational, individually focused forms of explanation, a fact that accounts for the highly selective early reception of his work in the United States (Morrison 2001), as well as the fact that, even today, he functions as a favoured *bête noir* to American sociologists who operate with more methodologically individualist orientations, such as rational choice theorists. Despite these challenges, however, his influence across a range of disciplines has been immense.

In anthropology, a functionalist reading of Durkheim very quickly achieved a great deal of influence through the work of Alfred Radcliffe-Brown, although Mauss, Durkheim's nephew and collaborator, did more than anyone to further the Durkheimian cause. Particularly worth noting is that Durkheim's arguments concerning the social origins and power of symbols were central to a number of later, highly influential studies of symbolic and ritual orders (e.g. Douglas 1966; Turner 1969). In sociology, they also had a decisive influence on well-known studies of the symbolic dimensions of contemporary culture (e.g. Berger 1967; Bellah 1970). More broadly, Durkheim's focus on the *conscience collective* inspired Talcott Parsons' (1937, 1951) renowned studies of the importance of values for social action and the integration of individuals into a social system. Many writers, however, including many self-professed 'Durkheimians', continued to doubt the viability of Durkheim's claims regarding the fundamental and permanent role of religion in social life. W. S. F. Pickering, in fact, claimed that "Durkheim's infatuation with religion blinded him to the nature of modern society" (1984: 516). Throughout much of the twentieth century, when the secularization of the modern world seemed to be advancing steadily, and when assumptions about the inevitability of secularization formed the dominant theoretical paradigm in sociological studies of religion and society, Pickering's comments made perfect sense: while Durkheim's arguments had proved fruitful for anthropologists studying non-Western, non-modern societies, modernity seemed to embody an entirely different type of social and cultural world. Nonetheless, in the early years of the twenty-first century, Durkheim's suggestion that, despite the apparent weakening of religious influence on modern life, "religion seems destined to transform itself rather than disappear" ([1912] 1995: 432) began to look more accurate than those confident declarations of the world's steady movement towards a non-religious, 'disenchanted' future.

THE RESURGENCE OF RELIGION

Despite Durkheim's position as one of the 'founding figures' of sociology being unassailable for most of the twentieth century, his popularity has waxed and waned. The growing dominance of Marxism in many European universities during the late 1960s and 1970s marked, perhaps, a low point for Durkheimian studies. Although Durkheim still has many vociferous critics, his influence has recently seen a notable resurgence. This resurgent influence has been intimately tied to the global resurgence of many traditional religious forms, confounding the expectations of secularization theorists, but has also signalled a broader interest in exploring the religious dimensions of social and cultural life in a more flexible and creative manner.

Durkheim's suggestion that we should understand religion as an emotionally potent grouping of people around collective experiences and symbols of the sacred offers a great deal of scope for what can be classed as 'religious', and this has been exploited by studies of a diverse range of contemporary social and cultural phenomena. Many writers are now beginning to draw attention to the spread of religious factors across diverse social and cultural domains, including patriotic or nationalist ceremonies (Tiryakian 1995, 2005; Alexander 2004; Collins 2004), everyday social interactions (Maffesoli 1996), consumerism (Featherstone 1991; Ritzer 1999), and communications media (Dayan & Katz 1988; Lundby 1997; Martín-Barbero 1997).

Nevertheless, the value of Durkheim's emphasis on the enduring significance of religious phenomena is also increasingly evident with regard to the more established connotations of the term 'religion'. Maurice Halbwachs (1995) and, more recently, Daniele Hervieu-Léger (2000) have drawn on Durkheim to account for the significance of specifically Christian collective memories in the Western world, while others have focused on collective memories associated with the Holocaust (Levy & Sznaider 2002; Misztal 2003). Durkheim has also been used to account for the resurgence of Christian and Islamic religious identities with regard to debates about the contemporary 'clash of civilizations' (Mellor 2004; see Huntington 1996). Here, in contrast to the approaches of Jeffrey Alexander (2004), Randall Collins (2004) and Edward Tiryakian (2005), who focus on the broadly Durkheimian 'religious' dimensions of post-September 11 2001 patterns of social solidarity, ritual performance and symbolic power in an era marked by Islamic terrorism, Durkheim's stress on the importance of the temporal aspects of society, strongly influenced by de Coulanges, is used to illuminate the fact that Western societies are considerably more Christian than they imagine themselves to be (Mellor 2004).

Further to this, it is notable that Samuel Huntington's (1996) highly influential and much debated 'clash of civilizations' thesis not only draws on Durkheim, but also gives religious factors a social and political significance lacking in much sociology precisely because of his attention to the endurance of collective memories. Huntington's notion of 'civilization' draws from a number of sources and includes a number of different features, although it relies heavily on Durkheim and Mauss's (1971) focus on civilization as an emergent 'moral milieu' encompassing particular groups of nations or societies (Huntington 1996: 41–4). It is particularly notable, however, that Huntington, following Durkheim, emphasizes the enduring importance of religion for civilizations. Indeed, in view of his arguments, a civilization can be considered as a phenomenon that encompasses a number of societies united by a common religious substratum: this applies not only to those societies defined by their identification with Islam, but also structures what we mean by 'the West', since this is constituted by societies that have evolved along specifically Christian lines (*ibid.*: 65, 70, 178; Mellor 2004: 162ff.).

While such studies build on Durkheim's legacy in order to highlight the historical and contemporary social significance of particular religious forms, others have sought to combine a focus on the substantive contents of religions with an interest in broader philosophical questions about what it is to be human. Charles Lemert (1999), for example, builds on Durkheim's suggestion that religion is to do with 'the serious life', and he seeks to distinguish religious forms from other types of social phenomena. For him, religion has a specific capacity for illuminating the contingency, frailty and finitude of human existence, grounded in the human experience of family and community, yet always allowing for an element of critical distance from them. In a similar vein, Anne Warfield Rawls (2001) builds on Durkheim's arguments to identify a 'fallacy of misplaced abstraction' that has characterized much twentieth-century sociological theorizing. This fallacy, manifest as the prioritization of ideas and beliefs over practices, has led to the conclusion, evident in much postmodern theorizing and cultural studies, "that there is no escape from the relativism of competing sets of beliefs, and competing sets of meanings, each of which defines a competing reality" (Rawls 2001: 63). For her, in contrast, conflicts concerning phenomena such as oppression, racism and sexism need to be understood *primarily* as phenomena "enacted and experienced concretely by real people in real time and in real places" (*ibid.*).

Some Durkheimians, of course, would question the neglect of belief encouraged by such arguments and would argue that Durkheim actually prioritizes belief over practice (Pickering 1984: 379; Stedman Jones 2001: 206–7). What is notable, however, is that even where this objection is raised it is often located within a broader picture of the inherent dispositions and potentialities of human beings that allow beliefs to attain their social significance. As Robert Alun Jones points out, Durkheim may have argued that the plasticity of human nature was greater than many suspect, but he also asserted that it "cannot become just anything at all" (1999: 81). Thus, it might be said that Durkheim does not suggest that the *capacity* to believe is socially constituted, only that the *nature* of beliefs is shaped by social relationships: there is an embodied basis for religious belief, in the sense that beliefs are propositional attitudes that play causal roles in generating actions, and that human beings have an innate capacity for adopting such attitudes.

Further to this, though very much emphasizing practice above belief, Margaret Archer's (2000) critical realist account of religion is in many respects quite close to Durkheim's. Like Durkheim, she emphasizes that religion arises on the basis of practice, arguing that religious knowledge entails a 'feel for' the sacred rather than a propositional knowledge about it, an exercise of spiritual 'know how' rather than a cognitive acceptance of abstract principles (Archer 2000: 185). Like Archer, in fact, Durkheim emphasizes a *natural* reality out of which society is an emergent phenomenon (Durkheim [1912] 1995: 17). Like her, his *homo duplex* view of human beings emphasizes the pre-social embodied capacities and potentialities of individuals, and he stresses that the power of the religious ideas we encounter in society "cannot add anything to our natural vitality", but "can only release the emotive forces that are already within us" (*ibid*.: 419). Thus, he stresses that, rather than individuals being constituted entirely by collective forces, there are purely individual as well as collective states of consciousness within us, and that the former constitute the basis of our individual personalities (Durkheim [1893] 1984: 61). What he emphasizes, however, as does Archer, is the power of society to constitute these properties that are emergent from the interrelationship between individuals and social forces (Archer 1995: 38; 2000: 215).

In conclusion, it is precisely for this reason that his vision of society as a *sui generis* reality and his account of the 'fundamental and permanent' significance of religion are inextricably linked. Durkheim has an abiding interest in the social, psychological and philosophical aspects of what it is to be human, and he always attempts to illuminate an embodied, anthropological basis for social life. He saw social realities as a complex interweaving of emergent cognitive and emotional elements in which religion plays an essential and continuing role, and the common interpretation of his view of religion as a 'social cement' binding a society together through sacred symbols (e.g. Turner 1991) hardly does justice to his understanding of religion as a dynamic and creative emergent social phenomenon. A proper engagement with Durkheim's social realism reveals a much more complex, multi-layered picture of society, and a vision of the religious dimensions of social life that is not only more subtle than that implied by a functionalist perspective, but also more radical in the elementary social, and sociological, significance it accords to religion. Taken together, these intimately related aspects of his sociological project constitute his philosophical legacy, a legacy that continues to be of immense value for making sense of the contemporary world.

FURTHER READING

Allen, N., W. Pickering & W. Watts Miller 1998. *On Durkheim's Elementary Forms of Religious Life*. London: Routledge

Jones, R. 1999. *The Development of Durkheim's Social Realism*. Cambridge: Cambridge University Press.

Lukes, S. 1973. *Emile Durkheim: His Life and Work*. Harmondsworth: Penguin.

Pickering, W. 1984. *Durkheim's Sociology of Religion*. London: Routledge & Kegan Paul.

Poggi, G. 2000. *Durkheim*. Oxford: Oxford University Press.

On PRIMITIVE RELIGION see also Ch. 7. On RITUAL see also Chs 9, 20; Vol. 1, Chs 12, 20. On SOCIETY see also Ch. 14; Vol. 3, Ch. 2; Vol. 5, Ch. 4.

CHRONOLOGY

1800   Foundation of the US Library of Congress.
        Washington DC is chosen as the capital of the United States.
        The Althing of Iceland, one of the world's oldest parliamentary institutions, is disbanded (although it was restored in 1844).

1801   Birth of **John Henry Newman**, English clergyman who led the Oxford Movement in the Church of England and later became a Roman Catholic cardinal.

1802   Napoleon re-establishes slavery in the French colonies.
        The world's human population reaches one billion people for the first time.

1803   Birth of **Ralph Waldo Emerson**, American essayist, philosopher and leading exponent of New England Transcendentalism.
        Death of Johann Gottfried Herder, German critic, theologian and philosopher who initiated the *Sturm und Drang* literary movement.

1804   Birth of **Ludwig Feuerbach**, German philosopher best known for his critique of religion in *The Essence of Christianity*.
        Deaths of **Immanuel Kant** (*see* Vol. 3, Ch. 21) and Joseph Priestley, Presbyterian minister and scientist, noted for his discovery of oxygen.
        Napoleon crowns himself emperor of France in the presence of the pope.
        New Jersey becomes the last northern state to abolish slavery.

1805   Death of Friederich Schiller, great German poet, dramatist and historian.
        Admiral Horatio Nelson is fatally shot at the Battle of Trafalgar.
        Start of the modernization of Egypt under Muhammad Ali.

1806   Birth of **John Stuart Mill**, who was to become the most important English-speaking philosopher of the nineteenth century, contributing especially to the British traditions of empiricism and political liberalism.
        Death of Kitagawa Utamaro, Japanese print artist.
        After his defeat at the hands of Napoleon, Emperor Francis II lays down the imperial crown and the Holy Roman Empire comes officially to an end.
        Napoleon captures Warsaw.

1809   Birth of **Charles Darwin**, English natural scientists who formulated the theory of evolution by means of natural selection.
        Death of Franz Joseph Haydn, Austrian composer.

Conclusion of the treaty of the Dardanelles between Great Britain and the Ottoman Empire.

1811   Death of Heinrich von Kleist, German playwright and poet.
Honoré Flaugergues discovers the 'Great Comet of 1811'.
Paraguay and Venezuela declare their independence from Spain.
Start of the Luddite uprisings in northern England and the Midlands.

1812   Start of the war between the United States and Great Britain.

1813   Birth of **Søren Kierkegaard**, Danish religious philosopher and first major existentialist.
Start of the 'Great Game', the contest between Britain and Russia for control of Central Asia.
French physician Mathieu Orfila institutes the discipline of toxicology with his *Traité des poisons*.

1814   Deaths of **Johann Gottlieb Fichte**, German idealist philosopher, and the Marquis de Sade, French author with a taste for sexual perversion.
Scottish poet and novelist Walter Scott anonymously publishes his first novel, *Waverley*.

1815   The European map is redrawn at the Congress of Vienna.
End of the war between the United States and Great Britain.
After defeat at Waterloo, Napoleon is exiled to Saint Helena, a desolate island in the Atlantic Ocean,

1816   Shaka, king of the Zulu nation, begins to expand the Zulu empire in southern Africa.

1817   Death of Jane Austen, English novelist.
The Elgin Marbles are displayed in the British Museum.

1818   Birth of **Karl Marx**, German social philosopher whose writings formed the basis of modern socialism and communism.
Publication of Mary Shelley's *Frankenstein*.
Chile attains independence from Spain.
Old Glory is adopted as the flag of the United States.

1819   Founding of Singapore by the British East India Company.
SS *Savannah* is the first steamship to cross the Atlantic Ocean.
The Panic of 1819 is the first major financial crisis in the United States.

1820   Birth of **Friedrich Engels**, German socialist philosopher and, with Marx, founder of communism.

1821   Deaths of John Keats, principal poet of the English Romantic movement, and Napoleon.

1822   Thomas Young and Jean-François Champollion decipher hieroglyphs using the Rosetta Stone.

1823   Restoration of absolute monarchy in Spain by Ferdinand VII.
Pronouncement of the Monroe Doctrine of separate spheres of influence between Europe and the Americas.

1824   Death of Lord Byron, English Romantic poet who died in Greece while supporting the Greek war of independence against the Ottomans.

1825   The world's first public railway opens in the industrial north-east of England.

1826   Death of Thomas Jefferson, third president of the United States of America and principal drafter of the American Declaration of Independence.

1827   Deaths of Ludwig van Beethoven, German composer and pianist, Pierre-Simon Laplace, French physicist and astronomer and William Blake, English painter and poet.

1828   Deaths of Francisco Goya, Spanish painter, and Franz Schubert, Austrian composer.

1829   Death of Jean-Baptiste Lamarck, French biologist who defended the heritability of acquired traits.
Premiere of Goethe's *Faust*.
James Smithson leaves £100,000 to fund the Smithsonian Institute.

1830   Joseph Smith founds the Mormon church.
The French conquest of Algeria begins.

1831   Death of **G. W. F. Hegel**, major German idealist philosopher.

1832   Death of Johann Wolfgang von Goethe, extraordinary German poet, playwright, novelist, journalist and scientist.

1833   Birth of **William Dilthey**, German philosopher who made important contributions to hermeneutics and our understanding of the human sciences.
Slavery is abolished throughout the British colonies.

1834   Deaths of **Friedrich Schleiermacher**, influential German Protestant theologian best known for his works *On Religion* (1799) and *The Christian Faith* (1821–2), and Thomas Malthus, English economist and demographer who theorized that population growth, unless checked, would always outstrip the food supply.
Official end of the Spanish Inquisition.

1835   Birth of **Edward Caird**, influential Scottish exponent of Hegelian idealism.
Darwin arrives in the Galapagos Islands.

1837   Death of Alexander Pushkin, Russian poet, novelist and dramatist.
Queen Victoria ascends to the British throne.

1839   Birth of **Charles S. Peirce**, American philosopher who helped found the school of pragmatism.
Start of the Opium Wars between Great Britain and China.

1842   Birth of **William James** (*see* Vol. 5, Ch. 2), American psychologist and pragmatic philosopher, and brother of novelist Henry James.
Death of Marie-Henri Beyle ('Stendhal'), great French novelist.
Crawford Long performs the first operation using anaesthetic.

1844   Birth of **Friedrich Nietzsche**, German philosopher who challenged traditional Western religion and morality by famously declaring, "God is dead".
Death of John Dalton, English chemist who formulated of the atomic theory of the elements.

1845   **Newman** converts from Anglicanism to Catholicism.
Beginning of the Irish potato famine, which leads to the Irish diaspora.
Scientific American begins publication.

1848   Deaths of Emily Bronte, English novelist and poet best remembered for *Wuthering Heights*, and George Stephenson, English mechanic and principal inventor of the railway locomotive.
Publication of *The Communist Manifesto* by **Engels** and **Marx**.
Wave of European revolutions.
Start of the Californian gold rush.

1849   Deaths of Katsushika Hokusai, greatest Japanese print painter, Frédéric Chopin, renowned Polish composer and pianist, and Edgar Allan Poe, American poet and writer, considered the originator of the modern detective story.
Elizabeth Blackwell becomes the United States' first female doctor.

1850   Deaths of Honoré de Balzac, French novelist who introduced 'realism' into literature, and Margaret Fuller, American critic, teacher and woman of letters.
Approximate date of the end of the Little Ice Age.

1851   Death of Joseph William Turner, English landscape painter.
Beginning of gold rushes in Victoria, Australia.
Start of the Taiping Rebellion in China, which led to the loss of at least twenty million lives.
The Great Exhibition, the world's first industrial exposition, takes place in London.

1854   Death of **Friedrich Wilhelm Joseph Schelling**, leading German idealist philosopher.
Doctrine of Immaculate Conception, according to which Mary (the mother of Jesus) was conceived without original sin, is proclaimed by Pope Pius IX.
Japan's policy of isolation is formally ended by the Convention of Kanagawa.
Start of the Crimean War, with France, Britain and the Ottoman Empire allied against Russia.

1855   Birth of **Josiah Royce**, Harvard philosopher who defended absolute idealism.
Death of **Kierkegaard**.

1856   Birth of **Sigmund Freud**, founder of psychoanalysis.
Deaths of Robert Schumann, German Romantic composer and pianist, and Heinrich Heine, German poet.
The world's first oil refinery commences operations in Romania.
Discovery of the first Neanderthal remains, in the Neander Valley, near Düsseldorf, Germany.

1857   Death of **Auguste Comte**, French philosopher and founder of positivism.

1858   Birth of **Émile Durkheim**, regarded as one of the founders of sociology.
Alleged appearance of the Virgin Mary to St Bernadette of Lourdes, the town of Lourdes thereafter becoming a popular Catholic pilgrimage

1859   Births of **Henri Bergson** (*see* Vol. 5, Ch. 3), French philosopher and winner of Nobel Prize for Literature (1927) and **John Dewey** (*see* Vol. 5, Ch. 4), American philosopher and educator.
Deaths of Alexander Humboldt, great German naturalist and explorer, and Alexis Tocqueville, French politician and writer.
Publication of **Darwin's** *The Origin of Species by Means of Natural Selection*, which sells out immediately.
Edwin Drake drills the first oil well in Pennsylvania.

1860   Death of **Arthur Schopenhauer**, German 'philosopher of pessimism', and author of *The World as Will and Representation*.

1861   Birth of **Alfred North Whitehead** (*see* Vol. 5, Ch. 5), professor of mathematics and philosophy.
Start of the American Civil War.

1862   Death of Henry David Thoreau, American author and transcendentalist philosopher best known for his book *Walden*.

1865   Assassination of President Abraham Lincoln.
The 13th Amendment to the US Constitution, prohibiting slavery, becomes law.
The Salvation Army is founded by William Booth in the slums of London.

1866   Death of Bernard Riemann, German mathematician who provided the mathematical tools for Einstein's theory of general relativity.

1869   Pope Pius IX opens the First Vatican Council, which proclaims the doctrine of papal infallibility.

1870   Death of Charles Dickens, the most popular Victorian novelist.
The 15th Amendment to the US Constitution gives blacks the right to vote.
Start of the Franco-Prussian War.

1872   Birth of **Bertrand Russell** (*see* Vol. 5, Ch. 6), leading British philosopher, mathematician and social reformer.
Death of **Feuerbach**.

1873   Death of **Mill**.

1875   Deaths of Georges Bizet, French composer best known for his opera *Carmen*, and Hans Christian Andersen, Danish writer and storyteller.
The Theosophical Society is founded in New York.

1876   Deaths of Mikhail Bakunin, Russian anarchist and revolutionary, and Amandine Dudevant (George Sand), French novelist.
Alexander Graham Bell's first telephone transmission.

1878   Birth of **Martin Buber** (*see* Vol. 5, Ch. 8), religious existentialist.

1879   Death of James Clerk Maxwell, Scottish physicist who produced a unified theory of electricity and magnetism.
Mary Baker Eddy founds the Christian Science Church.

1880   Deaths of Gustave Flaubert, pioneer of French 'realist' writing, and Mary Ann Evans (George Eliot), great Victorian novelist.
Ned Kelly, infamous Australian outlaw, is hanged in Melbourne.

1881   Deaths of Fyodor Dostoyevsky, Russian author of *Crime and Punishment* and *The Brothers Karamazov*, and Benjamin Disraeli, noted British statesman.
Assassination of Alexander II, Czar of Russia.
The first electrical power plant and grid is established at Godalming in Britain.

1882   Birth of **Jacques Maritain** (*see* Vol. 5, Ch. 9), French Thomist philosopher.
Deaths of **Darwin** and **Emerson**.

1883   Birth of **Karl Jaspers** (*see* Vol. 5, Ch. 10), German philosopher and one of the founders of existentialism.
Deaths of **Marx**, Richard Wagner, German dramatic composer, Édouard Manet, French painter who inspired the Impressionist movement, and Ivan Turgenev, Russian novelist.
Eruption of Krakatoa kills at least 36,000 people.

1884   Publication of the first edition of the *Oxford English Dictionary*.
The Greenwich meridian is fixed as the world's prime meridian.

1886   Births of **Paul Tillich** (*see* Vol. 5, Ch. 11), religious existentialist, and **Karl Barth** (*see* Vol. 5, Ch. 12), Swiss Protestant theologian and author of the monumental *Church Dogmatics*.
Death of Franz Liszt, noted Hungarian composer and pianist.
Karl Benz patents the first successful petrol-fuelled automobile.

1887   900,000 die when the Yellow River floods in China.

1889   Births of **Martin Heidegger** (*see* Vol. 5, Ch. 14) and **Ludwig Wittgenstein** (*see* Vol. 5, Ch. 13), regarded by many as the greatest philosophers of the twentieth century.
The Eiffel Tower opens in Paris.

1890   Deaths of **Newman**, and Vincent van Gogh, brilliant Dutch painter who led a turbulent and tragic life.

1893   Death of Peter Illyich Tchaikovsky, leading Russian composer best known for composing the music for the ballets *Swan Lake* and *Sleeping Beauty*.
Gandhi's first act of civil disobedience in South Africa.

1895   Deaths of **Engels**, and Louis Pasteur, French chemist and microbiologist credited with some of the most valuable contributions to science and industry.
Oscar Wilde is convicted of 'sodomy and gross indecency'.

1896   Death of Harriet Beecher Stowe, American author of the anti-slavery novel *Uncle Tom's Cabin*.
Revival of the Olympic Games in Athens,

1897   Birth of **Charles Hartshorne** (*see* Vol. 5, Ch. 5), American process philosopher and theologian.
Deaths of Johannes Brahms, noted Viennese German composer, and Felix Mendelssohn, German composer and pianist.
English scientist J. J. Thomson discovers the electron, the first known subatomic particle.

1900   Deaths of **Nietzsche**, and Oscar Wilde, Irish poet and dramatist.
German physicist Max Planck discovers the law of black body emission, thus inaugurating the science of quantum physics.
Formation of the British Labour Party.

BIBLIOGRAPHY

Abrams, M. 1971. *Natural Supernaturalism: Tradition and Revolution in Romantic Literature*. New York: W. W. Norton.

Alexander, J. 2004. "From the Depths of Despair: Performance, Counterperformance and September 11". *Sociological Theory* **22**: 88–105.

Allison, H. 1966. *Lessing and the Enlightenment*. Ann Arbor, MI: University of Michigan Press.

Archer, M. 1995. *Realist Social Theory*. Cambridge: Cambridge University Press.

Archer, M. 2000. *Being Human*. Cambridge: Cambridge University Press.

Argyll, Duke of 1867. *The Reign of Law*. London: Alexander Strahan.

Aristotle 1935. "The Metaphysics Books X–XIV". In *Metaphysics Books X–XIV, Oeconomica, Magna Moralia*, H. Tredennick & G. Armstrong (trans.), 1–320. Cambridge, MA: Harvard University Press.

Aristotle 1996. *Physics*, R. Waterfield (trans.). Oxford: Oxford University Press.

Balfour, A. 1888. *The Religion of Humanity*, address delivered at the Church Congress, Manchester, October 1888. Edinburgh: David Douglas.

Barrett, C. 1997. "Newman and Wittgenstein on the Rationality of Religious Belief". In *Newman and Conversion*, I. Ker (ed.), 89–99. Edinburgh: T&T Clark.

Barrett, L. 2002. "Faith, Works, and the Uses of the Law: Kierkegaard's Appropriation of Lutheran Doctrine". In *International Kierkegaard Commentary Volume 21: For Self-Examination and Judge for Yourself!*, R. Perkins (ed.), 77–109. Macon, GA: Mercer University Press.

Barrett, L. 2003. "Love's Grateful Striving: A Commentary on Kierkegaard's *Works of Love*". *Journal of the American Academy of Religion* 71(2): 442–5.

Barrett, P., P. Gautrey, S. Herbert, D. Kohn & S. Smith (eds) 1987. *Charles Darwin's Notebooks, 1836–1844*. Ithaca, NY: Cornell University Press.

Barth, K. 1957. "Introductory Essay", J. Adams (trans.). In L. Feuerbach, *The Essence of Christianity*, G. Eliot (trans.), x–xxxii. New York: Harper Torchbooks.

Barth, K. 1968. *The Epistle to the Romans*, E. Hoskyns (trans.). Oxford: Oxford University Press.

Bauer, B. 1838. *Kritik der Geschichte der Offenbarung: Die Religion des alten Testaments in der geschichtlichen Entwicklung ihrer Prinzipien dargestellt*. Berlin: Ferdinand Dümmler.

Bauer, B. 1840. *Kritik der evangelischen Geschichte des Johannes*. Bremen: Karl Schünemann.

Bauer, B. 1841. *Kritik der evangelischen Geschichte der Synoptiker*, 2 vols. Leipzig: Otto Wigand.

Bauer, B. 1842. *Kritik der evangelischen Geschichte der Synoptiker und des Johannes, Dritter und letzter Band*. Braunschweig: Fr. Otto.

305

Beierwaltes, W. 2004. *Platonismus und Idealismus*. Frankfurt: Klostermann.

Bellah, R. 1970. *Beyond Belief*. New York: Harper & Row.

Bellah, R. 1973. "Introduction". In *Emile Durkheim on Morality and Society: Selected Writings*, R. Bellah (ed.), ix–lv. Chicago, IL: University of Chicago Press.

Berger, P. 1967. *The Sacred Canopy*. New York: Doubleday.

Bernhardi, F. von 1912. *Germany and the Next War*. London: Edward Arnold.

Bloch, E. 1969. *Thomas Münzer als Theologe der Revolution*, 2nd edn, Ernst Bloch Werkausgabe 2. Frankfurt: Suhrkamp.

Bosanquet, B. 1913. *The Value and Destiny of the Individual: The Gifford Lectures for 1912 Delivered in Edinburgh University*. London: Macmillan.

Bosanquet, B. 1920. *What Religion Is*. London: Macmillan.

Breazeale, D. & T. Rockmore (eds) 2002. *New Essays on Fichte's Later Jena: Wissenschaftslehr*. Evanston, IL: Northwestern University Press.

Brosses, C. 1760. *Du Culte des dieux fétiches ou parallèle de l'ancienne religion de l'Égypte avec la religion actuelle de Nigritie*. Paris.

Browne, J. 1995. *Charles Darwin, vol. 1: Voyaging*. New York: Knopf.

Burgess, A. 2004. "Kierkegaard, Brorson, and Moravian Music". In *International Kierkegaard Commentary, Volume 20: Practice in Christianity*, R. L. Perkins (ed.), 211–43. Macon, GA: Mercer University Press.

Caird, E. 1866. "The Roman Element in Civilisation". *North British Review* **44**: 249–71.

Caird, E. 1883. *Hegel*. Edinburgh: William Blackwood.

Caird, E. 1885. *The Social Philosophy and Religion of Comte*. Glasgow: MacLehose.

Caird, E. 1892. "Goethe and Philosophy". In his *Essays on Literature and Philosophy*, vol. 1, 54–104. Glasgow: MacLehose.

Caird, E. 1893. *The Evolution of Religion*, 2 vols. Glasgow: MacLehose.

Caird, E. 1897. "Christianity and the Historical Christ". *New World* **6**, 1–13. Reprinted in *The Collected Works of Edward Caird*, C. Tyler (ed.), vol. 12, v–xvii (Bristol: Thoemmes, 1999).

Caird, E. 1899. "Anselm's Argument for the Being of God – Its History and What It Proves". *Journal of Theological Studies* **1**: 23–39.

Caird, E. 1903–4. "St Paul and the Idea of Evolution". *Hibbert Journal* **2**: 1–19.

Caird, E. 1904. *The Evolution of Theology in the Greek Philosophers*, 2 vols. Glasgow: MacLehose.

Caird, E. 1907. *Lay Sermons and Addresses: Delivered in the Hall of Balliol College, Oxford*. Glasgow: MacLehose.

Caird, E. [1893] 1999. "Letter to Francis Herbert Bradley". In *The Collected Works of F. H. Bradley*, W. Mander & C. Keene (eds), vol. 4, 77. Bristol: Thoemmes.

Caird, E. [*c*.1866] 2005a. "Reform and Reformation". See Tyler (2005), vol. 2, 1–39.

Caird, E. 2005b. "Lectures on Moral Philosophy: Social Ethics". See Tyler (2005), vol. 2, 40–152.

Caird, E. [*c*.1890s] 2005c. "Essay on Mysticism". See Tyler (2005), vol. 2, 164–83.

Caird, E. [*c*.1874] 2006. "Spencer", C. Tyler (ed.). *Collingwood and British Idealism Studies* **12**: 5–38.

Caird, J. 1880. *Introduction to the Philosophy of Religion*. Glasgow: MacLehose.

Calvin, J. 1960. *Institutes of the Christian Religion*, J. McNeill (ed.), F. Lewis Battles (trans.). Philadelphia, PA: Westminster Press.

Campbell, R. (ed.) 1970. *Psychiatric Dictionary*, 4th edn. New York: Oxford University Press.

Campbell, R. (ed.) 1981. *Psychiatric Dictionary*, 5th edn. New York: Oxford University Press.

Clendenning, J. (ed.) 1970. *The Letters of Josiah Royce*. Chicago, IL: University of Chicago Press.

Clendenning, J. 1999. *The Life and Thought of Josiah Royce*, rev. & exp. edn. Nashville, TN: Vanderbilt University Press.

Coleridge, S. 1817. *Biographia Literaria, or Biographical Sketches of My Literary Life and Opinions*. New York: C. Wiley.

Coleridge, S. & W. Wordsworth 1798. *Lyrical Ballads, With a Few Other Poems*. London: T. N. Longman.

Collins, R. 2004. "Rituals of Solidarity and Security in the Wake of Terrorist Attack". *Sociological Theory* **22**: 53–87.

Comte, A. 1830–42. *Cours de philosophie positive*, 6 vols. Paris: Bachelier.

Comte, A. 1865. *A General View of Positivism*, J. Bridges (trans.). London: Trübner.

Comte, A. 1875–7. *System of Positive Polity or Treatise on Sociology, Instituting the Religion of Humanity*, 4 vols. London: Longmans, Green and Co.

Comte, A. 1909. *Catéchisme positiviste ou Sommaire exposition de la religion universelle*, P-F. Pécaut (ed.). Paris: Garnier.

Comte, A. 1998. *Early Political Writings*, H. Jones (ed. & trans.). Cambridge: Cambridge University Press.

Conybeare, W. 1855. "The Neology of the Cloister". *Quarterly Review* **97**: 148–88. Reprinted in *Early Responses to British Idealism, vol. 1: Responses to B. Jowett, T. H. Green, E. Caird and W. Wallace*, C. Tyler (ed.), 5–53 (Bristol: Thoemmes Continuum, 2004).

Darwin, C. 1859. *On the Origin of Species*. London: John Murray.

Darwin, C. 1871. *The Descent of Man*. London: John Murray.

Darwin, C. 1959. *The Origin of Species by Charles Darwin: A Variorum Text*, M. Peckham (ed.). Philadelphia, PA: University of Pennsylvania Press.

Darwin, C. 1985– . *The Correspondence of Charles Darwin*. Cambridge: Cambridge University Press.

Darwin, C. 1996. *The Origin of Species by Means of Natural Selection*, G. Beer (ed.). Oxford: Oxford University Press.

Dawkins, R. 1976. *The Selfish Gene*. Oxford: Oxford University Press.

Dawkins, R. 1983. "Universal Darwinism". In *Evolution from Molecules to Men*, D. Bendall (ed.), 403–25. Cambridge: Cambridge University Press.

Dawkins, R. 1986. *The Blind Watchmaker*. New York: W. W. Norton.

Dawkins, R. 1995. *A River Out of Eden*. New York: Basic Books.

Dawkins, R. 2006. *The God Delusion*. Boston, MA: Houghton Mifflin.

Dayan, D. & E. Katz 1988. "Articulating Consensus: The Ritual and Rhetoric of Media Events". In *Durkheimian Sociology: Cultural Studies*, J. Alexander (ed.), 161–86. Cambridge: Cambridge University Press.

Derrida, J. 1976. *Of Grammatology*, G. Spivak (trans.). Baltimore, MD: Johns Hopkins University Press.

Dilthey, W. 1957. *Gesammelte Schriften, Vol. II*. Göttingen: Vandenhoeck & Ruprecht.

Dilthey, W. 1958. *Gesammelte Schriften, Vol. VI*. Göttingen: Vandenhoeck & Ruprecht.

Dilthey, W. 1960. *Der junge Dilthey*, C. Misch (ed.). Leipzig: B. G. Teubner.

Dilthey, W. 1961. *Gesammelte Schriften, Vol. V*. Göttingen: Vandenhoeck & Ruprecht.

Dilthey, W. 1962. *Gesammelte Schriften, Vol. VIII*. Göttingen: Vandenhoeck & Ruprecht.

Dilthey, W. 1979a. *Gesammelte Schriften, Vol. I*. Göttingen: Vandenhoeck & Ruprecht.

Dilthey, W. 1979b. *Gesammelte Schriften, Vol. XIII*. Göttingen: Vandenhoeck & Ruprecht.

Dilthey, W. 1991. *Selected Works, Vol. 1: Introduction to the Human Sciences*, R. Makkreel & F. Rodi (eds). Princeton, NJ: Princeton University Press.

Dilthey, W. 1996. *Selected Works, Vol. 4: Hermeneutics and the Study of History*, R. Makkreel & F. Rodi (eds). Princeton, NJ: Princeton University Press.

Dilthey, W. 2002. *Selected Works, Vol. 3: The Formation of the Historical World in the Human Sciences*, R. Makkreel & F. Rodi (eds). Princeton, NJ: Princeton University Press.

Dole, A. 2004. "Schleiermacher and Otto on Religion". *Religious Studies* **40**: 389–413.

Douglas, M. 1966. *Purity and Danger*. London: Routledge & Kegan Paul.

Durkheim, E. [1897] 1952. *Suicide: A Study in Sociology*. London: Routledge.

Durkheim, E. [1905] 1973. "The Dualism of Human Nature and Its Social Conditions". In *Emile*

Durkheim on Morality and Society: Selected Writings, R. Bellah (ed.), 149–63. Chicago, IL: University of Chicago Press.

Durkheim, E. [1906] 1974a. "The Determination of Moral Facts". In his *Sociology and Philosophy*, D. F. Pocock (trans.), 35–62. New York: Free Press.

Durkheim, E. [1898] 1974b. "Individual and Collective Representations". In his *Sociology and Philosophy*, D. F. Pocock (trans.), 1–34. New York: Free Press.

Durkheim, E. [1899] 1975. "Concerning the Definition of Religious Phenomena". In *Durkheim on Religion: A Selection of Readings with Bibliographies*, W. Pickering (ed.), 74–99. London: Routledge & Kegan Paul.

Durkheim, E. [1895] 1982. *The Rules of Sociological Method*. London: Macmillan.

Durkheim, E. [1893] 1984. *The Division of Labor in Society*. London: Macmillan.

Durkheim, E. [1912] 1995. *The Elementary Forms of Religious Life*. New York: Free Press.

Durkheim, E. & M. Mauss 1971. "Note on the Notion of Civilization". *Social Research* **38**: 808–13.

Elrod, J. W. 1981. *Kierkegaard and Christendom*. Princeton, NJ: Princeton University Press.

Emerson, R. 1960–82. *The Journals and Miscellaneous Notebooks of Ralph Waldo Emerson*, William Gillman *et al.* (eds), 16 vols. Cambridge: Belknap Press.

Emerson, R. 1962–72. *The Early Lectures of Ralph Waldo Emerson*, 3 vols, S. Whicher, R. Spiller & W. Williams (eds). Cambridge, MA: Harvard University Press.

Emerson, R. 1971– . *The Collected Works of Ralph Waldo Emerson*, R. Spiller *et al.* (eds), 7 vols. Cambridge, MA: Harvard University Press.

Engels, F. [1839] 1975a. *F. W. Krummacher's Sermon on Joshua*. In *Marx and Engels Collected Works*, vol. 2, 28. Moscow: Progress Publishers.

Engels, F. [1842] 1975b. *The Insolently Threatened Yet Miraculously Rescued Bible or: The Triumph of Faith, To Wit, the Terrible, Yet True and Salutary History of the Erstwhile Licentiate Bruno Bauer; How the Same, Seduced by the Devil, Fallen from the True Faith, Became Chief Devil, and Was Well and Truly Ousted in the End: A Christian Epic in Four Cantos*. In *Marx and Engels Collected Works*, vol. 2, 313–51. Moscow: Progress Publishers.

Engels, F. [1839] 1975c. *Letters from Wuppertal*. In *Marx and Engels Collected Works*, vol. 2, 7–25. Moscow: Progress Publishers.

Engels, F. [1840] 1975d. *Reports from Bremen* (1). In *Marx and Engels Collected Works*, vol. 2, 102–6. Moscow: Progress Publishers.

Engels, F. [1840] 1975e. *Reports from Bremen* (2). In *Marx and Engels Collected Works*, vol. 2, 126–30. Moscow: Progress Publishers.

Engels, F. [1841] 1975f. *Reports from Bremen* (3). In *Marx and Engels Collected Works*, vol. 2, 155–60. Moscow: Progress Publishers.

Engels, F. [1842] 1975g. *Schelling and Revelation: Critique of the Latest Attempt of Reaction Against the Free Philosophy*. In *Marx and Engels Collected Works*, vol. 2, 189–240. Moscow: Progress Publishers.

Engels, F. [1841] 1975h. *Schelling on Hegel*. In *Marx and Engels Collected Works*, vol. 2, 181–7. Moscow: Progress Publishers.

Engels, F. [1842] 1975i. *Schelling, Philosopher in Christ, or the Transfiguration of Worldly Wisdom into Divine Wisdom: For Believing Christians Who Do Not Know the Language of Philosophy*. In *Marx and Engels Collected Works*, vol. 2, 241–64. Moscow: Progress Publishers.

Engels, F. [1839] 1975j. *To Friedrich Graeber in Berlin, Bremen, about April 23–May 1, 1839*. In *Marx and Engels Collected Works*, vol. 2, 425–37. Moscow: Progress Publishers.

Engels, F. [1840] 1975k. *To Friedrich Graeber in Berlin, Bremen, December 9, 1839–February 5, 1840*. In *Marx and Engels Collected Works*, vol. 2, 487–93. Moscow: Progress Publishers.

Engels, F. [1839] 1975l. *To Friedrich Graeber in Berlin, Bremen, July 12–27, 1839*. In *Marx and Engels Collected Works*, vol. 2, 457–63. Moscow: Progress Publishers.

Engels, F. [1839] 1975m. *To Friedrich Graeber in Berlin, Bremen, June 15, 1839*. In *Marx and Engels Collected Works*, vol. 2, 453–6. Moscow: Progress Publishers.

Engels, F. [1839] 1975n. *To Friedrich Graeber, Bremen, April 8, 1839*. In *Marx and Engels Collected Works*, vol. 2, 420–23. Moscow: Progress Publishers.

Engels, F. [1839] 1975o. *To Friedrich Graeber, Bremen, February 19, 1839*. In *Marx and Engels Collected Works*, vol. 2, 414–17. Moscow: Progress Publishers.

Engels, F. [1839] 1975p. *To Friedrich Graeber, Bremen, October 29, 1839*. In *Marx and Engels Collected Works*, vol. 2, 476–81. Moscow: Progress Publishers.

Engels, F. [1841] 1975q. *To Friedrich Graeber, February 22, 1841*. In *Marx and Engels Collected Works*, vol. 2, 525–8. Moscow: Progress Publishers.

Engels, F. [1840] 1975r. *To Wilhelm Graeber in Barmen, Bremen, November 20, 1840*. In *Marx and Engels Collected Works*, vol. 2, 513–16. Moscow: Progress Publishers.

Engels, F. [1839] 1975s. *To Wilhelm Graeber in Berlin, Bremen, about April 28–30, 1839*. In *Marx and Engels Collected Works*, vol. 2, 422–7. Moscow: Progress Publishers.

Engels, F. [1839] 1975t. *To Wilhelm Graeber in Berlin, Bremen, July 30, 1839*. In *Marx and Engels Collected Works*, vol. 2, 464–9. Moscow: Progress Publishers.

Engels, F. [1839] 1975u. *To Wilhelm Graeber in Berlin, Bremen, May 24–June 15, 1839*. In *Marx and Engels Collected Works*, vol. 2, 448–52. Moscow: Progress Publishers.

Engels, F. [1839] 1975v. *To Wilhelm Graeber in Berlin, Bremen, November 13–20, 1839*. In *Marx and Engels Collected Works*, vol. 2, 481–7. Moscow: Progress Publishers.

Engels, F. [1839] 1975w. *To Wilhelm Graeber in Berlin, Bremen, October 8, 1839*. In *Marx and Engels Collected Works*, vol. 2, 471–4. Moscow: Progress Publishers.

Engels, F. [1839] 1975x. *To Wilhelm Graeber in Berlin, Bremen, October 20–21, 1839*. In *Marx and Engels Collected Works*, vol. 2, 474–5. Moscow: Progress Publishers.

Engels, F. [1840] 1975y. *Two Sermons by F. W. Krummacher*. In *Marx and Engels Collected Works*, vol. 2, 121–2. Moscow: Progress Publishers.

Engels, F. [1850] 1978. *The Peasant War in Germany*. In *Marx and Engels Collected Works*, vol. 10, 397–482. Moscow: Progress Publishers.

Engels, F. [1883] 1990a. *The Book of Revelation*. In *Marx and Engels Collected Works*, vol. 26, 112–17. Moscow: Progress Publishers.

Engels, F. [1886] 1990b. *Ludwig Feuerbach and the End of Classical German Philosophy*. In *Marx and Engels Collected Works*, vol. 26, 353–98. Moscow: Progress Publishers.

Engels, F. [1894–5] 1990c. *On the History of Early Christianity*. In *Marx and Engels Collected Works*, vol. 27, 445–69. Moscow: Progress Publishers.

Erdelyi, M. 1985. *Psychoanalysis*. New York: Freeman.

Featherstone, M. 1991. *Postmodernism and Consumer Culture*. London: Sage.

Fenichel, O. 1945. *The Psychoanalytic Theory of Neurosis*. New York: W. W. Norton.

Feuer, L. (ed.) 1959. *Basic Writings on Politics and Philosophy: Karl Marx and Friedrich Engels*. Garden City, NJ: Doubleday.

Feuerbach, L. 1957. *The Essence of Christianity*, G. Eliot (trans.). New York: Harper Torchbooks.

Feuerbach, L. 1967a. *Lectures on the Essence of Religion*. New York: Harper & Row.

Feuerbach, L. 1967b. *The Essence of Faith According to Luther*. New York: Harper & Row.

Feuerbach, L. 1980. *Thoughts on Death and Immortality from the Papers of a Thinker, along with an Appendix of Theological-Satirical Epigrams, Edited by One of his Friends*. Berkeley, CA: University of California Press.

Feuerbach, L. [1841] 1986. *Das Wesen des Christentums*. Stuttgart: Reclam, Ditzingen.

Feuerbach, L. 1989. *The Essence of Christianity*, G. Eliot (trans.). Amherst, NY: Prometheus Books.

Feuerbach, L. 2004. *The Essence of Religion*. Amherst, NY: Prometheus Books.

Fichte, J. 1910. *Die Anweisung zum seligen Leben, oder auch der Religionslehre*, F. Medicus (ed.). Hamburg: Felix Meiner.

Fichte, J. 1978. *Attempt at a Critique of All Revelation*, G. Green (trans.). Cambridge: Cambridge University Press.

Fichte, J. 1982. *Science of Knowledge: With the First and Second Introductions*, P. Heath & J. Lachs (eds & trans.). Cambridge: Cambridge University Press.

Fichte, J. 1987. *Vocation of Man*, P. Preuss (trans.). Indianapolis, IN: Hackett.

Fichte, J. 1992. *Foundations of Transcendental Philosophy (Wissenschaftslehre) Nova Methodo*, D. Breazeale (ed. & trans.). Ithaca, NY: Cornell University Press.

Fichte, J. 1994. *Introductions to the Wissenschaftslehre and Other Writings*, D. Breazeale (ed. & trans.). Indianapolis, IN: Hackett.

Fichte, J. 2005a. *System of Ethics*, D. Breazeale & G. Zöller (eds & trans). Cambridge: Cambridge University Press.

Fichte, J. 2005b. *Science of Knowing*, W. Wright (ed. & trans.). Albany, NY: SUNY Press.

Foot, P. 1973. "Nietzsche: The Revaluation of Values". In *Nietzsche: A Collection of Critical Essays*, R. Solomon (ed.), 156–68. Garden City, NY: Doubleday. Reprinted in *Nietzsche*, J. Richardson & B. Leiter (eds), 210–20 (Oxford: Oxford University Press, 2001).

Forberg, F. [1798] 1969. "The Development of the Concept of Religion", P. Edwards (trans.). In *Nineteenth-Century Philosophy*, P. Gardiner (ed.), 19–26. New York: Free Press.

Forster, M. 2002. "Introduction". In J. Herder, *Philosophical Writings*, M. Forster (ed. & trans.), vii–xxxv. Cambridge: Cambridge University Press.

Fourier, C. 1996. *The Theory of the Four Movements*, G. Stedman Jones & I. Patterson (eds & trans.). Cambridge: Cambridge University Press.

Freud, S. 1901. "The Psychopathology of Everyday Life". In *The Standard Edition of the Complete Psychological Works of Sigmund Freud*, J. Strachey (ed.), vol. 6, 1–279. London: Hogarth Press, 1960.

Freud, S. 1907. "Obsessive Actions and Religious Practices". In *The Standard Edition of the Complete Psychological Works of Sigmund Freud*, J. Strachey (ed.), vol. 9, 115–27. London: Hogarth Press, 1959.

Freud, S. 1909. "Notes Upon a Case of Obsessional Neurosis". In *The Standard Edition of the Complete Psychological Works of Sigmund Freud*, J. Strachey (ed.), vol. 10, 155–318. London: Hogarth Press, 1955.

Freud, S. 1910. "Leonardo da Vinci and a Memory of His Childhood". In *The Standard Edition of the Complete Psychological Works of Sigmund Freud*, J. Strachey (ed.), vol. 11, 63–137. London: Hogarth Press, 1957.

Freud, S. 1911. "Psycho-analytic Notes on an Autobiographical Account of a Case of Paranoia (dementia paranoides)". In *The Standard Edition of the Complete Psychological Works of Sigmund Freud*, J. Strachey (ed.), vol. 12, 9–82. London: Hogarth Press, 1958.

Freud, S. 1913a. "Animism, Magic and the Omnipotence of Thought". In *The Standard Edition of the Complete Psychological Works of Sigmund Freud*, J. Strachey (ed.), vol. 13, 75–99. London: Hogarth Press, 1955.

Freud, S. 1913b. "The Claims of Psycho-analysis to Scientific Interest". In *The Standard Edition of the Complete Psychological Works of Sigmund Freud*, J. Strachey (ed.), vol. 13, 163–90. London: Hogarth Press, 1955.

Freud, S. 1913c. "Totem and Taboo". In *The Standard Edition of the Complete Psychological Works of Sigmund Freud*, J. Strachey (ed.), vol. 13, 100–62. London: Hogarth Press, 1955.

Freud, S. 1914. "On the History of the Psycho-analytic Movement". In *The Standard Edition of the Complete Psychological Works of Sigmund Freud*, J. Strachey (ed.), vol, 14, 7–66. London: Hogarth Press, 1957.

Freud, S. 1915a. "A Case of Paranoia Running Counter to the Psycho-analytic Theory of the Disease". In *The Standard Edition of the Complete Psychological Works of Sigmund Freud*, J. Strachey (ed.), vol. 14, 263–72. London: Hogarth Press, 1957.

Freud, S. 1915b. "Instincts and their Vicissitudes". In *The Standard Edition of the Complete*

Psychological Works of Sigmund Freud, J. Strachey (ed.), vol. 14, 117–40. London: Hogarth Press, 1957.

Freud, S. 1915c. "Thoughts for the Times on War and Death". In *The Standard Edition of the Complete Psychological Works of Sigmund Freud*, J. Strachey (ed.), vol. 14, 275–302. London: Hogarth Press, 1957.

Freud, S. 1921. "Group Psychology and the Analysis of the Ego". In *The Standard Edition of the Complete Psychological Works of Sigmund Freud*, J. Strachey (ed.), vol. 18, 65–143. London: Hogarth Press, 1955.

Freud, S. 1922. "Some Neurotic Mechanisms in Jealousy, Paranoia and Homosexuality". In *The Standard Edition of the Complete Psychological Works of Sigmund Freud*, J. Strachey (ed.), vol. 18, 223–32. London: Hogarth Press, 1955.

Freud, S. 1923. "The Ego and the Id". In *The Standard Edition of the Complete Psychological Works of Sigmund Freud*, J. Strachey (ed.), vol. 19, 12–59. London: Hogarth Press, 1961.

Freud, S. 1925. "An Autobiographical Study". In *The Standard Edition of the Complete Psychological Works of Sigmund Freud*, J. Strachey (ed.), vol. 20, 7–70. London: Hogarth Press, 1959.

Freud, S. 1926. "Address to the Society of B'nai B'rith". In *The Standard Edition of the Complete Psychological Works of Sigmund Freud*, J. Strachey (ed.), vol. 20, 273–4. London: Hogarth Press, 1959.

Freud, S. 1927. "The Future of an Illusion". In *The Standard Edition of the Complete Psychological Works of Sigmund Freud*, J. Strachey (ed.), vol. 21, 1–56. London: Hogarth Press, 1961.

Freud, S. 1930. "Civilization and its Discontents". In *The Standard Edition of the Complete Psychological Works of Sigmund Freud*, J. Strachey (ed.), vol. 21, 59–145. London: Hogarth Press, 1961.

Freud, S. 1933. "New Introductory Lectures on Psycho-analysis". In *The Standard Edition of the Complete Psychological Works of Sigmund Freud*, J. Strachey (ed.), vol. 22, 5–182. London: Hogarth Press, 1960.

Freud, S. 1939. "Moses and Monotheism: Three Essays". In *The Standard Edition of the Complete Psychological Works of Sigmund Freud*, J. Strachey (ed.), vol. 23, 1–137. London: Hogarth Press, 1964.

Freud, S. 1985. "Why War?". In *The Pelican Freud Library, Volume 12: Civilization, Society and Religion*, J. Strachey (trans.), A. Dickson (ed.), 3499-62. Harmondsworth: Penguin.

Fuller, L. 1958. "Positivism and Fidelity to Law – A Reply to Professor Hart". *Harvard Law Review* **71**: 630–72.

Gadamer, H. 1992. *Truth and Method*. New York: Crossroads.

Garff, J. 2005. *Søren Kierkegaard: A Biography*, B. Kirmmse (trans.). Princeton, NJ: Princeton University Press.

Gaus, G. 2006. "The Rights Recognition Thesis: Defending and Extending Green". In *T. H. Green: Ethics, Metaphysics, and Political Philosophy*, M. Dimova-Cookson & W. Mander (eds), 209–35. Oxford: Clarendon.

Gay, P. 1987. *A Godless Jew: Freud, Atheism, and the Making of Psychoanalysis*. New Haven, CT: Yale University Press.

Gay, P. 1988. *Freud, A Life for Our Time*. New York: W.W. Norton.

Gerrish, B. 1984. *A Prince of the Church: Schleiermacher and the Beginnings of Modern Theology*. Philadelphia, PA: Fortress Press.

Giovanni, G. Di 1989. "From Jacobi's Philosophical Novel to Fichte's Idealism: Some Comments on the 1798–99 'Atheism Dispute'". *Journal of the History of Philosophy* **27**: 75–100.

Gould, S. 1988. "On Replacing the Idea of Progress with an Operational Notion of Directionality". In *Evolutionary Progress*, M. H. Nitecki (ed.), 319–38. Chicago, IL: University of Chicago Press.

Gould, S. 1989. *Wonderful Life: The Burgess Shale and the Nature of History*. New York: W. W. Norton.

Green, T. H. 1997a. "Review of J. Caird, 'Introduction to the Philosophy of Religion'". In his *Works*, vol. 3, R. L. Nettleship & P. P. Nicholson (eds), 138–46. Bristol: Thoemmes.

Green, T. H. 1997b. "Fragment on Immortality". In his *Works*, vol. 3, R. L. Nettleship & P. P. Nicholson (eds), 159–60. Bristol: Thoemmes.

Grøn, A. 1993. *Begreget Angst Hos Søren Kierkegaard*. Copenhagen: Gyldendal.

Grünbaum, A. 1984. *The Foundations of Psychoanalysis: A Philosophical Critique*. Berkeley, CA: University of California Press.

Grünbaum, A. 1993. *Validation in the Clinical Theory of Psychoanalysis: A Study in the Philosophy of Psychoanalysis*. Madison, CT: International Universities Press.

Grünbaum, A. 2002. "Critique of Psychoanalysis". In *The Freud Encyclopedia: Theory, Therapy, and Culture*, E. Erwin (ed.), 117–36. New York: Routledge.

Grünbaum, A. 2004. "The Poverty of Theistic Cosmology". *British Journal for the Philosophy of Science* **55**: 561–614.

Halbfass, W. 1988. *India and Europe: An Essay in Philosophical Understanding*. Albany, NY: SUNY Press.

Halbwachs, M. 1995. *On Collective Memory*. Chicago, IL: University of Chicago Press.

Hamburger, J. 1999. *John Stuart Mill on Liberty and Control*. Princeton, NJ: Princeton University Press.

Hart, H. 1994. *The Concept of Law*, 2nd edn. Oxford: Clarendon Press.

Hayman, R. 1980. *Nietzsche: A Critical Life*. New York: Penguin.

Hegel, G. 1948. *Early Theological Writing*, T. Knox (trans.). Chicago, IL: University of Chicago Press.

Hegel, G. 1969. *Werke in zwanig Bänden*, E. Moldenhauer & K. Michel (eds). Frankfurt: Suhrkamp.

Hegel, G. 1971. *Hegel's Philosophy of Mind, Being Part Three of the Encyclopaedia of the Philosophical Sciences (1830)*, W. Wallace & A. Miller (trans.). Oxford: Oxford University Press.

Hegel, G. 1977. *Phenomenology of Spirit*, A. Miller (trans.). Oxford: Clarendon Press.

Hegel, G. 1985. *Introduction to the Lectures on the History of Philosophy*, T. Knox & A. Miller (trans.). Oxford: Clarendon Press.

Hegel, G. 1991. *Elements of the Philosophy of Right*, A. Wood (ed.), H. Nisbet (trans.). Cambridge: Cambridge University Press.

Hegel, G. 1995. *Lectures on the History of Philosophy, in 3 volumes*, E. Haldane & F. Simson (trans.). Lincoln, NE: University of Nebraska Press.

Hegel, G. 2002. "Foreword to H. F. W. Hinrichs, *Religion in Its Inner Relation to Science*". In *Miscellaneous Writings of G. W. F. Hegel*, J. Stewart (ed.), 337–53. Evanston, IL: Northwestern University Press.

Hegel, G. 2006. *Lectures on the Philosophy of Religion: One-Volume Edition, The Lectures of 1827*, R. Brown, P. Hodgson & J. Stewart (trans. with the assistance of H. Harris). Oxford: Oxford University Press.

Heiberg, J. 1843. "Litterær Vintersæd". *Intelligensblade* **24**: 285–92.

Herder, J. [1782–3] 1833. *The Spirit of Hebrew Poetry*, J. Marsh (trans.). Burlington, VT: E. Smith.

Herder, J. 2002. *Philosophical Writings*, M. Forster (ed. & trans.). Cambridge: Cambridge University Press.

Hervieu-Léger, D. 2000. *Religion as a Chain of Memory*. Cambridge: Polity.

Hinchliff, P. 1987. *Benjamin Jowett and the Christian Religion*. Oxford: Clarendon.

Hook, S. 1950. *From Hegel to Marx: Studies in the Intellectual Development of Karl Marx*. New York: Humanities Press.

Hook, S. 1985. "An Interview with Sidney Hook". *Free Inquiry* **5**: 24–33.

Hume, D. [1779] 1947. *Dialogues Concerning Natural Religion*, N. Smith (ed.). Indianapolis, IN: Bobbs-Merrill.

Hume, D. 1993. "A Letter Concerning the Dialogues". In *Dialogues and Natural History of Religion*, J. Gaskin (ed.), 25–8. Oxford: Oxford University Press.

Hume, D. 2000. *An Enquiry Concerning Human Understanding*, T. Beauchamp (ed.). Oxford: Clarendon Press.

Huntington, S. 1996. *The Clash of Civilizations and the Remaking of World Order*. New York: Simon & Schuster.

Iremonger, F. 1948. *William Temple, Archbishop of Canterbury: His Life and Letters*. Oxford: Oxford University Press.

Iverach, J. 2004. "Edward Caird". Reprinted in *Early Responses to British Idealism, vol. 1: Responses to B. Jowett, T. H. Green, E. Caird and W. Wallace*, C. Tyler (ed.), 193–202. Bristol: Thoemmes Continuum. Originally published in *Expository Times* 5 (October 1893–September 1894), 205–9.

Jacobi, F. 1785. *Über die Lehre des Spinoza in Briefen an den Herrn Moses Mendelssohn*. Breslau: G. Löwe.

Jacobi, F. 1787. *David Hume über den Glauben, oder Idealismus und Realismus: ein Gespräch*. Breslau: G. Löwe.

Jacobi, F. 1987. "Open Letter to Fichte", D. I. Behler (trans.). In *Philosophy of German Idealism*, E. Behler (ed.), 119–41. New York: Continuum.

Jacobi, F. 2005. "Recollections of Conversations with Lessing in July and August 1780". In Gotthold Ephraim Lessing, *Philosophical and Theological Writings*, H. Nisbet (ed.), 241–56. Cambridge: Cambridge University Press.

Jaeschke, W. 1990. *Reason in Religion: The Foundations of Hegel's Philosophy of Religion*, J. Stewart & P. Hodgson (trans.). Berkeley, CA: University of California Press.

James, W. 1979. *The Will to Believe, and Other Essays in Popular Philosophy*. Cambridge, MA: Harvard University Press.

James, W. [1902] 1985. *The Varieties of Religious Experience*. Cambridge, MA: Harvard University Press.

Janaway, C. 2007. *Beyond Selflessness: Reading Nietzsche's Genealogy*. Oxford: Oxford University Press.

John Paul II 1998. *Fides et Ratio: Encyclical Letter of John Paul II to the Catholic Bishops of the World*. Vatican City: L'Osservatore Romano.

Jones, H. & J. Muirhead 1921. *Life and Philosophy of Edward Caird, LLD, DCL, FBA*. Glasgow: MacLehose, Jackson.

Jones, R. 1999. *The Development of Durkheim's Social Realism*. Cambridge: Cambridge University Press.

Jones, W. 1799. *Institutes of Hindu Law; or, The Ordinances of Menu*. In *The Works of Sir William Jones*, vol. 3. London: Printed for G.G. and J. Robinson.

Kant, I. 1960. *Religion Within the Limits of Reason Alone*, T. Greene & H. Hudson (trans.). La Salle, IL: Open Court.

Kant, I. 1991. "What is Orientation in Thinking?". In *Kant's Political Writings*, H. Reiss (ed.), H. Nisbet (trans.), 237–49. Cambridge: Cambridge University Press.

Kant, I. 1996. *Religion Within the Boundaries of Mere Reason*, G. Di Giovani (trans.). In his *Religion and Rational Theology*, A. Wood & G. Di Giovanni (eds), 39–215. Cambridge: Cambridge University Press.

Kant, I. 1997a. *Prolegomena to Any Future Metaphysic that will be able to Come Forward as Science*, G. Hatfield (ed. & trans.). Cambridge: Cambridge University Press.

Kant, I. 1997b. *Critique of Practical Reason*, M. Gregor (ed. & trans.). Cambridge: Cambridge University Press.

Kant, I. 1998. *Critique of Pure Reason*, P. Guyer & A. Wood (eds & trans.). Cambridge: Cambridge University Press.

Kant, I. 2000. *Critique of the Power of Judgment*, P. Guyer (ed.), P. Guyer & E. Matthews (trans.). Cambridge: Cambridge University Press.

Kant, I. 2001. "What Real Progress Has Metaphysics Made in Germany Since the Time of

Leibniz and Wolff?". In his *Theoretical Philosophy after 1781*, H. Allison & P. Heath (eds), P. Heath (trans.), 337–42. Cambridge: Cambridge University Press.

Kant, I. 2004. *Prolegomena to Any Future Metaphysics*, G. Hatfield (ed.). Cambridge: Cambridge University Press.

Kautsky, K. 2002. *Communism in Central Europe in the Time of the Reformation*, J. Mulliken & E. Mulliken (trans.), http://marxists.org/archive/kautsky/1897/europe/index.htm (accessed June 2009). Originally published (London: Fisher & Unwin, 1897).

Kennedy, E. 1994. "The French Revolution and the Genesis of a Religion of Man". In *Modernity and Religion*, R. McInerny (ed.), 61–87. London: University of Notre Dame Press.

Kent, C. 1978. *Brains and Numbers: Elitism, Comtism, and Democracy in Mid-Victorian England*. Toronto: University of Toronto Press.

Ker, I. & T. Gornall 1978. *The Letters and Diaries of John Henry Newman*, vol. I. Oxford: Clarendon Press.

Kierkegaard, S. 1968–78. *Søren Kierkegaards Papirer*, 2nd edn, P. Heiberg, V. Kuhr, E. Torsting, N. Thulstrup & N. Cappelørn (eds). Copenhagen: Gyldendal.

Kierkegaard, S. 1969. *Philosophical Fragments, or a Fragment of Philosophy; by Johannes Climacus*, D. Swenson (trans. & intro.), N. Thulstrup (comm. & new intro.) H. Hong (rev. trans. & rev. comm.). Princeton, NJ: Princeton University Press.

Kierkegaard, S. 1978–2000. *Kierkegaard's Writings*, vols I–XXVI, H. Hong & E. Hong (eds & trans.). Princeton, NJ: Princeton University Press.

Kierkegaard, S. 1985. *Fear and Trembling: Dialectical Lyric by Johannes de silentio*, A. Hannay (trans.). Harmondsworth: Penguin.

Kirmmse, B. 1990. *Kierkegaard in Golden Age Denmark*. Bloomington, IN: Indiana University Press.

Kirmmse, B. 1994. "Kierkegaard, Jews, and Judaism" *Kierkegaardiana* **17**: 83–97.

Kolakowski, L. 1981. *Main Currents of Marxism*, vol. 1, P. Falla (trans.). Oxford: Oxford University Press.

Kuklick, B. 1985. *Josiah Royce: An Intellectual Biography*. Indianapolis, IN: Hackett.

Küng, H. 1979. *Freud and the Problem of God*. New Haven, CT: Yale University Press.

Laplanche, J. & J. B. Pontalis 1973. *The Language of Psychoanalysis*. New York: W. W. Norton.

Le Bon, G. [1895] 1975. *Psychologie des Foules*. Paris: Presses Universitaires de France.

Leighton, D. 2004. *The Greenian Moment: T. H. Green, Religion and Political Argument in Victorian Britain*. Exeter: Imprint Academic.

Lemert, C. 1999. "The Might Have Been and Could Be of Religion in Social Theory". *Sociological Theory* **17**: 240–63.

Levy, D. & N. Sznaider 2002. "Memory Unbound: The Holocaust and the Formation of Cosmopolitan Memory". *European Journal of Social Theory* **5**: 87–106.

Lindbeck, G. 1984. *The Nature of Doctrine: Religion and Theology in a Postliberal Age*. Louisville, KY: Westminster John Knox.

Littré, E. 1863. *Auguste Comte et la philosophie positive*. Paris: Hachette.

Locke, J. [1701] 1958. *A Discourse of Miracles*. In his *The Reasonableness of Christianity, and A Discourse of Miracles*, I. Ramsey (ed.). Palo Alto, CA: Stanford University Press.

Loeb, P. 2009. *The Death of Zarathustra*. Cambridge: Cambridge University Press.

Lübcke, P. 1991. "An Analytical Interpretation of Kierkegaard as Moral Philosopher". *Kierkegaardiana* **15**: 93–103.

Lukes, S. 1973. *Emile Durkheim: His Life and Work*. Harmondsworth: Penguin.

Lundby, K. 1997. "The Web of Collective Representations". In *Rethinking Media, Religion, and Culture*, S. Hoover & K. Lundby (eds), 146–64. London: Sage.

Maffesoli, M. 1996. *The Times of the Tribes*. London: Sage.

Martín-Barbero, J. 1997. "Mass Media as a Site of Resacralisation of Contemporary Cultures". In *Rethinking Media, Religion and Culture*, S. Hoover & K. Lundby (eds), 106–16. London: Sage.

Marx, K. [1867] 1962. *Das Kapital. Kritik der politischen Ökonomie, Erster Band, Buch I: Der Produktionsprozeß des Kapitals. Karl Marx/Friedrich Engels – Werke*, vol. 23. Berlin: Dietz.

Marx, K. [1843] 1975a. *Contribution to the Critique of Hegel's Philosophy of Law*. In *Marx and Engels Collected Works*, vol. 3, 3–129. Moscow: Progress Publishers.

Marx, K. [1844] 1975b. *Contribution to the Critique of Hegel's Philosophy of Law: Introduction*. In *Marx and Engels Collected Works*, vol. 3, 175–87. Moscow: Progress Publishers.

Marx, K. [1844] 1975c. *Economic and Philosophic Manuscripts of 1844*. In *Marx and Engels Collected Works*, vol. 3, 229–346. Moscow: Progress Publishers.

Marx, K. [1842] 1975d. *The Leading Article in No. 179 of the* Kölnische Zeitung. In *Marx and Engels Collected Works*, vol. 1, 184–202. Moscow: Progress Publishers.

Marx, K. [1842] 1975e. *Proceedings of the Sixth Rhine Province Assembly. First Article: Debates on Freedom of the Press and Publication of the Proceedings of the Assembly of the Estates*. In *Marx and Engels Collected Works*, vol. 1, 132–81. Moscow: Progress Publishers.

Marx, K. [1842] 1975f. *Yet Another Word on* Bruno Bauer und die Akademische Lehrfreiheit *by Dr. O. F. Gruppe, Berlin, 1842*. In *Marx and Engels Collected Works*, vol. 1, 211–14. Moscow: Progress Publishers.

Marx, K. [1845] 1976a. *Theses on Feuerbach*. In *Marx and Engels Collected Works*, vol. 5, 3–5. Moscow: Progress Publishers.

Marx, K. [1844] 1976b. *Zur Kritik der Hegelschen Rechtsphilosophie. Einleitung*. In *Karl Marx/ Friedrich Engels – Werke*, vol. 1, 378–91. Berlin: Dietz.

Marx, K. [1867] 1996. *Capital: A Critique of Political Economy*, vol. I. *Marx and Engels Collected Works*, vol. 35. Moscow: Progress Publishers.

Marx, K. & F. Engels [1845] 1975. *The Holy Family, or Critique of Critical Criticism*. In *Marx and Engels Collected Works*, vol. 4, 5–244. Moscow: Progress Publishers.

Marx, K. & F. Engels [1845–6] 1976. *The German Ideology: Critique of Modern German Philosophy According to Its Representatives Feuerbach, B. Bauer and Stirner, and of German Socialism According to Its Various Prophets*. In *Marx and Engels Collected Works*, vol. 5. Moscow: Progress Publishers.

Marx, K. & F. Engels 2002. *The Communist Manifesto*, S. Moore (trans.). Harmondsworth: Penguin.

Masuzawa, T. 2005. *The Invention of World Religions*. Chicago, IL: University of Chicago Press.

May, S. 1999. *Nietzsche's Ethics and his 'War on Morality'*. Oxford: Clarendon Press.

McDonald, W. 1997. "Retracing the Circular Ruins of Hegel's *Encyclopedia*". In *International Kierkegaard Commentary, Volume 12: Concluding Unscientific Postscript*, R. L. Perkins (ed.), 227–46. Macon, GA: Mercer University Press.

McDonald, W. 2003. "Love in Kierkegaard's *Symposia*". *Minerva – An Internet Journal of Philosophy* 7: 60–93.

Meissner, W. 1984. *Psychoanalysis and Religious Experience*. New Haven, CT: Yale University Press.

Mellor, P. 2004. *Religion, Realism and Social Theory: Making Sense of Society*. London: Sage/TCS.

Middleton, C. (ed. & trans.) 1969. *Selected Letters of Friedrich Nietzsche*. Chicago, IL: Chicago University Press.

Mill, J. S. 1963–91. *The Collected Works of John Stuart Mill*. Toronto: University of Toronto Press.

Mill, J. S. 1969a. *The Collected Works of John Stuart Mill, vol. 10: Essays on Ethics, Religion and Society*, J. M. Robson (ed.). Toronto: University of Toronto Press.

Mill, J. S. 1969b. "The Utility of Religion". In his *Three Essays on Religion*, reprinted in *The Collected Works of John Stuart Mill, vol. 10: Essays on Ethics, Religion and Society*, J. M. Robson (ed.), 403–28. Toronto: University of Toronto Press.

Mill, J. S. 1972. *The Collected Works of John Stuart Mill, vol. 14: Later Letters, 1848–1873*, J. M. Robson (ed.). Toronto: University of Toronto Press.

Mill, J. S. 1977. *The Collected Works of John Stuart Mill, vol. 18: Essays on Politics and Society*, J. M. Robson (ed.). Toronto: University of Toronto Press.

Mill, J. S. 1980. *The Collected Works of John Stuart Mill, vol. 1: Autobiography and Literary Essays*, J. M. Robson (ed.). Toronto: University of Toronto Press.

Mill, J. S. 1993. *Auguste Comte and Positivism*. Bristol: Thoemmes.

Milton, J. [1644] 1953–82. "Areopagitica". In his *Complete Prose Works*, D. Wolfe (ed.), vol. 2, 515–16. Oxford: Oxford University Press.

Misztal, B. 2003. "Durkheim on Collective Memory". *Journal of Classical Sociology* **3**: 123–43.

Mitchell, B. 1990. "Newman as a Philosopher". In *Newman after a Hundred Years*, I. Ker & A. Hill (eds), 223–46. Oxford: Clarendon Press.

Morrison, K. 2001. "The Disavowal of the Social in the American Reception of Durkheim". *Journal of Classical Sociology* **1**: 95–125.

Mossner, E. 1980. *The Life of David Hume*. Oxford: Oxford University Press.

Myerson, J. 2000. *Transcendentalism: A Reader*. Oxford: Oxford University Press.

Nettleship, R. L. 1997. "Memoir". In *Collected Works of T. H. Green*, 5 vols, R. L. Nettleship & P. P. Nicholson (eds), vol. 3, xi–clxi. Bristol: Thoemmes.

Neville, R. 1992. *The Highroad Around Modernism*. Albany, NY: SUNY Press.

Newman, J. 1872. *Oxford University Sermons*. London: Longmans, Green.

Newman, J. 1973. *The Letters and Diaries of John Henry Newman*, vol. 25. C. Dessain & T. Gornall (eds). Oxford: Clarendon Press.

Newman, J. 1985. *An Essay in Aid of a Grammar of Assent*, I. Ker (ed.). Oxford: Clarendon Press.

Nietzsche, F. 1954a. *The Antichrist*, W. Kaufmann (trans.). In *The Portable Nietzsche*. New York: Viking Press.

Nietzsche, F. 1954b. *The Twilight of the Idols*, W. Kaufmann (trans.). In *The Portable Nietzsche*. New York: Viking Press.

Nietzsche, F. 1966a. *Beyond Good and Evil*, W. Kaufmann (trans.). New York: Vintage Press.

Nietzsche, F. 1966b. *The Birth of Tragedy*, W. Kaufmann (trans.). New York: Vintage Press.

Nietzsche, F. 1968a. *Ecce Homo*, W. Kaufmann (trans.). New York: Vintage Press.

Nietzsche, F. 1968b. *The Genealogy of Morals*, W. Kaufmann (trans.). New York: Vintage Press.

Nietzsche, F. 1968c. *The Will to Power*, W. Kaufmann (trans.). New York: Vintage Press.

Nietzsche, F. 1974. *The Gay Science*, W. Kaufmann (trans.). New York: Vintage Press.

Nietzsche, F. 1976. "The Antichrist". In *The Portable Nietzsche*, W. Kaufman (ed. & trans.), 568–656. Harmondsworth: Penguin.

Nietzsche, F. 1982. *Daybreak: Thoughts on the Prejudices of Morality*. Cambridge: Cambridge University Press.

Nietzsche, F. 1983. *Untimely Meditations*, R. Hollingdale (trans.). Cambridge: Cambridge University Press.

Nietzsche, F. 1986. *Human, All Too Human*, R. Hollingdale (trans.). Cambridge: Cambridge University Press.

Nietzsche, F. 1988. *Kritische Studienausgabe*, G. Colli & M. Montinari (eds). Munich: Walter de Gruyter.

Nietzsche, F. 1990. *Twilight of the Idols*. In *The Twilight of the Idols and The Anti-Christ*, R. Hollingdale (trans.). Harmondsworth: Penguin.

Nietzsche, F. 1994. *On the Genealogy of Morality*, K. Ansell-Pearson (ed.), C. Diethe (trans.). Cambridge: Cambridge University Press.

Nietzsche, F. 2005. *Thus Spoke Zarathustra*, C. Martin (trans.). New York: Barnes & Noble Classics.

Oppenheim, F. 1987. *Royce's Mature Philosophy of Religion*. Notre Dame, IN: University of Notre Dame Press.

Oppenheim, F. 1993. *Royce's Mature Ethics*. Notre Dame, IN University of Notre Dame Press.

Oppenheim, F. 2007. "Royce's Windows to the East". *Transactions of the Charles S. Peirce Society* **43**: 288–318.

Packe, M. 1954. *The Life of John Stuart Mill*. London: Secker & Warburg.

Packer, B. 1995. "The Transcendentalists". In *The Cambridge History of American Literature*, S. Bercovitch (ed.), vol. 2, 329–604. Cambridge: Cambridge University Press.

Paley, W. [1802] 1819. *Natural Theology*, Collected Works, vol. 4. London: Rivington.

Pannenberg, W. 1993. *Towards a Theology of Nature*. Louisville, KY: Westminster John Knox Press.

Parsons, T. 1937. *The Structure of Social Action*. New York: Free Press.

Parsons, T. 1951. *The Social System*. London: Routledge.

Pattison, G. 1997. "'Before God' as a Regulative Concept". In *Kierkegaard Studies Yearbook 1997*, N. Cappelørn & H. Deuser (eds), 70–84. Berlin: Walter de Gruyter.

Pattison, G. 2002. *Kierkegaard, Religion and the Nineteenth-Century Crisis of Culture*. Cambridge: Cambridge University Press.

Peirce, C. 1931–58. *The Collected Papers of Charles Sanders Peirce*, 8 vols, C. Hartshorne, P. Weiss & A. Burks (eds). Cambridge, MA: Harvard University Press.

Peirce, C. 1963–6. *The Charles S. Peirce Papers*, The Houghton Library, Harvard University Library, Cambridge, MA.

Peirce, C. 1992. *The Essential Peirce: Selected Philosophical Writings, Volume 1 (1867–1893)*, N. Houser & C. Kloesel (eds). Bloomington, IN: Indiana University Press.

Peirce, C. 1998. *The Essential Peirce: Selected Philosophical Writings, Volume 2 (1893–1913)*, Peirce Edition Project (ed.). Bloomington, IN: Indiana University Press.

Pickering, M. 1993. *Auguste Comte: An Intellectual Biography*, vol. 1. Cambridge: Cambridge University Press.

Pickering, W. 1984. *Durkheim's Sociology of Religion*. London: Routledge & Kegan Paul.

Pinkard, T. 2000. *Hegel: A Biography*. Cambridge: Cambridge University Press.

Plato [1941] 1961. *Euthyphro*, L. Cooper (trans.). In *Plato: Collected Dialogues*, E. Hamilton & H. Cairns (eds), 169–85. Princeton, NJ: Princeton University Press.

Poggi, G. 2000. *Durkheim*. Oxford: Oxford University Press.

Raposa, M. L. 1989. *Peirce's Philosophy of Religion*. Bloomington, IN: Indiana University Press.

Rawls, A. 2001. "Durkheim's Treatment of Practice". *Journal of Classical Sociology* **1**: 33–68.

Reardon, B. 1985. *Religion in the Age of Romanticism*. Cambridge: Cambridge University Press.

Richardson, J. & B. Leiter (eds) 2001. *Nietzsche*. Oxford: Oxford University Press.

Ricoeur, P. 1977. "Schleiermacher's Hermeneutics". *Monist* **60**: 181–97.

Ricoeur, P. 1991. *From Text to Action*. Evanston, IL: Northwestern University Press.

Rieff, P. 1959. *Freud: the Mind of the Moralist*. Chicago, IL: University of Chicago Press.

Ritschl, A. 1900. *The Christian Doctrine of Justification and Reconciliation: The Positive Development of the Doctrine*, H. Mackintosh & A. Macaulay (eds & trans.). Edinburgh: T&T Clark.

Ritzer, G. 1999. *Enchanting a Disenchanted World*. Thousand Oaks, CA: Pine Forge.

Robertson Smith, W. [1889] 1927. *Lectures on the Religion of the Semites*. London: A. & C. Black.

Robinson, D. (ed.) 1951. *Royce's Logical Essays: Collected Logical Essays of Josiah Royce*. Dubuque, IA: W. C. Brown Co.

Royce, J. 1897. *The Conception of God*. New York: Macmillan.

Royce, J. 1900. *The Conception of Immortality*. New York: Houghton, Mifflin.

Royce, J. 1903. "What Should Be the Attitude of Teachers of Philosophy Towards Religion?". *International Journal of Ethics* **13**: 280–85.

Royce, J. 1965. *The Religious Aspect of Philosophy*. Gloucester: Peter Smith.

Royce, J. 1968. *The Problem of Christianity*. Chicago, IL: University of Chicago Press.

Royce, J. 1976. *The World and the Individual*, 2 vols. Gloucester: Peter Smith.

Royce, J. 1995. *The Philosophy of Loyalty*. Nashville, TN: Vanderbilt University Press.

Royce, J. 2001a. *The Sources of Religious Insight.* Washington, DC: Catholic University of America Press.

Royce, J. 2001b. *The Problem of Christianity.* Washington, DC: Catholic University of America Press.

Ruse, M. 1979. *The Darwinian Revolution: Science Red in Tooth and Claw.* Chicago, IL: University of Chicago Press.

Ruse, M. 2001. *Can a Darwinian be a Christian? The Relationship between Science and Religion.* Cambridge: Cambridge University Press.

Ruse, M. 2003. *Darwin and Design: Does Evolution Have A Purpose?* Cambridge, MA: Harvard University Press.

Ruse, M. 2005. *The Evolution–Creation Struggle.* Cambridge, MA: Harvard University Press.

Ruse, M. 2006. *Darwinism and Its Discontents.* Cambridge: Cambridge University Press.

Ruse, M. 2008. *Charles Darwin.* Oxford: Blackwell.

Russell, B. 1946. *History of Western Philosophy.* London: Allen & Unwin.

Sanctis, A. de 2005. *The "Puritan" Democracy of Thomas Hill Green, With Some Unpublished Writings.* Exeter: Imprint Academic.

Schelling, F. 1856–61. *Sämmtliche Werke*, K. Schelling (ed.). Stuttgart: Cotta.

Schelling, F. 1936. *Of Human Freedom*, J. Gutman (trans.). Chicago, IL: Open Court.

Schelling, F. 1977. *Schellings Philosophie der Offenbarung 1841/2*, M. Frank (ed.). Frankfurt: Suhrkamp.

Schelling, F. 1978. *System of Transcendental Idealism*, P. Heath (trans.). Charlottesville, VA: University Press of Virginia.

Schelling, F. 1988. *Ideas for a Philosophy of Nature: As Introduction to the Study of this Science, 1797, second edition, 1803*, E. Harris & P. Heath (trans.). Cambridge: Cambridge University Press.

Schleiermacher, F. 1966. *A Brief Outline on the Study of Theology*, T. Tice (trans.). Atlanta, GA: John Knox.

Schleiermacher, F. 1984. *The Christian Faith*, H. Mackintosh & J. Stewart (eds). Edinburgh: T&T Clark.

Schleiermacher, F. 1984– . *Kritische Gesamtausgabe.* Berlin: de Gruyter.

Schleiermacher, F. 1991. "Occasional Thoughts on Universities in the German Sense With an Appendix", T. Tice & E. Lawler (trans.). Lewiston, NY: Edwin Mellen Press.

Schleiermacher, F. 1996. *On Religion: Speeches to its Cultured Despisers*, 2nd edn, R. Crouter (ed.). Cambridge: Cambridge University Press.

Schleiermacher, F. 1998. *Hermeneutics and Criticism*, A. Bowie (ed.). Cambridge: Cambridge University Press.

Schneewind, J. 1997. "Bayle, Locke, and the Concept of Toleration". In *Philosophy, Religion, and the Question of Intolerance*, M. Razavi & D. Ambuel (eds). Albany, NY: SUNY Press.

Schopenhauer. A. 1891. *On the Fourfold Root of the Principle of Sufficient Reason and On the Will in Nature: Two Essays by Schopenhauer*, K. Hillebrand (trans.). London: George Bell & Sons.

Schopenhauer. A. 1966a. *The World as Will and Representation*, vol. I, E. Payne (trans.). New York: Dover.

Schopenhauer. A. 1966b. *The World as Will and Representation*, vol. II, E. Payne (trans.). New York: Dover.

Schopenhauer. A. 1974a. *Parerga and Paralipomena: Short Philosophical Essays*, vol. 1, E. Payne (trans.). Oxford: Oxford University Press.

Schopenhauer. A. 1974b. *Parerga and Paralipomena: Short Philosophical Essays*, vol. 2, E. Payne (trans.). Oxford: Oxford University Press.

Schopenhauer, A. 1988a. *Manuscript Remains in Four Volumes*, vol. III, A. Hübscher (ed.), E. Payne (trans.). Oxford: Berg.

Schopenhauer, A. 1988b. *Manuscript Remains in Four Volumes*, vol. IV, A. Hübscher (ed.), E. Payne (trans.). Oxford: Berg.

Sell, A. (ed.) 1997. *Mill and Religion: Contemporary Responses to Three Essays on Religion*. Bristol: Thoemmes Press.

Shilling, C. & P. Mellor 2001. *The Sociological Ambition: Elementary Forms of Social and Moral Life*. London: Sage.

Shinn, R. 1986. "Tillich as Interpreter and Disturber of Contemporary Civilization". *Bulletin of the American Academy of Arts and Sciences* **39**: 7–27.

Sober, E. & D. Wilson 1997. *Unto Others: The Evolution of Altruism*. Cambridge, MA: Harvard University Press.

Sockness, B. 2004. "Schleiermacher and the Ethics of Authenticity". *Journal of Religious Ethics* **32**: 477–517.

Spinoza, B. 2000. *Ethics*, G. Parkinson (ed. and trans.). Oxford: Oxford University Press.

Spinoza, B. 2007. *Theological-Political Treatise*, J. Israel (ed.), M. Silverthorne (trans.). Cambridge: Cambridge University Press.

Stedman Jones, S. 2001. *Durkheim Reconsidered*. Cambridge: Polity.

Stepansky, P. 1986. "Feuerbach and Jung as Religious Critics – With a Note on Freud's Psychology of Religion". In *Freud: Appraisals and Reappraisals: Contributions to Freud Studies*, vol. 1, P. Stepansky (ed.), 215–39. Hillsdale, NJ: Analytic Press.

Stewart, J. 2003. *Kierkegaard's Relations to Hegel Reconsidered*. Cambridge: Cambridge University Press.

Stirner, M. 1845. *Der Einzige und Sein Eigentum*. Leipzig: Philipp Reclam.

Stirner, M. 2005. *The Ego and His Own: The Case of the Individual Against Authority*, S. Byington (trans.). Mineola, NY: Dover.

Strauss, D. 1835–6. *Das Leben Jesu, kritisch bearbeitet*. Tübingen: C. F. Osiander.

Strauss, D. 2006. *The Life of Jesus Critically Examined*, G. Eliot (trans.). Bristol: Thoemmes Continuum.

Suárez, F. 1619. *Disputationes Metaphysicae*. Paris: Apud I Mestais.

Sulloway, F. 1977. *Freud, Biologist of the Mind*. New York: Basic Books.

Svaglic, M. (ed.) 1967. *Apologia pro Vita Sua*. Oxford: Clarendon Press.

Taylor, C. 1975. *Hegel*. Cambridge: Cambridge University Press.

Temple, W. 1924. *Christus Veritas*. London: Macmillan.

Ten, C. 1980. *Mill on Liberty*. Oxford: Clarendon Press.

Ten, C. 2002. "Was Mill a Liberal?". *Politics, Philosophy, and Economics* **1**: 355–70.

Ten, C. 2007. "Constitutionalism and the Rule of Law". In *A Companion to Contemporary Political Philosophy*, 2nd edn, R. Goodin, P. Pettit & T. Pogge (eds), vol. 2, 493–502. Oxford: Blackwell.

Tiryakian, E. 1995. "Collective Effervescence, Social Change and Charisma: Durkheim, Weber and 1989". *International Sociology* **10**: 269–81.

Tiryakian, E. 2005. "Durkheim, Solidarity, and September 11". In *The Cambridge Companion to Durkheim*, J. Alexander & P. Smith (eds), 305–21. Cambridge: Cambridge University Press.

Turner, B. 1991. *Religion and Social Theory*. London: Sage.

Turner, V. 1969. *The Ritual Process*. London: Routledge.

Tyler, C. 1998. "The Evolution of the Epistemic Self: A Critique of the Evolutionary Epistemology of Thomas Hill Green and His Followers". *Bradley Studies* **4**: 175–94.

Tyler, C. (ed.) 2004. *Early Responses to British Idealism, vol. 1: Responses to B. Jowett, T. H. Green, E. Caird and W. Wallace*. Bristol: Thoemmes Continuum.

Tyler, C. 2005. *Unpublished Manuscripts in British Idealism: Political Philosophy, Theology and Social Thought*, 2 vols. Bristol: Thoemmes Continuum.

Tyler, C. 2006a. "Thomas Hill Green". In *Stanford Encyclopaedia of Philosophy* (summer 2006 edition), E. Zalta (ed.), http://plato.stanford.edu/archives/sum2006/entries/green/ (accessed June 2009).

Tyler, C. 2006b. *Idealist Political Philosophy: Pluralism and Conflict in the Absolute Idealist Tradition*. London: Continuum.

Vaughan, R. 1861. "Review of *Essays and Reviews*". *British Quarterly Review* **33**: 3–80. Reprinted in *Early Responses to British Idealism, vol. 1: Responses to B. Jowett, T. H. Green, E. Caird and W. Wallace*, C. Tyler (ed.), 54–68 (Bristol: Thoemmes Continuum, 2004).

Vieillard-Baron, J.-L. 1979. *Platon et L'Idéalism Allemand (1770–1830)*. Paris: Editions Beauchesne.

Voegelin, E. 1975. *From Enlightenment to Revolution*. Durham, NC: Duke University Press.

Wallace, E. 1983. *Freud and Anthropology: A History and Reappraisal*. New York: International Universities Press.

Wallace, E. 1984. "Freud and Religion: A History and Reappraisal". In *The Psychoanalytic Study of Society*, vol. 10, L. Boyer, W. Muensterberger & S. Grolnick (eds), 113–61. Hillsdale, NJ: Analytic Press.

Wartofsky, M. 1977. *Feuerbach*. Cambridge: Cambridge University Press.

Wernick, A. 2001. *Auguste Comte and the Religion of Humanity*. Cambridge: Cambridge University Press.

West, C. 1989. *The American Evasion of Philosophy*. Madison, WI: University of Wisconsin Press.

West, C. 1999. *The Cornel West Reader*. New York: Basic Civitas Books.

Wilson, E. O. 1978. *On Human Nature*. Cambridge: Cambridge University Press.

Wilson, E. O. 1992. *The Diversity of Life*. Cambridge, MA: Harvard University Press.

Wilson, H. (trans.) 1840. *The Vishnu Purana: A System of Hindu Mythology and Tradition*. London: J. Murray.

Wyman, W. 2007. "The Role of the Protestant Confessions in The Christian Faith". *Journal of Religion* **87**: 665–75.

Young, J. 2006. *Nietzsche's Philosophy of Religion*. Cambridge: Cambridge University Press.

INDEX

absolute (or objective) idealism 70
Adler, Adolph 176
Adler, Alfred 277
agape, central role in Peirce's philosophy of
    religion 226–7
altruism 102
American transcendentalists 224
anthropology 294
anthropomorphism
    at core of Christian faith 140
    Kant's critique of 3, 4, 11
    in Schopenhauer's concept of the will in
      nature 14, 16
Archer, Margaret 296–7
asceticism 243
associationalism 209
atheism
    charge against Fitche 8, 24–6
    dispute over implications of
      transcendental idealism 24–6
    and moral consequentialism 24
    of Nietzsche 18
    of Schopenhauer 18
    of Spinoza 6

Baader, Franz von 10
Balfour, Arthur 102–3
Barth, Karl
    his influence and significance 32
    influence of Kierkegaard 14
    on war as divine judgement 18
Bauer, Bruno
    A-theology 190–91

application of Hegelian method to sources
    and doctrines of Christianity 13
democratic self-consciousness 188
Bayle, Pierre 154
Bentham, Jeremy 151
Bergson, Henri, influence of Darwin's theory
    of evolution 16
Berkeley, George 1
Bhagavad Gita 127
Bible
    historical criticism of 35–6
    and information on the historical Jesus
      36–7, 49, 188
biblical authority
    and historical criticism during the
      Enlightenment 35
    and Protestantism 35
    Schleiermacher's stance 36–7
Böhme, Jakob 10, 53
Bosanquet, Bernard 215, 218
Bradley, F. H. 218
Bridgewater Treatises 166
British empiricism 105, 106, 107, 171
British idealist movement 209, 210, 211,
    215, 217, 218
Browne, Borden Parker 249
Bruno, Giordano 10
Buddhism 84–5, 245, 246
Butler, Joseph, *The Analogy of Religion* 109

Caird, Edward
    afterlife of the soul 211
    Aritotelianism 213